A GIFT FOR:

....

FROM:

....

MORNING & EVENING EDITION

GRACE

FOR THE MOMENT®

*Inspirational Thoughts for
Each Day of the Year*

Max Lucado

THOMAS NELSON
Since 1798

NASHVILLE   DALLAS   MEXICO CITY   RIO DE JANEIRO

CONTENTS

Each Day . . .

I t's quiet. It's early. My coffee is hot. The sky is still black. The world is still asleep. The day is coming.

In a few moments the day will arrive. It will roar down the track with the rising of the sun. The stillness of the dawn will be exchanged for the noise of the day. The calm of solitude will be replaced by the pounding pace of the human race. The refuge of the early morning will be invaded by decisions to be made and deadlines to be met.

For the next twelve hours I will be exposed to the day's demands. It is now that I must make a choice. Because of Calvary, I'm free to choose. And so I choose.

I CHOOSE LOVE . . .

No occasion justifies hatred;
no injustice warrants bitterness. I choose love.
Today I will love God and what God loves.

I CHOOSE JOY . . .

I will invite my God to be the God of circumstance.
I will refuse the temptation to be cynical . . .
the tool of the lazy thinker. I will refuse to see

people as anything less than human beings, created by God.
I will refuse to see any problem as anything less than
an opportunity to see God.

I CHOOSE PEACE . . .

I will live forgiven. I will forgive so that I may live.

I CHOOSE PATIENCE . . .

I will overlook the inconveniences of the world. Instead of
cursing the one who takes my place, I'll invite him to do so.
Rather than complain that the wait is too long,
I will thank God for a moment to pray. Instead of clenching my
fist at new assignments, I will face them with joy and courage.

I CHOOSE KINDNESS . . .

I will be kind to the poor, for they are alone.
Kind to the rich, for they are afraid. And kind to the unkind,
for such is how God has treated me.

I CHOOSE GOODNESS . . .

I will go without a dollar before
I take a dishonest one. I will be overlooked before I will boast.
I will confess before I will accuse. I choose goodness.

I CHOOSE FAITHFULNESS . . .

Today I will keep my promises.
My debtors will not regret their trust. My associates will not
question my word. My wife will not question my love.
And my children will never fear that
their father will not come home.

I CHOOSE GENTLENESS . . .

Nothing is won by force. I choose to be gentle.
If I raise my voice, may it be only in praise.
If I clench my fist, may it be only in prayer.
If I make a demand, may it be only of myself.

I CHOOSE SELF-CONTROL . . .

I am a spiritual being. . . .
After this body is dead, my spirit will soar.
I refuse to let what will rot rule the eternal.
I choose self-control. I will be drunk only by joy.
I will be impassioned only by my faith.
I will be influenced only by God.
I will be taught only by Christ.
I choose self-control.

Love, joy, peace, patience, kindness,
goodness, faithfulness, gentleness, and self-control.
To these I commit my day.
If I succeed, I will give thanks.
If I fail, I will seek his grace.
And then, when this day is done,
I will place my head on my pillow
and rest.

———————

MAX LUCADO
When God Whispers Your Name

January

I have chosen the way of truth;
I have obeyed your laws.

—Psalm 119:30

God Listens

I cry out to the LORD;
I pray to the LORD for mercy.

PSALM 142:1

Y ou can talk to God because God listens. Your voice matters in heaven. He takes you very seriously. When you enter his presence, he turns to you to hear your voice. No need to fear that you will be ignored. Even if you stammer or stumble, even if what you have to say impresses no one, it impresses God, and he listens. He listens to the painful plea of the elderly in the rest home. He listens to the gruff confession of the death-row inmate. When the alcoholic begs for mercy, when the spouse seeks guidance, when the businessman steps off the street into the chapel, God listens.

Intently. Carefully.

THE GREAT HOUSE OF GOD

God wants to hear what you have to say. How does that make you feel?

_____

_____

_____

_____

_____

_____

_____

Packed for a Purpose

He has filled them with skill.

EXODUS 35:35 NKJV

You were born prepacked. God looked at your entire life, determined your assignment, and gave you the tools to do the job.

Before traveling, you do something similar. You consider the demands of the journey and pack accordingly. Cold weather? Bring a jacket. Business meeting? Carry the laptop. Time with grandchildren? Better take some sneakers and pain medication.

God did the same with you. *Joe will research animals . . . install curiosity. Meagan will lead a private school . . . an extra dose of management. I need Eric to comfort the sick . . . include a healthy share of compassion. Denalyn will marry Max . . . instill a double portion of patience.*

God packed you on purpose for a purpose.

CURE FOR THE COMMON LIFE

How has God packaged your life? List some tools he has given you and describe how you might use them for his purpose.

_____

_____

_____

_____

_____

A Chosen People

*You are a chosen people, royal priests,
a holy nation, a people for God's own possession.*

1 PETER 2:9

Do you ever feel unnoticed? New clothes and styles may help for a while. But if you want permanent change, learn to see yourself as God sees you: "He has covered me with clothes of salvation and wrapped me with a coat of goodness, like a bridegroom dressed for his wedding, like a bride dressed in jewels" (Isaiah 61:10).

Does your self-esteem ever sag? When it does, remember what you are worth. "You were bought, not with something that ruins like gold or silver, but with the precious blood of Christ, who was like a pure and perfect lamb" (1 Peter 1:18–19).

The challenge is to remember that. To meditate on it. To focus on it. To allow his love to change the way you look at you.

WHEN CHRIST COMES

You are so valuable to God that he sent his Son to die for you. Does that encourage you? In what other ways has he shown you his love?

_____

_____

_____

_____

_____

The Lord Is with Me

You are with me; Your rod and Your staff, they comfort me.

PSALM 23:4 NKJV

Y ou are with me."

Yes, you, Lord, are in heaven. Yes, you rule the universe. Yes, you sit upon the stars and make your home in the deep. But yes, yes, yes, you are with me.

The Lord is with me. The Creator is with me. Yahweh is with me.

Moses proclaimed it: "What great nation has a god as near to them as the LORD our God is near to us" (Deuteronomy 4:7 NLT).

Paul announced it: "He is not far from each one of us" (Acts 17:27 NIV).

And David discovered it: "You are with me."

Somewhere in the pasture, wilderness, or palace, David discovered that God meant business when he said: "I will not leave you" (Genesis 28:15).

TRAVELING LIGHT

God is always with you. How can this truth bring positive changes to your life?

_____

_____

_____

_____

_____

Worthless Worry

I was young, and now I am old,
but I have never seen good people left helpless
or their children begging for food.

PSALM 37:25

We worry. We worry about the IRS and the SAT and the FBI. We worry that we won't have enough money, and when we have money we worry that we won't manage it well. We worry that the world will end before the parking meter expires. We worry what the dog thinks if he sees us step out of the shower. We worry that someday we'll learn that fat-free yogurt was fattening.

Honestly, now. Did God save you so you would fret? Would he teach you to walk just to watch you fall? Would he be nailed to the cross for your sins and then disregard your prayers? Come on. Is Scripture teasing us when it reads, "He has put his angels in charge of you to watch over you wherever you go" (Psalm 91:11)?

I don't think so either.

IN THE GRIP OF GRACE

What things do you tend to worry about? List some of God's promises in Scripture that will remind you not to worry.

_____

_____

_____

_____

_____

Loaded with Love

He . . . loads me with love and mercy.

PSALM 103:4

It's time to let God's love cover all things in your life. All secrets. All hurts. All hours of evil, minutes of worry.

The mornings you awoke in the bed of a stranger? His love will cover that. The years you peddled prejudice and pride? His love will cover that. Every promise broken, drug taken, penny stolen. Every cross word, cuss word, and harsh word. His love covers all things.

Let it. Discover along with the psalmist: "He . . . loads me with love and mercy." Picture a giant dump truck full of love. There you are behind it. God lifts the bed until the love starts to slide. Slowly at first, then down, down, down until you are hidden, buried, covered in his love.

"Hey, where are you?" someone asks.

"In here, covered in love."

A LOVE WORTH GIVING

God has loaded your life with mercy and love. What hurts and worries do you need to bury beneath that love?

_____

_____

_____

_____

_____

A Complete Restoration

*You will know that God's power is
very great for us who believe.*

EPHESIANS 1:19

God loves to decorate. God *has* to decorate. Let him live long enough in a heart, and that heart will begin to change. Portraits of hurt will be replaced by landscapes of grace. Walls of anger will be demolished and shaky foundations restored. God can no more leave a life unchanged than a mother can leave her child's tear untouched.

This might explain some of the discomfort in your life. Remodeling of the heart is not always pleasant. We don't object when the Carpenter adds a few shelves, but he's been known to gut the entire west wing. He has such high aspirations for you. God envisions a complete restoration. He won't stop until he is finished. He wants you to be just like Jesus.

JUST LIKE JESUS

How has God been changing your heart? What is different in your life today because of those changes?

_____

_____

_____

_____

_____

The Author of Life

He who was dead sat up and began to speak.
And [Jesus] presented him to his mother.

LUKE 7:15 NKJV

The mourners didn't cause him to stop. Nor did the large crowd, or even the body of the dead man on the stretcher. It was the woman—the look on her face and the redness in her eyes. He knew immediately what was happening. It was her son who was being carried out, her only son. And if anyone knows the pain that comes from losing your only son, God does.

So he did it; he went into action. "Don't cry," he told the mother. "Arise!" he told the boy. The dead man spoke, the devil ran, and the people were reminded of this truth: For those who know the Author of Life, death is nothing more than Satan's dead-man's-bluff.

GOD CAME NEAR

How has the Author of Life brought healing and hope to your life? What difference has this made to your life?

Don't Miss God's Answer

"Is anything too hard for the LORD? No!"

GENESIS 18:14

The God of surprises strikes again. God does that for the faithful. Just when the womb gets too old for babies, Sarai gets pregnant. Just when the failure is too great for grace, David is pardoned.

The lesson? Three words. Don't give up.

Is the road long? Don't stop.

Is the night black? Don't quit.

God is watching. For all you know right at this moment . . . the check may be in the mail.

The apology may be in the making.

The job contract may be on the desk.

Don't quit. For if you do, you may miss the answer to your prayers.

HE STILL MOVES STONES

God is faithful. God is always on time. Describe some other characteristics of God that will encourage you to "hang in there."

_____

_____

_____

_____

_____

_____

God Honors Work

Whatever work you do, do your best.

ECCLESIASTES 9:10

Heaven's calendar has seven Sundays a week. God sanctifies each day. He conducts holy business at all hours and in all places. He uncommons the common by turning kitchen sinks into shrines, cafés into convents, and nine-to-five workdays into spiritual adventures.

Workdays? Yes, workdays. He ordained your work as something good. Before he gave Adam a wife or a child, even before he gave Adam britches, God gave Adam a job. "Then the LORD God took the man and put him into the garden of Eden to cultivate it and keep it" (Genesis 2:15 NASB). Innocence, not indolence, characterized the first family.

God unilaterally calls all the physically able to till the gardens he gives. God honors work. So honor God in your work.

CURE FOR THE COMMON LIFE

God ordained work as something good. List some ways you can honor God in your work or daily responsibilities.

At Home with God

"If people love me, they will obey my teaching.
My Father will love them, and we will come
to them and make our home with them."

JOHN 14:23

God wants to be your dwelling place. He has no interest in being a weekend getaway or a Sunday bungalow or a summer cottage. Don't consider using God as a vacation cabin or an eventual retirement home. He wants you under his roof now and always. He wants to be your mailing address, your point of reference; he wants to be your home.

For many this is a new thought. We think of God as a deity to discuss, not a place to dwell. We think of God as a mysterious miracle worker, not a house to live in. We think of God as a Creator to call on, not a home to reside in. But our Father wants to be much more. He wants to be the One in whom "we live and move and have our being" (Acts 17:28 NIV).

THE GREAT HOUSE OF GOD

What does God provide for you as your "dwelling place"?

_____

_____

_____

_____

_____

_____

Miraculous Moments

In Christ there is all of God in a human body.
COLOSSIANS 2:9 TLB

Jesus was not a godlike man, nor a manlike God. He was God-man.

Midwifed by a carpenter.

Bathed by a peasant girl.

The Maker of the world with a belly button.

The Author of the Torah being taught the Torah.

Heaven's human. And because he was, we are left with scratch-your-head, double-blink, what's-wrong-with-this-picture? moments like these:

A cripple sponsoring the town dance.

A sack lunch satisfying five thousand tummies.

What do we do with such moments?

What do we do with such a *person*? We applaud men for doing good things. We enshrine God for doing great things. But when a man does God things?

One thing is certain: we can't ignore him.

NEXT DOOR SAVIOR

What God things have you seen happen in your life or the lives of others? How do you respond to those things?

_____

_____

_____

_____

_____

The Foundation of Courage

*"I will forgive their wickedness
and will remember their sins no more."*

HEBREWS 8:12 NIV

Therefore, there is now no condemnation for those who are in Christ Jesus" (Romans 8:1 NIV).

"[God] justifies those who have faith in Jesus" (v. 3:26).

For those in Christ, these promises are not only a source of joy. They are also the foundations of true courage. You are guaranteed that your sins will be filtered through, hidden in, and screened out by the sacrifice of Jesus. When God looks at you, he doesn't see you; he sees the One who surrounds you. That means that failure is not a concern for you. Your victory is secure. How could you not be courageous?

THE APPLAUSE OF HEAVEN

Why does God want us to confess our sins and admit our need of forgiveness? Is this for his benefit or for ours?

_____

_____

_____

_____

_____

_____

_____

_____

We Need a Big God

"I am Yahweh."
EXODUS 6:2 TJB

The Israelites considered the name *Yahweh* too holy to be spoken by human lips. Whenever they needed to say *Yahweh*, they substituted the word *Adonai*, which means "Lord." If the name needed to be written, the scribes would take a bath before they wrote it and destroy the pen afterward.

The name I AM sounds strikingly close to the Hebrew verb *to be—havah.* It's quite possibly a combination of the present tense form (I am) and the causative tense (I cause to be). *Yahweh*, then, seems to mean "I AM" and "I cause." God is the "One who is" and the "One who causes."

Why is that important? Because we need a big God. And if God is the "One who is," then he is an unchanging God.

TRAVELING LIGHT

We have a big God who is an unchanging God. Describe how you have personally experienced the wonder of God.

_____

_____

_____

_____

_____

_____

_____

The Water of the Servant

He poured water into a bowl and began
to wash the followers' feet, drying them with
the towel that was wrapped around him.

JOHN 13:5

To place our feet in the basin of Jesus is to place the filthiest parts of our lives into his hands. In the ancient East, people's feet were caked with mud and dirt. The servant of the feast saw to it that the feet were cleaned. Jesus is assuming the role of the servant. He will wash the grimiest part of your life.

If you let him. The water of the Servant comes only when we confess that we are dirty. Only when we confess that we are caked with filth, that we have walked forbidden trails and followed the wrong paths.

We will never be cleansed until we confess we are dirty. We will never be pure until we admit we are filthy. And we will never be able to wash the feet of those who have hurt us until we allow Jesus, the one we have hurt, to wash ours.

A GENTLE THUNDER

How do these promises help you to live with courage and joy?

_____

_____

_____

_____

_____

A Yoke of Kindness

*"Take My yoke upon you and learn from Me, for I am
gentle and lowly in heart, and you will find rest for your souls."*

MATTHEW 11:29 NKJV

Farmers in ancient Israel used to train an inexperienced ox by yoking it to an experienced one with a wooden harness. The straps around the older animal were tightly drawn. He carried the load. But the yoke around the younger animal was loose. He walked alongside the more mature ox, but his burden was light. In this verse Jesus is saying, "I walk alongside you. We are yoked together. But I pull the weight and carry the burden."

I wonder, how many burdens is Jesus carrying for us that we know nothing about? We're aware of some. He carries our sin. He carries our shame. He carries our eternal debt. But are there others? Has he lifted fears before we felt them? Has he carried our confusion so we wouldn't have to? Those times when we have been surprised by our own sense of peace? Could it be that Jesus has lifted our anxiety onto his shoulders and placed a yoke of kindness on ours?

A LOVE WORTH GIVING

Jesus wants to carry your burdens. What heavy loads do you need to place on his shoulders?

_____

_____

_____

_____

_____

Our High Priest

Our high priest is able to understand our weaknesses.
When he lived on earth, he was tempted in every
way that we are, but he did not sin.

HEBREWS 4:15

Read how J. B. Phillips translates Hebrews 4:15:

For we have no superhuman High Priest to whom our weaknesses are unintelligible—he himself has shared fully in all our experience of temptation, except that he never sinned.

It's as if he knows that we will say to God . . . : "God, it's easy for you up there. You don't know how hard it is from down here." So he boldly proclaims Jesus' ability to understand. Look at the wording again.

He himself. Not an angel. Not an ambassador. Not an emissary, but Jesus himself.

Shared fully. Not partially. Not nearly. Not to a large degree. Entirely! Jesus shared fully.

In all our experience. Every hurt. Each ache. All the stresses and all the strains. No exceptions. No substitutes. Why? So he could sympathize with our weaknesses.

IN THE EYE OF THE STORM

Jesus lived the stresses and strains of human life. How does this affect your life?

_____

_____

_____

Our Forgiving Christ

"Father, forgive them, for they do not know what they are doing."

LUKE 23:34 NIV

Have you ever wondered how Jesus kept from retaliating against the mob that killed him? Have you ever asked how he kept his control? Here's the answer. It's . . . this statement: "for they do not know what they are doing." Look carefully. It's as if Jesus considered this bloodthirsty, death-hungry crowd not as murderers, but as victims. It's as if he saw in their faces not hatred but confusion. It's as if he regarded them not as a militant mob but, as he put it, as "sheep without a shepherd" (Matthew 9:36).

"They don't know what they are doing."

And when you think about it, they didn't. They hadn't the faintest idea what they were doing. They were a stir-crazy mob, mad at something they couldn't see, so they took it out on, of all people, God. But they didn't know what they were doing.

NO WONDER THEY CALL HIM THE SAVIOR

Think about someone who has hurt you. How can Christ's example help you respond graciously to that person?

29

Made for Heaven

"My kingdom does not belong to this world."

JOHN 18:36

Unhappiness on earth cultivates a hunger for heaven. By gracing us with a deep dissatisfaction, God holds our attention. The only tragedy, then, is to be satisfied prematurely. To settle for earth. To be content in a strange land.

We are not happy here because we are not at home here. We are not happy here because we are not supposed to be happy here. We are "like foreigners and strangers in this world" (1 Peter 2:11).

And you will never be completely happy on earth simply because you were not made for earth. Oh, you will have your moments of joy. You will catch glimpses of light. You will know moments or even days of peace. But they simply do not compare with the happiness that lies ahead.

WHEN GOD WHISPERS YOUR NAME

Does it bother you to feel unrest here on earth? What joys are you looking forward to when you finally get "home"?

_____

_____

_____

_____

_____

_____

Headed Home

He chose us in Him before the foundation of the world.
EPHESIANS 1:4 NKJV

Search the faces of the Cap Haitian orphanage for Carinette. The girl with the long nose and bushy hair and a handful of photos. The photos bear the images of her future family. She's been adopted.

Her adoptive parents are friends of mine. They brought her pictures, a teddy bear, granola bars, and cookies. Carinette shared the goodies and asked the director to guard her bear, but she keeps the pictures. They remind her of her home-to-be. Within a month, two at the most, she'll be there. She knows the day is coming. Any day now her father will appear. He came once to claim her. He'll come again to carry her home. Till then she lives with a heart headed home.

Shouldn't we all? Our Father paid us a visit too. Have we not been claimed? Adopted? God searched you out. Before you knew you needed adopting, he'd already filed the papers and selected the wallpaper for your room.

COME THIRSTY

God searched you out and adopted you. Describe how that makes you feel.

_____

_____

_____

_____

_____

Faithfully Present

"The Son of Man came to find
lost people and save them."

LUKE 19:10

Our God is the God who follows. Have you sensed him following you? He is the One who came to seek and save the lost. Have you sensed him seeking you?

Have you felt his presence through the kindness of a stranger? Through the majesty of a sunset or the mystery of romance? Through the question of a child or the commitment of a spouse? Through a word well spoken or a touch well timed, have you sensed him?

God gives us himself. Even when we choose our hovel over his house and our trash over his grace, still he follows. Never forcing us. Never leaving us. Patiently persistent. Faithfully present. He uses all his power to convince us that he is who he is and he can be trusted to lead us home.

THE GIFT FOR ALL PEOPLE

Describe a vivid experience that spoke to you of God's presence.

_____

_____

_____

_____

_____

_____

_____

The Gift of Choice

I haven chosen the way of truth; I have obeyed your laws.

PSALM 119:30

We can choose:
- a narrow gate or a wide gate (Matthew 7:13–14)
- a narrow road or a wide road (Matthew 7:13–14)
- the big crowd or the small crowd (Matthew 7:13–14)

We can choose to:
- build on rock or sand (Matthew 7:24–27)
- serve God or riches (Matthew 6:24)
- be numbered among the sheep or the goats (Matthew 25:32–33)

God gives eternal choices, and these choices have eternal consequences.

One of God's greatest gifts? The gift of choice.

HE CHOSE THE NAILS

List some important choices you have made and the consequences of those choices.

Who Is the Servant?

*"Martha was distracted with much serving. . . .
But . . . Mary has chosen that good part, which
will not be taken away from her."*

LUKE 10:40, 42 NKJV

Martha is worried about something good. She's having Jesus over for dinner. She's literally serving God. Her aim was to please Jesus. But she made a common yet dangerous mistake. As she began to work for him, her work became more important than her Lord. What began as a way to serve Jesus, slowly and subtly became a way to serve self. She has forgotten that the meal is to honor Jesus, not Martha.

It's easy to forget who is the servant and who is to be served.

HE STILL MOVES STONES

*The wrong motive can sabotage even the best of intentions.
What can you do to safeguard good intentions?*

_____

_____

_____

_____

_____

_____

_____

_____

Ask and Believe

"If you believe, you will get anything you ask for in prayer."
MATTHEW 21:22

I f you believe, you will get anything you ask for in prayer."
Don't reduce this grand statement to the category of new cars
and paychecks. Don't limit the promise of this passage to the
selfish pool of perks and favors. The fruit God assures is far greater
than earthly wealth. His dreams are much greater than promotions
and proposals.

God wants you to fly. He wants you to fly free of yesterday's guilt.
He wants you to fly free of today's fears. He wants you to fly free of
tomorrow's grave. Sin, fear, and death. These are the mountains he
has moved. These are the prayers he will answer. That is the fruit
he will grant. This is what he longs to do.

AND THE ANGELS WERE SILENT

God's dreams for your life are greater than promotions and
proposals. What things does God want you to fly free of?

_____

_____

_____

_____

_____

_____

Thinking of You

*Pray and ask God for everything
you need, always giving thanks.*

PHILIPPIANS 4:6

Heaven knows no difference between Sunday morning and Wednesday afternoon. God longs to speak as clearly in the workplace as he does in the sanctuary. He longs to be worshiped when we sit at the dinner table and not just when we come to his communion table. You may go days without thinking of him, but there's never a moment when he's not thinking of you.

Knowing this, we understand Paul's rigorous goal: "We capture every thought and make it give up and obey Christ" (2 Corinthians 10:5). We can fathom why he urges us to "pray without ceasing" (1 Thessalonians 5:17 NKJV), "be constant in prayer" (Romans 12:12 ESV) . . . and "let heaven fill your thoughts" (Colossians 3:2 TLB).

THE GREAT HOUSE OF GOD

If we thought more of God, would we think of him more often? What difference would this make in your life?

_____

_____

_____

_____

_____

_____

He Lives in You

*I work and struggle, using Christ's great strength
that works so powerfully in me.*

COLOSSIANS 1:29

God was *with* Adam and Eve, walking with them in the cool of the evening.

God was *with* Abraham, even calling the patriarch his friend.

God was *with* Moses and the children of Israel. He was *with* the apostles. Peter could touch God's beard. John could watch God sleep. Multitudes could hear his voice. God was *with* them!

But he is *in* you. He will do what you cannot. Imagine a million dollars being deposited into your checking account. To any observer you look the same, except for the goofy smile, but are you? Not at all! With God *in* you, you have a million resources that you did not have before!

Can't stop worrying? Christ can. And he lives within you.

Can't forgive the jerk, forget the past, or forsake your bad habits? Christ can! And he lives within you.

NEXT DOOR SAVIOR

What resources do you have with God in you?

_____

_____

_____

_____

_____

Just the Way You Are

*In your lives you must
think and act like Christ Jesus.*

PHILIPPIANS 2:5

It's dangerous to sum up grand truths in one statement, but I'm going to try. If a sentence or two could capture God's desire for each of us, it might read like this:

God loves you just the way you are, but he refuses to leave you that way. He wants you to be just like Jesus.

God loves you just the way you are. If you think his love for you would be stronger if your faith were, you are wrong. If you think his love would be deeper if your thoughts were, wrong again. Don't confuse God's love with the love of people. The love of people often increases with performance and decreases with mistakes. Not so with God's love. He loves you right where you are.

JUST LIKE JESUS

God's love does not increase with performance or decrease with mistakes. How do you respond to that kind of love?

_____

_____

_____

_____

_____

_____

Divine Miracles

All things were made by him, and nothing was made without him.

From where I write I can see several miracles.

White-crested waves slap the beach with rhythmic regularity. One after the other, the rising swells of saltwater gain momentum, humping, rising, then standing to salute the beach before crashing onto the sand. How many billions of times has this simple mystery repeated itself since time began?

In the distance lies a miracle of colors—twins of blue. The ocean-blue of the Atlantic encounters the pale blue of the sky, separated only by the horizon.

Miracles. Divine miracles.

These are miracles because they are mysteries. Scientifically explainable? Yes. Reproducible? To a degree.

But still they are mysteries. Events that stretch beyond our understanding and find their origins in another realm. They are every bit as divine as divided seas, walking cripples, and empty tombs.

GOD CAME NEAR

What comes to mind when you think of divine miracles?
In creation? In your life?

_____

_____

_____

_____

_____

God's Good Gifts

Every good action and every perfect gift is from God.
JAMES 1:17

Ever feel like you have nothing? Just look at the gifts [God] has given you:

He has sent his angels to care for you, his Holy Spirit to dwell in you, his church to encourage you, and his Word to guide you.

Anytime you speak, he listens; make a request and he responds.

He will never let you be tempted too much or stumble too far.

Let a tear appear on your cheek, and he is there to wipe it.

Let a love sonnet appear on your lips, and he is there to hear it.

As much as you want to see him, he wants to see you more.

You have been chosen by Christ. He has claimed you as his beloved.

WHEN CHRIST COMES

Every good gift is from God. Remind yourself of some of these gifts you tend to take for granted.

_____

_____

_____

_____

_____

_____

Know Your Knack

Make a careful exploration of who you are and the work you have been given, and then sink yourself into that.

GALATIANS 6:4 MSG

God never prefabs or mass-produces people. No slapdash shaping. "I make all things new," he declares (Revelations 21:5 NKJV). He didn't hand you your granddad's bag or your aunt's life; he personally and deliberately packed *you.*

You can do something no one else can do in a fashion no one else can do it. Exploring and extracting your uniqueness excites you, honors God, and expands his kingdom. So "make a careful exploration of who you are and the work you have been given, and then sink yourself into that."

Discover and deploy your knacks. When you do the most what you do the best, you put a smile on God's face. What could be better than that?

CURE FOR THE COMMON LIFE

You can do something no one else can do. List some of the things that make you unique.

_____

_____

_____

_____

_____

God's Good Timing

*"God will always give what is right
to his people who cry to him night and day,
and he will not be slow to answer them."*

LUKE 18:7

Why does God wait until the money is gone? Why does he wait until the sickness has lingered? Why does he choose to wait until the other side of the grave to answer the prayers for healing?

I don't know. I only know his timing is always right. I can only say he will do what is best.

Though you hear nothing, he is speaking. Though you see nothing, he is acting. With God there are no accidents. Every incident is intended to bring us closer to him.

A GENTLE THUNDER

God does what is best when it is best. What should your attitude be while you wait? Why?

_____

_____

_____

_____

_____

_____

Water of Eternal Life

*"The water I give will become a spring of water
gushing up inside that person, giving eternal life."*

JOHN 4:14

Remember the words of Jesus to the Samaritan woman? "The water I give will become a spring of water gushing up inside that person, giving eternal life." Jesus offers, not a singular drink of water, but a perpetual artesian well! And the well isn't a hole in your backyard but the Holy Spirit of God in your heart:

> "If anyone believes in me, rivers of living water will flow out from that person's heart, as the Scripture says." Jesus was talking about the Holy Spirit. The Spirit had not yet been given, because Jesus had not yet been raised to glory. But later, those who believed in Jesus would receive the Spirit. (John 7:38–39)

Water, in this verse, is a picture of the Spirit of Jesus working in us. He's not working to save us, mind you; that work is done. He's working to change us.

HE CHOSE THE NAILS

*The Spirit of Jesus is working to change us. What changes
has he made in your life?*

_____

_____

_____

_____

Clothes of Salvation

*This body that dies must clothe itself
with something that can never die.*

1 CORINTHIANS 15:53

D oes Jesus care what clothes we wear?

Apparently so. In fact, the Bible tells us exactly the wardrobe God desires.

"But clothe yourselves with the Lord Jesus Christ and forget about satisfying your sinful self" (Romans 13:14).

"You were all baptized into Christ, and so you were all clothed with Christ. This means that you are all children of God through faith in Christ Jesus" (Galatians 3:26–27).

This clothing has nothing to do with dresses and jeans and suits. God's concern is with our spiritual garment. He offers a heavenly robe that only heaven can see and only heaven can give. Listen to the words of Isaiah: "The LORD makes me very happy; all that I am rejoices in my God. He has covered me with clothes of salvation and wrapped me with a coat of goodness"(Isaiah 61:10).

WHEN CHRIST COMES

When you are clothed with Christ you will not want to satisfy your sinful longings. What will you do instead?

_____

_____

_____

_____

_____

A Worry-Free Life

Do not worry about anything,
but pray and ask God for everything you need.

PHILIPPIANS 4:6

Look around you. You have reason to worry. The sun blasts cancer-causing rays. Air vents blow lung-clotting molds. Potato chips have too many carbs. Vegetables, too many toxins. And do they have to call an airport a terminal?

Some of us have postgraduate degrees from the University of Anxiety. We go to sleep worried that we won't wake up; we wake up worried that we didn't sleep. We worry that someone will discover that lettuce was fattening all along. The mother of one teenager bemoaned, "My daughter doesn't tell me anything. I'm a nervous wreck." Another mother replied, "My daughter tells me everything. I'm a nervous wreck." Wouldn't you love to stop worrying? Could you use a strong shelter from life's harsh elements?

God offers you just that: the possibility of a worry-free life. Not just less worry, but no worry.

COME THIRSTY

God offers the possibility of a worry-free life. How would
your life be different if you were truly worry free?

Sowing Seeds of Peace

Plant goodness, harvest the fruit of loyalty,
plow the new ground of knowledge.

HOSEA 10:12

Want to see a miracle? Plant a word of love heart-deep in a person's life. Nurture it with a smile and a prayer, and watch what happens.

An employee gets a compliment. A wife receives a bouquet of flowers. A cake is baked and carried next door. A widow is hugged. A gas-station attendant is honored. A preacher is praised.

Sowing seeds of peace is like sowing beans. You don't know why it works; you just know it does. Seeds are planted, and topsoils of hurt are shoved away.

Don't forget the principle. Never underestimate the power of a seed.

THE APPLAUSE OF HEAVEN

Think of a time when someone planted a word of love in your heart. How did this make you feel? How did you respond?

_____

_____

_____

_____

_____

_____

_____

We Need a Savior

Christt was offered once to bear the sins of many.

HEBREWS 9:28 NKJV

Y ou can't forgive me for my sins nor can I forgive you for yours. Two kids in a mud puddle can't clean each other. They need someone clean. Someone spotless. We need someone clean too.

That's why we need a savior.

Trying to make it to heaven on our own goodness is like trying to get to the moon on a moonbeam; nice idea, but try it and see what happens.

Listen. Quit trying to quench your own guilt. You can't do it. There's no way. Not with a bottle of whiskey or perfect Sunday school attendance. Sorry. I don't care how bad you are. You can't be bad enough to forget it. And I don't care how good you are. You can't be good enough to overcome it.

You need a Savior.

NO WONDER THEY CALL HIM THE SAVIOR

Have you done things to earn salvation? Why is impossible for us to save ourselves?

_____

_____

_____

_____

_____

One Secure Place

"I will be with you always."

MATTHEW 28:20

David, the man after God's own heart, said: "I'm asking GOD for one thing, only one thing: to live with him in his house my whole life long" (Psalm 27:4 MSG).

What is this house of God which David seeks? Is David describing a physical structure? Does he long for a building with four walls and a door through which he can enter but never exit? No. "He does not live in temples built by human hands" (Acts 17:24). When David says, "I will live in the house of the LORD forever" (Psalm 23:6), he's not saying he wants to get away from people. He's saying that he yearns to be in God's presence, wherever he is.

THE GREAT HOUSE OF GOD

Is God with us at all times whether we think of him or not? Why is this good news for us?

_____

_____

_____

_____

_____

_____

_____

The Cure for Selfishness

*If there is any fellowship of the Spirit, if any affection
and compassion, make my joy complete by being of the same mind.*

PHILIPPIANS 2:1–2 NASB

What's the cure for selfishness?

Get your self out of your eye by getting your eye off your self. Quit staring at that little self, and focus on your great Savior.

A friend who is an Episcopalian minister explains the reason he closes his prayers with the sign of the cross. "The touching of my forehead and chest makes a capital 'I.' The gesture of touching first one shoulder, then the other, cuts the 'I' in half."

Isn't that a work of the cross? A smaller "I" and a greater Christ? Don't focus on yourself; focus on all that you have in Christ. Focus on the fellowship of the Spirit, the affection and compassion of heaven.

A LOVE WORTH GIVING

Are there things you could do to change your focus from self to the Savior? How will this improve your life?

_____

_____

_____

_____

_____

_____

A World Without Sin

Then wolves will live in peace with lambs,
and leopards will lie down to rest with goats.

ISAIAH 11:6

C an you imagine a world minus sin? Have you done anything recently because of sin?

At the very least, you've complained. You've worried. You've grumbled. You've hoarded when you should have shared. You've turned away when you should have helped.

Because of sin, you've snapped at the ones you love and argued with the ones you cherish. You have felt ashamed, guilty, bitter.

Sin has sired a thousand heartaches and broken a million promises. Your addiction can be traced back to sin. Your mistrust can be traced back to sin. Bigotry, robbery, adultery—all because of sin. But in heaven, all of this will end.

Can you imagine a world without sin? If so, you can imagine heaven.

WHEN CHRIST COMES

Think of some of the noisy distractions in your life. What do you do to give God your quiet attention?

_____

_____

_____

_____

_____

_____

One Step at a Time

Your word is like a lamp for my feet and a light for my path.
PSALM 119:105

A rthur Hays Sulzberger was the publisher of the *New York Times* during the Second World War. Because of the world conflict, he found it almost impossible to sleep. He was never able to banish worries from his mind until he adopted as his motto these five words—"one step enough for me"—taken from the hymn "Lead Kindly Light."

God isn't going to let you see the distant scene either. So you might as well quit looking for it. He promises a lamp unto our feet, not a crystal ball into the future. We do not need to know what will happen tomorrow.

God is leading you. Leave tomorrow's problems until tomorrow.

TRAVELING LIGHT

Most people tend to worry about tomorrow's troubles today. How can this have a negative effect on life?

_____

_____

_____

_____

_____

_____

_____

A Heart Like His

We are like clay, and you are the potter;
your hands made us all.

ISAIAH 64:8

God wants us to be just like Jesus.

Isn't that good news? You aren't stuck with today's personality. You aren't condemned to "grumpydom." You are tweakable. Even if you've worried each day of your life, you needn't worry the rest of your life. So what if you were born a bigot? You don't have to die one.

Where did we get the idea we can't change? From whence come statements such as, "It's just my nature to worry," or "I'll always be pessimistic. I'm just that way." Who says? Would we make similar statements about our bodies? "It's just my nature to have a broken leg. I can't do anything about it." Of course not. If our bodies malfunction, we seek help. Shouldn't we do the same with our hearts? Shouldn't we seek aid for our sour attitudes? Can't we request treatment for our selfish tirades? Of course we can. Jesus can change our hearts. He wants us to have a heart like his.

JUST LIKE JESUS

Sometimes we get "stuck in a rut" with a bad habit. What is the first step to getting out of the rut?

_____

_____

_____

_____

God Never Gives Up

GOD's business is putting things right.
PSALM 11:7 MSG

God never gives up.

When Joseph was dropped into a pit by his own brothers, God didn't give up.

When Moses said, "Here I am, send Aaron," God didn't give up.

When the delivered Israelites wanted Egyptian slavery instead of milk and honey, God didn't give up.

When Peter worshiped him at the supper and cursed him at the fire, he didn't give up.

And when human hands fastened the divine hands to a cross with spikes, it wasn't the soldiers who held the hands of Jesus steady. It was God who held them steady. God, who would give up his only son before he'd give up on you.

SIX HOURS ONE FRIDAY

God never gives up. Explain how this is good news for you and the people you know.

_____

_____

_____

_____

_____

_____

The Reachable Jesus

He remembered us when we were
in trouble. His love continues forever.

PSALM 136:23

God chose to reveal himself through a human body.

The tongue that called forth the dead was a human one. The hand that touched the leper had dirt under its nails. The feet upon which the woman wept were calloused and dusty. And his tears . . . oh, don't miss the tears . . . they came from a heart as broken as yours or mine ever has been.

So, people came to him. My, how they came to him! They came at night; they touched him as he walked down the street; they followed him around the sea; they invited him into their homes and placed their children at his feet. Why? Because he refused to be a statue in a cathedral or a priest in an elevated pulpit. He chose instead to be a touchable, approachable, reachable Jesus.

GOD CAME NEAR

Jesus came near to us in our need. Does he want us to respond to others in the same way? What are some practical ways to do this?

_____

_____

_____

_____

_____

Applaud Loud and Often

Sing to Him, sing psalms to Him;
talk of all His wondrous works!

PSALM 105:2 NKJV

God has never taken his eyes off you. Not for a millisecond. He's always near. He lives to hear your heartbeat. He loves to hear your prayers. He'd die for your sin before he'd let you die in your sin, so he did.

What do you do with such a Savior? Don't you sing to him? Don't you declare, confess, and proclaim his name? Don't you bow a knee, lower a head, hammer a nail, feed the poor, and lift up your gift in worship? Of course you do.

Worship God. Applaud him loud and often. For your sake, you need it.

And for heaven's sake, he deserves it.

CURE FOR THE COMMON LIFE

Describe some of the reasons you want to applaud God loud and often.

Blessings at God's Table

You prepare a meal for me in front of my enemies.

PSALM 23:5

P ause and envision the scene in [God's] royal dining room. Driven not by our beauty but by his promise, he calls us to himself and invites us to take a permanent place at his table. We take our place next to the other sinners-made-saints and we share in God's glory.

May I share a partial list of what awaits you at his table?

- You are beyond condemnation (Romans 8:1).
- You are a member of his kingdom (Colossians 1:13).
- You have been adopted (Romans 8:15).
- You have access to God at any moment (Ephesians 2:18).
- You will never be abandoned (Hebrews 13:5).
- You have an imperishable inheritance (1 Peter 1:4).

IN THE GRIP OF GRACE

You sit at God's table that overflows with blessings. List some of his personal blessings to you. Thank him for his goodness.

_____

_____

_____

_____

_____

Love Accepts All Things

Love . . . bears all things, believes all things.
1 Corinthians 13:4–7 nkjv

Wouldn't it be nice if love were like a cafeteria line? What if you could look at the person with whom you live and select what you want and pass on what you don't? What if parents could do this with kids? "I'll take a plate of good grades and cute smiles, and I'm passing on the teenage identity crisis and tuition bills."

What if kids could do the same with parents? "Please give me a helping of allowances and free lodging but no rules or curfews, thank you."

And spouse with spouse? "Hmmm, how about a bowl of good health and good moods. But job transfers, in-laws, and laundry are not on my diet."

Wouldn't it be great if love were like a cafeteria line? It would be easier. It would be neater. It would be painless and peaceful. But you know what? It wouldn't be love. Love doesn't accept just a few things. Love is willing to accept all things.

A Love Worth Giving

"Love is willing to accept all things." Do you find this difficult? Why?

The Compassionate Christ

When he arrived, he saw a
great crowd waiting. He felt sorry for them. . . .
So he began to teach them many things.

MARK 6:34

When Jesus lands on the shore of Bethsaida, he leaves the Sea of Galilee and steps into a sea of humanity. Keep in mind, he has crossed the sea to get away from the crowds. He needs to grieve. He longs to relax with his followers. He needs anything but another crowd of thousands to teach and heal.

But his love for people overcomes his need for rest.

Many of those he healed would never say "thank you," but he healed them anyway. Most would be more concerned with being healthy than being holy, but he healed them anyway. Some of those who asked for bread today would cry for his blood a few months later, but he healed them anyway. He had compassion on them.

IN THE EYE OF THE STORM

What does it mean to be a compassionate person? How has Christ's compassion touched your life?

_____

_____

_____

_____

_____

Our Work Is God's Work

Jesus got into one of the boats . . . that belonged to [Peter], and asked him to push off a little from the land.

LUKE 5:3

Jesus claims Peter's boat. He doesn't *request* the use of it. Christ doesn't fill out an application or ask permission; he simply boards the boat and begins to preach.

He can do that, you know. All boats belong to Christ. Your boat is where you spend your day, make your living, and to a large degree live your life. The taxi you drive, the dental office you manage, the family you feed and transport—this is your boat. Christ shoulder-taps us and reminds:

"You drive my truck."

"You work on my job site."

"You serve my hospital wing."

To us all, Jesus says, "Your work is my work."

CURE FOR THE COMMON LIFE

Your "boat belongs to Christ." Is there anything in your life that is not completely his?

Adopted by God

*The Spirit himself bears witness with
our Spirit that we are children of God.*

ROMANS 8:16 ESV

When we come to Christ, God not only forgives us, he also adopts us. Through a dramatic series of events, we go from condemned orphans with no hope to adopted children with no fear. Here is how it happens. You come before the judgment seat of God full of rebellion and mistakes. Because of his justice he cannot dismiss your sin, but because of his love he cannot dismiss you. So, in an act which stunned the heavens, he punished himself on the cross for your sins. God's justice and love are equally honored. And you, God's creation, are forgiven. But the story doesn't end with God's forgiveness.

It would be enough if God just cleansed your name, but he does more. He gives you *his* name.

THE GREAT HOUSE OF GOD

What are some of our privileges as members of God's family? What are some of our obligations?

_____

_____

_____

_____

_____

_____

Love for the Least

"I was thirsty, and you gave me something to drink."

MATTHEW 25:35

What is the sign of the saved? Their scholarship? Their willingness to go to foreign lands? Their ability to amass an audience and preach? Their skillful pens and hope-filled volumes? Their great miracles? No.

The sign of the saved is their love for the least.

Those put on the right hand of God will be those who gave food to the hungry, drink to the thirsty, warmth to the lonely, clothing to the naked, comfort to the sick, and friendship to the imprisoned.

Did you note how simple the works are? Jesus doesn't say, "I was sick and you healed me. I was in prison and you liberated me. I was lonely and you built a retirement home for me." He doesn't say, "I was thirsty and you gave me spiritual counsel."

No fanfare. No hoopla. No media coverage. Just good people doing good things.

AND THE ANGELS WERE SILENT

Describe what it means to "love the least."

_____

_____

_____

_____

_____

Guard Your Attitude

May our Lord Jesus Christ himself and
God our Father encourage you and strengthen
you in every good thing you do and say.

2 THESSALONIANS 2:16

L ord, don't you care that my sister has left me alone to do all the work?" (Luke 10:40).

Martha's life was cluttered. She needed a break. "Martha, Martha, you are worried and upset about many things," the Master explained to her. "Only one thing is important. Mary has chosen [it]" (Luke 10:41–42).

What had Mary chosen? She had chosen to sit at the feet of Christ. God is more pleased with the quiet attention of a sincere servant than the noisy service of a sour one.

What matters more than the type of service is the heart behind the service. A bad attitude spoils the gift we leave on the altar for God.

HE STILL MOVES STONES

How can a bad attitude spoil the gifts we give to God?

_____

_____

_____

_____

_____

Blind Ambition

Before destruction the heart of a man is haughty,
and before honor is humility.

PROVERBS 18:12 NKJV

Blind ambition. Success at all cost. Becoming a legend in one's own time. Climbing the ladder to the top. King of the mountain. Top of the heap. "I did it my way."

We make heroes out of people who are ambitious. We hold them up as models for our kids and put their pictures on the covers of our magazines.

And rightly so. This world would be in sad shape without people who dream of touching the heavens. Ambition is that grit in the soul which creates disenchantment with the ordinary and puts the dare into dreams.

But left unchecked it becomes an insatiable addiction to power and prestige, a roaring hunger for achievement that devours people as a lion devours an animal, leaving behind only the skeletal remains of relationships.

God won't tolerate it. Blind ambition is a giant step away from God and one step closer to catastrophe.

GOD CAME NEAR

Why is unchecked ambition a step away from God?

_____

_____

_____

_____

You're Something Special

*Nothing . . . in the whole world will ever
be able to separate us from the love of God.*

ROMANS 8:39

We want to know how long God's love will endure. Not just on Easter Sunday when our shoes are shined and our hair is fixed. Not when I'm peppy and positive and ready to tackle world hunger. Not then. I know how he feels about me then. Even I like me then.

I want to know how he feels about me when I snap at anything that moves, when my thoughts are gutter-level, when my tongue is sharp enough to slice a rock. How does he feel about me then?

Can anything separate us from the love Christ has for us?

God answered our question before we asked it. So we'd see his answer, he lit the sky with a star. So we'd hear it, he filled the night with a choir; and so we'd believe it, he did what no man had ever dreamed. He became flesh and dwelt among us.

He placed his hand on the shoulder of humanity and said, "You're something special."

IN THE GRIP OF GRACE

*God thinks you're special. Does this make a difference in
what you think about yourself? About others?*

_____

_____

_____

_____

Look at the Son

*Let us run with endurance the race that is set
before us, looking unto Jesus, the author and finisher of our faith.*

HEBREWS 12:1–2 NKJV

More mornings than not I drag myself out of bed and onto the street. I run because I don't like cardiologists.

Since heart disease runs in our family, I run in our neighborhood. As the sun is rising, I am running. And as I am running, my body is groaning. It doesn't want to cooperate. My knee hurts. My hip is stiff. My ankles complain.

Things hurt. And as things hurt, I've learned that I have three options. Go home. (Denalyn would laugh at me.) Meditate on my hurts until I start imagining I'm having chest pains. (Pleasant thought.) Or I can keep running and watch the sun come up. If I watch God's world go from dark to golden, guess what? The same happens to my attitude. The pain passes and the joints loosen. Everything improves as I fix my eyes on the sun.

Wasn't that the counsel of the Hebrew epistle—"looking unto Jesus"?

TRAVELING LIGHT

*Describe a time when your attitude improved because you
kept your focus on the Son.*

_____

_____

_____

_____

A Hunch and a Hope

"Daughter, your faith has made you well.
Go in peace, and be healed of your affliction."

MARK 5:34 NKJV

Maybe all you have [is] a crazy hunch and a high hope. You have nothing to give. But you are hurting. And all you have to offer him is your hurt.

Maybe that has kept you from coming to God. Oh, you've taken a step or two in his direction. But then you saw the other people around him. They seemed so clean, so neat, so trim and fit in their faith. And when you saw them, they blocked your view of him. So you stepped back.

If that describes you, note carefully one person [whom Christ] commended for having faith. It wasn't a wealthy giver. It wasn't a loyal follower. It wasn't an acclaimed teacher. It was a shame-struck, penniless outcast—a woman who had been bleeding for twelve years—who clutched onto her hunch that he could and her hope that he would.

Which, by the way, isn't a bad definition of faith. *A conviction that he can and a hope that he will.*

HE STILL MOVES STONES

Describe a time when you believed God could help you and he did.

_____

_____

_____

Two Sisters

Since we have been made right with God
by our faith, we have peace with God.

ROMANS 5:1

Pride and shame. You'd never know they are sisters. They appear so different. Pride puffs out her chest. Shame hangs her head. Pride boasts. Shame hides. Pride seeks to be seen. Shame seeks to be avoided.

But don't be fooled, the emotions have the same parentage. And the emotions have the same impact. They keep you from your Father.

Pride says, "You're too good for him."

Shame says, "You're too bad for him."

Pride drives you away.

Shame keeps you away.

If pride is what goes before a fall, then shame is what keeps you from getting up after one.

HE CHOSE THE NAILS

Do you face the challenge of pride or shame? How does this affect your relationship with God?

_____

_____

_____

_____

_____

A Heart at Peace

The wisdom that comes from God is first of all pure,
then peaceful, gentle, and easy to please.

JAMES 3:17

The heart of Jesus was pure. The Savior was adored by thousands, yet content to live a simple life. He was cared for by women (Luke 8:1–3), yet never accused of lustful thoughts; scorned by his own creation, but willing to forgive them before they even requested his mercy. Peter, who traveled with Jesus for three and a half years, described him as a "lamb unblemished and spotless" (1 Peter 1:19 NASB).

After spending the same amount of time with Jesus, John concluded, "And in him is no sin" (1 John 3:5 NIV).

Jesus' heart was peaceful. The disciples fretted over the need to feed the thousands, but not Jesus. He thanked God for the problem. The disciples shouted for fear in the storm, but not Jesus. He slept through it. Peter drew his sword to fight the soldiers, but not Jesus. He lifted his hand to heal. His heart was at peace.

JUST LIKE JESUS

What upsets you that Jesus would probably take in stride?

_____

_____

_____

_____

_____

An Everlasting Love

As high as the sky is above the earth,
so great is his love for those who respect him.

PSALM 103:11

The big news of the Bible is not that you love God but that God loves you; not that you can know God but that God already knows you! He tattooed your name on the palm of his hand. His thoughts of you outnumber the sand on the shore. You never leave his mind, escape his sight, flee his thoughts. He sees the worst of you and loves you still. Your sins of tomorrow and failings of the future will not surprise him; he sees them now. Every day and deed of your life has passed before his eyes and been calculated in his decision. He knows you better than you know you and has reached his verdict: he loves you still. No discovery will disillusion him; no rebellion will dissuade him. He loves you with an everlasting love.

COME THIRSTY

God knows everything about you and loves you still. Describe how that can positively affect your life.

God Heals Our Hurts

He had compassion on them.

MATTHEW 14:14 NIV

The Greek word for compassion is *splanchnizomai*, which won't mean much to you unless you are in the health professions and studied "splanchnology" in school. If so, you remember that "splanchnology" is a study of . . . the gut.

When Matthew writes that Jesus had compassion on the people, he is not saying that Jesus felt casual pity for them. No, the term is far more graphic. Matthew is saying that Jesus felt their hurt in his gut:

He felt the limp of the crippled.

He felt the hurt of the diseased.

He felt the loneliness of the leper.

He felt the embarrassment of the sinful.

And once he felt their hurts, he couldn't help but heal their hurts.

THE EYE OF THE STORM

Do you think there is a difference between compassion and concern? How would each cause you to respond to a need?

_____

_____

_____

_____

_____

The World Needs Servants

*"The Son of Man did not come to be served,
but to serve, and to give His life a ransom for many."*

MARK 10:45 NKJV

The world needs servants. People like Jesus who "did not come to be served, but to serve." He chose remote Nazareth over center-stage Jerusalem, his dad's carpentry shop over a marble-columned palace, and three decades of anonymity over a life of popularity.

Jesus came to serve. He selected prayer over sleep, the wilderness over the Jordan, irascible apostles over obedient angels. I'd have gone with the angels. Given the choice, I would have built my apostle team out of cherubim and seraphim or Gabriel and Michael, eyewitnesses of Red Sea rescues and Mount Carmel falling fires. I'd choose the angels.

Not Jesus. He picked the people. Peter, Andrew, John, and Matthew. When they feared the storm, he stilled it. When they had no coin for taxes, he supplied it. And when they had no wine for the wedding or food for the multitude, he made both.

CURE FOR THE COMMON LIFE

Make a list of things you can do to serve others.

_____

_____

_____

_____

The Lord Is Peace

*God's peace, which is so great we
cannot understand it, will keep your hearts
and minds in Christ Jesus.*

PHILIPPIANS 4:7

The Lord came to Gideon and told him he was to lead his people in victory over the Midianites. That's like God telling a housewife to stand up to her abusive husband or a high school student to take on drug peddlers or a preacher to preach the truth to a congregation of Pharisees. "Y-y-you b-b-better get somebody else," we stammer. But then God reminds us that he knows we can't, but he can, and to prove it he gives a wonderful gift. He brings a spirit of peace. A peace before the storm. A peace beyond logic. He gave it to David after he showed him Goliath; he gave it to Saul after he showed him the gospel; he gave it to Jesus after he showed him the cross. And he gave it to Gideon. So Gideon, in turn, gave the name to God. He built an altar and named it Jehovah-shalom, the Lord is peace (Judges 6:24).

THE GREAT HOUSE OF GOD

List some of the ways God calms your heart on a daily basis.

_____

_____

_____

_____

_____

The Last Step

He will change our simple bodies
and make them like his own glorious body.

PHILIPPIANS 3:21

Which word describes your body? My *cancerous* body? My *arthritic* body? My *deformed* body? My *crippled* body? My *addicted* body? My *ever-expanding* body? The word may be different, but the message is the same: These bodies are weak. They began decaying the minute we began breathing.

And, according to God, that's a part of the plan. Every wrinkle and every needle take us one step closer to the last step when Jesus will change our simple bodies into forever bodies. No pain. No depression. No sickness. No end.

This is not our forever house. It will serve for the time being. But there is nothing like the moment we enter his door.

TRAVELING LIGHT

Your body is not your "forever house." Think of some reasons why that is such good news.

February

The LORD is close to everyone who
prays to him, to all who truly pray to him.

—PSALM 145:18

The Greenhouse of the Heart

People harvest only what they plant.

GALATIANS 6:7

Think for a moment of your heart as a greenhouse. And your heart, like a greenhouse, has to be managed.

Consider for a moment your thoughts as seed. Some thoughts become flowers. Others become weeds. Sow seeds of hope and enjoy optimism. Sow seeds of doubt and expect insecurity.

The proof is everywhere you look. Ever wonder why some people have the Teflon capacity to resist negativism and remain patient, optimistic, and forgiving? Could it be that they have diligently sown seeds of goodness and are enjoying the harvest?

Ever wonder why others have such a sour outlook? Such a gloomy attitude? You would, too, if your heart were a greenhouse of weeds and thorns.

JUST LIKE JESUS

Make a list of some positive seeds you would like to sow in the "greenhouse" of your heart. Beside each, write how it will improve your attitude.

_____

_____

_____

_____

_____

_____

Have You Seen Him?

We . . . were eyewitnesses of His majesty.

2 PETER 1:16 NKJV

Jesus. The man. The bronzed Galilean who spoke with such thunderous authority and loved with such childlike humility.

The One who claimed to be older than time and greater than death.

Have you seen him?

Those who first did were never the same.

"My Lord and my God!" cried Thomas.

"I have seen the Lord," exclaimed Mary Magdalene.

"We have seen his glory," declared John.

"Were not our hearts burning within us while he talked?" rejoiced the two Emmaus-bound disciples.

But Peter said it best. "We were eyewitnesses of his majesty."

GOD CAME NEAR

How would you describe the majesty of Jesus? Imagine having him as your Savior!

Holiness Among Us

"Shout and be glad, Jerusalem.
I am coming, and I will live among you," says the LORD.

ZECHARIAH 2:10

God became a baby. He entered a world of problems and heartaches.

"The Word became human and lived here on earth among us. He was full of unfailing love and faithfulness" (John 1:14 NLT).

The operative word of the verse is *among*. He lived *among* us. He donned the costliest of robes: a human body. He made a throne out of a manger and a royal court out of some cows. He took a common name—Jesus—and made it holy. He took common people and made them the same. He could have lived over us or away from us. But he didn't. He lived *among* us.

He became a friend of the sinner and brother of the poor.

WHEN CHRIST COMES

Christ comes as a friend. Describe what this divine friendship means to you.

_____

_____

_____

_____

_____

_____

Living Loved

*God showed how much he loved us by
sending his only Son into the world. . . . This is real love.*

1 JOHN 4:9–10 NLT

Apart from God, "the heart is deceitful above all things" (Jeremiah 17:9 NIV). A marriage-saving love is not within us. A friendship-preserving devotion cannot be found in our hearts. We need help from an outside source. A transfusion. Would we love as God loves? Then we start by receiving God's love.

We preachers have been guilty of skipping the first step. "Love each other!" we tell our churches. "Be patient, kind, forgiving," we urge. But instructing people to love without telling them they are loved is like telling them to write a check without our making a deposit in their accounts. No wonder so many relationships are overdrawn. Hearts have insufficient love.

The secret to loving is living loved.

A LOVE WORTH GIVING

List some things that remind you of God's great love.

_____

_____

_____

_____

_____

_____

_____

Your Day Is Coming

"Hold on to what you have,
so that no one will take your crown."
REVELATION 3:11 NIV

Some of you have never won a prize in your life. Oh, maybe you were quartermaster in your Boy Scout troop or in charge of sodas at the homeroom Christmas party, but that's about it. You've never won much. You've watched the Mark McGwires of this world carry home the trophies and walk away with the ribbons. All you have are "almosts" and "what ifs."

If that hits home, then you'll cherish this promise: "And when the Chief Shepherd appears, you will receive the crown of glory that will never fade away" (1 Peter 5:4 NIV).

Your day is coming. What the world has overlooked, your Father has remembered, and sooner than you can imagine, you will be blessed by him.

WHEN CHRIST COMES

Hidden acts of unselfish love will be heralded with heavenly honor. How does this make you want to live your life?

_____

_____

_____

_____

_____

_____

Defined by Grace

Christ . . . raised us up together . . . that . . .
He might show the exceeding riches of His grace.

EPHESIANS 2:5–7 NKJV

Grace defines you. As grace sinks in, earthly labels fade. Society labels you like a can on an assembly line. Stupid. Unproductive. Slow learner. Fast talker. Quitter. Cheapskate. But as grace infiltrates, criticism disintegrates. You know you aren't who they say you are. You are who God says you are. Spiritually alive. Heavenly positioned. Connected to the Father. A billboard of mercy. An honored child.

Of course, not all labels are negative. Some people regard you as handsome, clever, successful, or efficient. But even a White House office doesn't compare with being "seated . . . with him in the heavenly realms" (Ephesians 2:6 NLT). Grace creates the Christian's résumé.

COME THIRSTY

You are who God says you are. What difference should this make in your life?

_____

_____

_____

_____

_____

_____

God's Help Is Near

The LORD is close to everyone who
prays to him, to all who truly pray to him.

PSALM 145:18

Healing begins when we do something. Healing begins when we reach out. Healing starts when we take a step. God's help is near and always available, but it is only given to those who seek it. Nothing results from apathy.

God honors radical, risk-taking faith.

When arks are built, lives are saved. When soldiers march, Jerichos tumble. When staffs are raised, seas still open. When a lunch is shared, thousands are fed. And when a garment is touched—whether by the hand of an anemic woman in Galilee or by the prayers of a beggar in Bangladesh—Jesus stoPsalm He stops and responds.

HE STILL MOVES STONES

God is looking for risk-takers. What do we gain by making ourselves totally available to him?

_____

_____

_____

_____

_____

_____

A Quiet Day of Rest

"Remember to keep the Sabbath holy."

EXODUS 20:8

Ever feel the wheels of your life racing faster and faster as you speed past the people you love? Could you use a reminder on how to slow it all down?

If so, read what Jesus did during the last Sabbath of his life. Start in the Gospel of Matthew. Didn't find anything? Try Mark. Read what Mark recorded about the way Jesus spent the Sabbath. Nothing there either? Strange. What about Luke? What does Luke say? Not a reference to the day? Not a word about it? Well, try John. Surely John mentions the Sabbath. He doesn't? No reference? Hmmm. Looks like Jesus was quiet that day.

"Wait a minute. That's it?" That's it.

"You mean with one week left to live, Jesus observed the Sabbath?" As far as we can tell.

"You mean with all those apostles to train and people to teach, he took a day to rest and worship?" Apparently so.

AND THE ANGELS WERE SILENT

What can you do to make time for rest and worship?

_____

_____

_____

_____

_____

God of Purpose

*"He came to serve others and to give his life
as a ransom for many people."*

MATTHEW 20:28

Jesus refused to be guided by anything other than his high call. His heart was purposeful. Most lives aim at nothing in particular and achieve it. Jesus aimed at one goal—to save humanity from its sin. He could summarize his life with one sentence: "The Son of man came to seek and to save the lost" (Luke 19:10 RSV). Jesus was so focused on his task that he knew when to say, "It is finished" (John 19:30). But he was not so focused on his goal that he was unpleasant.

Quite the contrary. How pleasant were his thoughts! Children couldn't resist Jesus. He could find beauty in lilies, joy in worship, and possibilities in problems. He would spend days with multitudes of sick people and still feel sorry for them. He spent over three decades wading through the muck and mire of our sin yet still saw enough beauty in us to die for our mistakes.

JUST LIKE JESUS

How can you maintain a balanced focus on your goals?

_____

_____

_____

_____

_____

_____

Love Isn't Easy

"Love your enemies. Pray for those who hurt you."
MATTHEW 5:44

Love isn't easy. Not for you. Not for me. Not even for Jesus. Want proof? Listen to his frustration: "You people have no faith. How long must I stay with you? How long must I put up with you?" (Mark 9:19).

How long must I put up with you?

"Long enough to be called crazy by my brothers and a liar by my neighbors. Long enough to be run out of my town and my temple."

How long? "Until the rooster sings and the sweat stings and the mallet rings and a hillside of demons smirk at a dying God."

How long? "Long enough for every sin to so soak my sinless soul that heaven will turn in horror until my swollen lips pronounce the final transaction: 'It is finished.'"

How long? "Until it kills me."

A LOVE WORTH GIVING

Do you sometimes find it difficult to love others? Why is it important for us to love, even though it can be frustrating?

_____

_____

_____

_____

_____

God Always Gives Grace

"God can do all things."

MARK 10:27

Our questions betray our lack of understanding:

How can God be everywhere at one time? (Who says God is bound by a body?)

How can God hear all the prayers which come to him? (Perhaps his ears are different from yours.)

How can God be the Father, the Son, and the Holy Spirit? (Could it be that heaven has a different set of physics than earth?)

If people down here won't forgive me, how much more am I guilty before a holy God? (Oh, just the opposite. God is always able to give grace when we humans can't—he invented it.)

THE GREAT HOUSE OF GOD

Do you tend to limit God to your human understanding? How can you avoid this?

_____

_____

_____

_____

_____

_____

_____

_____

A Next Door Savior

Who is this? Even the wind and the waves obey him!

MARK 4:41

He was, at once, man and God.

There he was, the single most significant person who ever lived. Forget MVP; he is the entire league. The head of the parade? Hardly. No one else shares the street. Who comes close? Humanity's best and brightest fade like dime-store rubies next to him.

Dismiss him? We can't.

Resist him? Equally difficult. Don't we need a God-man Savior? A just-God Jesus could make us but not understand us. A just-man Jesus could love us but never save us. But a God-man Jesus? Near enough to touch. Strong enough to trust. A next door Savior.

A Savior found by millions to be irresistible.

NEXT DOOR SAVIOR

We have a Savior who is near enough to touch and strong enough to trust. Write a note of praise to him for his love and care and power.

_____

_____

_____

_____

_____

A Home for Your Heart

LORD, I love the Temple
where you live, where your glory is.

PSALM 26:8

When it comes to resting your soul, there is no place like the Great House of God. "I'm asking GOD for one thing," [David] wrote, "only one thing: to live with him in his house my whole life long. I'll contemplate his beauty; I'll study at his feet. That's the only quiet, secure place in a noisy world" (Psalm 27:4–5 MSG).

If you could ask God for one thing, what would you request? David tells us what he would ask. He longs to *live* in the house of God. I emphasize the word *live*, because it deserves to be emphasized. David doesn't want to chat. He doesn't desire a cup of coffee on the back porch. He doesn't ask for a meal or to spend an evening in God's house. He wants to move in with him . . . forever. He's asking for his own room . . . permanently. He doesn't want to be stationed in God's house; he longs to retire there. He doesn't seek a temporary assignment, but rather lifelong residence.

THE GREAT HOUSE OF GOD

What one thing would you ask of God?

_____

_____

_____

_____

_____

Our Unchanging God

"When you go to the people of Israel,
tell them, 'I AM sent me to you.'"

EXODUS 3:14

Do you know anyone who goes around saying, "I am"? Neither do I. When we say "I am," we always add another word. "I am *happy*." "I am *sad*." "I am *strong*." "I am *Max*." God, however, starkly states, "I AM" and adds nothing else.

"You are what?" we want to ask. "I AM," he replies. God needs no descriptive word because he never changes. God is what he is. He is what he has always been. His immutability motivated the psalmist to declare, "But thou art the same" (Psalm 102:27 KJV). The writer is saying, "You are the One who is. You never change." Yahweh is an unchanging God.

TRAVELING LIGHT

We have an unchanging God. How does this encourage you to live for him?

_____

_____

_____

_____

_____

_____

Jesus Understands

*He took our suffering on him
and felt our pain for us.*

ISAIAH 53:4

Jesus knows how you feel. You're under the gun at work? Jesus knows how you feel. You've got more to do than is humanly possible? So did he. People take more from you than they give? Jesus understands. Your teenagers won't listen? Your students won't try? Jesus knows how you feel.

You are precious to him. So precious that he became like you so that you would come to him.

When you struggle, he listens. When you yearn, he responds. When you question, he hears. He has been there.

IN THE EYE OF THE STORM

God knows how you feel. In what area of life is this most encouraging to you?

_____

_____

_____

_____

_____

_____

_____

Kindness Makes the Coffee

"He is kind even to people who are ungrateful and full of sin."

LUKE 6:35

How often do we thank God for his kindness? Not often enough. But does our ingratitude restrict his kindness? No. "Because he is kind even to people who are ungrateful and full of sin."

In the original language, the word for *kindness* carries an added idea the English word does not. Chiefly it refers to an act of grace. But it also refers to a deed or person who is "useful, serviceable, adapted to its purpose." *Kindness* was even employed to describe food that was tasty as well as healthy. Sounds odd to our ears. "Hey, honey, what a great meal. The salad is especially *kind* tonight."

But the usage makes sense. Isn't kindness good *and* good for you? Pleasant *and* practical? Kindness not only says "good morning"; kindness makes the coffee.

A LOVE WORTH GIVING

"Kindness is an act of grace." Think of times when you have received kindness and times when you have been blessed to give kindness.

A Letter of Joy

Rejoice in the Lord always.
Again I will say, rejoice!
PHILIPPIANS 4:4 NKJV

G o with me back in history a couple of thousand years. Let's go to Rome . . . to a rather drab little room, surrounded by high walls. Inside we see a man seated on the floor. He's an older fellow, shoulders stooped and balding. Chains are on his hands and feet.

It is the apostle Paul. The apostle who was bound only by the will of God is now in chains—stuck in a dingy house—attached to a Roman officer.

He is writing a letter. No doubt it is a complaint letter to God. No doubt it is a list of grievances. He has every reason to be bitter and complain. But he doesn't. Instead, he writes a letter that two thousand years later is still known as the treatise on joy— Philippians.

Why don't you spend some time with it?

THE INSPIRATIONAL STUDY BIBLE

Make a list of "joy" verses from Philippians.

_____

_____

_____

_____

_____

An Amazing Destiny

I will extol You, O LORD, for You have lifted me up.

I n God's book, man is heading somewhere. He has an amazing destiny. We are being prepared to walk down the church aisle and become the bride of Jesus. We are going to live with him. Share the throne with him. Reign with him. We count. We are valuable. And what's more, our worth is built in! Our value is inborn.

You see, if there was anything that Jesus wanted everyone to understand, it was this: A person is worth something simply because he is a person. That is why he treated people like he did. Think about it. The girl caught making undercover thunder with someone she shouldn't—he forgave her. The untouchable leper who asked for cleansing—he touched him. And the blind welfare case that cluttered the roadside—he honored him. And the worn-out old windbag addicted to self-pity near the pool of Siloam—he healed him!

NO WONDER THEY CALL HIM THE SAVIOR

How would Jesus want us to treat others?

Preparing the Heart

*As far as the east is from
the west, so far has He removed
our transgressions from us.*

PSALM 103:12 NKJV

onfession does for the soul what preparing the land does for the field. Before the farmer sows the seed he works the acreage, removing the rocks and pulling the stumps. He knows that seed grows better if the land is prepared. Confession is the act of inviting God to walk the acreage of our hearts. "There is a rock of greed over here, Father. I can't budge it. And that tree of guilt near the fence? Its roots are long and deep. And may I show you some dry soil, too crusty for seed?" God's seed grows better if the soil of the heart is cleared.

And so the Father and the Son walk the field together; digging and pulling, preparing the heart for fruit. Confession invites the Father to work the soil of the soul.

IN THE GRIP OF GRACE

It is not always comfortable to have God "walk the acreage of our hearts." But it is necessary. Why?

The Place of Prayer

*They went back to Jerusalem from the Mount
of Olives. . . . They all continued praying together.*

ACTS 1:12, 14

Desire power for your life? It will come as you pray. For ten days the disciples prayed. Ten days of prayer plus a few minutes of preaching led to three thousand saved souls. Perhaps we invert the numbers. We're prone to pray for a few minutes and preach for ten days. Not the apostles. Like the boat waiting for Christ, they lingered in his presence. They never left the place of prayer.

The Upper Room was occupied by 120 disciples. Since there were about 4,000,000 people in Palestine at the time, this means that fewer than 1 in 30,000 was a Christian. Yet look at the fruit of their work. Better said, look at the fruit of God's Spirit in them. We can only wonder what would happen today if we, who *still* struggle, did what they did: wait on the Lord in the right place.

COME THIRSTY

The disciples lingered in God's presence. What would happen today if we did what they did?

_____

_____

_____

_____

A Morsel of Kindness

*Suppose someone has enough to live and
sees a brother or sister in need, but does not help.
Then God's love is not living in that person.*

1 JOHN 3:17

Leo Tolstoy, the great Russian writer, tells of the time he was walking down the street and passed a beggar. Tolstoy reached into his pocket to give the beggar some money, but his pocket was empty. Tolstoy turned to the man and said, "I'm sorry, my brother, but I have nothing to give."

The beggar brightened and said, "You have given me more than I asked for—you have called me brother."

To the loved, a word of affection is a morsel, but to the love-starved, a word of affection can be a feast.

HE STILL MOVES STONES

*Do you know people who are starving for a morsel of love?
How can you reach out to them?*

_____

_____

_____

_____

_____

_____

_____

Freedom to Choose

We are people who have faith and are saved.
HEBREWS 10:39

God honors us with the freedom to choose where we spend eternity.

And what an honor it is! In so many areas of life we have no choice. Think about it. You didn't choose your gender. You didn't choose your siblings. You didn't choose your race or place of birth.

Sometimes our lack of choices angers us. "It's not fair," we say. It's not fair that I was born in poverty or that I sing so poorly or that I run so slowly. But the scales of life were forever tipped on the side of fairness when God planted a tree in the Garden of Eden. All complaints were silenced when Adam and his descendants were given free will, the freedom to make whatever eternal choice we desire. Any injustice in this life is offset by the honor of choosing our destiny in the next.

HE CHOSE THE NAILS

God has given us the freedom to choose our destiny. How have you honored him with this freedom?

_____

_____

_____

_____

_____

See What God Has Done!

The heavens tell the glory of God.

PSALM 19:1

How vital that we pray, armed with the knowledge that God is in heaven. Pray with any lesser conviction and your prayers are timid, shallow, and hollow. But spend some time walking in the workshop of the heavens, seeing what God has done, and watch how your prayers are energized.

Behold the sun! Every square yard of the sun is constantly emitting 130,000 horsepower, or the equivalent of 450 eight-cylinder automobile engines. And yet our sun, as powerful as it is, is but one minor star in the 100 billion orbs which make up our Milky Way galaxy. Hold a dime in your fingers and extend it arm's length toward the sky, allowing it to eclipse your vision, and you will block out fifteen million stars from your view. By showing us the heavens, Jesus is showing us his Father's workshop. He taps us on the shoulder and says, "Your Father can handle that for you."

THE GREAT HOUSE OF GOD

Write some thoughts about God that help to energize your prayers.

_____

_____

_____

_____

_____

No Price Is Too High

"We had to celebrate and be happy because
your brother . . . was lost, but now he is found."

LUKE 15:32

When our oldest daughter, Jenna, was two, I lost her in a department store. One minute she was at my side and the next she was gone. I panicked. All of a sudden only one thing mattered—I had to find my daughter. Shopping was forgotten. The list of things I came to get was unimportant. I yelled her name. What people thought didn't matter. For a few minutes, every ounce of energy had one goal—to find my lost child. (I did, by the way. She was hiding behind some jackets!)

No price is too high for a parent to pay to redeem his child. No energy is too great. No effort too demanding. A parent will go to any length to find his or her own.

So will God.

Mark it down. God's greatest creation is not the flung stars or the gorged canyons; it's his eternal plan to reach his children.

AND THE ANGELS WERE SILENT

Do you know someone who is hiding from God? Write a prayer for that person to be found.

_____

_____

_____

_____

_____

Pursue the Wonder of Life

"Those who try to keep their lives
will lose them. But those who give up
their lives will save them."

LUKE 17:33

There is a rawness and a wonder to life. Pursue it. Hunt for it. Sell out to get it. Don't listen to the whines of those who have settled for a second-rate life and want you to do the same so they won't feel guilty. Your goal is not to live long; it's to live.

Jesus says the options are clear. On one side there is the voice of safety. You can build a fire in the hearth, stay inside, and stay warm and dry and safe.

Or you can hear the voice of adventure—God's adventure. Instead of building a fire in your hearth, build a fire in your heart. Follow God's impulses. Adopt the child. Move overseas. Teach the class. Change careers. Run for office. Make a difference. Sure it isn't safe, but what is?

HE STILL MOVES STONES

What adventure do you feel compelled to follow? What steps can you take to achieve it?

_____

_____

_____

_____

_____

He Chose the Cross

You did not save yourselves; it was a gift from God.

Ephesians 2:8

Jesus' obedience began in a small-town carpentry shop. His uncommon approach to his common life groomed him for his uncommon call. "When Jesus entered public life he was about thirty years old" (Luke 3:23 MSG). In order for Jesus to change the world, he had to say good-bye to his world.

He had to give Mary a kiss. Have a final meal in the kitchen, a final walk through the streets. Did he ascend one of the hills of Nazareth and think of the day he would ascend the hill near Jerusalem?

He knew what was going to happen. "God chose him for this purpose long before the world began" (1 Peter 1:20 NLT). Every ounce of suffering had been scripted—it just fell to him to play the part.

Not that he had to. Nazareth was a cozy town. Why not build a carpentry business? Keep his identity a secret? To be forced to die is one thing, but to willingly take up your own cross is something else.

Next Door Savior

Is there something you need to leave to follow Christ?

_____

_____

_____

_____

_____

Your Personal Blessing

God will praise each one of them.

1 CORINTHIANS 4:5

W hat an incredible sentence. *God will praise each one of them.* Not "the best of them" nor "a few of them" nor "the achievers among them," but "God will praise each one of them."

You won't be left out. God will see to that. In fact, God himself will give the praise. When it comes to giving recognition, God does not delegate the job. Michael doesn't hand out the crowns. Gabriel doesn't speak on behalf of the throne. God himself does the honors. God himself will praise his children.

And what's more, the praise is personal! Awards aren't given a nation at a time, a church at a time, or a generation at a time. The crowns are given one at a time. God himself will look you in the eye and bless you with the words, "Well done, good and faithful servant!" (Matthew 25:23 NIV).

WHEN CHRIST COMES

How awesome to think that God will reward us personally. How can this thought help when your days are discouraging?

_____

_____

_____

_____

_____

_____

"God Is! God Is!"

If I go up to the heavens, you are there;
if I make my bed in the depths, you are there.

PSALM 139:8 NIV

It is the normality not the uniqueness of God's miracles that causes them to be so staggering. Rather than shocking the globe with an occasional demonstration of deity, God has opted to display his power daily. Proverbially. Pounding waves. Prism-cast colors. Birth, death, life. We are surrounded by miracles. God is throwing testimonies at us like fireworks, each one exploding, "God is! God is!"

The psalmist marveled at such holy handiwork. "Where can I go from your Spirit?" he questioned with delight. "Where can I flee from your presence? If I go up to the heavens, you are there; if I make my bed in the depths, you are there" (Psalm 139:7–8 NIV).

We wonder, with so many miraculous testimonies around us, how we could escape God. But somehow we do. We live in an art gallery of divine creativity and yet are content to gaze only at the carpet

GOD CAME NEAR

Describe some of the most beautiful things you have seen in God's art gallery.

_____

_____

_____

_____

The Heart of Jesus

"The Son does whatever the Father does."

JOHN 5:19

The crowning attribute of Christ was this: his heart was spiritual. His thoughts reflected his intimate relationship with the Father. "I am in the Father and the Father is in me," he stated (John 14:11).

Jesus took his instructions from God. It was his habit to go to worship (Luke 4:16). It was his practice to memorize Scripture (v. 4:4). Luke says Jesus "often slipped away to be alone so he could pray" (v. 5:16). His times of prayer guided him. He once returned from prayer and announced it was time to move to another city (Mark 1:35–38). Another time of prayer resulted in the selection of the disciples (Luke 6:12–13). Jesus was led by an unseen hand.

The heart of Jesus was spiritual.

JUST LIKE JESUS

What actions and attitudes come from a spiritual heart? What are some possible results from demonstrating them?

_____

_____

_____

_____

_____

_____

You Are God's Idea

"Before I made you in your mother's womb, I chose you."

God planned and packed you on purpose for his purpose. Heaven's custom design.

At a moment before moments existed, the sovereign Star Maker resolved, "I will make _____." Your name goes in the blank. Then he continued with, "And I will make him/her _____, _____ and _____ and _____ and _____." Fill those blanks with your characteristics. Insightful. Clever. Detail oriented. Restless. And since you are God's idea, you are a good idea. What God said about Jeremiah, he said about you: "Before I made you in your mother's womb, I chose you. Before you were born, I set you apart for a special work."

Set apart for a special work.

CURE FOR THE COMMON LIFE

How have your unique characteristics prepared you to do a special work for God?

_____

_____

_____

_____

_____

_____

_____

Sacred Delight

*"Those people who know they have great spiritual needs
are happy, because the kingdom of heaven belongs to them."*

MATTHEW 5:3

God promises sacred delight. And he promises it to an unlikely crowd:

• "The poor in spirit" (v. 3). Beggars in God's soup kitchen.

• "Those who mourn" (v. 4). Sinners Anonymous bound together by the truth of their introduction: "Hi, I am me. I'm a sinner."

• "The merciful" (v. 7). Winners of the million-dollar lottery who share the prize with their enemies.

• "The pure in heart" (v. 8)/ Physicians who love lepers and escape infection.

• "The peacemakers" (v. 9). Architects who build bridges with wood from a Roman cross.

• "The persecuted" (v. 10). Those who manage to keep an eye on heaven while walking through hell on earth.

It is to this band of pilgrims that God promises a special blessing. A heavenly joy. A sacred delight.

THE APPLAUSE OF HEAVEN

What characteristics are common to all of these pilgrims?

_____

_____

_____

_____

A Daily Development

God is working in you to help you
want to do and be able to do what pleases him.

PHILIPPIANS 2:13

Wouldn't a bride and groom have to be more married on their fiftieth anniversary than on their wedding day?

Yet, on the other hand, how could they be? The marriage certificate hasn't matured. Ah, but the relationship has, and there is the difference. Technically, they are no more united than they were when they left the altar. But relationally, they are completely different.

The same is true of our walk with God. Can you be more saved than you were the first day of your salvation? No. But can a person grow in salvation? Absolutely. It, like marriage, is a done deal and a daily development.

HE CHOSE THE NAILS

Make a list of some of the ways you have grown in your
walk with God over the past weeks and months.

_____

_____

_____

_____

_____

The Sum of Christianity

*"I did this as an example so that you
should do as I have done for you."*

JOHN 13:15

Mark it down. We are what we see. If we see only ourselves, our tombstones will have the same epitaph Paul used to describe enemies of Christ: "Their god is their own appetite, their pride is in what they should be ashamed of, and this world is the limit of their horizon" (Philippians 3:19 PHILLIPS).

Humans were never meant to dwell in the stale fog of the lowlands with no vision of their Creator.

Seeing Jesus is what Christianity is all about. Christian service, in its purest form, is nothing more than imitating him whom we see. To see his majesty and to imitate him, that is the sum of Christianity.

GOD CAME NEAR

Describe some of Jesus' actions that you would like to imitate. Pray that God would help you to imitate his Son.

_____

_____

_____

_____

_____

_____

Why Worry?

Continue praying, keeping alert, and always thanking God.

COLOSSIANS 4:2

Two words summarize Christ's opinion of worry: *irrelevant* and *irreverent*.

"Can all your worries add a single moment to your life? Of course not" (Matthew 6:27 NLT). Worry is irrelevant. It alters nothing. When was the last time you solved a problem by worrying about it? Imagine someone saying, "I got behind in my bills, so I resolved to worry my way out of debt. And, you know, it worked! A few sleepless nights, a day of puking and hand wringing. I yelled at my kids and took some pills, and—glory to worry—money appeared on my desk."

It doesn't happen! Worry changes nothing. You don't add one day to your life or one bit of life to your day by worrying. Your anxiety earns you heartburn, nothing more.

Ninety-two percent of our worries are needless! Not only is worry irrelevant, doing nothing; worry is irreverent, distrusting God.

COME THIRSTY

"Worry is irreverent, distrusting God." Explain what that sentence means and why it is true.

_____

_____

_____

_____

God Cares About You

"Look at the birds in the air. They don't plant or harvest or store food in barns, but your heavenly Father feeds them."

MATTHEW 6:26

Consider the earth! Our globe's weight has been estimated at six sextillion tons (a six with twenty-one zeroes). Yet it is precisely tilted at twenty-three degrees; any more or any less and our seasons would be lost in a melted polar flood. Though our globe revolves at the rate of one-thousand miles per hour or twenty-five thousand miles per day or nine million miles per year, none of us tumbles into orbit.

As you stand . . . observing God's workshop, let me pose a few questions. If he is able to place the stars in their sockets and suspend the sky like a curtain, do you think it is remotely possible that God is able to guide your life? If your God is mighty enough to ignite the sun, could it be that he is mighty enough to light your path? If he cares enough about the planet Saturn to give it rings or Venus to make it sparkle, is there an outside chance that he cares enough about you to meet your needs?

THE GREAT HOUSE OF GOD

God cares about Saturn and Venus, the sunflowers and violets. How does this help you realize he cares for you?

_____

_____

_____

_____

The Reason for the Cross

We have been sanctified through the
offering of the body of Jesus Christ once for all.

HEBREWS 10:10 NKJV

Man by himself cannot deal with his own guilt. He must have help from the outside. In order to forgive himself, he must have forgiveness from the One he has offended. Yet man is unworthy to ask God for forgiveness.

That, then, is the whole reason for the cross.

The cross did what sacrificed lambs could not do. It erased our sins, not for a year, but for eternity. The cross did what man could not do. It granted us the right to talk with, love, and even live with God.

You can't do that by yourself. I don't care how many worship services you attend or good deeds you do, your goodness is insufficient. You can't be good enough to deserve forgiveness. No one bats a thousand. No one bowls three hundred. No one. Not you, not me, not anyone.

That's why we need a savior.

NO WONDER THEY CALL HIM THE SAVIOR

The cross erased our sins for eternity. Christ did what we
could not do. Write sentences of praise for his sacrificial love

_____

_____

_____

_____

Good Habits

So let us go on to grown-up teaching.
Let us not go back over the beginning lessons
we learned about Christ.

HEBREWS 6:1

I like the story of the little boy who fell out of bed. When his mom asked him what happened, he answered, "I don't know. I guess I stayed too close to where I got in."

Easy to do the same with our faith. It's tempting just to stay where we got in and never move.

Pick a time in the not-too-distant past. A year or two ago. Now ask yourself a few questions. How does your prayer life today compare with then? How about your giving? Have both the amount and the joy increased? What about your church loyalty? Can you tell you've grown? And Bible study? Are you learning to learn?

Don't make the mistake of the little boy. Don't stay too close to where you got in. It's risky resting on the edge.

WHEN GOD WHISPERS YOUR NAME

How does your prayer life today compare with a year or two ago? Your giving, church loyalty, and Bible study?

Reasons for Joy

Rejoice in the Lord always. Again I will say, rejoice!
PHILIPPIANS 4:4 NKJV

How's life?" someone asks. And we who've been resurrected from the dead say, "Well, things could be better." Or "Couldn't get a parking place." Or "My parents won't let me move to Hawaii." Or "People won't leave me alone so I can finish my sermon on selfishness."

Are you so focused on what you don't have that you are blind to what you do?

> You have a ticket to heaven no thief can take,
> an eternal home no divorce can break.

> Every sin of your life has been cast to the sea.
> Every mistake you've made is nailed to the tree.

> You're blood-bought and heaven-made.
> A child of God—forever saved.

> So be grateful, joyful—for isn't it true?
> What you don't have is much less
> than what you do.

A LOVE WORTH GIVING

List some of the things you can be thankful for in your life.

_____

_____

_____

_____

Prayers Make a Difference

We all know that God does not listen to sinners,
but he listens to anyone who worships and obeys him.

JOHN 9:31

Most of our prayer lives could use a tune-up.

Some prayer lives lack consistency. They're either a desert or an oasis. Long, arid, dry spells interrupted by brief plunges into the waters of communion.

Others of us need sincerity. Our prayers are a bit hollow, memorized, and rigid. More liturgy than life. And though they are daily, they are dull.

Still others lack, well, honesty. We honestly wonder if prayer makes a difference. Why on earth would God in heaven want to talk to me? If God knows all, who am I to tell him anything? If God controls all, who am I to do anything?

Our prayers may be awkward. Our attempts may be feeble. But since the power of prayer is in the one who hears it and not the one who says it, our prayers do make a difference.

HE STILL MOVES STONES

Do you ever wonder if your prayers make a difference?
How can you be assured they do?

_____

_____

_____

_____

It's a Jungle out There!

My help comes from the LORD, who made heaven and earth.

PSALM 121:2

For many people, life is—well, life is a jungle. Not a jungle of trees and beasts. Our jungles are comprised of the thicker thickets of failing health, broken hearts, and empty wallets. We don't hear the screeching of birds or the roaring of lions, but we do hear the complaints of neighbors and the demands of bosses.

Whether you are a lamb lost on a craggy ledge or a city slicker alone in a deep jungle, everything changes when your rescuer appears.

Your loneliness diminishes, because you have fellowship. Your despair decreases, because you have vision. Your confusion begins to lift, because you have direction.

You haven't left the jungle. The trees still eclipse the sky, and the thorns still cut the skin. It hasn't changed, but you have. You have changed because you have hope. And you have hope because you have met someone who can lead you out.

TRAVELING LIGHT

Have you met that Someone who can lead you out of the "jungle of life"? How has this changed the way you live your life?

_____

_____

_____

_____

_____

Beyond Imagination

"There are many rooms in my Father's house; . . .
I am going there to prepare a place for you."

JOHN 14:2

Rest on this earth is a false rest. Beware of those who urge you to find happiness here; you won't find it. Guard against the false physicians who promise that joy is only a diet away, a marriage away, a job away, or a transfer away.

Try this. Imagine a perfect world. Whatever that means to you, imagine it. Does that mean peace? Then envision absolute tranquility. Does a perfect world imply joy? Then create your highest happiness. Will a perfect world have love? If so, ponder a place where love has no bounds. Whatever heaven means to you, imagine it. Get it firmly fixed in your mind.

And then smile as the Father reminds you, *No one has ever imagined what God has prepared for those who love him.*

When it comes to describing heaven, we are all happy failures.

WHEN GOD WHISPERS YOUR NAME

Describe the wonders you imagine are waiting for you in heaven.

_____

_____

_____

_____

_____

Don't Forget

May our Lord Jesus Christ himself . . . encourage you and
strengthen you in every good thing you do and say.

2 THESSALONIANS 2:16

Are you still in love with Jesus? Before you remember anything, remember him. If you forget anything, don't forget him. Oh, but how quickly we forget. So much happens through the years. So many changes within. So many alterations without. And, somewhere, back there, we leave him. We don't turn away from him . . . we just don't take him with us. Assignments come. Promotions come. Budgets are made. Kids are born, and the Christ . . . the Christ is forgotten.

Has it been awhile since you stared at the heavens in speechless amazement? Has it been awhile since you realized God's divinity and your carnality?

If it has, then you need to know something. He is still there. He hasn't left.

SIX HOURS ONE FRIDAY

Make a list of things you can look for in the world and
people around you that testify to God's divinity.

_____

_____

_____

_____

_____

Changed to His Likeness

We Christians actually do have within us
a portion of the very thoughts and mind of Christ.

1 CORINTHIANS 2:16 TLB

The distance between our hearts and [Jesus' heart] seems so immense. How could we ever hope to have the heart of Jesus?

Ready for a surprise? You already do. If you are in Christ, you already have the heart of Christ. One of the supreme yet unrealized promises of God is simply this: if you have given your life to Jesus, Jesus has given himself to you. He has made your heart his home. It would be hard to say it more succinctly than Paul does: "Christ lives in me" (Galatians. 2:20 MSG).

He has moved in and unpacked his bags and is ready to change you "into his likeness from one degree of glory to another" (2 Corinthians 3:18 RSV).

JUST LIKE JESUS

Think back over your life. How has Christ been changing you into his likeness?

_____

_____

_____

_____

_____

_____

God Warrants Our Worship

Oh, give thanks to the LORD, for He is good!
For His mercy endures forever.

PSALM 107:1 NKJV

The chief reason for applauding God? He deserves it. If singing did nothing but weary your voice, if giving only emptied your wallet—if worship did nothing for you—it would still be right to do. God warrants our worship.

How else do you respond to a Being of blazing, blistering, unadulterated, unending holiness? What do you do with such holiness if not adore it?

And his power. He churns forces that launch meteors, orbit planets, and ignite stars. Commanding whales to spout salty air, petunias to perfume the night, and songbirds to chirp joy into spring. Above the earth, flotillas of clouds endlessly shape and reshape; within the earth, strata of groaning rocks shift and turn. Who are we to sojourn on a trembling, wonderful orb so shot through with wonder?

CURE FOR THE COMMON LIFE

Why does God deserve our praise and worship?

_____

_____

_____

_____

_____

God's Help Is Near

Faith means being sure of the things we hope for
and knowing that something is real even if we do not see it.

Faith is the belief that God is real and that God is good. It is a choice to believe that the One who made it all hasn't left it all and that he still sends light into the shadows and responds to gestures of faith.

Faith is the belief that God will do what is right.

God says that the more hopeless your circumstances, the more likely your salvation. The greater your cares, the more genuine your prayers. The darker the room, the greater the need for light.

God's help is near and always available, but it is only given to those who seek it.

HE STILL MOVES STONES

Sometimes we need to look beyond the "little picture" of our problems to the "big picture" of God's provision. What steps will help you to do this?

_____

_____

_____

_____

_____

_____

_____

Working Well

"My Father never stops working, and so I keep working, too."

JOHN 5:17

God views work worthy of its own engraved commandment: "You shall work six days, but on the seventh day you shall rest" (Exodus 34:21 NASB). We like the second half of that verse. But emphasis on the day of rest might cause us to miss the command to work: "You shall work six days." Whether you work at home or in the marketplace, your work matters to God.

And your work matters to society. We need you! Cities need plumbers. Nations need soldiers. Stoplights break. Bones break. We need people to repair the first and set the second. Someone has to raise kids, raise cane, and manage the kids who raise Cain.

Whether you log on or lace up for the day, you imitate God. Jehovah himself worked for the first six days of creation. Jesus said, "My Father never stops working, and so I keep working, too."

CURE FOR THE COMMON LIFE

Name some ways you can honor God through your work.

_____

_____

_____

_____

_____

_____

A Cut Above

"Be still, and know that I am God."

PSALM 46:10 NIV

The word *holy* means "to separate." The ancestry of the term can be traced back to an ancient word which means "to cut." To be holy, then, is to be a cut above the norm, superior, extraordinary. The Holy One dwells on a different level from the rest of us. What frightens us does not frighten him. What troubles us does not trouble him.

I'm more a landlubber than a sailor, but I've puttered around in a bass boat enough to know the secret for finding land in a storm. You don't aim at another boat. You certainly don't stare at the waves. You set your sights on an object unaffected by the wind—a light on the shore—and go straight toward it.

When you set your sights on our God, you focus on One "a cut above" any storm life may bring. You find peace.

THE GREAT HOUSE OF GOD

What is the purpose of setting your sights on God?

Assurance of Victory

This is the victory that conquers the world—our faith.

1 JOHN 5:4

What is unique about the kingdom of God is that you are assured of victory. You have won! You are assured that you will someday stand before the face of God and see the King of kings. You are assured that someday you will enter a world where there will be no more pain, no more tears, no more sorrow.

If you have no faith in the future, then you have no power in the present. If you have no faith in the life beyond this life, then your present life is going to be powerless. But if you believe in the future and are assured of victory, then there should be a dance in your step and a smile on your face.

THE INSPIRATIONAL STUDY BIBLE

Remind yourself of some of the many victories you have experienced because of God. Are you smiling?

_____

_____

_____

_____

_____

_____

_____

Come and See

*Nathanael said to Philip, "Can anything good
come from Nazareth?" Philip answered, "Come and see."*

JOHN 1:46

Nathanael's question still lingers, even two thousand years later. Can anything good come out of Nazareth? Come and see.

Come and see the changed lives:

>the alcoholic now dry,
>the embittered now joyful,
>the shamed now forgiven,
>marriages rebuilt, the orphans embraced,
>the imprisoned inspired.

Come and see the pierced hand of God touch the most common heart, wipe the tear from the wrinkled face, and forgive the ugliest sin.

Come and see. He avoids no seeker. He ignores no probe. He fears no search. Come and see.

A GENTLE THUNDER

List people you know who have been changed by God's touch.

_____

_____

_____

_____

To See God

*"Anything you did for even the least
of my people here, you also did for me."*

Matthew 25:40

When Francis of Assisi turned his back on wealth to seek God in simplicity, he stripped naked and walked out of the city. He soon encountered a leper on the side of the road. He passed him, then stopped and went back and embraced the diseased man. Francis then continued on his journey. After a few steps he turned to look again at the leper, but no one was there.

For the rest of his life, he believed the leper was Jesus Christ. He may have been right.

Jesus lives in the forgotten. He has taken up residence in the ignored. He has made a mansion amid the ill. If we want to see God, we must go among the broken and beaten and there we will see him.

AND THE ANGELS WERE SILENT

We will find Christ among the "broken and beaten." Yet so often these are the very ones we tend to avoid. What will compel us to reach out to them in love?

God's Goodness

*The rich and the poor are alike
in that the LORD made them all.*

PROVERBS 22:2

Have you noticed that God doesn't ask you to prove that you will put your salary to good use? Have you noticed that God doesn't turn off your oxygen supply when you misuse his gifts? Aren't you glad that God doesn't give you only that which you remember to thank him for?

God's goodness is spurred by his nature, not by our worthiness.

Someone asked an associate of mine, "What biblical precedent do we have to help the poor who have no desire to become Christians?"

My friend responded with one word: "God."

God does it daily, for millions of people.

IN THE EYE OF THE STORM

*How has God demonstrated his love and goodness to you?
Does this help you want to do the same for others?*

_____

_____

_____

_____

_____

_____

_____

Wisdom in Warnings

Do not be deceived: God cannot be mocked.
A man reaps what he sows.

GALATIANS 6:7 NIV

We're often surprised at life's mishaps, but when pressed against the wall of honesty we have to admit that if we had just fired that silly receptionist and done something about those calls, we could have avoided many problems. We usually knew that trouble was just around the bend. Christians who have fallen away felt the fire waning long before it went out. Unwanted pregnancies or explosions of anger may appear to be the fruit of a moment's waywardness, but in reality, they're usually the result of a history of ignoring warnings about an impending fire.

Are you close to the falls? Are your senses numb? Are your eyes trained to turn and roll when they should pause and observe?

Then maybe you need to repair your warning detector.

GOD CAME NEAR

Have you developed a habit of ignoring God's warnings? What can you do to keep your "warning detector" in good working order?

_____

_____

_____

_____

What God Has Done

You have been saved by God's grace.
EPHESIANS 2:5

Read slowly and carefully Paul's description of what God has done for you: "When you were spiritually dead because of your sins and because you were not free from the power of your sinful self, God made you alive with Christ, and he forgave all our sins. He canceled the debt, which listed all the rules we failed to follow. He took away that record with its rules and nailed it to the cross. God stripped the spiritual rulers and powers of their authority. With the cross, he won the victory and showed the world that they were powerless" (Colossians 2:13–15).

As you look at the words above, answer this question. Who is doing the work? You or God? Who is active? You or God? Who is doing the saving? You or God?

HE STILL MOVES STONES

God has given us new life in Christ. Why is that good news for you?

_____

_____

_____

_____

_____

_____

Open Your Heart

When I am afraid, I put my trust in you.

PSALM 56:3 NLT

How did Jesus endure the terror of the crucifixion? He went first to the Father with his fears. He modeled the words of Psalm 56:3: "When I am afraid, I will trust you."

Do the same with yours. Don't avoid life's Gardens of Gethsemane. Enter them. Just don't enter them alone. And while there, be honest. Pounding the ground is permitted. Tears are allowed. And if you sweat blood, you won't be the first. Do what Jesus did; open your heart.

And be specific. Jesus was. "Take *this* cup," he prayed (Mark 14:36 NIV). Give God the number of the flight. Tell him the length of the speech. Share the details of the job transfer. He has plenty of time. He also has plenty of compassion.

He doesn't think your fears are foolish or silly. He won't tell you to "buck up" or "get tough." He's been where you are. He knows how you feel.

And he knows what you need.

TRAVELING LIGHT

How can God's love help you to be honest with him?

_____

_____

_____

_____

Godless Living

Their thinking became useless. Their foolish minds were filled with darkness. They said they were wise, but they became fools.

ROMANS 1:21–22

Since the hedonist has never seen the hand who made the universe, he assumes there is no life beyond the here and now. He believes there is no truth beyond this room. No purpose beyond his own pleasure. No divine factor. He has no concern for the eternal.

The hedonist says, "Who cares? I may be bad, but so what? What I do is my business." He's more concerned about satisfying his passions than in knowing the Father. His life is so desperate for pleasure that he has no time or room for God.

Is he right? Is it okay to spend our days thumbing our noses at God and living it up?

Paul says, "Absolutely not!"

According to Romans 1, we lose more than stained glass windows when we dismiss God. We lose our standard, our purpose, and our worship.

IN THE GRIP OF GRACE

How do we lose our standard, our purpose, and our worship if we dismiss God?

_____

_____

_____

_____

The Love of God

"I'll call the unloved and make them beloved."
ROMANS 9:25 MSG

Our love depends on the receiver of the love. Let a thousand people pass before us, and we will not feel the same about each. Our love will be regulated by their appearance, by their personalities. Even when we find a few people we like, our feelings will fluctuate. How they treat us will affect how we love them. The receiver regulates our love.

Not so with the love of God. We have no thermostatic impact on his love for us. The love of God is born from within him, not from what he finds in us. His love is uncaused and spontaneous.

Does he love us because of our goodness? Because of our kindness? Because of our great faith? No, he loves us because of *his* goodness, kindness, and great faith.

A LOVE WORTH GIVING

God's love is uncaused and spontaneous. It does not depend on the qualities of the receiver. How can this guide us as we love others?

March

*Depend on the L*ORD*; trust him,*
and he will take care of you.

—PSALM 37:5

Only One Thing Counts

No one has ever imagined what
God has prepared for those who love him.

1 CORINTHIANS 2:9

Think about the day Christ comes. There you are in the great circle of the redeemed. Though you are one of a throng, it's as if you and Jesus are all alone.

I'm speculating now, but I wonder if Christ might say these words to you: "I'm so proud that you let me use you. Because of you, others are here today. Would you like to meet them?"

At that point Jesus might turn to the crowd and invite them. One by one, they begin to step out and walk forward.

The first is your neighbor, a crusty old sort who lived next door. To be frank, you didn't expect to see him. "You never knew I was watching," he explains, "but I was. And because of you, I am here."

It's not long before you and your Savior are encircled by the delightful collection of souls you've touched. Some you know, most you don't, but for each you feel the same. You feel what Paul felt . . . "I'm so proud of your faith" (1 Thessalonians 2:19).

WHEN CHRIST COMES

Will people step forward in heaven because of your faith?
What can you do to share Christ with others?

_____

_____

_____

_____

The Reward of Christianity

*All things are worth nothing compared
with the greatness of knowing Christ Jesus my Lord.*

PHILIPPIANS 3:8

The reward of Christianity is Christ.

Do you journey to the Grand Canyon for the souvenir T-shirt or the snow globe with the snowflakes that fall when you shake it? No. The reward of the Grand Canyon is the Grand Canyon. The wide-eyed realization that you are part of something ancient, splendid, powerful, and greater than you.

The cache of Christianity is Christ. Not money in the bank or a car in the garage or a healthy body or a better self-image. Secondary and tertiary fruits perhaPsalm But the Fort Knox of faith is Christ. Fellowship with him. Walking with him. Pondering him. Exploring him. The heart-stopping realization that in him you are part of something ancient, endless, unstoppable, and unfathomable. And that he, who can dig the Grand Canyon with his pinkie, thinks you're worth his death on Roman timber. Christ is the reward of Christianity.

NEXT DOOR SAVIOR

Explain how Christ is the reward of Christianity.

_____

_____

_____

_____

Live a Holy Life

"You should be a light for other people.
Live so that they will see the good things you do
and will praise your Father in heaven."

MATTHEW 5:16

Y ou want to make a difference in your world? Live a holy life:

Be faithful to your spouse.

Be the one at the office who refuses to cheat.

Be the neighbor who acts neighborly.

Be the employee who does the work and doesn't complain.

Pay your bills.

Do your part and enjoy life.

Don't speak one message and live another.

People are watching the way we act more than they are listening to what we say.

A GENTLE THUNDER

Add to this list other ways of living out a holy life.

_____

_____

_____

_____

_____

_____

_____

Anger Does No Good

An angry person causes trouble.
PROVERBS 29:22

Anger. It's a peculiar yet predictable emotion. It begins as a drop of water. An irritant. A frustration. Nothing big, just an aggravation. Someone gets your parking place. Someone pulls in front of you on the freeway. A waitress is slow and you are in a hurry. The toast burns. Drops of water. Drip. Drip. Drip. Drip.

Yet, get enough of these seemingly innocent drops of anger and before long you've got a bucket full of rage. Walking revenge. Blind bitterness.

Now, is that any way to live? What good has hatred ever brought? What hope has anger ever created? What problems have ever been resolved by revenge?

NO WONDER THEY CALL HIM THE SAVIOR

Think of a time when you allowed anger and revenge to build in your heart. What was the result of this? Did it resolve a problem or create more problems?

_____

_____

_____

_____

_____

_____

Boldness Before the Throne

*Let us, then, feel very sure that we can
come before God's throne where there is grace.*

HEBREWS 4:16

Jesus tells us, "When you pray, pray like this. 'Our Father who is in heaven, hallowed be thy name. Thy kingdom come.'"

When you say, "Thy kingdom come," you are inviting the Messiah himself to walk into your world. "Come, my King! Take your throne in our land. Be present in my heart. Be present in my office. Come into my marriage. Be Lord of my family, my fears, and my doubts." This is no feeble request; it's a bold appeal for God to occupy every corner of your life.

Who are you to ask such a thing? Who are you to ask God to take control of your world? You are his child, for heaven's sake! And so you ask boldly.

THE GREAT HOUSE OF GOD

Have you invited Christ to be King in your heart? Your place of employment? Your home?

_____

_____

_____

_____

_____

_____

_____

Our Problem

*The wages of sin is death, but the gift of God
is eternal life in Christ Jesus our Lord.*

ROMANS 6:23 NIV

We have a problem: We are not holy, and "anyone whose life is not holy will never see the Lord" (Hebrews 12:14).

Our deeds are ugly. Our actions are harsh. We don't do what we want to do, we don't like what we do, and what's worse—yes, there is something worse—we can't change.

We try, oh, how we try. But "can a leopard change his spots? In the same way, Jerusalem, you cannot change and do good, because you are accustomed to doing evil" (Jeremiah 13:23).

We, like Adam, were under a curse, but Jesus "changed places with us and put himself under that curse" (Galatians 3:13).

The sinless One took on the face of a sinner so that we sinners could take on the face of a saint.

HE CHOSE THE NAILS

There is One who can change our lives because he changed places with us at Calvary. What does that mean to you personally?

_____

_____

_____

_____

_____

Removing Doubt

"Who is more important: the one sitting at the table or the one serving? You think the one at the table is more important, but I am like a servant among you."

In Jesus' day the washing of feet was a task reserved not just for servants but for the lowest of servants. Every circle has its pecking order, and the circle of household workers was no exception. The servant at the bottom of the totem pole was expected to be the one on his knees with the towel and basin.

In this case the one with the towel and basin is the King of the universe. Hands that shaped the stars now wash away filth. Fingers that formed mountains now massage toes. And the One before whom all nations will one day kneel now kneels before his disciples. Hours before his own death, Jesus' concern is singular. He wants his disciples to know how much he loves them. More than removing dirt, Jesus is removing doubt.

JUST LIKE JESUS

Think of Jesus kneeling to wash away the filth of your life. What is your response to such love?

_____

_____

_____

_____

_____

Work and Worship

"Work and get everything done during six days each week, but the seventh day is a day of rest to honor the LORD."

EXODUS 20:9–10

We need one day in which work comes to a screeching halt. We need one twenty-four-hour period in which the wheels stop grinding and the motor stops turning. We need to stop.

There is a verse that summarizes many lives: "Man is a mere phantom as he goes to and fro: He bustles about, but only in vain; he heaps up wealth, not knowing who will get it" (Psalm 39:6 NIV).

Does that sound like your life? Are you so seldom in one place that your friends regard you as a phantom? Are you so constantly on the move that your family is beginning to question your existence? Do you take pride in your frenzy at the expense of your faith?

Slow down. If God commanded it, you need it. If Jesus modeled it, you need it. Take a day to say no to work and yes to worship.

AND THE ANGELS WERE SILENT

Do you take pride in a life of frenzy at the expense of your faith? What steps can you take to set aside a day of rest and worship?

_____

_____

_____

_____

_____

Sole Provider, Sole Comforter

*"Come to me, all of you who are tired
and have heavy loads, and I will give you rest."*

MATTHEW 11:28

As long as Jesus is one of many options, he is no option.
As long as you can carry your burdens alone, you
don't need a burden bearer. As long as your situation
brings you no grief, you will receive no comfort. And as long as you
can take him or leave him, you might as well leave him, because he
won't be taken halfheartedly.

But when you mourn, when you get to the point of sorrow for
your sins, when you admit that you have no other option but to cast
all your cares on him, and when there is truly no other name that
you can call, then cast all your cares on him, for he is waiting in the
midst of the storm.

THE APPLAUSE OF HEAVEN

*What does the statement mean: "If Jesus is one of many
options, he is no option"? Do you agree with the statement?*

_____

_____

_____

_____

_____

_____

_____

Uncommonly Unique

I will praise You, for I am fearfully and wonderfully made.
PSALM 139:14 NKJV

How would you answer this multiple-choice question?
I am

_____ a coincidental collision of particles.

_____ an accidental evolution of molecules.

_____ soulless flotsam in the universe.

_____ "fearfully and wonderfully made."

Don't dull your life by missing this point: You are more than statistical chance, more than a marriage of heredity and society, more than a confluence of inherited chromosomes and childhood trauma. More than a walking weather vane whipped about by the cold winds of fate. Thanks to God you have been "sculpted from nothing into something" (Psalm 139:15 MSG).

CURE FOR THE COMMON LIFE

God has sculpted you from nothing. What difference should this make in the way you live? In your attitudes toward life?

_____

_____

_____

_____

_____

The Cost of His Gift

[Jesus] was not guilty, but he suffered
for those who are guilty to bring you to God.

1 PETER 3:18

C hrist came to earth for one reason: to give his life as a
ransom for you, for me, for all of us. He sacrificed himself
to give us a second chance. He would have gone to any
lengths to do so. And he did. He went to the cross, where man's
utter despair collided with God's unbending grace. And in that
moment when God's great gift was complete, the compassionate
Christ showed the world the cost of his gift.

He who was perfect gave that perfect record to us, and our
imperfect record was given to him. As a result, God's holiness is
honored and his children are forgiven.

THE APPLAUSE OF HEAVEN

What a privilege to have our imperfect record replaced with
the perfect record of Christ. How should this affect our lives
from day to day?

_____

_____

_____

_____

_____

_____

He's Been There

He had to enter into every detail of human life.

HEBREWS 2:17 MSG

You've barely dipped a toe into Matthew's Gospel when you realize Jesus hails from the Tilted-Halo Society. Rahab was a Jericho harlot. Grandpa Jacob was slippery enough to warrant an electric ankle bracelet. David had a personality as irregular as a Picasso painting—one day writing psalms, another day seducing his captain's wife. But did Jesus erase his name from the list? Not at all.

Why did Jesus hang his family's dirty laundry on the neighborhood clothesline?

Because your family has some too. The dad who never came home. The grandparent who ran away with the coworker. If your family tree has bruised fruit, then Jesus wants you to know, "I've been there."

NEXT DOOR SAVIOR

How can the "bruised fruit" of Jesus' family tree encourage you?

_____

_____

_____

_____

_____

_____

Just in Time

May the God you serve all the time save you!

DANIEL 6:16

Look at Jonah in the fish belly—surrounded by gastric juices and sucked-in seaweed. He prays. Before he can say amen, the belly convulses, the fish belches, and Jonah lands face first on the beach.

Look at Daniel in the lions' den; his prospects aren't much better than Jonah's. Jonah had been swallowed, and Daniel is about to be. Or look at Joseph in the pit, a chalky hole in a hot desert. The lid has been pulled over the top and the wool has been pulled over his eyes. Like Jonah and Daniel, Joseph is trapped. He is out of options. There is no exit. There is no hope. Though the road to the palace takes a detour through a prison, it eventually ends up at the throne.

Such are the stories in the Bible. One near-death experience after another. Just when the neck is on the chopping block, just when the noose is around the neck, Calvary comes.

HE STILL MOVES STONES

Why are these illustrations from the Bible important to our faith?

_____

_____

_____

_____

_____

God Has No Limitations

Where can I go to get away from your Spirit?

PSALM 139:7

You and I are governed. The weather determines what we wear. The terrain tells us how to travel. Gravity dictates our speed, and health determines our strength. We may challenge these forces and alter them slightly, but we never remove them.

God—our Shepherd—doesn't check the weather; he makes it. He doesn't defy gravity; he created it. He isn't affected by health; he has no body. Jesus said, "God is spirit" (John 4:24). Since he has no body, he has no limitations—equally active in Cambodia as he is in Connecticut. "Where can I go to get away from your Spirit?" asked David. "Where can I run from you? If I go up to the heavens, you are there. If I lie down in the grave, you are there" (Psalm 139:7–8).

TRAVELING LIGHT

There is no place we can go where God is not. Describe what an amazing and uplifting thought that is!

_____

_____

_____

_____

_____

_____

Led by the Spirit

The true children of God are
those who let God's Spirit lead them.

ROMANS 8:14

To hear many of us talk, you'd think we didn't believe that verse. You'd think we didn't believe in the Trinity. We talk about the Father and study the Son—but when it comes to the Holy Spirit, we are confused at best and frightened at worst. Confused because we've never been taught. Frightened because we've been taught to be afraid.

May I simplify things a bit? The Holy Spirit is the presence of God in our lives, carrying on the work of Jesus. The Holy Spirit helps us in three directions—inwardly (by granting us the fruits of the Spirit, Galatians 5:22–24), upwardly (by praying for us, Romans 8:26), and outwardly (by pouring God's love into our hearts, Romans 5:5).

WHEN GOD WHISPERS YOUR NAME

List some examples of how the Holy Spirit has helped you inwardly, upwardly, and outwardly.

_____

_____

_____

_____

_____

_____

Kind Hearts

Love suffers long and is kind.

1 CORINTHIANS 13:4 NKJV

What is your kindness quotient? When was the last time you did something kind for someone in your family—e.g., got a blanket, cleaned off the table, prepared the coffee—without being asked?

Think about your school or workplace. Which person is the most overlooked or avoided? A shy student? A grumpy employee? Maybe he doesn't speak the language. Maybe she doesn't fit in. Are you kind to this person?

Kind hearts are quietly kind. They let the car cut into traffic and the young mom with three kids move up in the checkout line. They pick up the neighbor's trash can that rolled into the street. And they are especially kind at church. They understand that perhaps the neediest person they'll meet all week is the one standing in the foyer or sitting on the row behind them in worship. Paul writes: "When we have the opportunity to help anyone, we should do it. But we should give special attention to those who are in the family of believers" (Galatians 6:10).

A LOVE WORTH GIVING

List some people who could use a little of your kindness quotient.

_____

_____

_____

_____

God's Will Be Done

"May your kingdom come and what you want be done,
here on earth as it is in heaven."

MATTHEW 6:10

To pray, "Thy will be done" is to seek the heart of God. The word *will* means "strong desire." [So] what is his heart? His passion? He wants you to know it.

Shall God hide from us what he is going to do? Apparently not, for he has gone to great lengths to reveal his will to us. Could he have done more than send his Son to lead us? Could he have done more than give his word to teach us? Could he have done more than orchestrate events to awaken us? Could he have done more than send his Holy Spirit to counsel us?

God is not the God of confusion, and wherever he sees sincere seekers with confused hearts, you can bet your sweet December that he will do whatever it takes to help them see his will.

THE GREAT HOUSE OF GOD

What steps have you taken to find God's will, to know his heart?

_____

_____

_____

_____

_____

_____

The Pioneer of Salvation

He was wounded for our transgressions,
He was bruised for our iniquities.

ISAIAH 53:5 NKJV

The One to whom we pray knows our feelings. He knows temptation. He has felt discouraged. He has been hungry and sleepy and tired. He knows what we feel like when the alarm clock goes off. He knows what we feel like when our children want different things at the same time. He nods in understanding when we pray in anger. He is touched when we tell him there is more to do than can ever be done. He smiles when we confess our weariness.

He wants us to remember that he, too, was human. He wants us to know that he, too, knew the drone of the humdrum and the weariness that comes with long days. He wants us to remember that our trailblazer didn't wear bulletproof vests or rubber gloves or an impenetrable suit of armor. No, he pioneered our salvation through the world that you and I face daily.

No Wonder They Call Him the Savior

Jesus walked through our world. He was hungry. He was
discouraged. How can this help you face difficult days?

_____

_____

_____

_____

God Is Crazy About You

"God even knows how
many hairs are on your head."

MATTHEW 10:30

There are many reasons God saves you: to bring glory to himself, to appease his justice, to demonstrate his sovereignty. But one of the sweetest reasons God saved you is because he is fond of you. He likes having you around. He thinks you are the best thing to come down the pike in quite a while.

If God had a refrigerator, your picture would be on it. If he had a wallet, your photo would be in it. He sends you flowers every spring and a sunrise every morning. Whenever you want to talk, he'll listen. He can live anywhere in the universe, and he chose your heart.

Face it, friend. He's crazy about you.

A GENTLE THUNDER

How does it make you feel to know that God is "crazy about you"? How do you respond to such compassionate love?

_____

_____

_____

_____

_____

_____

_____

Redefining Prayer

Continue earnestly in prayer,
being vigilant in it with thanksgiving.

COLOSSIANS 4:2 NKJV

Early Christians were urged to
- "pray without ceasing" (1 Thessalonians 5:17 NASB);
- "always be prayerful" (Romans 12:12 NLT);
- "pray at all times and on every occasion" (Ephesians 6:18 NLT).

Sound burdensome? Are you wondering, *My business needs attention, my children need dinner, my bills need paying. How can I stay in a place of prayer?*

Do this. Change your definition of prayer. Think of prayers less as an activity for God and more as an awareness of God. Seek to live in uninterrupted awareness. Acknowledge his presence everywhere you go. As you stand in line to register your car, think, *Thank you, Lord, for being here.* In the grocery as you shop, *Your presence, my King, I welcome.* As you wash the dishes, worship your Maker.

COME THIRSTY

Does the idea of praying without ceasing seem burdensome to you? What can you do to live in uninterrupted awareness of God?

_____

_____

_____

_____

Behold His Mercy!

Be kind and loving to each other,
and forgive each other just as God forgave you in Christ.

EPHESIANS 4:32

Jesus wraps a servant's girdle around his waist, takes up the basin, and kneels before one of the disciples. He unlaces a sandal and gently lifts the foot and places it in the basin, covers it with water, and begins to bathe it. One by one, one grimy foot after another, Jesus works his way down the row.

You can be sure Jesus knows the future of these feet he is washing. These twenty-four feet will not spend the next day following their Master, defending his cause. These feet will dash for cover at the flash of a Roman sword. Only one pair of feet won't abandon him in the garden. One disciple won't desert him at Gethsemane—Judas won't even make it that far!

Behold the gift Jesus gives his followers! He knows what these men are about to do. And when they do, he wants them to remember how his knees knelt before them and he washed their feet. He wants them to realize those feet are still clean. He forgave their sin before they even committed it. He offered mercy before they even sought it.

JUST LIKE JESUS

How can you demonstrate mercy to others?

The Sin of the World

Christ carried our sins in his body on the cross.

1 PETER 2:24

Every aspect of the crucifixion was intended not only to hurt the victim but to shame him. Death on a cross was usually reserved for the most vile offenders: slaves, murderers, assassins, and the like. The condemned person was marched through the city streets, shouldering his crossbar and wearing a placard about his neck that named his crime. At the execution site he was stripped and mocked.

Crucifixion was so abhorrent that Cicero wrote, "Let the very name of the cross be far away, not only from the body of a Roman citizen, but even from his thoughts, his eyes, his ears."

Jesus was not only shamed before people, he was shamed before heaven.

Since he bore the sin of the murderer and adulterer, he felt the shame of the murderer and adulterer. Though he never lied, he bore the disgrace of a liar. Though he never cheated, he felt the embarrassment of a cheater. Since he bore the sin of the world, he felt the collective shame of the world.

HE CHOSE THE NAILS

Write a prayer of thanks to Jesus for his grace, mercy, and love.

_____

_____

_____

_____

Slaves to Goodness

*Now you are free from sin and have
become slaves of God. This brings you a life that is
only for God, and this gives you life forever.*

ROMANS 6:22

How could we who have been freed from sin return to it? Before Christ our lives were out of control, sloppy, and indulgent. We didn't even know we were slobs until we met him.

Then he moved in. Things began to change. What we threw around we began putting away. What we neglected we cleaned up. What had been clutter became order. Oh, there were and still are occasional lapses of thought and deed, but by and large he got our house in order.

Suddenly we find ourselves wanting to do good. Go back to the old mess? Are you kidding? "In the past you were slaves to sin—sin controlled you. But thank God, you fully obeyed the things that you were taught. You were made free from sin, and now you are slaves to goodness" (Romans 6:17–18).

IN THE GRIP OF GRACE

List some of the differences God has made in your life.

_____

_____

_____

_____

He Is Your God

"I am God and not a human;
I am the Holy One, and I am among you."

HOSEA 11:9

Before you read any further, reflect on those last four words, "I am among you." Do you believe that? Do you believe God is near? He wants you to. He wants you to know he is in the midst of your world. Wherever you are as you read these words, he is present. In your car. On the plane. In your office, your bedroom, your den. He's near.

God is in the thick of things in your world. He has not taken up residence in a distant galaxy. He has not removed himself from history. He has not chosen to seclude himself on a throne in an incandescent castle.

He has drawn near. He has involved himself in the carpools, heartbreaks, and funeral homes of our day. He is as near to us on Monday as on Sunday. In the schoolroom as in the sanctuary. At the coffee break as much as the communion table.

AND THE ANGELS WERE SILENT

God is in the midst of your world. How does this affect you?

_____

_____

_____

_____

A Burst of Love

"Seek God's kingdom, and all the
other things you need will be given to you."

LUKE 12:31

S
ometimes God is so touched by what he sees that he gives
us what we need and not simply that for which we ask.

It's a good thing. For who would have ever thought to
ask God for what he gives? Which of us would have dared to say:
"God, would you please hang yourself on a tool of torture as a
substitution for every mistake I have ever committed?" And then
have the audacity to add: "And after you forgive me, could you
prepare me a place in your house to live forever?"

And if that wasn't enough: "And would you please live within
me and protect me and guide me and bless me with more than I
could ever deserve?"

Honestly, would we have the chutzpah to ask for that?

Jesus already knows the cost of grace. He already knows the
price of forgiveness. But he offers it anyway. Love burst his heart.

HE STILL MOVES STONES

Why do so many people refuse to accept Christ's offer of love?
Does this diminish his love or defeat the purpose of his love?

_____

_____

_____

_____

God's Greatest Blessings

"The Son of Man will die, just as the Scriptures say."
MATTHEW 26:24

God's greatest blessings often come costumed as disasters. Any doubters need to do nothing more than ascend the hill of Calvary.

Jerusalem's collective opinion that Friday was this: Jesus is finished. What other conclusion made sense? The religious leaders had turned him in. Rome had refused to bail him out. His followers had tucked their tails and scattered. He was nailed to a cross and left to die, which he did. They silenced his lips, sealed his tomb, and, as any priest worth the price of a phylactery would tell you, Jesus is history. Three years of power and promises are decomposing in a borrowed grave. Search the crucifixion sky for one ray of hope, and you won't find it.

Such is the view of the disciples, the opinion of the friends, and the outlook of the enemies.

But God is not surprised. His plan is right on schedule. Even in—especially in—death, Christ is still the King, the King over his own crucifixion.

NEXT DOOR SAVIOR

God isn't surprised by world events. Why is this good news?

_____

_____

_____

Heaven's on Your Side

The One who died for us . . . is in the presence of God
at this very moment sticking up for us.

ROMANS 8:34 MSG

Jesus is praying for us. Jesus has spoken and Satan has listened. The devil may land a punch or two. He may even win a few rounds, but he never wins the fight. Why? Because Jesus takes up for you. "He is able always to save those who come to God through him because he always lives, asking God to help them" (Hebrews 7:25).

Jesus, at this very moment, is protecting you. Evil must pass through Christ before it can touch you. And God will "never let you be pushed past your limit; he'll always be there to help you come through it" (1 Corinthians 10:13 MSG).

WHEN CHRIST COMES

"Jesus is praying for us." Describe what this means to you.
How should it affect the way you live?

_____

_____

_____

_____

_____

_____

God Loves to Surprise Us

People receive God's promise by having faith.
This happens so the promise can be a free gift.

ROMANS 4:16

Our problem is not so much that God doesn't give us what we hope for as it is that we don't know the right thing for which to hope. (You may want to read that sentence again.)

Hope is not what you expect; it is what you would never dream. It is a wild, improbable tale with a pinch-me-I'm-dreaming ending. It's Abraham adjusting his bifocals so he can see not his grandson, but his son. It's Moses standing in the promised land not with Aaron or Miriam at his side, but with Elijah and the transfigured Christ.

Hope is not a granted wish or a favor performed; no, it is far greater than that. It is a zany, unpredictable dependence on a God who loves to surprise us out of our socks and be there in the flesh to see our reaction.

GOD CAME NEAR

We can depend on God to "surprise us out of our socks"
with things beyond our wildest dreams. Describe a time
when this happened in your life.

_____

_____

_____

_____

The Fire Within

Jesus began to explain everything that
had been written about himself in the Scriptures.

LUKE 24:27

When [the disciples] saw who he was, he disappeared. They said to each other, 'It felt like a fire burning in us when Jesus talked to us on the road and explained the Scriptures to us'" (Luke 24:31–32).

Don't you love that verse? They knew they had been with Jesus because of the fire within them. God reveals his will by setting a torch to your soul. He gave Jeremiah a fire for hard hearts. He gave Nehemiah a fire for a forgotten city. He set Abraham on fire for a land he'd never seen. He set Isaiah on fire with a vision he couldn't resist. Forty years of fruitless preaching didn't extinguish the fire of Noah.

Mark it down: Jesus comes to set you on fire! He walks as a torch from heart to heart, warming the cold and thawing the chilled and stirring the ashes. He comes to purge infection and illuminate your direction.

THE GREAT HOUSE OF GOD

Has God set your life on fire? What is the fire that will not be extinguished in your heart?

_____

_____

_____

_____

Designed by God

*If anyone ministers, let him do it
as with the ability which God supplies.*

1 PETER 4:11 NKJV

God shaped you according to your purpose. How else can you explain yourself? Your ability to diagnose an engine problem by the noise it makes, to bake a cake without a recipe. You knew the Civil War better than your American history teacher. You know the name of every kid in the orphanage. How do you explain such quirks of skill?

God. He knew young Israel would need a code, so he gave Moses a love for the law. He knew the doctrine of grace would need a fiery advocate, so he set Paul ablaze. And in your case, he knew what your generation would need and gave it. He designed you. And *his design defines your destiny.* Remember Peter's admonition? "If anyone ministers, let him do it as with the ability which God supplies."

CURE FOR THE COMMON LIFE

What abilities has God given you? How are they shaping your destiny?

Listen for His Voice

"Never will I leave you;
never will I forsake you."

HEBREWS 13:5 NIV

L et me state something important. There is never a time during which Jesus is not speaking. Never. There is never a place in which Jesus is not present. Never. There is never a room so dark . . . a lounge so sensual . . . an office so sophisticated . . . that the ever-present, ever-pursuing, relentlessly tender Friend is not there, tapping gently on the doors of our hearts—waiting to be invited in.

Few hear his voice. Fewer still open the door.

But never interpret our numbness as his absence. For amidst the fleeting promises of pleasure is the timeless promise of his presence.

"Surely I am with you always, to the very end of the age" (Matthew 28:20 NIV).

There is no chorus so loud that the voice of God cannot be heard . . . if we will but listen.

IN THE EYE OF THE STORM

What things try to drown out the voice of God in your life?
How can you overcome them?

_____

_____

_____

_____

How Wide God's Love

"For God so loved the world, that he gave his only begotten Son."

JOHN 3:16 KJV

As boldly as the center beam of the cross proclaims God's holiness, the crossbeam declares his love. And, oh, how wide his love reaches.

Aren't you glad the verse does not read:

"For God so loved the rich . . . "?

Or, "For God so loved the famous . . . "?

Or, "For God so loved the thin . . . "?

It doesn't. Nor does it state, "For God so loved the Europeans or Africans . . . " "the sober or successful . . . " "the young or the old . . . "

No, when we read John 3:16, we simply (and happily) read, "For God so loved the world."

How wide is God's love? Wide enough for the whole world.

HE CHOSE THE NAILS

Aren't you glad God loves the whole world? Write some sentences that describe the amazing wideness of God's love and mercy.

_____

_____

_____

_____

_____

_____

Because of His Gift

*I want to know Christ and the power that
raised him from the dead. I want to share in his
sufferings and become like him in his death.*

PHILIPPIANS 3:10

Trace the path of this Savior, the God who swapped heavenly royalty for earthly poverty. His bed became, at best, a borrowed pallet—and usually the hard earth. He was dependent on handouts for his income. He was sometimes so hungry he would eat raw grain or pick fruit off a tree. He knew what it meant to have no home. He was ridiculed. His neighbors tried to lynch him. Some called him a lunatic. His family tried to confine him to their house. His friends weren't always faithful to him.

He was accused of a crime he never committed. Witnesses were hired to lie. The jury was rigged. A judge swayed by politics handed down the death penalty.

They killed him.

And why? Because of the gift that only he could give.

THE APPLAUSE OF HEAVEN

*Think what it cost Christ to die for our salvation. Write a
note of praise for this gift.*

_____

_____

_____

_____

_____

Peace Through Prayer

God's peace . . . will keep your hearts and minds in Christ Jesus.

PHILIPPIANS 4:7

The worrisome heart pays a high price for doing so. *Worry* comes from the Greek word that means "to divide the mind." Anxiety splits us right down the middle, creating a double-minded thinker. Rather than take away tomorrow's trouble, worry voids today's strength. Perception is divided, distorting your vision. Strength is divided, wasting your energy. Who can afford to lose power?

But how can we stop doing so? Paul offers a two-pronged answer: God's part and our part. Our part includes prayer and gratitude. "Don't worry about anything; instead, *pray* about everything. Tell God what you need, and *thank him* for all he has done" (Philippians 4:6 NLT, emphasis mine).

God's part? "If you do this, you will experience God's peace, which is far more wonderful than the human mind can understand" (v. 7).

COME THIRSTY

What happens when we replace worry with prayer and gratitude?

Doing What's Right

This is the victory that conquers the world—our faith.

1 JOHN 5:4

You get impatient with your own life, trying to master a habit or control a sin—and in your frustration begin to wonder where the power of God is. Be patient. God is using today's difficulties to strengthen you for tomorrow. He is *equipping* you. The God who makes things grow will help you bear fruit.

Dwell on the fact that God lives within you. Think about the power that gives you life. The realization that God is dwelling within you may change the places you want to go and the things you want to do today.

Do what is right this week, whatever it is, whatever comes down the path, whatever problems and dilemmas you face—just do what's right. Maybe no one else is doing what's right, but you do what's right. You be honest. You take a stand. You be true. After all, regardless of what you do, God does what is right: he saves you with his grace.

WALKING WITH THE SAVIOR

Think of a difficulty God has brought you through. How does that affect your life today?

_____

_____

_____

_____

_____

God's Testimony

The testimony of the LORD is sure, making wise the simple.
PSALM 19:7 NKJV

A small seed becoming a towering tree.
A thin stalk pushing back the earth.
A rainbow arching in the midst of the thundercloud.
"God's testimony," wrote David, "makes wise the simple."

God's testimony. When was the last time you witnessed it? A stroll through knee-high grass in a green meadow. An hour listening to seagulls or looking at seashells on the beach. Or witnessing the shafts of sunlight brighten the snow on a crisp winter dawn.

There comes a time when we should lay down our pens and commentaries and step out of our offices and libraries. To really understand and believe in the miracle on the cross, we'd do well to witness God's miracles every day.

No Wonder They Call Him the Savior

What are the benefits of simply walking in nature and admiring the handiwork of God?

_____

_____

_____

_____

_____

_____

The Basin of God's Grace

The blood of Jesus, God's Son, cleanses us from every sin.

1 JOHN 1:7

John tells us, "We are *being cleansed* from every sin by the blood of Jesus." In other words, we are *always being cleansed.* The cleansing is not a promise for the future but a reality in the present. Let a speck of dust fall on the soul of a saint, and it is washed away. Let a spot of filth land on the heart of God's child, and the filth is wiped away.

Our Savior kneels down and gazes upon the darkest acts of our lives. But rather than recoil in horror, he reaches out in kindness and says, "I can clean that if you want." And from the basin of his grace, he scoops a palm full of mercy and washes away our sin.

But that's not all he does. Because he lives in us, you and I can do the same. Because he has forgiven us, we can forgive others.

JUST LIKE JESUS

Explain how we can forgive others because Christ has forgiven us.

_____

_____

_____

_____

_____

_____

Free to Enter His Presence

When Jesus had cried out again in a loud voice,
he gave up his spirit. At that moment the curtain of the temple
was torn in two from top to bottom.

MATTHEW 27:50–51 NIV

I t's as if the hands of heaven had been gripping the veil, waiting for this moment. Keep in mind the size of the curtain—sixty feet tall and thirty feet wide. One instant it was whole; the next it was ripped in two from top to bottom. No delay. No hesitation.

What did the torn curtain mean? For the Jews it meant no more barrier between them and the Holy of Holies. No more priests to go between them and God. No more animal sacrifices to atone for their sins.

And for us? What did the torn curtain signify for us?

We are welcome to enter into God's presence—any day, any time. God has removed the barrier that separates us from him. The barrier of sin? Down. He has removed the curtain.

HE CHOSE THE NAILS

We are welcome to enter God's presence—any day, any time.
Record some of the times you entered his presence today.

From Heaven Itself

God . . . forgave all our sins. He canceled the debt,
which listed all the rules we failed to follow.

COLOSSIANS 2:13–14

All the world religions can be placed in one of two camps: legalism or grace. Humankind does it or God does it. Salvation as a wage based on deeds done—or salvation as a gift based on Christ's death.

A legalist believes the supreme force behind salvation is you. If you look right, speak right, and belong to the right segment of the right group, you will be saved. The brunt of responsibility doesn't lie within God; it lies within you.

The result? The outside sparkles. The talk is good and the step is true. But look closely. Listen carefully. Something is missing. What is it? Joy. What's there? Fear. (That you won't do enough.) Arrogance. (That you have done enough.) Failure. (That you have made a mistake.)

Spiritual life is not a human endeavor. It is rooted in and orchestrated by the Holy Spirit. Every spiritual achievement is created and energized by God.

HE STILL MOVES STONES

Is salvation a wage or a gift? Why?

_____

_____

_____

_____

Love Makes the Difference

"The person who is forgiven only a little will love only a little."

LUKE 7:47

We can replace the word *forgiven* with *accepted* and maintain the integrity of the passage. "He who is *accepted* little loves little." If we think God is harsh and unfair, guess how we'll treat people. Harshly and unfairly. But if we discover that God has doused us with unconditional love, would that make a difference?

The apostle Paul would say so! Talk about a turnaround. He went from bully to teddy bear. Paul BC (Before Christ) sizzled with anger. He "made havoc of the church" (Acts 8:3 NKJV). Paul AD (After Discovery) brimmed with love.

His accusers beat him, stoned him, jailed him, mocked him. But can you find one occasion where he responded in kind? One temper tantrum? One angry outburst? *This is a different man.* His anger is gone. His passion is strong. His devotion is unquestioned. But rash outbursts of anger? A thing of the past.

What made the difference? He encountered Christ.

A LOVE WORTH GIVING

In what ways has encountering Christ changed your life?

God Hears Our Prayers

*The LORD hears good people when they cry out to him,
and he saves them from all their troubles.*

PSALM 34:17

When [a friend] told Jesus of the illness [of Lazarus] he said, "Lord, the one you love is sick" (John 11:3). He doesn't base his appeal on the imperfect love of the one in need, but on the perfect love of the Savior. He doesn't say, "The one *who loves you* is sick." He says, "The one you love is sick." The power of the prayer, in other words, does not depend on the one who makes the prayer, but on the One who hears the prayer.

We can and must repeat the phrase in manifold ways. "The one you love is tired, sad, hungry, lonely, fearful, depressed." The words of the prayer vary, but the response never changes. The Savior hears the prayer. He silences heaven, so he won't miss a word. He hears the prayer.

THE GREAT HOUSE OF GOD

The power of prayer does not depend on us but on the One who hears our prayer. Explain why this is true.

The Right Direction

You are like foreigners and strangers in this world.

1 PETER 2:11

Your Shepherd knows that you were not made for this place. He knows you are not equipped for this place. So he has come to guide you out.

He has come to restore your soul. He is the perfect One to do so. He has the right vision. He reminds you that "you are like foreigners and strangers in this world." And he urges you to lift your eyes from the jungle around you to the heaven above you.

He also has the right direction. He made the boldest claim in the history of man when he declared, "I am the way" (John 14:6). People wondered if the claim was accurate. He answered their questions by cutting a path through the underbrush of sin and death . . . and escaping alive. He's the only One who ever did. And he is the only One who can help you and me do the same.

TRAVELING LIGHT

We are "foreigners and strangers in this world." What does that phrase mean? Why do we need God to guide us day by day?

Dark Nights—God's Light

Pray for all people, asking God for
what they need and being thankful to him.

1 TIMOTHY 2:1

You wonder if it is a blessing or a curse to have a mind that never rests. But you would rather be a cynic than a hypocrite, so you continue to pray with one eye open and wonder: about starving children . . . about Christians in cancer wards . . .

Tough questions. Throw-in-the-towel questions. Questions the disciples must have asked in the storm.

All they could see were black skies as they bounced in the battered boat.

[Then] a figure came to them walking on the water. It wasn't what they expected. They almost missed seeing the answer to their prayers.

And unless we look and listen closely, we risk making the same mistake. God's lights in our dark nights are as numerous as the stars, if only we'll look for them.

IN THE EYE OF THE STORM

How does God want us to respond when the night is dark?

_____

_____

_____

_____

Remember Jesus

*Remember Jesus Christ, who was raised from the
dead. . . . This is the Good News I preach.*

2 TIMOTHY 2:8

In a letter written within earshot of the sharpening of the blade
that would sever his head, Paul urged Timothy to remember.
You can almost picture the old warrior smiling as he wrote the
words. "Remember Jesus Christ, who was raised from the dead. This
is the Good News I preach."

When times get hard, remember Jesus. When people don't
listen, remember Jesus. When tears come, remember Jesus. When
disappointment is your bed partner, remember Jesus.

Remember holiness in tandem with humanity. Remember
the sick who were healed with callused hands. Remember the
dead called from the grave with a Galilean accent. Remember
the eyes of God that wept human tears.

SIX HOURS ONE FRIDAY

*Explain why we are always better off to forget the negative and
focus on Jesus instead.*

_____

_____

_____

_____

_____

_____

The Cloak of Humanity

Jesus took Peter, James, and John with him, and he
began to be very sad and troubled.

MARK 14:33

Whiles Jesus lived on earth, he prayed with loud cries and tears to the One who could save him from death" (Hebrews 5:7).

My, what a portrait! Jesus is in pain. Jesus is on the stage of fear. Jesus is cloaked, not in sainthood, but in humanity.

The next time the fog finds you, you might do well to remember Jesus in the garden. The next time you think that no one understands, reread the fourteenth chapter of Mark. The next time your self-pity convinces you that no one cares, pay a visit to Gethsemane. And the next time you wonder if God really perceives the pain that prevails on this dusty planet, listen to him pleading among the twisted trees.

NO WONDER THEY CALL HIM THE SAVIOR

Take a moment to read the fourteenth chapter of Mark.
What are your impressions about Christ's prayer? How does
this encourage you to trust God?

God's Family of Friends

*His unchanging plan has always been to adopt us into
his own family by bringing us to himself through Jesus Christ.*

EPHESIANS 1:5 NLT

God offers you a family of friends and friends who are family—his church. When you transfer your trust into Christ, he not only pardons you; he places you in his family of friends.

Family far and away outpaces any other biblical term to describe the church. *Brothers* or *brothers and sisters* appears a whopping 148 times between the book of Acts and the book of Revelation.

God heals his family through his family. In the church we use our gifts to love each other, honor one another, keep an eye on troublemakers, and carry each other's burdens.

CURE FOR THE COMMON LIFE

Christ places us in his family of friends. How have you been helped by members of God's family? How can you reach out to help your brothers and sisters in Christ?

The Standard

We are made holy through the sacrifice
Christ made in his body once and for all time.

HEBREWS 10:10

O nly the holy will see God. Holiness is a prerequisite to heaven. Perfection is a requirement for eternity. We wish it weren't so. We act like it isn't so. We act like those who are "decent" will see God. We suggest that those who try hard will see God. We act as if we're good if we never do anything too bad. And that goodness is enough to qualify us for heaven.

Sounds right to us, but it doesn't sound right to God. And he sets the standard. And the standard is high. "You must be perfect, just as your Father in heaven is perfect" (Matthew 5:48).

You see, in God's plan, God is the standard for perfection. We don't compare ourselves to others; they are just as fouled up as we are. The goal is to be like him; anything less is inadequate.

HE STILL MOVES STONES

Are we qualified to set the standards for holiness? Why or why not? Who is qualified?

_____

_____

_____

_____

_____

_____

A Cloak of Love

Love . . . always protects.
1 CORINTHIANS 13:4–7 NIV

When Paul said, "Love always protects," he might have been thinking of a coat. One scholar thinks he was. *The Theological Dictionary of the New Testament* is known for its word studies, not its poetry. But the scholar sounds poetic as he explains the meaning of *protect* as used in 1 Corinthians 13:7. The word conveys, he says, "the idea of covering with a cloak of love."

Remember receiving one? You were nervous about the test, but the teacher stayed late to help you. You were far from home and afraid, but your mother phoned to comfort you. You were innocent and accused, so your friend stood to defend you. Covered with encouragement. Covered with tenderhearted care. Covered with protection. *Covered with a cloak of love.*

A LOVE WORTH GIVING

List some times you've been covered with a "cloak" of love. List some times you've covered others with a cloak of love.

_____

_____

_____

_____

_____

_____

A Few More Scenes

"In [this] world you will have tribulation;
but be of good cheer, I have overcome the world."

JOHN 16:33 NKJV

God has kept no secrets. He has told us that, while on this yellow brick road [of life], we will experience trouble. Disease will afflict bodies. Divorce will break hearts. Death will make widows and devastation will destroy countries. We should not expect any less. But just because the devil shows up and cackles, we needn't panic.

Our Master speaks of an accomplished deed. "It is finished" (John 19:30). The battle is over. Be alert. But don't be alarmed. The manuscript has been published. The book has been bound. Satan is loosed for a season, but the season is oh-so-brief. Just a few more scenes, just a few more turns in the road, and his end will come.

WHEN CHRIST COMES

How do Christ's words from the cross, "It is finished," encourage your Christian faith?

_____

_____

_____

_____

_____

What Is Grace?

*"My grace is enough for you.
When you are weak, my power is made perfect in you."*

2 CORINTHIANS 12:9

What is grace? It's what someone gives us out of the goodness of his heart, not out of the perfection of ours. The story of grace is the good news that says that when we come, he gives. That's what grace is.

Grace is something you did not expect. It is something you certainly could never earn. But grace is something you'd never turn down.

You know what happens when someone sees the grace of God? When someone really tastes the forgiving and liberating grace of God? Someone who tastes God's grace is the hardest worker, the most morally pure individual, and the person most willing to forgive.

THE INSPIRATIONAL STUDY BIBLE

God's generous grace changes our lives for the better. Describe how your life is different because of that grace.

_____

_____

_____

_____

_____

_____

A Godly Touch

*Jesus reached out his hand and
touched the man and said, "I will. Be healed!"*

MATTHEW 8:3

Oh, the power of a godly touch. Haven't you known it? The doctor who treated you, or the teacher who dried your tears? Was there a hand holding yours at a funeral? Another on your shoulder during a trial? A handshake of welcome at a new job?

Can't we offer the same?

Many of you already do. Some of you have the master touch of the Physician himself. You use your hands to pray over the sick and minister to the weak. If you aren't touching them personally, your hands are writing letters, dialing phones, baking pies. You have learned the power of a touch.

But others of us tend to forget. Our hearts are good; it's just that our memories are bad. We forget how significant one touch can be.

Aren't we glad Jesus didn't make the same mistake?

JUST LIKE JESUS

Describe a time when someone's touch made a difference in your life.

_____

_____

_____

_____

Life Is Not Fair

"Love your neighbor as you love yourself."

GALATIANS 5:14

As long as you hate your enemy, a jail door is closed and a prisoner is taken. But when you try to understand and release your foe from your hatred, then the prisoner is released, and that prisoner is you.

Perhaps you don't like that idea. Perhaps the thought of forgiveness is unrealistic. Perhaps the idea of trying to understand the Judases in our world is simply too gracious.

My response to you then is a question. What do you suggest? Will harboring the anger solve the problem? Will getting even remove the hurt? Does hatred do any good? Again, I'm not minimizing your hurt or justifying their actions. But I am saying that justice won't come this side of eternity. And demanding that your enemy get his or her share of pain will, in the process, be most painful to you.

May I gently but firmly remind you of something you know but may have forgotten? Life is not fair. That's not pessimism; it's fact.

AND THE ANGELS WERE SILENT

Explain why we are hurt if we harbor hatred.

_____

_____

_____

_____

God's Priority

Depend on the LORD; trust him,
and he will take care of you.

PSALM 37:5

God is committed to caring for our needs. Paul tells us that a man who won't feed his own family is worse than an unbeliever (1 Timothy 5:8). How much more will a holy God care for his children? After all, how can we fulfill his mission unless our needs are met? How can we teach or minister or influence unless we have our basic needs satisfied? Will God enlist us in his army and not provide a commissary? Of course not.

"I pray that the God of peace will give you every good thing you need so you can do what he wants" (Hebrews 13:20–21). Hasn't that prayer been answered in our lives? We may not have had a feast, but haven't we always had food? Perhaps there was no banquet, but at least there was bread. And many times there *was* a banquet.

THE GREAT HOUSE OF GOD

Make a list of the ways God cares for your needs each day.
What should your response be?

_____

_____

_____

_____

_____

Reliability

"He who is faithful in what is least is faithful also in much."

LUKE 16:10 NKJV

There is a common denominator in any form of greatness—reliability.

It's the bread and butter characteristic of achievement. It's the shared ingredient behind retirement pens, Hall of Fame awards, and golden anniversaries. It is the quality that produces not momentary heroics but monumental lives.

The Bible has its share. Consistent and predictable, these saints were spurred by a gut-level conviction that they had been called by no one less than God himself. As a result, their work wasn't affected by moods, cloudy days, or rocky trails. Their performance graph didn't rise and fall with roller-coaster irregularity. They weren't addicted to accolades or applause nor deterred by grumpy bosses or empty wallets. And since their loyalty was not determined by their comfort, they were just as faithful in dark prisons as they were in spotlighted pulpits.

GOD CAME NEAR

How have you benefited from people whose lives are consistent and predictable, who serve God and others reliably?

_____

_____

_____

_____

God's Child

*The Father has loved us so much that we are
called children of God. And we really are his children.*

1 JOHN 3:1

L et me tell you who you are. In fact, let me proclaim who
you are.

You are an heir of God and a co-heir with Christ (Romans
8:17).

You are eternal, like an angel (Luke 20:36).

You have a crown that will last forever (1 Corinthians 9:25).

You are a holy priest (1 Peter 2:5), a treasured possession
(Exodus 19:5).

But more than any of the above—more significant than any
title or position—is the simple fact that you are God's child.

"We really are his children."

As a result, if something is important to you, it's important
to God.

HE STILL MOVES STONES

*If something is important to you, it's important to God.
Does that mean we have no personal responsibility for the
events in our lives? Explain.*

_____

_____

_____

_____

_____

Hear His Music

The Lord disciplines those he loves.

HEBREWS 12:6

O h, how God wants you to hear his music. He has a rhythm that will race your heart and lyrics that will stir your tears. You want to journey to the stars? He can take you there. You want to lie down in peace? His music can soothe your soul.

But first, he's got to get rid of that country-western stuff. (Forgive me, Nashville. Only an example.)

And so he begins tossing the CDs. A friend turns away. The job goes bad. Your spouse doesn't understand. The church is dull. One by one he removes the options until all you have left is God.

He would do that? Absolutely. If he must silence every voice, he will. He wants you to hear his music.

TRAVELING LIGHT

God removes all the options until he is all that is left. Do you know someone who is still choosing other options? Write a prayer for that person.

Footprints of Discipleship

*"All people will know that you
are my followers if you love each other."*

JOHN 13:35

Watch a small boy follow his dad through the snow. He stretches to step where his dad stepped. Not an easy task. His small legs extend as far as they can so his feet can fall in his father's prints.

The father, seeing what the son is doing, smiles and begins taking shorter steps, so the son can follow.

It's a picture of discipleship.

In our faith we follow in someone's stePsalm A parent, a teacher, a hero—none of us are the first to walk the trail. All of us have someone we follow.

In our faith we leave footprints to guide others. A child, a friend, a recent convert. None should be left to walk the trail alone.

It's the principle of discipleship.

THE INSPIRATIONAL STUDY BIBLE

Think for a moment of the footprints you are leaving for others. Will others be blessed by following your steps?

_____

_____

_____

_____

_____

Loved by God

The LORD loves you.

DEUTERONOMY 7:8 NLT

God loves you simply because he has chosen to do so.

He loves you when you don't feel lovely.

He loves you when no one else loves you. Others may abandon you, divorce you, and ignore you, but God will love you. Always. No matter what.

This is his sentiment: "I'll call nobodies and make them somebodies; I'll call the unloved and make them beloved" (Romans 9:25 MSG).

This is his promise. "I have loved you, my people, with an everlasting love. With unfailing love I have drawn you to myself" (Jeremiah 31:3 NLT).

Do you know what else that means? You have a deep aquifer of love from which to draw. When you find it hard to love, then you need a drink! Drink deeply! Drink daily!

A LOVE WORTH GIVING

God's unfailing love is a deep resource to help us love others. List some circumstances when you need to draw deeply from the well of that love.

_____

_____

_____

_____

_____

One Incredible Plan

*He humbled himself and was fully obedient
to God, even when that caused his death—death on a cross.*

PHILIPPIANS 2:8

When human hands fastened the divine hands to a cross with spikes, it wasn't the soldiers who held the hands of Jesus steady. It was God who held them steady. Those same hands that formed the oceans and built the mountains. Those same hands that designed the dawn and crafted each cloud. Those same hands that blueprinted one incredible plan for you and me.

Take a stroll out to the hill. Out to Calvary. Out to the cross where, with holy blood, the hand that placed you on the planet wrote the promise, "God would give up his only Son before he'd give up on you."

SIX HOURS ONE FRIDAY

God has an incredible plan for your life. Write how you see his plan unfolding for your good and his glory.

_____

_____

_____

_____

_____

_____

_____

"You Are Mine"

Our lives are in the True One and in his Son, Jesus Christ.
1 JOHN 5:20

God knows your entire story, from first word to final breath, and with clear assessment declares, "You are mine."

My publisher made a similar decision with this book. Before agreeing to publish it, they read it—every single word. Multiple sets of editorial eyes scoured the manuscript, moaning at my bad jokes, grading my word crafting, suggesting a tune-up here and a tone-down there. We volleyed pages back and forth, writer to editor to writer, until finally we all agreed—this is it. It's time to publish or pass. The publisher could pass, mind you. Sometimes they do. But in this case, obviously they didn't. With perfect knowledge of this imperfect product, they signed on. What you read may surprise you, but not them.

What you do may stun you, but not God. With perfect knowledge of your imperfect life, God signed on.

COME THIRSTY

God knows your entire story from first word to final breath.
You are his. What positive effect can this have in your life?

193

The Shepherd's Voice

"A time is coming when all who are in their graves will hear his voice and come out—those who have done good will rise to live."

JOHN 5:28–29 NIV

A day is coming when everyone will hear [Jesus'] voice. A day is coming when all the other voices will be silenced; his voice—and his voice only—will be heard.

Some will hear his voice for the very first time. It's not that he never spoke, it's just that they never listened. For these, God's voice will be the voice of a stranger. They will hear it once—and never hear it again. They will spend eternity fending off the voices they followed on earth.

But others will be called from their graves by a familiar voice. For they are sheep who know their Shepherd. They are servants who opened the door when Jesus knocked.

Now the door will open again. Only this time, it won't be Jesus who walks into our house; it will be we, who walk into his.

IN THE EYE OF THE STORM

Do you know people who hear God's voice as the voice of a stranger? Write a prayer that they will hear the sound of his voice before it is too late.

_____

_____

_____

_____

Love the Overlooked

Put on the apron of humility, to serve one another.
1 PETER 5:5 TEV

Servanthood requires no unique skill or seminary degree. Regardless of your strengths, training, or church tenure, you can . . . love the overlooked.

Jesus sits in your classroom, wearing the thick glasses, outdated clothing, and a sad face. You've seen him. He's Jesus.

Jesus works in your office. Pregnant again, she shows up to work late and tired. No one knows the father. According to water-cooler rumors, even she doesn't know the father. You've seen her. She's Jesus.

When you talk to the lonely student, befriend the weary mom, you love Jesus. He dresses in the garb of the overlooked and ignored. "Whenever you did one of these things to someone overlooked or ignored, that was me—you did it to me" (Matthew 25:40 MSG).

CURE FOR THE COMMON LIFE

List some people you encounter every day who are overlooked and ignored. Think how you can reach out to them.

_____

_____

_____

_____

_____

April

Be strong in the Lord and in his great power.

—EPHESIANS 6:10

A Meeting of Moments

[They] put him to death by nailing him to a cross.
But this was God's plan which he had made long ago.

ACTS 2:23

The cross was no accident.

Jesus' death was not the result of a panicking cosmological engineer. The cross wasn't a tragic surprise. Calvary was not a knee-jerk response to a world plummeting toward destruction. It wasn't a patch-up job or a stop-gap measure. The death of the Son of God was anything but an unexpected peril.

No, it was part of an incredible plan. A calculated choice.

The moment the forbidden fruit touched the lips of Eve, the shadow of a cross appeared on the horizon. And between that moment and the moment the man with the mallet placed the spike against the wrist of God, a master plan was fulfilled.

GOD CAME NEAR

"The cross wasn't a tragic surprise. It was a calculated choice." What does that mean?

God's Name

The LORD is my shepherd; I have everything I need.

PSALM 23:1

Y ou want to know who God really is?" David asks. "Then read this." And he writes the name *Yahweh*. "Yahweh is my shepherd."

Though foreign to us, the name was rich to David. So rich, in fact, that David chose *Yahweh* over *El Shaddai* (God Almighty), *El Elyon* (God Most High), and *El Olam* (God the Everlasting). These and many other titles for God were at David's disposal. But when he considered all the options, David chose *Yahweh*.

Why *Yahweh*? Because *Yahweh* is God's name. You can call me preacher or writer or half-baked golfer—these are accurate descriptions, but these aren't my names. I might call you dad, mom, doctor, or student, and those terms may describe you, but they aren't your name. If you want to call me by my name, say *Max*. If I call you by your name, I say it. And if you want to call God by his name, say *Yahweh*.

TRAVELING LIGHT

God wants us to call him by name. He wants us to have a personal relationship with him. How is such divine friendship unique to Christianity?

_____

_____

_____

_____

A Cross-Shaped Shadow

John said, "Look, the Lamb of God,
who takes away the sin of the world!"

JOHN 1:29

Jesus was born crucified. Whenever he became conscious of who he was, he also became conscious of what he had to do. The cross-shaped shadow could always be seen. And the screams of hell's imprisoned could always be heard.

This explains the glint of determination on his face as he turned to go to Jerusalem for the last time. He was on his death march (Luke 9:51).

This explains the resoluteness in the words, "The reason my Father loves me is that I lay down my life—only to take it up again. No one takes it from me, but I lay it down of my own accord" (John 10:17–18 NIV).

So call it what you wish: An act of grace. A plan of redemption. A martyr's sacrifice. But whatever you call it, don't call it an accident. It was anything but that.

GOD CAME NEAR

Christ knew that pain and difficulties were part of his life plan, yet he marched toward them with determination. How does this encourage you?

_____

_____

_____

_____

A Man of Sorrows

He is despised and rejected by men,
a Man of sorrows and acquainted with grief.

ISAIAH 53:3 NKJV

The scene is very simple; you'll recognize it quickly. A grove of twisted olive trees. Ground cluttered with large rocks. A low stone fence. A dark, dark night.

See that solitary figure? Flat on the ground. Face stained with dirt and tears. Fists pounding the hard earth. Eyes wide with a stupor of fear. Hair matted with salty sweat. Is that blood on his forehead?

That's Jesus. Jesus in the Garden of Gethsemane.

We see an agonizing, straining, and struggling Jesus. We see a "Man of sorrows." We see a man struggling with fear, wrestling with commitments, and yearning for relief.

Seeing God like this does wonders for our own suffering. God was never more human than at this hour. God was never nearer to us than when he hurt. The incarnation was never so fulfilled as in the garden.

NO WONDER THEY CALL HIM THE SAVIOR

Jesus agonized and struggled in prayer. Describe ways that this can encourage you in your own prayers.

_____

_____

_____

_____

You Were in His Prayers

Then Jesus went about a stone's throw away from them.
He kneeled down and prayed.

LUKE 22:41

The final prayer of Jesus was about you. His final pain was for you. His final passion was for you. Before he went to the cross, Jesus went to the garden. And when he spoke with his Father, you were in his prayers.

And God couldn't turn his back on you. He couldn't because he saw you, and one look at you was all it took to convince him. Right there in the middle of a world which isn't fair. He saw you cast into a river of life you didn't request. He saw you betrayed by those you love. He saw you with a body which gets sick and a heart which grows weak.

On the eve of the cross, Jesus made his decision. He would rather go to hell for you than go to heaven without you.

AND THE ANGELS WERE SILENT

Jesus' final prayer was about you. How do you respond to that?

_____

_____

_____

_____

_____

_____

Patience Freely Offered

The Spirit produces the fruit of love, joy, peace, patience.
GALATIANS 5:22

I f you find patience hard to give, you might ask this question. How infiltrated are you with God's patience? You've heard about it. Read about it. Perhaps underlined Bible passages regarding it. But have you received it? The proof is in your patience. Patience deeply received results in patience freely offered.

God does more than demand patience from us; he offers it to us. Patience is a fruit of his Spirit. It hangs from the tree of Galatians 5:22: "The Spirit produces the fruit of love, joy, peace, patience." Have you asked God to give you some fruit? *Well I did once, but* . . . But what? Did you, h'm, grow impatient? Ask him again and again and again. He won't grow impatient with your pleading, and you will receive patience in your praying.

A LOVE WORTH GIVING

Most of us do not enjoy learning lessons of patience.
Describe some ways that God has taught you patience.

The Debt Is Paid

Though your sins are like scarlet,
they can be as white as snow. Though your sins
are deep red, they can be white like wool.

ISAIAH 1:18

When Jesus told us to pray for forgiveness of our debts as we forgive our own debtors, he knew who would be the one to pay the debt. As he would hang on the cross he would say, "It is finished". . . the debt is paid!

There are some facts that will never change. One fact is that you are forgiven. If you are in Christ, when he sees you, your sins are covered—he doesn't see them. He sees you better than you see yourself. And that is a glorious fact of your life.

WALKING WITH THE SAVIOR

Christ sees you better than you see yourself. How should this affect the way you see yourself? Others?

_____

_____

_____

_____

_____

_____

God's Work of Art

We are God's masterpiece.

EPHESIANS 2:10 NLT

Over a hundred years ago, a group of fishermen were relaxing in a Scottish seaside inn. One of the men gestured widely and his arm struck the serving maid's tea tray, sending the teapot flying into the whitewashed wall. The innkeeper surveyed the damage and sighed, "The whole wall will have to be repainted."

"Perhaps not," offered a stranger. "Let me work with it."

Having nothing to lose, the proprietor consented. The man pulled pencils, brushes, and pigment out of an art box. In time, an image began to emerge: a stag with a great rack of antlers. The man inscribed his signature at the bottom, paid for his meal, and left. His name: Sir Edwin Landseer, famous painter of wildlife.

In his hands, a mistake became a masterpiece. God's hands do the same, over and over. He draws together the disjointed blotches in our lives and renders them an expression of his love.

COME THIRSTY

In God's hands, a mistake can become a masterpiece. What does this mean to you personally?

The Worshipful Heart

Come, let's worship him and bow down.
Let's kneel before the LORD who made us.

PSALM 95:6

Worship. In two thousand years we haven't worked out the kinks. We still struggle for the right words in prayer. We still fumble over Scripture. We don't know when to kneel. We don't know when to stand. We don't know how to pray.

Worship is a daunting task.

For that reason, God gave us the Psalms—a praise book for God's people. This collection of hymns and petitions are strung together by one thread—a heart hungry for God.

Some are defiant. Others are reverent. Some are to be sung. Others are to be prayed. Some are intensely personal. Others are written as if the whole world would use them.

The very variety should remind us that worship is personal. No secret formula exists. What moves you may stymie another. Each worships differently. But each should worship.

THE INSPIRATIONAL STUDY BIBLE

Make note of some things Christ taught us about prayer,
both through his words and his life.

_____

_____

_____

_____

A Clear Vision of the Cross

*Christ died for sins once for all, the righteous
for the unrighteous, to bring you to God.*

1 PETER 3:18 NIV

O ne of the reference points of London is the Charing Cross. It is near the geographical center of the city and serves as a navigational tool for those confused by the streets.

A little girl was lost in the great city. A policeman found her. Between sobs and tears, she explained she didn't know her way home. He asked her if she knew her address. She didn't. He asked her phone number; she didn't know that either. But when he asked her what she knew, suddenly her face lit up.

"I know the Cross," she said. "Show me the Cross and I can find my way home from there."

So can you. Keep a clear vision of the cross on your horizon and you can find your way home.

AND THE ANGELS WERE SILENT

What are some practical ways that you can "keep a clear vision of the Cross" in your daily life?

Heaven's Solution

*"I pray these things while I am still in the world
so that these followers can have all of my joy in them."*

JOHN 17:13

What Jesus dreamed of doing and what he seemed able to do were separated by an impossible gulf. So Jesus prayed.

We don't know what he prayed about. But I have my guesses. He prayed for the impossible to happen.

Or maybe I'm wrong. Maybe he didn't ask for anything. Maybe he just stood quietly in the presence of Presence and basked in the Majesty. Perhaps he placed his war-weary self before the throne and rested.

Maybe he lifted his head out of the confusion of earth long enough to hear the solution of heaven. Perhaps he was reminded that hard hearts don't faze the Father. That problem people don't perturb the Eternal One.

IN THE EYE OF THE STORM

*Problem people don't perturb God . . . but they do perturb us.
Why is that? What can we do about it?*

_____

_____

_____

_____

_____

You Are *You-Nique*

Each of us is an original.

GALATIANS 5:26 MSG

God made you *you-nique.*

Secular thinking, as a whole, doesn't buy this. Secular society sees no author behind the book, no architect behind the house, no purpose behind or beyond life. It simply says, "You can be anything you want to be."

Be a butcher if you want to, a sales rep if you like. Be an ambassador if you really care. You can be anything you want to be. But can you? If God didn't pack within you the meat sense of a butcher, the people skills of a salesperson, or the world vision of an ambassador, can you be one? An unhappy, dissatisfied one perhaPsalm But a fulfilled one? No. Can an acorn become a rose, a whale fly like a bird, or lead become gold? Absolutely not. You cannot be anything you want to be. But you can be everything God wants you to be.

CURE FOR THE COMMON LIFE

Can you be anything you want to be in life? Why or why not?

One Word from His Lips

*I" have given you power . . .
that is greater than the enemy has."*

LUKE 10:19

Many players appear on the stage of Gethsemane. Judas and his betrayal. Peter and his sword. The soldiers and their weapons. And though these are crucial, they aren't instrumental. The encounter is not between Jesus and the soldiers; it is between God and Satan. Satan dares to enter yet another garden, but God stands and Satan hasn't a prayer.

Satan falls in the presence of Christ. One word from his lips, and the finest army in the world collapsed.

Satan is silent in the proclamation of Christ. Not once did the Enemy speak without Jesus' invitation. Before Christ, Satan has nothing to say.

Satan is powerless against the protection of Christ.

When Jesus says he will keep you safe, he means it. Hell will have to get through him to get to you. Jesus is able to protect you. When he says he will get you home, he will get you home.

A GENTLE THUNDER

Describe some ways you have experienced Christ's protection.

_____

_____

_____

_____

He Walked Among Us

We do not have a high priest who is
unable to sympathize with our weaknesses.

HEBREWS 4:15 NIV

When God chose to reveal himself, he did so (surprise of surprises) through a human body. The tongue that called forth the dead was a human one. The hand that touched the leper had dirt under its nails. The feet upon which the woman wept were calloused and dusty. And his tears . . . oh, don't miss the tears . . . they came from a heart as broken as yours or mine ever has been.

"For we do not have a high priest who is unable to sympathize with our weaknesses."

So, people came to him. My, how they came to him! They came at night; they touched him as he walked down the street; they followed him around the sea; they invited him into their homes and placed their children at his feet. Why? Because he refused to be a statue in a cathedral or a priest in an elevated pulpit. He chose instead to be Jesus.

GOD CAME NEAR

God chose to be Jesus. He chose to cry human tears. How should this affect the way we pray?

Faith Sees the Savior

Be strong in the Lord and in his great power.

EPHESIANS 6:10

I stand a few feet from a mirror and see the face of a man who failed, who failed his Maker. Again. I promised I wouldn't, but I did. I was quiet when I should have been bold. I took a seat when I should have taken a stand.

If this were the first time, it would be different. But it isn't. How many times can one fall and expect to be caught?

Your eyes look in the mirror and see a sinner, a failure, a promise-breaker. But by faith you look in the mirror and see a robed prodigal bearing the ring of grace on your finger and the kiss of your Father on your face.

Your eyes see your faults. Your faith sees your Savior.

Your eyes see your guilt. Your faith sees his blood.

WHEN GOD WHISPERS YOUR NAME

How does our faith "see" the Savior and his blood?

_____

_____

_____

_____

_____

_____

_____

Try Again

We worked hard all night and caught nothing.

LUKE 5:5 NASB

Do you have any worn, wet, empty nets? Do you know the feeling of a sleepless, fishless night? Of course you do. For what have you been casting?

Solvency? "My debt is an anvil around my neck . . ."

Faith? "I want to believe, but . . ."

Healing? "I've been sick so long . . ."

A happy marriage? "No matter what I do . . ."

"I've worked hard all night and caught nothing."

You've felt what Peter felt. You've sat where Peter sat. And now Jesus is asking you to go fishing. He knows your nets are empty. He knows your heart is weary. He knows you'd like nothing more than to turn your back on the mess and call it a life.

But he urges, "It's not too late to try again."

See if Peter's reply won't help you formulate your own. "I will do as You say and let down the nets" (Luke 5:5 NASB).

NEXT DOOR SAVIOR

What would you describe as the "empty nets" in your life? What does God want you to do with them? How do you respond to that?

_____

_____

_____

_____

Tipped Scales

*Christ's love is greater than anyone can ever know, but I
pray that you will be able to know that love.*

EPHESIANS 3:19

I t wasn't right that spikes pierced the hands that formed the earth. And it wasn't right that the Son of God was forced to hear the silence of God.

It wasn't right, but it happened.

For while Jesus was on the cross, God sat on his hands. He turned his back. He ignored the screams of the innocent.

He sat in silence while the sins of the world were placed upon his Son. And he did nothing while a cry a million times bloodier than John's echoed in the black sky: "My God, my God, why have you forsaken me?" (Matthew 27:46 NIV).

Was it right? No.

Was it fair? No.

Was it love? Yes.

THE APPLAUSE OF HEAVEN

*It is easy to get caught up in the struggle to protect our
"rights." How would your life be different if Christ had
struggled to protect his?*

Our Middle C

"I the LORD do not change."

MALACHI 3:6

When Lloyd Douglas, author of *The Robe* and other novels, attended college, he lived in a boardinghouse. A retired, wheelchair-bound music professor resided on the first floor. Each morning Douglas would stick his head in the door of the teacher's apartment and ask the same question, "Well, what's the good news?" The old man would pick up his tuning fork, tap it on the side of the wheelchair, and say, "That's middle C! It was middle C yesterday; it will be middle C tomorrow; it will be middle C a thousand years from now. The tenor upstairs sings flat. The piano across the hall is out of tune, but, my friend, that is middle C."

You and I need a middle C. Haven't you had enough change in your life? Relationships change. Health changes. The weather changes. But the Yahweh who ruled the earth last night is the same Yahweh who rules it today. Same convictions. Same plan. Same mood. Same love. He never changes.

TRAVELING LIGHT

The world around us changes almost daily if not hourly. Is it a comfort to you that God does not change? Explain why.

_____

_____

_____

_____

His Broken Heart

When he saw the crowds, he felt sorry for them because
they were hurting and helpless, like sheep without a shepherd.

MATTHEW 9:36

I can't understand it. I honestly cannot. Why did Jesus [die on the cross]? Oh, I know, I know. I have heard the official answers. "To gratify the old law." "To fulfill prophecy." And these answers are right. They are. But there is something more here. Something very compassionate. Something yearning. Something personal.

What is it?

Could it be that his heart was broken for all the people who cast despairing eyes toward the dark heavens and cry the same "Why?" Could it be that his heart was broken for the hurting?

I imagine him bending close to those who hurt. I imagine him listening. I picture his eyes misting and a pierced hand brushing away a tear. He who also was once alone understands.

No Wonder They Call Him the Savior

Imagine Christ bending close to touch your broken heart,
to heal your hurts. What areas of your life need his touch?

_____

_____

_____

_____

_____

_____

Be Kind to Yourself

Be kind to one another, tenderhearted,
forgiving one another, even as God in Christ forgave you.

EPHESIANS 4:32 NKJV

O ur heavenly Father is kind to us. And since he is so kind to us, can't we be a little kinder to ourselves? *Oh, but you don't know me, Max. You don't know my faults and my thoughts. You don't know the gripes I grumble and the complaints I mumble.* No, I don't, but he does. He knows everything about you, yet he doesn't hold back his kindness toward you. Has he, knowing all your secrets, retracted one promise or reclaimed one gift?

No, he is kind to you. Why don't you be kind to yourself? He forgives your faults. Why don't you do the same? He thinks tomorrow is worth living. Why don't you agree? He believes in you enough to call you his ambassador, his follower, even his child. Why not take his cue and believe in yourself?

A LOVE WORTH GIVING

Do you find it difficult to be kind to yourself? To believe in yourself? How can you be kinder to yourself?

217

Love Hung on a Cross

"God loved the world so much that he gave his one and only Son so that whoever believes in him may not be lost, but have eternal life."

JOHN 3:16

He looked around the hill and foresaw a scene. Three figures hung on three crosses. Arms spread. Heads fallen forward. They moaned with the wind.

Men clad in soldier's garb sat on the ground near the trio.

Women clad in sorrow huddled at the foot of the hill, faces tear-streaked.

All heaven stood to fight. All nature rose to rescue. All eternity poised to protect. But the Creator gave no command.

"It must be done . . ." he said, and withdrew.

The angel spoke again. "It would be less painful . . ."

The Creator interrupted softly. "But it wouldn't be love."

IN THE EYE OF THE STORM

The cross is a symbol of love, courage, and hope. Think of other things that the cross symbolizes.

Made in His Image

Then God said, "Let Us make man in Our image."
GENESIS 1:26 NKJV

Imagine God's creativity. Of all we don't know about the creation, there is one thing we do know—he did it with a smile. He must've had a blast. Painting the stripes on the zebra, hanging the stars in the sky, putting the gold in the sunset. What creativity! Stretching the neck of the giraffe, putting the flutter in the mockingbird's wings, planting the giggle in the hyena.

What a time he had. Like a whistling carpenter in his workshop, he loved every bit of it. He poured himself into the work. So intent was his creativity that he took a day off at the end of the week just to rest.

And then, as a finale to a brilliant performance, he made man. With his typical creative flair, he began with a useless mound of dirt and ended up with an invaluable species called a human. A human who had the unique honor to bear the stamp, "In His Image."

NO WONDER THEY CALL HIM THE SAVIOR

Can you imagine God creating this world with a smile? Make a list of some of the things that must have been the most fun for him to create.

_____

_____

_____

_____

The Message of God to Man

When Jesus tasted the vinegar, he said,
"It is finished." Then he bowed his head and died.

JOHN 19:30

It is finished."

Stop and listen a moment. Let the words wind through your heart. Imagine the cry from the cross. The sky is dark. The other two victims are moaning. Jeering mouths of the crowd are silent. Perhaps there is thunder. Perhaps there is weeping. Perhaps there is silence. Then Jesus draws in a deep breath, pushes his feet down on that Roman nail, and cries, "It is finished!" (NLT).

What was finished?

The history-long plan of redeeming man was finished. The message of God to man was finished. The works done by Jesus as a man on earth were finished. The sting of death had been removed. It was over.

NO WONDER THEY CALL HIM THE SAVIOR

Christ defeated death on the cross. How should this
encourage you?

_____

_____

_____

_____

_____

God Gets into Our Lives

I do not live anymore—it is Christ who lives in me.
GALATIANS 2:20

Y ou have leaves to rake. A steering wheel to grip. A neighbor's hand to shake. Simply put, you have things to do.

So does God. Babies need hugs. Children need good-night tucks. AIDS orphans need homes. Stressed-out executives need hope. God has work to do. And he uses our hands to do it.

What the hand is to the glove, the Spirit is to the Christian. God gets into us. At times, imperceptibly. Other times, disruptively. God gets his fingers into our lives, inch by inch reclaiming the territory that is rightfully his.

Your tongue. He claims it for his message.

Your feet. He requisitions them for his purpose.

Your mind? He made it and intends to use it for his glory.

Your eyes, face, and hands? Through them he will weep, smile, and touch.

COME THIRSTY

What areas of your life is God using for his message? What other areas rightfully belong to him?

The Key of Our Faith

Since Jesus died and broke loose from the grave,
God will most certainly bring back to life those who die in Jesus.

1 Thessalonians 4:14 MSG

For any follower of Christ, the promise is simply this: The resurrection of Jesus is proof and preview of our own.

But can we trust the promise? Is the resurrection a reality? Are the claims of the empty tomb true? This is not only a good question. It is *the* question. For as Paul wrote, "If Christ has not been raised, then your faith has nothing to it; you are still guilty of your sins" (1 Corinthians 15:17). In other words, if Christ has been raised, then his followers will join him; but if not, then his followers are fools. The resurrection, then, is the keystone in the arch of the Christian faith.

When Christ Comes

"The resurrection of Jesus is proof and preview of our own."
What does this mean to you now and in the life to come?

_____

_____

_____

_____

_____

_____

A Good Choice

Let us come near to God with a sincere heart and a sure faith.

HEBREWS 10:22

It would have been nice if God had let us order life like we order a meal. I'll take good health and a high IQ. I'll pass on the music skills, but give me a fast metabolism. Would've been nice. But it didn't happen. When it came to your life on earth, you weren't given a voice or a vote.

But when it comes to life after death, you were. In my book that seems like a good deal. Wouldn't you agree?

Have we been given any greater privilege than that of choice? Not only does this privilege offset any injustice, the gift of free will can offset any mistakes.

You've made some bad choices in life, haven't you? You've chosen the wrong friends, maybe the wrong career, even the wrong spouse. You look back over your life and say, "If only . . . if only I could make up for those bad choices." You can. One good choice for eternity offsets a thousand bad ones on earth.

The choice is yours.

HE CHOSE THE NAILS

God lets us make the important choices ourselves. Explain how this is a wonderful privilege.

A Noble Motivation

*At dawn on the first day, Mary Magdalene
and another woman named Mary went to look at the tomb.*

MATTHEW 28:1

It isn't hope that leads [Mary and Mary Magdalene] up the mountain to the tomb. It is duty. Naked devotion. They expect nothing in return. What could Jesus give? What could a dead man offer? The two women are not climbing the mountain to receive; they are going to the tomb to give. Period.

There is no motivation more noble.

Service prompted by duty. This is the call of discipleship.

HE STILL MOVES STONES

*Though these women thought the Savior was gone, they
continued to serve him. How do you respond to such devotion?*

_____

_____

_____

_____

_____

_____

_____

_____

It's Up to You

"Behold, I stand at the door, and knock: if any man hear my voice, and open the door, I will come in to him."

REVELATION 3:20 KJV

Perhaps you've seen Holman Hunt's painting of Jesus. Stone archway . . . ivy-covered bricks . . . Jesus standing before a heavy wooden door.

It was in a Bible I often held as a young boy. Beneath the painting were the words, "Behold, I stand at the door, and knock: if any man hear my voice, and open the door, I will come in to him."

Years later I read about a surprise in the painting. Holman Hunt had intentionally left out something that only the most careful eye would note as missing. I had not noticed it. When I was told about it I went back and looked. Sure enough, it wasn't there. There was no doorknob on the door. It could be opened only from the inside.

God comes to your house, steps up to the door, and knocks. But it's up to you to let him in.

AND THE ANGELS WERE SILENT

Do you know people who have not opened the door of their life to Jesus? Write a prayer for them.

A Holy Task

*Everything you do or say
should be done to obey Jesus your Lord.*

COLOSSIANS 3:17

Mary and Mary [Magdalene] knew a task had to be done—Jesus' body had to be prepared for burial. Peter didn't offer to do it. Andrew didn't volunteer. So the two Marys decide to do it.

I wonder if halfway to the tomb they had sat down and reconsidered. What if they'd looked at each other and shrugged, "What's the use?" What if they had given up? What if one had thrown up her arms in frustration and bemoaned, "I'm tired of being the only one who cares. Let Andrew do something for a change. Let Nathanael show some leadership."

Whether or not they were tempted to, I'm glad they didn't quit. That would have been tragic. You see, we know something they didn't. We know the Father was watching. Mary and Mary thought they were alone. They weren't. They thought their journey was unnoticed. They were wrong. God knew.

HE STILL MOVES STONES

These women demonstrated their love for Christ. How can you demonstrate your love for him?

_____

_____

_____

_____

The Empty Tomb

He has been raised from the dead. . . .
Come, see where his body was lying.

MATTHEW 28:6 NLT

Following Christ demands faith, but not blind faith. "Come and see," the angel invites. Shall we?

Take a look at the vacated tomb. Did you know the opponents of Christ never challenged its vacancy? No Pharisee or Roman soldier ever led a contingent back to the burial site and declared, "The angel was wrong. The body is here. It was all a rumor."

They would have if they could have. Within weeks disciples occupied every Jerusalem street corner, announcing a risen Christ. What quicker way for the enemies of the church to shut them up than to produce a cold and lifeless body? But they had no cadaver to display.

Helps explain the Jerusalem revival. When the apostles argued for the empty tomb, the people looked to the Pharisees for a rebuttal. But they had none to give. As A. M. Fairbairn put it long ago, "The silence of the Jews is as significant as the speech of the Christians."

NEXT DOOR SAVIOR

Why is the empty tomb such a joyful symbol for Christians?

The Only Path

*"I am the way, and the truth, and the life.
The only way to the Father is through me."*

JOHN 14:6

Tolerance. A prized virtue today. The ability to be understanding of those with whom you differ is a sign of sophistication. Jesus, too, was a champion of tolerance:

- tolerant of the disciples when they doubted.
- tolerant of the crowds when they misunderstood.
- tolerant of us when we fall.

But there is one area where Jesus was intolerant. There was one area where he was unindulgent and dogmatic.

As far as he was concerned, when it comes to salvation, there aren't several roads . . . there is only one road. There aren't several paths . . . there is only one path. And that path is Jesus himself.

That is why it is so hard for people to believe in Jesus. It's much easier to consider him one of several options rather than the option. But such a philosophy is no option.

A GENTLE THUNDER

Explain why Christ is not an option but is the option.

_____

_____

_____

_____

_____

Eternal Instants

You have done good things for your servant,
as you have promised, LORD.

PSALM 119:65

E ternal instants. You've had them. We all have.

Sharing a porch swing on a summer evening with your grandchild.

Seeing her face in the glow of a candle.

Putting your arm into your husband's as you stroll through the golden leaves and breathe the brisk autumn air.

Listening to your six-year-old thank God for everything from goldfish to Grandma.

Such moments are necessary because they remind us that everything is okay. The King is still on the throne and life is still worth living. Eternal instants remind us that love is still the greatest possession and the future is nothing to fear.

The next time an instant in your life begins to be eternal, let it.

GOD CAME NEAR

List some of the most memorable and touching "eternal instants" in your life. What is the benefit of these reminders?

_____

_____

_____

_____

_____

Insufficient Funds

*People cannot do any work
that will make them right with God.*

ROMANS 4:5

If Christ had not covered us with his grace, each of us would be overdrawn on [our heavenly bank] account. When it comes to goodness we would have insufficient funds. Inadequate holiness. God requires a certain balance of virtue in our account, and it's more than any of us has alone. Our holiness account shows insufficient funds, and only the holy will see the Lord; what can we do?

We could try making a few deposits. Maybe if I wave at my neighbor or compliment my husband or go to church next Sunday, I'll get caught up. But how do you know when you've made enough?

If you are trying to justify your own statement, forget ever having peace. You are trying to justify an account you can't justify. "It is God who justifies" (Romans 8:33 NIV).

THE GREAT HOUSE OF GOD

To be justified means that God sees you "just-as-if" you had never sinned. How does this give you hope?

_____

_____

_____

_____

_____

There's Only One You

From the place of His dwelling He looks on all the
inhabitants of the earth; He fashions their hearts individually.

PSALM 33:14–15 NKJV

Y ou are the only you God made.

He made you and broke the mold. Every single baby is a brand-new idea from the mind of God.

No one can duplicate your life. Scan history for your replica; you won't find it. God tailor-made you. He "personally formed and made each one" (Isaiah 43:7 MSG). No box of "backup yous" sits in God's workshop. You aren't one of many bricks in the mason's pile or one of a dozen bolts in the mechanic's drawer. You are it! And if you aren't you, we don't get you. The world misses out.

You are heaven's Halley's comet; we have one shot at seeing you shine.

CURE FOR THE COMMON LIFE

You are a brand-new idea from the mind of God. How can
you honor him with your tailor-made life?

Not Perfection, but Forgiveness

*Christ had no sin, but God made him
become sin so that in Christ we could become right with God.*

2 CORINTHIANS 5:21

It wasn't the Romans who nailed Jesus to the cross. It wasn't spikes that held Jesus to the cross. What held him to that cross was his conviction that it was necessary that he become sin—that he who is pure become sin and that the wrath of God be poured down, not upon the creation, but upon the Creator.

When the One who knew no sin became sin for us, when the sinless One was covered with all the sins of all the world, God didn't call his army of angels to save him. He didn't, because he knew he would rather give up his Son than give up on us.

Regardless of what you've done, it's not too late. Regardless of how far you've fallen, it's not too late. It doesn't matter how low the mistake is, it's not too late to dig down, pull out that mistake, and then let it go—and be free.

What makes a Christian a Christian is not perfection but forgiveness.

WALKING WITH THE SAVIOR

Is it possible to be perfect? Is it necessary?

_____

_____

_____

_____

_____

The Shadow of the Cross

God put the wrong on him who never did anything wrong,
so we could be put right with God.

2 CORINTHIANS 5:21 MSG

Envision the moment. God on his throne. You on the earth. And between you and God, suspended between you and heaven, is Christ on his cross. Your sins have been placed on Jesus. God, who punishes sin, releases his rightful wrath on your mistakes. Jesus receives the blow. Since Christ is between you and God, you don't. The sin is punished, but you are safe—safe in the shadow of the cross.

This is what God did, but why, why would he do it? Moral duty? Heavenly obligation? Paternal requirement? No. God is required to do nothing.

The reason for the cross? God loves the world.

HE CHOSE THE NAILS

"You are safe in the shadow of the cross." Explain what that means.

Whispered Wonderings

"She will have a son, and they will name him Immanuel,"
which means "God is with us."

MATTHEW 1:23

The white space between Bible verses is fertile soil for questions. One can hardly read Scripture without whispering, "I wonder . . ."

"I wonder if Eve ever ate any more fruit."

"I wonder if Noah slept well during storms."

But in our wonderings, there is one question we never need to ask. Does God care? Do we matter to God? Does he still love his children?

Through the small face of the stable-born baby, he says yes.

Yes, your sins are forgiven.

Yes, your name is written in heaven.

And yes, God has entered your world. Immanuel. God is with us.

HE STILL MOVES STONES

List some of the things you wonder about in the Bible.
Then make a "yes" list of things that are beyond doubt.

_____

_____

_____

_____

_____

_____

Pray About Everything

"Call to me in times of trouble.
I will save you, and you will honor me."

Psalm 50:15

W ant to worry less? Then pray more. Rather than look forward in fear, look upward in faith. This command surprises no one. Regarding prayer, the Bible never blushes. Jesus taught people that "it was necessary for them to pray consistently and never quit" (Luke 18:1 MSG). Paul told believers, "Devote yourselves to prayer with an alert mind and a thankful heart" (Colossians 4:2 NLT). James declared, "Are any among you suffering? They should keep on praying about it" (James 5:13 NLT).

Rather than worry about anything, "pray about everything" (Philippians 4:6 NLT). Everything? Diaper changes and dates? Business meetings and broken bathtubs? Procrastinations and prognostications? Pray about everything.

COME THIRSTY

Do you pray about everything? Or do some things seem too trivial for prayer? What is the advantage of praying about even the little things?

The Fire of Your Heart

My God, I want to do what you want.
Your teachings are in my heart.

PSALM 40:8

Want to know God's will for your life? Then answer this question: What ignites your heart? Forgotten orphans? Untouched nations? The inner city? The outer limits?

Heed the fire within!

Do you have a passion to sing? Then sing! Are you stirred to manage? Then manage! Do you ache for the ill? Then treat them! Do you hurt for the lost? Then teach them!

As a young man I felt the call to preach. Unsure if I was correct in my reading of God's will for me, I sought the counsel of a minister I admired. His counsel still rings true. "Don't preach," he said, "unless you have to."

As I pondered his words I found my answer: "I have to. If I don't, the fire will consume me."

What is the fire that consumes you?

THE GREAT HOUSE OF GOD

What passion has God placed in your heart? What are you doing to pursue it?

_____

_____

_____

_____

Covered with Christ

Your life is now hidden with Christ in God.

COLOSSIANS 3:3 NIV

The Chinese language has a great symbol for the truth of that verse. The word for *righteousness* is a combination of two pictures. On the top is a lamb. Beneath the lamb is a person. The lamb covers the person. Isn't that the essence of righteousness? The Lamb of Christ over the child of God? Whenever the Father looks down on you, what does he see? He sees his Son, the perfect Lamb of God, hiding you. Christians are like their ancestor Abel. We come to God by virtue of the flock. Cain came with the work of his own hands. God turned him away. Abel came, and we come, dependent upon the sacrifice of the Lamb, and we are accepted. Like the Chinese symbol, we are covered by the lamb, hidden in Christ.

When God looks at you, he doesn't see you; he sees Jesus. And how does he respond when he sees Jesus? He rends the heavens and vibrates the earth with the shout, "You are my Son, whom I love, and I am very pleased with you" (Mark 1:11).

A LOVE WORTH GIVING

When God looks at you, he sees Jesus. Why should this make you glad?

A Cleared Calendar

Jesus often withdrew to lonely places and prayed.

LUKE 5:16 NIV

How long has it been since you let God have you?

I mean really *have* you? How long since you gave him a portion of undiluted, uninterrupted time listening for his voice? Apparently, Jesus did. He made a deliberate effort to spend time with God.

Spend much time reading about the listening life of Jesus and a distinct pattern emerges. He spent regular time with God, praying and listening. Mark says, "Very early in the morning, while it was still dark, Jesus got up, left the house and went off to a solitary place, where he prayed" (Mark 1:35 NIV).

Let me ask the obvious. If Jesus, the Son of God, the sinless Savior of humankind, thought it worthwhile to clear his calendar to pray, wouldn't we be wise to do the same?

JUST LIKE JESUS

God wants you to make a deliberate effort to spend time with him. Why is this important to a victorious life of faith?

_____

_____

_____

_____

_____

_____

He Gives Us Himself

"I am with you always, to the very end of the age."

MATTHEW 28:20 NIV

The story is told of a man on an African safari deep in the jungle. The guide before him had a machete and was whacking away the tall weeds and thick underbrush. The traveler, wearied and hot, asked in frustration, "Where are we? Do you know where you are taking me? Where is the path?!" The seasoned guide stopped and looked back at the man and replied, "I am the path."

We ask the same questions, don't we? We ask God, "Where are you taking me? Where is the path?" And he, like the guide, doesn't tell us. Oh, he may give us a hint or two, but that's all. If he did, would we understand? Would we comprehend our location? No, like the traveler, we are unacquainted with this jungle. So rather than give us an answer, Jesus gives us a far greater gift. He gives us himself.

TRAVELING LIGHT

God is the pathway of life. How does he lead you along that path?

God's Magnum Opus

We know that when Christ comes, we will be like him,
because we will see him as he really is.

1 JOHN 3:2

When you arrive [in heaven] something wonderful will happen. A final transformation will occur. You will be just like Jesus.

Of all the blessings of heaven, one of the greatest will be you! You will be God's magnum opus, his work of art. The angels will gasp. God's work will be completed. At last, you will have a heart like his.

You will love with a perfect love.

You will worship with a radiant face.

You'll hear each word God speaks.

Your heart will be pure, your words will be like jewels, your thoughts will be like treasures.

You will be just like Jesus. You will, at long last, have a heart like his.

JUST LIKE JESUS

Make a list of other things that will be different in your life when you finally have "a heart like his."

_____

_____

_____

_____

Jesus Offers Peace

"Peace be with you."

JOHN 20:19

The church of Jesus Christ began with a group of frightened men in a second-floor room in Jerusalem.

Though they'd marched with Jesus for three years, they now sat . . . afraid. They were timid soldiers, reluctant warriors, speechless messengers.

Daring to dream that the Master had left them some word, some plan, some direction, they came back.

But little did they know their wildest dream wasn't wild enough. Just as someone mumbles, "It's no use," they hear a noise. They hear a voice: "Peace be with you."

The one betrayed sought his betrayers. What did he say to them? Not "What a bunch of flops!" Not "I told you so." No "Where-were-you-when-I-needed-you?" speeches. But simply one phrase, "Peace be with you." The very thing they didn't have was the very thing he offered: peace.

SIX HOURS ONE FRIDAY

Do you feel that your dreams for life are too timid? If you believed God's promises, what would your dreams look like?

Friends with God

"I no longer call you servants. . . . But I call you friends."

JOHN 15:15

Through Christ's sacrifice, our past is pardoned and our future secure. And, "since we have been made right with God by our faith, we have peace with God" (Romans 5:1). Peace with God. What a happy consequence of faith! Not just peace between countries, peace between neighbors, or peace at home; salvation brings peace with God.

God is no longer a foe, but a friend. We are at peace with him.

IN THE GRIP OF GRACE

Through Christ's sacrifice, God has become your friend. How does this affect the way you live from day to day?

_____

_____

_____

_____

_____

_____

_____

_____

_____

_____

We Are Family

Be devoted to one another in brotherly love.

ROMANS 12:10 NIV

Common belief identifies members of God's family. And common affection unites them. Paul gives this relationship rule for the church: "Be devoted to one another in brotherly love." The apostle plays the wordsmith here, bookending the verse with fraternal-twin terms. He begins with *philostorgos* (*philos* means friendly; *storgos* means family love) and concludes with *philadelphia* (*phileo* means tender affection; *adelphia* means brethren). An awkward but accurate translation of the verse might be "Have a friend/family devotion to each other in a friend/family sort of way." If Paul doesn't get us with the first adjective, he catches us with the second. In both he reminds us: the church is God's family.

You didn't pick me. I didn't pick you. You may not like me. I may not like you. But since God picked and likes us both, we are family.

CURE FOR THE COMMON LIFE

God's children are friends/family. Make a list of some of the blessings and challenges of relating to this family.

Confession Creates Peace

Happy is the person whose sins
are forgiven, whose wrongs are pardoned.

PSALM 32:1

I f we are already forgiven, then why does Jesus teach us to pray, "Forgive us our debts"?

The very reason you would want your children to do the same. If my children violate one of my standards or disobey a rule, I don't disown them. I don't kick them out of the house or tell them to change their last name. But I do expect them to be honest and apologize. And until they do, the tenderness of our relationship will suffer. The nature of the relationship won't be altered, but the intimacy will.

The same happens in our walk with God. Confession does not create a relationship with God; it simply nourishes it. If you are a believer, admission of sins does not alter your position before God, but it does enhance your peace with God.

THE GREAT HOUSE OF GOD

Confession nourishes our relationship with God. Can you think of other reasons why it is important to be totally honest with him?

_____

_____

_____

_____

_____

Love Protects

The LORD God made clothes from animal skins
for the man and his wife and dressed them.

GENESIS 3:21

That simple sentence suggests three powerful scenes.

Scene 1: God slays an animal. For the first time in the history of the earth, dirt is stained with blood. Innocent blood. The beast committed no sin. The creature did not deserve to die.

Adam and Eve did. The couple deserve to die, but they live.

Scene 2: Clothing is made. The shaper of the stars now becomes a tailor.

And in Scene 3: God dresses them. "The Lord . . . dressed them."

Adam and Eve are on their way out of the garden. They've been told to leave, but now God tells them to stop. "Those fig leaves," he says, shaking his head, "will never do." And he produces some clothing. But he doesn't throw the garments at their feet and tell them to get dressed. He dresses them himself. As a father would zip up the jacket of a preschooler. God covers them.

A LOVE WORTH GIVING

As God covered and protected Adam and Eve, so he covers and protects all his children. Write some ways you have experienced his divine protection.

_____

_____

_____

Something Deep Within

The heavens declare the glory of God.

PSALM 19:1 NIV

God's judgment [on the day Christ returns] is based upon humanity's response to the message received. He will never hold us accountable for what he doesn't tell us. At the same time, he will never let us die without telling us something. Even those who never heard of Christ are given a message about the character of God. "The heavens declare the glory of God" (Psalm 19:1 NIV). Nature is God's first missionary. Where there is no Bible, there are sparkling stars. Where there are no preachers, there are springtimes. If a person has nothing but nature, then nature is enough to reveal something about God. As Paul says: "God's law is not something alien, imposed on us from without, but woven into the very fabric of our creation. There is something deep within [people] that echoes God's yes and no, right and wrong. Their response to God's yes and no will become public knowledge on the day God makes his final decision about every man and woman" (Romans 2:15–16 MSG).

WHEN CHRIST COMES

What does the fabric of creation tell you about God?

_____

_____

_____

_____

_____

A Plea for Help

*"We deserve to die for our evil deeds,
but this man hasn't done one thing wrong."*

LUKE 23:41 TLB

We are guilty and he is innocent.

We are filthy and he is pure.

We are wrong and he is right.

He is not on that cross for his sins. He is there for ours.

And once the crook understands this, his request seems only natural. As he looks into the eyes of his last hope, he makes the same request any Christian has made: "Remember me when you come into your Kingdom" (Luke 23:42 TLB).

No stained glass homilies. No excuses. Just a desperate plea for help.

At this point Jesus performs the greatest miracle of the cross. Greater than the earthquake. Greater than the tearing of the temple curtain.

He performs the miracle of forgiveness: "Today you will be with me in Paradise. This is a solemn promise" (Luke 23:43 TLB).

SIX HOURS ONE FRIDAY

Explain why extending forgiveness to others is a miracle.

Character Creates Courage

All you who put your hope in the LORD be strong and brave.

PSALM 31:24

A legend from India tells about a mouse who was terrified of cats until a magician agreed to transform him into a cat. That resolved his fear . . . until he met a dog, so the magician changed him into a dog. The mouse-turned-cat-turned-dog was content until he met a tiger—so, once again, the magician changed him into what he feared. But when the tiger came complaining that he had met a hunter, the magician refused to help. "I will make you into a mouse again, for though you have the body of a tiger, you still have the heart of a mouse."

Sound familiar? How many people do you know who have built a formidable exterior, only to tremble inside with fear? We face our fears with force or we stockpile wealth. We seek security in things. We cultivate fame and seek status.

But do these approaches work?

Courage is an outgrowth of who we are. Exterior supports may temporarily sustain, but only inward character creates courage.

THE APPLAUSE OF HEAVEN

What things do you turn to for security? Can any of these deliver you from fear and anxiety? What can?

_____

_____

_____

_____

Think of Home

When you have many kinds of troubles, you should be full of joy, because you know that these troubles test your faith, and this will give you patience.

JAMES 1:2–3

God didn't say, "*If* you have many kinds of troubles. . . " He said, "*When* you have many kinds of troubles . . ." Troubles are part of the package. Betrayals are part of our troubles. Don't be surprised when betrayals come. Don't look for fairness here—look instead where Jesus looked.

While going through hell, Jesus kept his eyes on heaven. While surrounded by enemies, he kept his mind on his father. While abandoned on earth, he kept his heart on home. "In the future you will see the Son of Man sitting at the right hand of God, the Powerful One, and coming on clouds in the sky" (Matthew 26:64).

When all of earth turns against you, all of heaven turns toward you. To keep your balance in a crooked world, think of home.

AND THE ANGELS WERE SILENT

"While going through hell, Jesus kept his eyes on heaven." How can you apply that truth to your life and your experiences?

One of a Kind

You made my whole being; you formed me in my mother's body.
PSALM 139:13

In my closet hangs a sweater that I seldom wear. It is too small. I should throw that sweater away. But love won't let me.

It's the creation of a devoted mother expressing her love. Each strand was chosen with care. Each thread was selected with affection. It is valuable not because of its function, but because of its Maker.

That must have been what the psalmist had in mind when he wrote, "You knit me together in my mother's womb" (Psalm 139:13 NIV).

Think on those words. You were knitted together. You aren't an accident. You weren't mass-produced. You aren't an assembly-line product.

You were deliberately planned, specifically gifted, and lovingly positioned on this earth by the Master Craftsman. In a system that ranks the value of a human by the figures of his salary or the shape of her legs . . . let me tell you something: Jesus' plan is a reason for joy!

THE APPLAUSE OF HEAVEN

God lovingly placed you on this earth. How does that make you feel about yourself? About God?

_____

_____

_____

_____

Thank You

Oh, love the LORD, all you His saints!
For the LORD preserves the faithful.

PSALM 31:23 NKJV

Re-liable. *Liable* means responsible. *Re* means over and over again.

I'm wondering if this book has found its way into the hands of some contemporary saints of reliability. If such is the case I can't resist the chance to say one thing.

Thank you.

Thank you, senior saints, for a generation of prayer and forest clearing.

Thank you, teachers, for the countless Sunday school lessons, prepared and delivered with tenderness.

Thank you, missionaries, for your bravery in sharing the timeless truth in a foreign tongue.

Thank you, preachers. You thought we weren't listening, but we were. And your stubborn sowing of God's seed is bearing fruit you may never see this side of the great harvest.

GOD CAME NEAR

Why do we value people who are reliable and responsible?
How does God reward reliability?

Voice of Grace

"I tell you the truth, today you will be with me in paradise."

LUKE 23:43

Tell me, what has [the thief on the cross] done to warrant help? He has wasted his life. Who is he to beg for forgiveness? He publicly scoffed at Jesus. What right does he have to pray, "Jesus, remember me when you come into your kingdom" (Luke 23:42)?

Do you really want to know? The same right you have to pray.

You see, that is you and me on the cross. Naked, desolate, hopeless, and estranged. That is us. That is us asking.

We don't boast. We don't produce our list. Any sacrifice appears silly when placed before God on a cross.

We, like the thief, have one more prayer. And we, like the thief, pray.

And we, like the thief, hear the voice of grace.

HE STILL MOVES STONES

The dying thief heard the voice of God's grace. Have you heard that voice? How has it changed your life?

_____

_____

_____

_____

_____

_____

Never Alone

"I will . . . not forsake My people."

1 KINGS 6:13 NKJV

The Lord is with us. And, since the Lord is near, everything is different. Everything!

You may be facing death, but you aren't facing death alone; the Lord is with you. You may be facing unemployment, but you aren't facing unemployment alone; the Lord is with you. You may be facing marital struggles, but you aren't facing them alone; the Lord is with you. You may be facing debt, but you aren't facing debt alone; the Lord is with you.

Underline these words: *You are not alone.*

Your family may turn against you, but God won't. Your friends may betray you, but God won't. You may feel alone in the wilderness, but you are not. He is with you.

TRAVELING LIGHT

"You are not alone. God is with you." Describe how that thought makes you feel. How can this make a difference in your life?

Secondhand Spirituality

Come near to God, and God will come near to you.

JAMES 4:8

Some of us have tried to have a daily quiet time and have not been successful. Others of us have a hard time concentrating. And all of us are busy. So rather than spend time with God, listening for his voice, we'll let others spend time with him and then benefit from their experience. Let them tell us what God is saying. After all, isn't that why we pay preachers?

If that is your approach, if your spiritual experiences are secondhand and not firsthand, I'd like to challenge you with this thought: Do you do that with other parts of your life?

You don't do that with vacations. You don't do that with romance. You don't let someone eat on your behalf, do you? [There are] certain things no one can do for you.

And one of those is spending time with God.

JUST LIKE JESUS

Why is it important that we each spend time with God? Why can't we just listen to what others tell us about him?

_____

_____

_____

_____

_____

_____

Words of Strength

When you talk, do not say harmful things, but say
what people need—words that will help others become stronger.

EPHESIANS 4:29

Before you speak, ask: Will what I'm about to say help others become stronger? You have the ability, with your words, to make a person stronger. Your words are to their soul what a vitamin is to their body. If you had food and saw someone starving, would you not share it? If you had water and saw someone dying of thirst, would you not give it? Of course you would. Then won't you do the same for their hearts? Your words are food and water!

Do not withhold encouragement from the discouraged.

Do not keep affirmation from the beaten down!

Speak words that make people stronger. Believe in them as God has believed in you.

A LOVE WORTH GIVING

Can you think of a time when affirming words had a
positive effect on your life? Make a list of ways you can
speak words that will make others stronger.

Beggars in Need of Bread

"Give us the food we need for each day. Forgive us for our sins, just as we have forgiven those who sinned against us."

MATTHEW 6:11–12

We are sinners in need of grace, strugglers in need of strength. Jesus teaches us to pray, "Forgive our debts . . . and lead us not into temptation."

We've all made mistakes and we'll all make some more. The line that separates the best of us from the worst of us is a narrow one; hence we'd be wise to take seriously Paul's admonition: "Why do you judge your brothers or sisters in Christ? And why do you think you are better than they? We will all stand before the Lord to be judged" (Romans 14:10).

Your sister would like me to remind you that she needs grace. Just like you need forgiveness, so does she. There comes a time in every relationship when it's damaging to seek justice, when settling the score only stirs the fire. There comes a time when the best thing you can do is accept your brother and offer him the same grace you've been given.

THE GREAT HOUSE OF GOD

"We are strugglers in need of strength." What does that statement mean to you?

_____

_____

_____

He Knows How You Feel

He is able . . . to run to the cry of . . .
those who are being tempted and tested and tried.

HEBREWS 2:18 AMP

Jesus was angry enough to purge the temple, hungry enough to eat raw grain, distraught enough to weep in public, fun-loving enough to be called a drunkard, winsome enough to attract kids, weary enough to sleep in a storm-bounced boat, poor enough to sleep on dirt and borrow a coin for a sermon illustration, radical enough to get kicked out of town, responsible enough to care for his mother, tempted enough to know the smell of Satan, and fearful enough to sweat blood.

But why? Why would heaven's finest Son endure earth's toughest pain? So you would know that "he is able . . . to run to the cry of . . . those who are being tempted and tested and tried."

Whatever you are facing, he knows how you feel.

NEXT DOOR SAVIOR

God not only knows about your every pain and struggle, he knows how you feel. How does this truth change your thoughts about situations in your life?

May

*Your word is like a lamp for my feet
and a light for my path.*

—Psalm 119:105

Prayers Are Precious Jewels

The Lord sees the good people and listens to their prayers.

1 PETER 3:12

You and I live in a loud world. To get someone's attention is no easy task. He must be willing to set everything aside to listen: turn down the radio, turn away from the monitor, turn the corner of the page and set down the book. When someone is willing to silence everything else so he can hear us clearly, it is a privilege. A rare privilege, indeed.

[Your] prayers are honored [in heaven] as precious jewels. Purified and empowered, the words rise in a delightful fragrance to our Lord. Your words do not stop until they reach the very throne of God.

Your prayer on earth activates God's power in heaven, and God's will is done on earth as it is in heaven.

Your prayers move God to change the world. You may not understand the mystery of prayer. You don't need to. But this much is clear: Actions in heaven begin when someone prays on earth.

THE GREAT HOUSE OF GOD

"Your prayers move God to change the world." How do you respond to that truth?

_____

_____

_____

_____

Saturated in Love

Where God's love is, there is no fear,
because God's perfect love drives out fear.

1 JOHN 4:18

We fear rejection, so we follow the crowd. We fear not fitting in, so we take the drugs. For fear of standing out, we wear what everyone else wears. For fear of blending in, we wear what no one else wears. For fear of sleeping alone, we sleep with anyone. For fear of not being loved, we search for love in all the wrong places.

But God flushes those fears. Those saturated in God's love don't sell out to win the love of others. They don't even sell out to win the love of God.

Do you think you need to? Do you think, *If I cuss less, pray more, drink less, study more . . . if I try harder, God will love me more?* Sniff and smell Satan's stench behind those words. We all need improvement, but we don't need to woo God's love. We change because we already have God's love. God's perfect love.

COME THIRSTY

Have you ever found yourself trying to "woo God's love"?
Explain why this doesn't work.

_____

_____

_____

_____

_____

We Look to God

"Lord, if it's you," Peter replied, "tell me to come to you on the water."

Peter is not testing Jesus; he is pleading with Jesus. Stepping onto a stormy sea is not a move of logic; it is a move of desperation. Peter grabs the edge of the boat. Throws out a leg . . . follows with the other. Several steps are taken. It's as if an invisible ridge of rocks runs beneath his feet. At the end of the ridge is the glowing face of a never-say-die friend.

We do the same, don't we? We come to Christ in an hour of deep need. We abandon the boat of good works. We realize that human strength won't save us. So we look to God in desperation. We realize that all the good works in the world are puny when laid before the Perfect One.

IN THE EYE OF THE STORM

Think of a time when you cried out to God in desperation and he met your need. How does this encourage your faith?

_____

_____

_____

_____

_____

_____

Wounded by Words

When they hurled their insults at him, he did not retaliate.
1 PETER 2:23 NIV

Someone you love or respect slams you to the floor with a slur or slip of the tongue. And there you lie, wounded and bleeding. Perhaps the words were intended to hurt you, perhaps not; but that doesn't matter. The wound is deep. The injuries are internal. Broken heart, wounded pride, bruised feelings.

If you have suffered or are suffering because of someone else's words, you'll be glad to know that there is a balm for this laceration. Meditate on these words from 1 Peter 2:23: "When they hurled their insults at him, he did not retaliate. Instead, he entrusted himself to him who judges justly" (NIV).

Did you see what Jesus did? He left the judging to God. He did not take on the task of seeking revenge. He demanded no apology. He, to the astounding contrary, spoke on their defense. "Father, forgive them, for they do not know what they are doing" (Luke 23:34 NIV).

NO WONDER THEY CALL HIM THE SAVIOR

Why is forgiveness a balm for hurting hearts?

_____

_____

_____

_____

Sometimes God Says No

Continue praying, keeping alert, and always thanking God.
COLOSSIANS 4:2

Can you imagine the outcome if a parent honored each request of each child during a trip? We'd inch our bloated bellies from one ice-cream store to the next.

Can you imagine the chaos if God indulged each of ours?

"For God has not *destined* us [emphasis mine] to the terrors of judgment, but to the full attainment of salvation through our Lord Jesus Christ" (1 Thessalonians 5:9 NEB).

Note God's destiny for your life. Salvation.

God's overarching desire is that you reach that destiny. His itinerary includes stops that encourage your journey. He frowns on stops that deter you. When his sovereign plan and your earthly plan collide, a decision must be made. Who's in charge of this journey?

If God must choose between your earthly satisfaction and your heavenly salvation, which do you hope he chooses?

Me too.

IN THE EYE OF THE STORM

Do you hope he chooses your earthly satisfaction or your heavenly salvation? Why?

_____

_____

_____

_____

_____

Following Our Own Paths

All of us have strayed away like sheep.
We have left God's paths to follow our own.

ISAIAH 53:6 NLT

A dam and Eve turned their heads toward the hiss of the snake and for the first time ignored God. Eve did not ask, "God, what do you want?" Adam didn't suggest, "Let's consult the Creator." They acted as if they had no heavenly Father. His will was ignored, and sin, with death on its coattails, entered the world.

Sin sees the world with no God in it.

Where we might think of sin as slipups or missteps, God views sin as a godless attitude that leads to godless actions. "All of us have strayed away like sheep. We have left God's paths to follow our own." The sinful mind dismisses God. His counsel goes unconsulted. His opinion, unsolicited.

The lack of God-centeredness leads to self-centeredness. Sin celebrates its middle letter—s*I*n.

COME THIRSTY

Have there been times in your life when you have left God's path to follow your own? What have been the consequences?

_____

_____

_____

_____

_____

God's Passion and Plan

Your word is like a lamp for my feet and a light for my path.

PSALM 119:105

The purpose of the Bible is simply to proclaim God's plan to save his children. It asserts that man is lost and needs to be saved. And it communicates the message that Jesus is God in the flesh sent to save his children.

Though the Bible was written over sixteen centuries by at least forty authors, it has one central theme—salvation through faith in Christ. Begun by Moses in the lonely desert of Arabia and finished by John on the lonely Isle of Patmos, it is held together by a strong thread: God's passion and God's plan to save his children.

What a vital truth! Understanding the purpose of the Bible is like setting the compass in the right direction. Calibrate it correctly and you'll journey safely. But fail to set it, and who knows where you'll end up.

THE INSPIRATIONAL BIBLE

As you read through the Bible, look for the central theme—salvation through faith in Christ. Explain how this theme is central to the Christian faith.

_____

_____

_____

_____

_____

The Language God Speaks

Accept teaching from his mouth, and keep his words in your heart.

JOB 22:22

There is no language God will not speak. Which leads us to a delightful question. What language is he speaking to you? I'm not referring to an idiom or dialect but to the day-to-day drama of your life.

There are times he speaks the "language of abundance." Is your tummy full? Are your bills paid? Got a little jingle in your pocket? Don't be so proud of what you have that you miss what you need to hear. Could it be you have much so you can give much?

Or how about the "language of affliction"? Talk about an idiom we avoid. But you and I both know how clearly God speaks in hospital hallways and sickbeds.

God speaks all languages—including yours. What language is God speaking to you?

HE CHOSE THE NAILS

What language is God speaking to you right now? Think of some of the ways God speaks to us regardless of what is going on in life.

_____

_____

_____

_____

_____

Not Guilty

Who can accuse the people God has chosen?
No one, because God is the One who makes them right.

ROMANS 8:33

Every moment of your life, your accuser is filing charges against you. He has noticed every error and marked each slip. Try to forget your past; he'll remind you. Try to undo your mistakes; he will thwart you.

This expert witness has no higher goal than to take you to court and press charges. Who is he? The devil.

He rails: "This one you call your child, God. He is not worthy."

As he speaks, you hang your head. You have no defense. His charges are fair. "I plead guilty, your honor," you mumble.

"The sentence?" Satan asks.

"The wages of sin is death," explains the judge, "but in this case the death has already occurred. For this one died with Christ."

Satan is suddenly silent. And you are suddenly jubilant. You have stood before the judge and heard him declare, "Not guilty."

IN THE GRIP OF GRACE

When you stand before the judge of the heavens he declares you "not guilty." Why is this good news?

_____

_____

_____

_____

A Hardy Faith

"There is joy in the presence of the angels of God
when one sinner changes his heart and life."

LUKE 15:10

O ur faith is not in religion; our faith is in God. A hardy, daring faith that believes God will do what is right, every time. And that God will do what it takes—whatever it takes—to bring his children home.

He is the Shepherd in search of his lamb. His legs are scratched, his feet are sore, and his eyes are burning. He scales the cliffs and traverses the fields. He explores the caves. He cups his hands to his mouth and calls into the canyon.

And the name he calls is yours.

He is the housewife in search of the lost coin. No matter that he has nine others; he won't rest until he has found the tenth. He searches the house. He moves furniture. All other tasks can wait. Only one matters. The coin is of great value to him. He owns it. He will not stop until he finds it.

The coin he seeks is you.

AND THE ANGELS WERE SILENT

Has God searched for you and found you? How has this
changed your life?

God's in Charge

God's Spirit, who is in you,
is greater than the devil, who is in the world.

1 JOHN 4:4

S atan has no power except that which God gives him.

To the first-century church in Smyrna, Christ said, "Do not be afraid of what you are about to suffer. I tell you, the devil will put some of you in prison to test you, and you will suffer for ten days. But be faithful, even if you have to die, and I will give you the crown of life" (Revelation 2:10).

Analyze Jesus' words for a minute. Christ informs the church of the persecution, the duration of the persecution (ten days), the reason for the persecution (to test you), and the outcome of the persecution (a crown of life). In other words, Jesus uses Satan to fortify his church.

Even when [Satan] appears to win, he loses.

THE GREAT HOUSE OF GOD

Even when the devil appears to win, he loses. Can you
relate this truth to events in your life? In the world?

Heaven Came Down

*"I have come down from heaven, not to do
My own will, but the will of Him who sent Me."*

JOHN 6:38 NKJV

This is no run-of-the-mill messiah. His story was extraordinary. He called himself divine, yet allowed a minimum-wage Roman soldier to drive a nail into his wrist. He demanded purity, yet stood for the rights of a repentant whore. He called men to march, yet refused to allow them to call him King. He sent men into all the world, yet equipped them with only bended knees and memories of a resurrected carpenter.

Has it been awhile since you have seen him? If your prayers seem stale, it probably has. If your faith seems to be trembling, perhaps your vision of him has blurred. If you can't find power to face your problems, perhaps it is time to face him.

One warning. Something happens to a person who has witnessed his Majesty. One glimpse of the King and you are consumed by a desire to see more of him and say more about him.

GOD CAME NEAR

What steps can you take to spend more time in Christ's presence?

Grace Teaches Us

*He gave himself for us so he might pay the price to free us
from all evil and to make us pure people who belong only to him.*

TITUS 2:14

Do we ever compromise tonight, knowing we'll confess tomorrow?

It's easy to be like the fellow visiting Las Vegas who called the preacher, wanting to know the hours of the Sunday service. The preacher was impressed. "Most people who come to Las Vegas don't do so to go to church."

"Oh, I'm not coming for the church. I'm coming for the gambling and parties and wild women. If I have half as much fun as I intend to, I'll need a church come Sunday morning."

Is that the intent of grace? Is God's goal to promot disobedience? Hardly. "Grace . . . teaches us not to live against God nor to do the evil things the world wants to do. Instead, that grace teaches us to live now in a wise and right way and in a way that shows we serve God" (Titus 2:11–12). God's grace has released us from selfishness. Why return?

IN THE GRIP OF GRACE

*The goal of grace is not to promote disobedience but wise living.
How has God's grace taught you to live in the right way?*

_____

_____

_____

_____

God Is Uncaused

*"Remember that I am God, and there is no other God.
I am God, and there is no one like me."*

ISAIAH 46:9

No one breathed life into Yahweh. No one sired him. No one gave birth to him. No one caused him. No act brought him forth.

And since no act brought him forth, no act can take him out. Does he fear an earthquake? Does he tremble at a tornado? Hardly. Yahweh sleeps through storms and calms the winds with a word. Cancer does not trouble him, and cemeteries do not disturb him. He was here before they came. He'll be here after they are gone. He is uncaused.

And he is ungoverned. Counselors can comfort you *in* the storm, but you need a God who can *still* the storm. Friends can hold your hand at your deathbed, but you need a Yahweh who has defeated the grave. Philosophers can debate the meaning of life, but you need a Lord who can declare the meaning of life.

TRAVELING LIGHT

"You need a God who can still the storm." What storms are you facing that need God's peace?

_____

_____

_____

_____

Get Out of the Judgment Seat

"You will be judged in the same way that you judge others."

MATTHEW 7:2

We condemn a man for stumbling this morning, but we didn't see the blows he took yesterday. We judge a woman for the limp in her walk, but cannot see the tack in her shoe. We mock the fear in their eyes, but have no idea how many stones they have ducked or darts they have dodged.

Are they too loud? Perhaps they fear being neglected again. Are they too timid? Perhaps they fear failing again. Too slow? Perhaps they fell the last time they hurried. You don't know. Only one who has followed yesterday's steps can be their judge.

Not only are we ignorant about yesterday, we are ignorant about tomorrow. Dare we judge a book while chapters are yet unwritten? Should we pass a verdict on a painting while the artist still holds the brush? How can you dismiss a soul until God's work is complete? "God began doing a good work in you, and I am sure he will continue it until it is finished when Jesus Christ comes again" (Philippians 1:6).

IN THE GRIP OF GRACE

"We cannot judge a painting while the artist still holds the brush." How does this statement relate to the people in your life?

_____

_____

_____

_____

No Pecking Orders

*He humbled himself and became obedient
to death—even death on a cross!*

PHILIPPIANS 2:8 NIV

Jesus blasts the top birds of the church, those who roost at the top of the spiritual ladder and spread their plumes of robes, titles, jewelry, and choice seats. Jesus won't stand for it. It's easy to see why. How can I love others if my eyes are only on me? How can I point to God if I'm pointing at me? And, worse still, how can someone see God if I keep fanning my own tail feathers?

Jesus has no room for pecking orders. Love "does not boast, it is not proud" (1 Corinthians 13:4 NIV).

His solution to man-made caste systems? A change of direction. In a world of upward mobility, choose downward servility. Go down, not up. "Regard one another as more important than yourselves" (Philippians 2:3 NASB). That's what Jesus did.

He flip-flopped the pecking order. While others were going up, he was going down. "He humbled himself and became obedient to death—even death on a cross!"

A LOVE WORTH GIVING

In a world of upward mobility, how can you choose downward servility?

Listening for God

A rule here, a rule there. A little lesson here, a little lesson there.

ISAIAH 28:10

Equipped with the right tools, we can learn to listen to God. What are those tools? Here are the ones I have found helpful.

A regular time and place. Select a slot on your schedule and a corner of your world, and claim it for God. For some it may be the best to do this in the morning. Others prefer the evening.

A second tool you need [is] *an open Bible.* God speaks to us through his Word. The first step in reading the Bible is to ask God to help you understand it. Don't go to Scripture looking for your own idea; go searching for God's.

There is a third tool. Not only do we need a regular time and an open Bible, we also need *a listening heart.* If you want to be just like Jesus, let God have you. Spend time listening for him until you receive your lesson for the day—then apply it.

JUST LIKE JESUS

Have you set aside a regular time and place to meet with God? How can this make your Christian walk more meaningful?

_____

_____

_____

_____

_____

_____

Forgiveness Follows Failure

In the past God spoke . . . many times and in many different ways.
But now . . . God has spoken to us through his Son.

HEBREWS 1:1–2

God, motivated by love and directed by divinity, surprised everyone. He became a man. In an untouchable mystery, he disguised himself as a carpenter and lived in a dusty Judaean village. Determined to prove his love for his creation, he walked incognito through his own world. His callused hands touched wounds and his compassionate words touched hearts.

But as beautiful as this act of incarnation was, it was not the zenith. Like a master painter, God reserved his masterpiece until the end. All the earlier acts of love had been leading to this one. The angels hushed and the heavens paused to witness the finale. God unveils the canvas and the ultimate act of creative compassion is revealed.

God on a cross. The Creator being sacrificed for the creation. God convincing man once and for all that forgiveness still follows failure.

NO WONDER THEY CALL HIM THE SAVIOR

The cross is the ultimate act of compassion. What does that statement mean to you? How does that truth affect your life?

Faith Meets Grace

Let us come near to God with a sincere heart and a sure faith,
because we have been made free from a guilty conscience.

Faith is not born at the negotiating table where we barter our gifts in exchange for God's goodness. Faith is not an award given to the most learned. It's not a prize given to the most disciplined. It's not a title bequeathed to the most religious.

Faith is a desperate dive out of the sinking boat of human effort and a prayer that God will be there to pull us out of the water. The apostle Paul wrote about this kind of faith: "For it is by grace you have been saved, through faith—and this not from yourselves, it is the gift of God—not by works, so that no one can boast" (Ephesians 2:8–9 NIV).

The supreme force in salvation is God's grace.

IN THE EYE OF THE STORM

"Faith is a desperate dive out of the sinking boat of human effort." Explain why we can't save ourselves, why human effort is not sufficient.

The Spirit's Work

If Christ is in you, then the Spirit gives you life.

ROMANS 8:10

Receiving the unseen is not easy. Most Christians find the cross of Christ easier to accept than the Spirit of Christ. Good Friday makes more sense than Pentecost. Christ, our substitute. Jesus taking our place. The Savior paying for our sins. These are astounding, yet embraceable, concepts. They fall in the arena of transaction and substitution, familiar territory for us. But Holy Spirit discussions lead us into the realm of the supernatural and unseen. We grow quickly quiet and cautious, fearing what we can't see or explain.

It helps to consider the Spirit's work from this angle. What Jesus did in Galilee is what the Holy Spirit does in us. Jesus dwelt among the people, teaching, comforting, and convicting. The Holy Spirit dwells within us, teaching, comforting, and convicting.

COME THIRSTY

Are you uneasy discussing the work of the Spirit? Why or why not?

Itemized Grace

The Lord knows those who belong to him.

2 TIMOTHY 2:19

Imagine the event. You are before the judgment seat of Christ. The book is opened and the reading begins—each sin, each deceit, each occasion of destruction and greed. But as soon as the infraction is read, grace is proclaimed.

The result? God's merciful verdict will echo through the universe. For the first time in history, we will understand the depth of his goodness. Itemized grace. Catalogued kindness. Registered forgiveness. We will stand in awe as one sin after another is proclaimed, and then pardoned.

The devil will shrink back in defeat. The angels will step forward in awe. And we saints will stand tall in God's grace. As we see how much he has forgiven us, we will see how much he loves us. And we will worship him.

The result will be the first genuine community of forgiven people. Only One is worthy of the applause of heaven, and he's the One with the pierced hands and feet.

WHEN CHRIST COMES

Do you "stand tall in God's grace"? How can this make a difference in your life?

_____

_____

_____

_____

Uninterrupted Perfection

They divided his clothes among the four of them. They also took his robe, but it was seamless, woven in one piece from the top.

JOHN 19:23 NLT

I t must have been Jesus' finest possession. Jewish tradition called for a mother to make such a robe and present it to her son as a departure gift when he left home. Had Mary done this for Jesus? We don't know. But we do know the tunic was without seam, woven from top to bottom. Why is this significant?

Scripture often describes our behavior as the clothes we wear. Peter urges us to be "clothed with humility" (1 Peter 5:5 NKJV). David speaks of evil people who clothe themselves "with cursing" (Psalm 109:18 NKJV). Garments can symbolize character, and like his garment, Jesus' character was seamless. Coordinated. Unified. He was like his robe: uninterrupted perfection.

HE CHOSE THE NAILS

Jesus was uninterrupted perfection. Think of some of the attributes of his perfection. How can this encourage your walk of faith?

A Higher Standard

*I keep trying to reach the goal and
get the prize for which God called me.*

PHILIPPIANS 3:14

Most of my life I've been a closet slob. Then I got married.

I enrolled in a twelve-step program for slobs. ("My name is Max, I hate to vacuum.") A physical therapist helped me rediscover the muscles used for hanging shirts. My nose was reintroduced to the fragrance of Pine Sol.

Then came the moment of truth. Denalyn went out of town for a week. Initially I reverted to the old man. I figured I'd be a slob for six days and clean on the seventh. But something strange happened, a curious discomfort. I couldn't relax with dirty dishes in the sink.

What had happened to me? Simple. I'd been exposed to a higher standard.

Isn't that what has happened with us? Before Christ our lives were out of control, sloppy, and indulgent. We didn't even know we were slobs until we met him. Suddenly we find ourselves wanting to do good. Go back to the old mess? Are you kidding?

IN THE GRIP OF GRACE

How has God changed the direction of your life?

_____

_____

_____

_____

The Invitation

"All you who are thirsty, come and drink."

ISAIAH 55:1

To receive an invitation is to be honored—to be held in high esteem. For that reason all invitations deserve a kind and thoughtful response.

But the most incredible invitations are not found in envelopes or fortune cookies; they are found in the Bible. You can't read about God without finding him issuing invitations. He invited Eve to marry Adam, the animals to enter the ark, David to be king, Israel to leave bondage, Nehemiah to rebuild Jerusalem. God is an inviting God. He invited Mary to birth his Son, the disciples to fish for men, the adulterous woman to start over, and Thomas to touch his wounds. God is the King who prepares the palace, sets the table, and invites his subjects to come in.

God is a God who opens the door and waves his hand, pointing pilgrims to a full table.

His invitation is not just for a meal, however; it is for life. An invitation to come into his kingdom. Who can come? Whoever wishes.

AND THE ANGELS WERE SILENT

Make a list of the benefits of accepting God's invitation.

A Personal Query

He said to them, "But who do you say that I am?"

MARK 8:29 NKJV

Jesus turns [to his disciples] and asks them the question. *The* question. "But who do you say that I am?"

He doesn't ask, "What do you think about what I've done?" He asks, "Who do you say that I am?"

He doesn't ask, "Who do your friends think I am? Who do your parents think I am? Who do your peers think I am?" He poses instead a starkly personal query, "Who do *you* think I am?"

You have been asked some important questions in your life:

Will you marry me?

Would you be interested in a transfer?

What would you think if I told you I was pregnant?

You've been asked some important questions. But the grandest of them is an anthill compared to the Everest found in the eighth chapter of Mark.

Who do you say that I am?

THE INSPIRATIONAL STUDY BIBLE

How do you answer Jesus' question?

_____

_____

_____

_____

_____

_____

Our Plight

When we were unable to help ourselves,
at the moment of our need, Christ died for us.

ROMANS 5:6

God did for us what I did for one of my daughters in the shop at New York's La Guardia Airport. The sign above the ceramic pieces read Do Not Touch. But the wanting was stronger than the warning, and she touched. And it fell. By the time I looked up, ten-year-old Sara was holding the two pieces of a New York City skyline. Next to her was an unhappy store manager. Over them both was the written rule. Between them hung a nervous silence. My daughter had no money. He had no mercy. So I stepped in. "How much do we owe you?" I asked.

How was it that I owed anything? Simple. She was my daughter. And since she could not pay, I did.

Since you and I cannot pay, Christ did. We've broken so much more than souvenirs. We've . . . broken God's heart.

With the law on the wall and shattered commandments on the floor, Christ steps near (like a neighbor) and offers a gift (like a Savior).

NEXT DOOR SAVIOR

Write a note of praise to God for the gift of his Son.

God's Mountains

"My grace is enough for you. When you are weak,
my power is made perfect in you."

2 CORINTHIANS 12:9

There are certain mountains only God can climb.

It's not that you aren't welcome to try; it's just that you aren't able.

If the word *Savior* is in your job description, it's because you put it there. Your role is to help the world, not save it. Mount Messiah is one mountain you weren't made to climb.

Nor is Mount Self-Sufficient. You aren't able to run the world, nor are you able to sustain it. Some of you think you can. You are self-made. You don't bow your knees, you just roll up your sleeves and put in another twelve-hour day . . . which may be enough when it comes to making a living or building a business. But when you face your own grave or your own guilt, your power will not do the trick.

THE GREAT HOUSE OF GOD

We are taught from childhood to be self-reliant, to be self-sufficient. How can this actually be a detriment when it comes to our salvation?

_____

_____

_____

_____

_____

Seeing the Source

"Whoever has seen me has seen the Father."

JOHN 14:9

Should a man see only popularity, he becomes a mirror, reflecting whatever needs to be reflected to gain acceptance. Though in vogue, he is vague. Though in style, he is stodgy.

Should a man see only power, he becomes a wolf—prowling, hunting, and stalking the elusive game. Recognition is his prey and people are his prizes. His quest is endless.

Should a man see only pleasure, he becomes a carnival thrill-seeker, alive only in bright lights, wild rides, and titillating entertainment. With lustful fever he races from ride to ride, satisfying his insatiable passion for sensations only long enough to look for another.

Seekers of popularity, power, and pleasure. The end result is the same: painful unfulfillment.

Only in seeing his Maker does a man truly become man. For in seeing his Creator, man catches a glimpse of what he was intended to be.

GOD CAME NEAR

Only in seeing our Creator do we catch a glimpse of what we are intended to be. Explain what that sentence means.

_____

_____

_____

_____

The Correct Solution

The just shall live by faith.

ROMANS 1:17 NKJV

At the moment I don't feel too smart. I just got off the wrong plane that took me to the wrong city and left me at the wrong airport. I went east instead of west and ended up in Houston instead of Denver.

It didn't look like the wrong plane, but it was. I walked through the wrong gate, dozed off on the wrong flight, and ended up in the wrong place.

Paul says we've all done the same thing. Not with airplanes and airports, but with our lives and God. He tells the Roman readers,

There is none righteous, no, not one (Romans 3:10 NKJV).

All have sinned and fall short of the glory of God (Romans 3:23 NKJV).

We are all on the wrong plane, he says. All of us. Gentile and Jew. Every person has taken the wrong turn. And we need help. The wrong solutions are pleasure and pride (Romans 1 and 2); the correct solution is Christ Jesus (Romans 3:21–26).

THE INSPIRATIONAL STUDY BIBLE

Explain why Jesus is the correct solution.

_____

_____

_____

_____

_____

Live Your Life

God, who makes everything work together,
will work you into his most excellent harmonies.

PHILIPPIANS 4:9 MSG

T he Unseen Conductor prompts this orchestra we call living. When gifted teachers aid struggling students and skilled managers disentangle bureaucratic knots, when dog lovers love dogs and number crunchers zero balance the account, when you and I do the most what we do the best for the glory of God, we are "marvelously functioning parts in Christ's body" (Romans 12:5 MSG).

You play no small part, because there is no small part to be played. "All of you together are Christ's body, and each one of you is a separate and necessary part of it" (1 Corinthians 12:27 NLT). "Separate" and "necessary." Unique and essential. No one else has been given your lines. The Author of the human drama entrusted your part to you alone. Live your life, or it won't be lived. We need you to be you.

You need you to be you.

CURE FOR THE COMMON LIFE

God has a special part for you to play in the human drama.
Describe some of the ways you are living that part.

_____

_____

_____

_____

_____

This Isn't Home

"I have chosen you out of the world, so you don't belong to it."

JOHN 15:19

All of us know what it is like to be in a house that is not our own. Perhaps you've spent time in a dorm room or army barrack. Maybe you've slept in your share of hotels or bunked in a few hostels. They have beds. They have tables. They may have food and they may be warm, but they are a far cry from being "your father's house."

Your father's house is where your father is.

We don't always feel welcome here on earth. We wonder if there is a place here for us. People can make us feel unwanted. Tragedy leaves us feeling like intruders. Strangers. Interlopers in a land not ours. We don't always feel welcome here.

We shouldn't. This isn't our home. To feel unwelcome is no tragedy. Indeed it is healthy. We are not home here. This language we speak, it's not ours. This body we wear, it isn't us. And the world we live in, this isn't home.

A GENTLE THUNDER

Do you ever feel like a stranger in this world below, like you don't belong? Why can that be a good thing?

_____

_____

_____

_____

_____

No More Sacrifice

He came as High Priest of this better system which we now have.

HEBREWS 9:11 TLB

Even a casual student of Scripture notes the connection between blood and mercy. As far back as the son of Adam, worshipers knew "without the shedding of blood there is no forgiveness" (Hebrews 9:22 NIV).

With a field as his temple and the ground as his altar, Abel became the first to do what millions would imitate. He offered a blood sacrifice for sins.

Those who followed suit form a long line: Abraham, Moses, Gideon, Samson, Saul, David. They knew the shedding of blood was necessary for the forgiveness of sins. Jacob knew it too; hence, the stones were stacked for the altar.

But the line ended at the cross. What Abel sought to accomplish in the field, God achieved with his Son. What Abel began, Christ completed. After Christ's sacrifice there would be no more need to shed blood.

HE CHOSE THE NAILS

Christ's death on the cross finished forever the need to offer a sacrifice of blood. What does that mean to you?

No Nonsacred Moments

We are God's workers, working together.

1 CORINTHIANS 3:9

I t's a wonderful day indeed when we stop working for God and begin working with God.

For years I viewed God as a compassionate CEO and my role as a loyal sales representative. He had his office, and I had my territory. I could contact him as much as I wanted. He was always a phone or fax away. He encouraged me, rallied behind me, and supported me, but he didn't go with me. At least I didn't think he did. Then I read 2 Corinthians 6:1: We are "God's fellow workers" (NIV).

Fellow workers? Co-laborers? God and I work together? Imagine the paradigm shift this truth creates. Rather than report to God, we work *with* God. Rather than check in with him and then leave, we check in with him and then follow. We are always in the presence of God. There is never a nonsacred moment!

JUST LIKE JESUS

How would you explain the difference between working for God and with God?

_____

_____

_____

_____

_____

Perfect Peace

*His peace will guard your hearts and
minds as you live in Christ Jesus.*

PHILIPPIANS 4:7 NLT

Believing prayer ushers in God's peace. Not a random, nebulous, earthly peace, but his peace. Imported from heaven. The same tranquility that marks the throne room God offers to you.

Do you think he battles anxiety? You suppose he ever wrings his hands or asks the angels for antacids? Of course not. A problem is no more a challenge to God than a twig is to an elephant. God enjoys perfect peace because God enjoys perfect power.

And he offers his peace to you. A peace that will "guard your hearts and minds as you live in Christ Jesus." Paul employs a military metaphor here. The Philippians, living in a garrison town, were accustomed to the Roman sentries maintaining their watch. Before any enemy could get inside, he had to pass through the guards. God gives you the same offer. His supernatural peace overshadows you, guarding your heart.

COME THIRSTY

Describe a time when the peace of God helped you through a difficult time.

_____

_____

_____

_____

Found, Called, and Adopted

"It is not the healthy people who need a doctor, but the sick. . . .
I did not come to invite good people but to invite sinners."

MATTHEW 9:12–13

God didn't look at our frazzled lives and say, "I'll die for you when you deserve it."

No, despite our sin, in the face of our rebellion, he chose to adopt us. And for God, there's no going back. His grace is a come-as-you-are promise from a one-of-a-kind King. You've been found, called, and adopted; so trust your Father and claim this verse as your own: "God shows his great love for us in this way: Christ died for us while we were still sinners" (Romans 5:8). And you never again have to wonder who your father is—you've been adopted by God and are therefore an "heir of God through Christ" (Galatians 4:7 NKJV).

IN THE GRIP OF GRACE

You have been adopted by God. Describe some characteristics of life in his family.

_____

_____

_____

_____

_____

_____

God's Open Arms

Keep your roots deep in him and have your lives built on him.

COLOSSIANS 2:7

The people God used to change history were a ragbag of ne'er-do-wells and has-beens who found hope, not in their performance, but in God's proverbially open arms.

Let's start with Abraham. Though eulogized by Paul for his faith, this Father of a Nation wasn't without his weaknesses. He had a fibbing tongue that wouldn't stop! One time, in order to save his neck, he let the word get out that Sarah wasn't his wife but his sister, which was only half true. And then, not long later, he did it again! "And there Abraham said of his wife Sarah, 'She is my sister'" (Genesis 20:2 NIV).

Twice he traded in his integrity for security. That's what you call confidence in God's promises? Can you build a nation on that kind of faith? God can. God took what was good and forgave what was bad and used "old forked tongue" to start a nation.

NO WONDER THEY CALL HIM THE SAVIOR

Our hope is not in our performance but in God's open arms. How have you experienced God's open arms?

_____

_____

_____

_____

_____

Within Reach of Your Prayers

If God is for us, who can be against us?

ROMANS 8:31 NIV

The question is not simply, "Who can be against us?" You could answer that one. Who is against you? Disease, inflation, corruption, exhaustion. Calamities confront, and fears imprison. Were Paul's question, "Who can be against us?" we could list our foes much easier than we could fight them. But that is not the question. The question is, *"If God is for us,* who can be against us?"

God is for you. Your parents may have forgotten you, your teachers may have neglected you, your siblings may be ashamed of you; but within reach of your prayers is the Maker of the oceans. God!

IN THE GRIP OF GRACE

"God is for you." Make a list of the ways he has shown his loving care for you. Praise him for unfailing love.

_____

_____

_____

_____

_____

_____

Captured Thoughts

We capture every thought and make it give up and obey Christ.
2 CORINTHIANS 10:5

Capturing thoughts is serious business. It was for Jesus. Remember the thoughts that came his way courtesy of the mouth of Peter? Jesus had just prophesied his death, burial, and resurrection, but Peter couldn't bear the thought of it. "Peter took Jesus aside and told him not to talk like that. Jesus said to Peter, 'Go away from me, Satan! You are not helping me! You don't care about the things of God, but only about the things people think are important'" (Matthew 16:22–23).

See the decisiveness of Jesus? A trashy thought comes his way. He is tempted to entertain it. A cross-less life would be nice. But what does he do? He stands at the gangplank of the dock and says, "Get away from me." As if to say, "You are not allowed to enter my mind."

What if you did that? What if you took every thought captive?

A LOVE WORTH GIVING

What would you have done differently today if you had "taken every thought captive"?

_____

_____

_____

_____

_____

God Is Angry at Evil

So put all evil things out of your life. . . .
These things make God angry.

Colossians 3:5–6

Many don't understand God's anger because they confuse the wrath of God with the wrath of man. The two have little in common. Human anger is typically self-driven and prone to explosions of temper and violent deeds. We get ticked off because we've been overlooked, neglected, or cheated. This is the anger of man. It is not, however, the anger of God.

God doesn't get angry because he doesn't get his way. He gets angry because disobedience always results in self-destruction. What kind of father sits by and watches his child hurt himself?

In the Grip of Grace

Disobedience to God always results in self-destruction. Do you have friends or family who are living in disobedience to God? Write a prayer to pray for them.

_____

_____

_____

_____

_____

_____

God Is Righteous

He is gracious, and full of compassion, and righteous.

Righteousness is who God is. God's righteousness "endures forever" (Psalm 112:3 NIV) and "reaches to the skies (Psalm 71:19 NIV).

God is righteous. His decrees are righteous (Romans 1:32). His judgment is righteous (Romans 2:5). His requirements are righteous (Romans 8:4). His acts are righteous (Daniel 9:16). Daniel declared, "Our God is right in everything he does" (v. 14).

God is never wrong. He has never rendered a wrong decision, experienced the wrong attitude, taken the wrong path, said the wrong thing, or acted the wrong way. He is never too late or too early, too loud or too soft, too fast or too slow. He has always been and always will be right. He is righteous.

TRAVELING LIGHT

Write out each of the verses mentioned above. How do these truths affect your faith in God?

God Knows You by Name

"I have written your name on my hand."

ISAIAH 49:16

Quite a thought, isn't it? Your name on God's hand. Your name on God's lips. Maybe you've seen your name in some special places. On an award or diploma. But to think that your name is on God's hand and on God's lips . . . my, could it be?

Or perhaps you have never seen your name honored. And you can't remember when you heard it spoken with kindness. If so, it may be more difficult for you to believe that God knows your name.

But he does. Written on his hand. Spoken by his mouth. Whispered by his lips. Your name.

WHEN GOD WHISPERS YOUR NAME

Can you think of a time when your name was honored? How did you feel? How does it make you feel to know that your name is on God's hand?

They Couldn't Forget Him

Jesus is the One whom God raised from the dead.
And we are all witnesses to this.

ACTS 2:32

W e don't know where the disciples went when they fled the garden, but we do know what they took: a memory. They took a heart-stopping memory of a man who called himself no less than God in the flesh. And they couldn't get him out of their minds. Try as they might to lose him in the crowd, they couldn't forget him.

If they saw a leper, they thought of his compassion.

If they heard a storm, they would remember the day he silenced one.

If they saw a child, they would think of the day he held one.

And if they saw a lamb being carried to the temple, they would remember his face streaked with blood and his eyes flooded with love.

No, they couldn't forget him. As a result, they came back. And, as a result, the church of our Lord began with a group of frightened men in an Upper Room.

SIX HOURS ONE FRIDAY

List some things that make it impossible for you to forget God.

The Brief Journey of Life

Our days on earth are like a shadow.

1 CHRONICLES 29:15 NIV

He who "lives forever" has placed himself at the head of a band of pilgrims who mutter, "How long, O LORD? . . . How long?" (Psalm 89:46 NIV).

"How long must I endure this sickness?"

"How long must I endure this spouse?"

"How long must I endure this paycheck?"

Do you really want God to answer? He could, you know. He could answer in terms of the here and now with time increments we know. "Two more years on the illness." "The rest of your life in the marriage." "Ten more years for the bills."

But he seldom does that. He usually opts to measure the *here and now* against the *there and then*. And when you compare *this* life to *that* life, this life ain't long.

IN THE EYE OF THE STORM

Do you ever find yourself asking God, "How long?" Can you trust his grace to meet your needs?

_____

_____

_____

_____

_____

The Proper View of Self

To Him who is able to do exceedingly abundantly above all that we ask or think . . . be glory.

EPHESIANS 3:20–21 NKJV

There are two extremes of poor I-sight. Self-loving and self-loathing. We swing from one side to the other. Promotions and demotions bump us back and forth. One day too high on self, the next too hard on self. Neither is correct. Self-elevation and self-deprecation are equally inaccurate. Where is the truth?

Smack-dab in the middle. Dead center between "I can do anything" and "I can't do anything" lies "I can do all things through Christ who strengthens me" (Philippians 4:13 NKJV).

Neither omnipotent nor impotent, neither God's MVP nor God's mistake. Not self-secure or insecure, but God-secure—a self-worth based in our identity as children of God. The proper view of self is in the middle.

CURE FOR THE COMMON LIFE

Do you find yourself leaning toward one extreme of poor I-sight or the other? What areas of your life are most affected by this tendency?

Keep Unity

May the Lord lead your hearts into God's love and Christ's patience.
2 THESSALONIANS 3:5

All people will know that you are my followers if you love each other" (John 13:35). Stop and think about this verse for a minute. Could it be that *unity* is the key to reaching the world for Christ?

If unity is the key to evangelism, shouldn't it have precedence in our prayers? Should we, as Paul said, "make every effort to keep the unity of the Spirit through the bond of peace" (Ephesians 4:3 NIV)? If unity matters to God, then shouldn't unity matter to us? If unity is a priority in heaven, then shouldn't it be a priority on earth?

Nowhere, by the way, are we told to *build* unity. We are told simply to *keep* unity. From God's perspective there is but "one flock and one shepherd" (John 10:16). Unity does not need to be created; it simply needs to be protected.

How do we do that? Does that mean we compromise our convictions? No. Does that mean we abandon the truths we cherish? No. But it does mean we look long and hard at the attitudes we carry.

IN THE GRIP OF GRACE

What can we each do to protect the unity of God's flock?

_____

_____

_____

_____

A Robe of Righteousness

You were all clothed with Christ.

GALATIANS 3:27

We eat our share of forbidden fruit. We say what we shouldn't say. Go where we shouldn't go. Pluck fruit from trees we shouldn't touch.

And when we do, the door opens, and the shame tumbles in. And we hide. We sew fig leaves. We cover ourselves in good works and good deeds, but one gust of the wind of truth, and we are naked again—stark naked in our own failure.

So what does God do? Exactly what he did for our parents in the garden. He sheds innocent blood. He offers the life of his Son. And from the scene of the sacrifice the Father takes a robe—the robe of righteousness. And does he throw it in our direction and tell us to shape up? No, he dresses us himself. He dresses us with himself. "You were all baptized into Christ, and so you were all clothed with Christ" (Galatians 3:26–27).

We hide. He seeks. We bring sin. He brings a sacrifice. We try fig leaves. He brings the robe of righteousness.

A LOVE WORTH GIVING

Think of a time when you brought sin and God brought a robe of righteousness. What did that robe do to your sin?

_____

_____

_____

_____

Sorrow for Sin

If we confess our sins, he will forgive
our sins, because we can trust God to do what is right.

1 JOHN 1:9

I f we confess our sins . . ." The biggest word in Scriptures just might be that two-letter one, *if.* For confessing sins—admitting failure—is exactly what prisoners of pride refuse to do.

"Me a sinner? Oh sure, I get rowdy every so often, but I'm a pretty good ol' boy."

"Listen, I'm just as good as the next guy. I pay my taxes."

Justification. Rationalization. Comparison. They sound good. They sound familiar. They even sound American. But in the kingdom, they sound hollow.

When you get to the point of having sorrow for your sins, when you admit that you have no other option, then cast all your cares on him, for he is waiting.

THE APPLAUSE OF HEAVEN

Why is it so difficult for us to admit our sins and our
failures? Why is it so necessary?

_____

_____

_____

_____

_____

_____

The Other Side of the River

I want to know Christ and the power that
raised him from the dead. . . . Then I have hope
that I myself will be raised from the dead.

PHILIPPIANS 3:10–11

Jesus saw people enslaved by their fear of death. He explained that the river of death was nothing to fear. The people wouldn't believe him. He touched a boy and called him back to life. The followers were still unconvinced. He whispered life into the dead body of a girl. The people were still cynical. He let a dead man spend four days in a grave and then called him out. Was that enough? Apparently not. For it was necessary for him to enter the river, to submerge himself in the water of death before people would believe that death had been conquered.

But after he did, after he came out on the other side of death's river, it was time to sing . . . it was time to celebrate.

SIX HOURS ONE FRIDAY

Do you fear death or do you know someone who fears death?
How can the death and resurrection of Jesus help us overcome
that fear?

Finding Courage in Grace

I was given mercy so that in me, the worst of all sinners,
Christ Jesus could show that he has patience without limit.

1 TIMOTHY 1:16

During the early days of the Civil War a Union soldier was arrested on charges of desertion. Unable to prove his innocence, he was condemned and sentenced to die a deserter's death. His appeal found its way to the desk of Abraham Lincoln. The president felt mercy for the soldier and signed a pardon. The soldier returned to service, fought the entirety of the war, and was killed in the last battle. Found within his breast pocket was the signed letter of the president.

Close to the heart of the soldier were his leader's words of pardon. He found courage in grace. I wonder how many thousands more have found courage in the emblazoned cross of their heavenly King.

IN THE GRIP OF GRACE

Describe some ways the cross of Christ gives you courage.

_____

_____

_____

_____

_____

_____

_____

Two Choices

What should I do with Jesus, the one called the Christ?
MATTHEW 27:22

Pilate is correct in his question. "What should I do with Jesus, the one called the Christ?"

Perhaps you, like Pilate, are curious about this one called Jesus.

What do you do with a man who claims to be God, yet hates religion? What do you do with a man who calls himself the Savior, yet condemns systems? What do you do with a man who knows the place and time of his death, yet goes there anyway?

You have two choices.

You can reject him. That is an option. You can, as have many, decide that the idea of God's becoming a carpenter is too bizarre—and walk away.

Or you can accept him. You can journey with him. You can listen for his voice amid the hundreds of voices and follow him.

AND THE ANGELS WERE SILENT

Every person must make one of two choices: reject Christ or accept him. Explain your choice.

God Still Comes

The LORD is close to the brokenhearted,
and he saves those whose spirits have been crushed.

PSALM 34:18

Everything that was written in the past was written to teach us," Paul penned. "The Scriptures give us patience and encouragement so that we can have hope" (Romans 15:4).

These are not just Sunday school stories. Not romantic fables. They are historical moments in which a real God met real pain so we could answer the question, "Where is God when I hurt?"

How does God react to dashed hopes? Read the story of Jairus. How does the Father feel about those who are ill? Stand with him at the pool of Bethesda. Do you long for God to speak to your lonely heart? Then listen as he speaks to the Emmaus-bound disciples.

He's not doing it just for them. He's doing it for me. He's doing it for you.

The God who spoke still speaks. The God who came still comes. He comes into our world. He comes into your world. He comes to do what you can't.

HE STILL MOVES STONES

Explain how the Bible gives you patience and encouragement and hope.

_____

_____

_____

_____

Wrestling with God

"Your name will now be Israel, because you have
wrestled with God and with people, and you have won."

GENESIS 32:28

The word *Jabbok* in Hebrew means "wrestle," and wrestle is what Jacob did. He wrestled with his past: all the white lies, scheming, and scandalizing. He wrestled with his situation: a spider trapped in his own web of deceit and craftiness. But more than anything, he wrestled with God.

Jacob wrestled with God the entire night. On the banks of Jabbok he rolled in the mud of his mistakes. He met God face-to-face, sick of his past and in desperate need of a fresh start. And because Jacob wanted it so badly, God honored his determination. God gave him a new name and a new promise. But he also gave him a wrenched hip as a reminder of that mysterious night at the river.

We too should unmask our stained hearts and grimy souls and be honest with the One who knows our most secret sins.

The result could be refreshing. We know it was for Jacob. After his encounter with God, Jacob was a new man.

GOD CAME NEAR

Do you find it difficult to believe that you can meet God
face-to-face and be honest with him? Why?

_____

_____

_____

_____

Intimacy with the Almighty

As a deer thirsts for streams of water, so I thirst for you, God.

PSALM 42:1

Jesus didn't act unless he saw his Father act. He didn't judge until he heard his Father judge. No act or deed occurred without his Father's guidance.

Because Jesus could hear what others couldn't, he acted differently than they did. Remember when everyone was troubled about the man born blind? Jesus wasn't. Somehow he knew that the blindness would reveal God's power (John 9:3). Remember when everyone was distraught about Lazarus's illness? Jesus wasn't. It was as if Jesus could hear what no one else could. Jesus had unbroken communion with his Father.

Do you suppose the Father desires the same for us? Absolutely! God desires the same abiding intimacy with you that he had with his Son.

JUST LIKE JESUS

Jesus did not listen to the voices around him. He listened to the voice above him. What difference did this make in his life?

_____

_____

_____

_____

_____

_____

Perfect Love

Perfect love casts out fear.
1 JOHN 4:18 NKJV

Have you ever gone to the grocery on an empty stomach? You're a sitting duck. You buy everything you don't need. Doesn't matter if it is good for you—you just want to fill your tummy. When you're lonely, you do the same in life, pulling stuff off the shelf, not because you need it, but because you are hungry for love.

Why do we do it? Because we fear facing life alone. For fear of not fitting in, we take the drugs. For fear of standing out, we wear the clothes. For fear of appearing small, we go into debt and buy the house. For fear of going unnoticed, we dress to seduce or to impress. For fear of sleeping alone, we sleep with anyone. For fear of not being loved, we search for love in all the wrong places.

But all that changes when we discover God's perfect love. And "perfect love casts out fear."

TRAVELING LIGHT

What happens when people search for love in all the wrong places? What is God's solution?

A Work in Progress

Jesus will keep you strong until the end so that there will
be no wrong in you on the day our Lord Jesus Christ comes again.

1 CORINTHIANS 1:8

God is not finished with you yet. Oh, you may think he is. You may think you've peaked. You may think he's got someone else to do the job.

If so, think again.

"God began doing a good work in you, and I am sure he will continue it until it is finished when Jesus Christ comes again" (Philippians 1:6).

Did you see what God is doing? *A good work in you.*

Did you see when he will be finished? *When Jesus comes again.*

May I spell out the message? *God ain't finished with you yet.*

WHEN GOD WHISPERS YOUR NAME

We are God's work in progress until he takes us home. Why
should this encourage us?

_____

_____

_____

_____

_____

_____

_____

Watch and Pray

"Watch and pray so that you will not fall into temptation."
MARK 14:38 NIV

Watch." They don't come any more practical than that. Watch. Stay alert. Keep your eyes open. When you see sin coming, duck. When you anticipate an awkward encounter, turn around. When you sense temptation, go the other way.

All Jesus is saying is, "Pay attention." You know your weaknesses. You also know the situations in which your weaknesses are most vulnerable. Stay out of those situations. Backseats. Late hours. Movie theaters. Whatever it is that gives Satan a foothold in your life, stay away from it. Watch out!

"Pray." Prayer isn't telling God anything new. There is not a sinner nor a saint who would surprise him. What prayer does is invite God to walk the shadowy pathways of life with us. Prayer is asking God to watch ahead for falling trees and tumbling boulders and to bring up the rear, guarding our backside from the poison darts of the devil.

NO WONDER THEY CALL HIM THE SAVIOR

Describe some specific ways you can avoid situations in which you are vulnerable to temptation.

_____

_____

_____

_____

Love Hates Evil

Many of those who sleep in the dust of the earth shall awake, some to everlasting life, and some to shame and everlasting contempt.

DANIEL 12:2 RSV

Does hell serve a purpose? Remove it from the Bible and, at the same time, remove any notion of a just God and a trustworthy Scripture.

If there is no hell, God is not just. If there is no punishment of sin, heaven is apathetic toward the rapists and pillagers and mass murderers of society. If there is no hell, God is blind toward the victims and has turned his back on those who pray for relief. If there is no wrath toward evil, then God is not love, for love hates that which is evil.

To say there is no hell is also to say God is a liar and his Scripture untrue. The Bible repeatedly and stoutly affirms the dualistic outcome of history. Some will be saved. Some will be lost.

WHEN CHRIST COMES

What purpose does hell serve? Why is hell important to God's justice? What difference does this make to your life?

What Will You Bring?

If we confess our sins, he will forgive our sins, because we
can trust God to do what is right.

1 JOHN 1:9

In order for the cross of Christ to be the cross of our lives, you and I need to bring something to the hill.

We have seen what Jesus brought. With scarred hands he offered forgiveness. Through torn skin he promised acceptance. He took the path to take us home. He wore our garment to give us his own. We have seen the gifts he brought.

Now we ask, what will we bring?

Why don't you start with your bad moments?

Those bad habits? Leave them at the cross. Your selfish moods and white lies? Give them to God. Your binges and bigotries? God wants them all. Every flop, every failure. He wants every single one. Why? Because he knows we can't live with them.

HE CHOSE THE NAILS

What will you bring to the cross? Bad moments? Bad habits?
Selfish moods? Make a list and then thank God that you can
leave them at the cross.

_____

_____

_____

_____

Beyond Our Faults

He felt sorry for them and healed those who were sick.

MATTHEW 14:14

Matthew writes that Jesus "healed their sick." Not *some* of their sick. Not the *righteous* among the sick. Not the *deserving* among the sick. But *the sick*.

Surely, among the many thousands, there were a few people unworthy of good health. The same divinity that gave Jesus the power to heal also gave him the power to perceive. I wonder if Jesus was tempted to say to the bigot, "Get out of here, buddy, and take your arrogance with you."

And he could see not only their past, he could see their future.

Undoubtedly, there were those in the multitude who would use their newfound health to hurt others. Jesus released tongues that would someday curse. He gave sight to eyes that would lust. He healed hands that would kill.

Each time Jesus healed, he had to overlook the future and the past.

Something, by the way, that he still does.

IN THE EYE OF THE STORM

Why is it comforting to know that Jesus healed all the sick?

_____

_____

_____

_____

Each Day Matters

You were chosen to tell about the
excellent qualities of God.

1 PETER 2:9 GW

Let's spend a lifetime making our heavenly Father proud. Use your uniqueness to do so. You exited the womb called. Don't see yourself as a product of your parents' DNA, but rather as a brand-new idea from heaven.

Make a big deal out of God. Become who you are for him! Has he not transferred you from a dull, death-destined life to a rich, heaven-bound adventure? Remember, "You were chosen to tell about the excellent qualities of God." And do so every day of your life.

With God, every day matters, every person counts.

And that includes you.

CURE FOR THE COMMON LIFE

Describe some ways your life makes a big deal out of God.

_____

_____

_____

_____

_____

_____

_____

Play Sublimely

I praise you because you made me
in an amazing and wonderful way.

PSALM 139:14

Antonio Stradivari was a seventeenth-century violin maker whose name in its Latin form, *Stradivarius*, has become synonymous with excellence. He once said that to make a violin less than his best would be to rob God, who could not make Antonio Stradivari's violins without Antonio.

He was right. God could not make Stradivarius violins without Antonio Stradivari. Certain gifts were given to that craftsman that no other violin maker possessed.

In the same vein, there are certain things you can do that no one else can. Perhaps it is parenting, or constructing houses, or encouraging the discouraged. There are things that *only* you can do, and you are alive to do them. In the great orchestra we call life, you have an instrument and a song, and you owe it to God to play them both sublimely.

THE APPLAUSE OF HEAVEN

What gifts has God given to you? Are you developing them and using them for his glory?

_____

_____

_____

_____

_____

Imitate Christ

Live a life of love, just as Christ loved us.
EPHESIANS 5:2 NIV

Long to be more loving? Begin by accepting your place as a dearly loved child. "Be imitators of God, therefore, as dearly loved children and live a life of love, just as Christ loved us" (Ephesians 5:1–2 NIV).

Want to learn to forgive? Then consider how you've been forgiven. "Be kind and compassionate to one another, forgiving each other, just as in Christ God forgave you" (Ephesians 4:32 NIV).

Finding it hard to put others first? Think of the way Christ put you first. "Though he was God, he did not demand and cling to his rights as God" (Philippians 2:6 NLT).

Need more patience? Drink from the patience of God (2 Peter 3:9). Is generosity an elusive virtue? Then consider how generous God has been with you (Romans 5:8). Having trouble putting up with ungrateful relatives or cranky neighbors? God puts up with you when you act the same. "He is kind to the ungrateful and wicked" (Luke 6:35 NIV).

A LOVE WORTH GIVING

Think of some times when you have seen godly traits in the lives of others. How did this affect you? Why?

June

What we see will last only a short time, but what we cannot see will last forever.

—2 Corinthians 4:18

God's Favorite Word

Jesus said, "Come follow me."

MATTHEW 4:19

God is an inviting God. He invited Mary to birth his Son, the disciples to fish for men, the adulteress woman to start over, and Thomas to touch his wounds. God is the King who prepares the palace, sets the table, and invites his subjects to come in.

In fact, it seems his favorite word is *come.*

"*Come,* let us talk about these things. Though your sins are like scarlet, they can be as white as snow" (Isaiah 1:18).

"All you who are thirsty, *come* and drink" (Isaiah 55:1).

"*Come* to me, all of you who are tired and have heavy loads, and I will give you rest" (Matthew 11:28).

God is a God who invites. God is a God who calls.

AND THE ANGELS WERE SILENT

What does God's invitation for any and all to come to him say about his character?

_____

_____

_____

_____

_____

_____

_____

Jesus Honors You

It is good to . . . sing praises to Your name. . .
to declare Your lovingkindness in the morning.

PSALM 92:1–2 NKJV

Listen closely. Jesus' love does not depend upon what we do for him. Not at all. In the eyes of the King, you have value simply because you are. You don't have to look nice or perform well. Your value is inborn.

Period.

Think about that for just a minute. You are valuable just because you exist. Not because of what you do or what you have done, but simply because you are. Remember that the next time you are left bobbing in the wake of someone's steamboat ambition. Remember that the next time some trickster tries to hang a bargain basement price tag on your self-worth. The next time someone tries to pass you off as a cheap buy, just think about the way Jesus honors you . . . and smile.

I do. I smile because I know I don't deserve love like that. None of us do.

NO WONDER THEY CALL HIM THE SAVIOR

God says you are valuable just because you exist. In what ways does that affect your outlook on life? Yourself? Others?

The Branch and the Vine

*"Remain in me, and I will remain in you. A branch
cannot produce fruit alone but must remain in the vine."*

JOHN 15:4

God wants to be as close to us as a branch is to a vine. One is an extension of the other. It's impossible to tell where one starts and the other ends. The branch isn't connected only at the moment of bearing fruit. The gardener doesn't keep the branches in a box and then, on the day he wants grapes, glue them to the vine. No, the branch constantly draws nutrition from the vine.

God also uses the temple to depict the intimacy he desires. "Don't you know," Paul writes, "that your body is the temple of the Holy Spirit, who lives in you and who was given to you by God?" (1 Corinthians 6:19 TEV). Think with me about the temple for a moment. God didn't come and go, appear and disappear. He was a permanent presence, always available.

What incredibly good news for us! We are *never* away from God!

JUST LIKE JESUS

How do you draw nutrition from the Vine for your soul?

The Flagship of Patience

Love is patient.

1 CORINTHIANS 13:4

Paul presents patience as the premiere expression of love. Positioned at the head of the apostle's Love Armada—a boat-length or two in front of kindness, courtesy, and forgiveness—is the flagship known as patience. "Love is patient."

The Greek word used here for patience is a descriptive one. It figuratively means "taking a long time to boil." Think about a pot of boiling water. What factors determine the speed at which it boils? The size of the stove? No. The pot? The utensil may have an influence, but the primary factor is the intensity of the flame. Water boils quickly when the flame is high. It boils slowly when the flame is low. Patience "keeps the burner down."

Helpful clarification, don't you think? Patience isn't naive. It doesn't ignore misbehavior. It just keeps the flame low. It waits. It listens. It's slow to boil. This is how God treats us. And, according to Jesus, this is how we should treat others.

A LOVE WORTH GIVING

Think of some ways that life would be better for all of us if we each practiced a little more patience.

A Hidden Hero

*I have learned the secret of being
happy at any time in everything that happens.*

PHILIPPIANS 4:12

Peer into the prison and see [Paul] for yourself: bent and frail, shackled to the arm of a Roman guard. Behold the apostle of God.

Dead broke. No family. No property. Nearsighted and worn-out.

Doesn't look like a hero.

Doesn't sound like one either. He introduced himself as the worst sinner in history. He was a Christian-killer before he was a Christian leader. At times his heart was so heavy, Paul's pen drug itself across the page. "What a miserable man I am! Who will save me from this body that brings me death?" (Romans 7:24).

Only heaven knows how long he stared at the question before he found the courage to defy logic and write, "I thank God for saving me through Jesus Christ our Lord!" (Romans 7:25).

WHEN GOD WHISPERS YOUR NAME

*Why is Paul's changed life from Christian-killer to
Christian leader an example of hope for us all?*

_____

_____

_____

_____

The Price of Self-Obsession

"I am the LORD. There is no other God."

ISAIAH 45:18

We pay a high price for . . . self-obsession. "God isn't pleased at being ignored" (Romans 8:8 MSG). Paul speaks of sinners when he describes those who "knew God, but they wouldn't worship him as God. So God let them go ahead and do whatever shameful things their hearts desired" (Romans 1:21, 24 NLT).

You've seen the chaos. The husband ignoring his wife. The dictator murdering the millions. Grown men seducing the young. The young propositioning the old. When you do what you want, and I do what I want, and no one gives a lick as to what God wants, humanity implodes. The infection of the person leads to the corruption of the populace.

Extract God; expect earthly chaos and, many times worse, expect eternal misery.

COME THIRSTY

Why is self-obsession so destructive to ourselves and to others?

Power Can Be Painful

The wisdom of this world is foolishness with God.

1 CORINTHIANS 3:19

Power comes in many forms.

It's the husband who refuses to be kind to his wife.

It's the employee who places personal ambition over personal integrity.

It's the wife who withholds sex both to punish and persuade.

It might be the taking of someone's life, or it might be the taking of someone's turn.

But they are all spelled the same: p-o-w-e-r. And all have the same goal: "I will get what I want at your expense."

And all have the same end: futility. Absolute power is unreachable. When you stand at the top—if there is a top—the only way to go is down. And the descent is often painful.

A thousand years from now, will it matter what title the world gave you? No, but it will make a literal hell of a difference whose child you are.

THE APPLAUSE OF HEAVEN

Use the life of Christ to list examples of positive ways to use power.

_____

_____

_____

_____

_____

Our Servant Master

"The Son of Man did not come to be served. He came
to serve others and to give his life as a ransom for many people."
MATTHEW 20:28

As a young boy, I read a Russian fable about a master and a servant who went on a journey to a city. Many of the details I've forgotten but the ending I remember. Before the two men could reach the destination they were caught in a blinding blizzard. They lost their direction and were unable to reach the city before nightfall.

The next morning concerned friends went searching for the two men. They finally found the master, frozen to death, face-down in the snow. When they lifted him they found the servant—cold but alive. He survived and told how the master had voluntarily placed himself on top of the servant so the servant could live.

I hadn't thought of that story in years. But when I read what Christ said he would do for us, the story surfaced—for Jesus is the Master who died for the servants.

AND THE ANGELS WERE SILENT

Write a note of praise to Jesus for his death on the cross.

God's Mighty Hand

Through his power all things were made—
things in heaven and on earth, things seen and unseen.

COLOSSIANS 1:16

With one decision, history began. Existence became measurable.

Out of nothing came light.

Out of light came day.

Then came sky . . . and earth.

And on this earth? A mighty hand went to work.

Canyons were carved. Oceans were dug. Mountains erupted out of flatlands. Stars were flung. A universe sparkled.

Look to the canyons to see the Creator's splendor. Touch the flowers and see his delicacy. Listen to the thunder and hear his power.

Today you will encounter God's creation. When you see the beauty around you, let each detail remind you to lift your head in praise. Express your appreciation for God's creation. Encourage others to see the beauty of his creation.

IN THE EYE OF THE STORM

Write your own psalm of praise to God for the beauty of his creation.

_____

_____

_____

_____

A Second Transformation

We shall all be changed—in a moment, in the twinkling of an eye.

1 CORINTHIANS 15:51–52 NKJV

I am with you always" are the words of a God who in one instant did the impossible to make it all possible for you and me (Matthew 28:20 NKJV).

It all happened in a moment. In one moment . . . a most remarkable moment. The Word became flesh.

There will be another. The world will see another instantaneous transformation. You see, in becoming man, God made it possible for man to see God. When Jesus went home he left the back door open. As a result, "we shall all be changed—in a moment, in the twinkling of an eye."

The first moment of transformation went unnoticed by the world. But you can bet your sweet September that the second one won't.

GOD CAME NEAR

Explain why God's children wait with eager expectation for Christ's return.

The Oldest and Choicest

"Even when you are old, I will be the same.
Even when your hair has turned gray, I will take care of you."

ISAIAH 46:4

Growing old can be dangerous. The trail is treacherous and the pitfalls are many. One is wise to be prepared. You know it's coming. It's not like God kept the process a secret. It's not like you are blazing a trail as you grow older. It's not as if no one has ever done it before. Look around you. You have ample opportunity to prepare and ample case studies to consider. If growing old catches you by surprise, don't blame God. He gave you plenty of warning. He also gave you plenty of advice.

Your last chapters can be your best. Your final song can be your greatest. It could be that all of your life has prepared you for a grand exit. God's oldest have always been among his choicest.

HE STILL MOVES STONES

Make a list of the positive things we gain with age. Does our culture value old age? Does the church?

_____

_____

_____

_____

_____

_____

_____

Travel Light

Give all your worries to him, because he cares about you.

1 Peter 5:7

God has a great race for you to run. Under his care you will go where you've never been and serve in ways you've never dreamed. But you have to drop some stuff. How can you share grace if you are full of guilt? How can you offer comfort if you are disheartened? How can you lift someone else's load if your arms are full with your own?

For the sake of those you love, travel light.

For the sake of the God you serve, travel light.

For the sake of your own joy, travel light.

There are certain weights in life you simply cannot carry. Your Lord is asking you to set them down and trust him.

TRAVELING LIGHT

Think about things in your life that are weighing you down and keeping you from traveling light. What do you need to do about these things?

_____

_____

_____

_____

_____

God Will Get You Home

What we see will last only a short time,
but what we cannot see will last forever.

2 CORINTHIANS 4:18

For some of you, the journey has been long. Very long and stormy. In no way do I wish to minimize the difficulties that you have had to face along the way. Some of you have shouldered burdens that few of us could ever carry. You have bid farewell to lifelong partners. You have been robbed of lifelong dreams. You have been given bodies that can't sustain your spirit. You have spouses who can't tolerate your faith. You have bills that outnumber the paychecks and challenges that outweigh the strength.

And you are tired.

It's hard for you to see the City in the midst of the storms. The desire to pull over to the side of the road and get out entices you. You want to go on, but some days the road seems so long.

Let me encourage you. God never said that the journey would be easy, but he did say that the arrival would be worthwhile.

IN THE EYE OF THE STORM

What encourages you to keep pressing on when the road seems long?

_____

_____

_____

_____

What Love Does

Christ Jesus . . . made himself nothing,
taking the very nature of a servant.
PHILIPPIANS 2:5–7 NIV

Would you do what Jesus did? He swapped a spotless castle for a grimy stable. He exchanged the worship of angels for the company of killers. He could hold the universe in his palm but gave it up to float in the womb of a maiden.

If you were God, would you sleep on straw, nurse from a breast, and be clothed in a diaper? I wouldn't, but Christ did.

If you knew that only a few would care that you came, would you still come? If you knew that those you loved would laugh in your face, would you still care? Christ did.

He humbled himself. He went from commanding angels to sleeping in the straw. From holding stars to clutching Mary's finger. The palm that held the universe took the nail of a soldier.

Why? Because that's what love does. It puts the beloved before itself.

A LOVE WORTH GIVING

Love puts others before itself. Describe some practical ways you can apply this to your life.

Set Apart

Anyone who wants to be a
friend of the world becomes God's enemy.
JAMES 4:4

John the Baptist would never get hired today. No church would touch him. He was a public relations disaster. He "wore clothes made from camel's hair, had a leather belt around his waist, and ate locusts and wild honey" (Mark 1:6). Who would want to look at a guy like that every Sunday?

His message was as rough as his dress: a no-nonsense, bare-fisted challenge to repent because God was on his way.

John the Baptist set himself apart for one task: to be a voice of Christ. Everything about John centered on his purpose. His dress. His diet. His actions. His demands.

You don't have to be like the world to have an impact on the world. You don't have to be like the crowd to change the crowd. You don't have to lower yourself down to their level to lift them up to your level. Holiness doesn't seek to be odd. Holiness seeks to be like God.

A GENTLE THUNDER

"Holiness seeks to be like God." What does that statement mean to you? Does that affect the choices you make each day?

_____

_____

_____

_____

Don't Give Up!

"It is finished."
JOHN 19:30

Our inability to finish what we start is seen in the smallest of things:
A partly mowed lawn.
A half-read book.
Or, it shows up in life's most painful areas:
An abandoned child.
A wrecked marriage.

Any chance I'm addressing someone who is considering giving up? If I am, I want to encourage you to remain. I want to encourage you to remember Jesus' determination on the cross.

Jesus didn't quit. But don't think for one minute that he wasn't tempted to. Did he ever want to quit? You bet.

That's why his words are so splendid. "It is finished."

NO WONDER THEY CALL HIM THE SAVIOR

Jesus finished his God-given task here on earth. How does his example encourage you not to give up?

God Honors Our Choice

We all have wandered away
like sheep; each of us has gone his own way.

ISAIAH 53:6

How could a loving God send people to hell? That's a commonly asked question. The question itself reveals a couple of misconceptions.

First, God does not *send* people to hell. He simply honors their choice. Hell is the ultimate expression of God's high regard for the dignity of man. He has never forced us to choose him, even when that means we would choose hell.

No, God does not *send* people to hell. Nor does he send *people* to hell. That is the second misconception.

The word *people* is neutral, implying innocence. Nowhere does Scripture teach that innocent people are condemned. People do not go to hell. Sinners do. The rebellious do. The self-centered do. So how could a loving God send people to hell? He doesn't. He simply honors the choice of sinners.

WHEN CHRIST COMES

God honors our choice. How does that affect our relationship with him?

_____

_____

_____

_____

_____

Taking Inventory

Don't you know that you are
God's temple and that God's Spirit lives in you?

1 CORINTHIANS 3:16

All believers have God in their heart. But not all believers have given their whole heart to God. Remember, the question is not, "How can I have more of the Spirit?" but rather, "How can the Spirit have more of me?" Take inventory. As you look around your life, do you see any resistant pockets? Go down the list.

Your tongue. Do you tend to stretch the truth? Puff up the facts? Your language? Is your language a sewer of profanities and foul talk? And grudges? Do you keep resentments parked in your "garudge"? Are you unproductive and lazy? Do you live off the system, assuming that the church or the country should take care of you?

Do your actions interrupt the flow of the Spirit in your life?

COME THIRSTY

Are there areas of your life you have resisted giving to God?
What can you do to give him your whole heart?

Shortcuts

*"They continue saying things that mean nothing,
thinking that God will hear them because of their many words."*

MATTHEW 6:7

I love the short sentence. What follows are cuts from some of my books and a couple of others. Keep the ones you like. Forgive the ones you don't. Share them when you can.

Pray all the time. If necessary, use words.

God forgets the past. Imitate him.

Greed I've often regretted. Generosity—never.

Don't ask God to do what you want. Ask God to do what is right.

No one is useless to God. No one.

Nails didn't hold God to a cross. Love did.

You will never forgive anyone more than God has already forgiven you.

WHEN GOD WHISPERS YOUR NAME

Choose one of the sentences above and write what it means to you.

_____

_____

_____

_____

_____

The Clothing on the Cross

He himself bore our sins in his body on the tree,
so that we might die to sins and live for righteousness.

1 PETER 2:24 NIV

When Christ was nailed to the cross, he took off his robe of seamless perfection and assumed a different wardrobe, the wardrobe of indignity.

The indignity of nakedness. Stripped before his own mother and loved ones. Shamed before his family.

The indignity of failure. For a few pain-filled hours, the religious leaders were the victors, and Christ appeared the loser. Shamed before his accusers.

Worst of all, he wore *the indignity of sin.* "He himself bore our sins in his body on the tree, so that we might die to sins and live for righteousness."

The clothing of Christ on the cross? Sin—yours and mine. The sins of all humanity.

HE CHOSE THE NAILS

How do you respond to Christ's humiliation on the cross?
How does this affect the way you live for him?

Who's in Charge?

Give all your worries to him, because he cares about you.
1 PETER 5:7

Worry makes you forget who's in charge.

And when the focus is on yourself . . . you worry. You become anxious about many things. You worry that:

Your coworkers won't appreciate you.

Your leaders will overwork you.

Your superintendent won't understand you.

Your congregation won't support you.

With time, your agenda becomes more important than God's. You're more concerned with presenting self than pleasing him. And you may even find yourself doubting God's judgment.

God has gifted you with talents. He has done the same to your neighbor. If you concern yourself with your neighbor's talents, you will neglect yours. But if you concern yourself with yours, you could inspire both.

HE STILL MOVES STONES

Do you find that you worry more when you focus on yourself rather than on God? Why is that so?

_____

_____

_____

_____

The God You Need

*The LORD created the heavens. He is
the God who formed the earth and made it.*

ISAIAH 45:18

You don't need what Dorothy found. Remember her discovery in *The Wonderful Wizard of Oz*? She and her trio followed the yellow-brick road only to discover that the wizard was a wimp! Nothing but smoke and mirrors and tin-drum thunder. Is that the kind of god you need?

You don't need to carry the burden of a lesser god . . . a god on a shelf, a god in a box, or a god in a bottle. No, you need a God who can place 100 billion stars in our galaxy and 100 billion galaxies in the universe. You need a God who can shape two fists of flesh into 75 to 100 billion nerve cells, each with as many as 10,000 connections to other nerve cells, place it in a skull, and call it a brain.

And you need a God who, while so mind-numbingly mighty, can come in the soft of night and touch you with the tenderness of an April snow.

TRAVELING LIGHT

Write a psalm of praise for your great and mighty God.

_____

_____

_____

_____

Walking with God

*You were taught to be made new in your hearts,
to become a new person. . . . Made to be like God—
made to be truly good and holy.*

EPHESIANS 4:23–24

Healthy marriages have a sense of "remaining." The husband remains in the wife, and she remains in him. There is a tenderness, an honesty, an ongoing communication. The same is true in our relationship with God. Sometimes we go to him with our joys, and sometimes we go with our hurts, but we always go. And as we go, the more we go, the more we become like him. Paul says we are being changed from "glory to glory" (2 Corinthians 3:18 KJV).

People who live long lives together eventually begin to sound alike, to talk alike, even to think alike. As we walk with God, we take on his thoughts, his principles, his attitudes. We take on his heart.

JUST LIKE JESUS

Are there times when you hesitate to go to God with your joys or your hurts? How does this affect the growth of your spiritual faith?

God Authored Your Life

My frame was not hidden from you when I was made in the secret place. When I was woven together in the depths of the earth.

PSALM 139:15 NIV

David emphasizes the pronoun "you" as if to say "you, God, and you alone." "The secret place" suggests a hidden and safe place, concealed from intruders and evil. Just as an artist takes a canvas into a locked studio, so God took you into his hidden chamber where you were "woven together." Moses used the same word to describe the needlework of the temple's inner curtains—stitched together by skillful hands for the highest purpose (Exodus 26:1; 36:8; 38:9). The Master Weaver selected your temperament threads, your character texture, the yarn of your personality—all before you were born. God did not drop you into the world utterly defenseless and empty-handed. You arrived fully equipped.

What motivates you, what exhausts you . . . God authored— and authors—it all.

CURE FOR THE COMMON LIFE

Write a note of praise to God for the tapestry of your life.

A Promise Delivered

I saw the holy city, the new Jerusalem, coming down out of heaven from God. It was prepared like a bride dressed for her husband.

REVELATION 21:2

The Holy City, John says, is like "a bride beautifully dressed for her husband" (NLT).

What is more beautiful than a bride?

Maybe it is the aura of whiteness that clings to her as dew clings to a rose. Or perhaps it is the diamonds that glisten in her eyes. Or maybe it's the blush of love that pinks her cheeks or the bouquet of promises she carries.

A bride. A commitment robed in elegance. "I'll be with you forever." Tomorrow bringing hope today. Promised purity faithfully delivered.

When you read that our heavenly home is similar to a bride, tell me, doesn't it make you want to go home?

THE APPLAUSE OF HEAVEN

Christ says he is preparing a beautiful new home for us. How does that home contrast with our earthly home?

_____

_____

_____

_____

_____

God Sees What We Can't

No one is like the LORD our God, who rules from heaven.

PSALM 113:5

On a trip to the United Kingdom, our family visited a castle. In the center of the garden sat a maze. Row after row of shoulder-high hedges, leading to one dead end after another. Successfully navigate the labyrinth, and discover the door to a tall tower in the center of the garden. Were you to look at our family pictures of the trip, you'd see four of our five family members standing on the top of the tower. Hmmm, someone is still on the ground. Guess who? I was stuck in the foliage. I just couldn't figure out which way to go.

Ah, but then I heard a voice from above. "Hey, Dad." I looked up to see Sara, peering through the turret at the top. "You're going the wrong way," she explained. "Back up and turn right."

Do you think I trusted her? I didn't have to. But do you know what I did? I listened. Her vantage point was better than mine. She was above the maze. She could see what I couldn't.

Don't you think we should do the same with God?

NEXT DOOR SAVIOR

List some reminders of God's power.

_____

_____

_____

_____

A Reason to Sit Tight

*"I am the LORD, the God of every person on the earth.
Nothing is impossible for me."*

JEREMIAH 32:27

We need to hear that God is still in control. We need to hear that it's not over until he says so. We need to hear that life's mishaps and tragedies are not a reason to bail out. They are simply a reason to sit tight.

Corrie ten Boom used to say, "When the train goes through a tunnel and the world gets dark, do you jump out? Of course not. You sit still and trust the engineer to get you through."

The way to deal with discouragement? The cure for disappointment? Go back and read the story of God. Read it again and again. Be reminded that you aren't the first person to weep. And you aren't the first person to be helped.

Read the story and remember, the story is yours!

HE STILL MOVES STONES

*What does "sitting tight" during life's tragedies have to do
with trust in God?*

_____

_____

_____

_____

_____

_____

He Doesn't Remember

"I will remember their sins no more."
Hebrews 8:12 rsv

I was thanking the Father today for his mercy. I began listing the sins he'd forgiven. One by one I thanked God for forgiving my stumbles and tumbles. My motives were pure and my heart was thankful, but my understanding of God was wrong. It was when I used the word *remember* that it hit me.

"Remember the time I . . ." I was about to thank God for another act of mercy. But I stopped. Something was wrong. The word *remember* seemed displaced. "Does he remember?"

Then *I* remembered. I remembered his words. "I will remember their sins no more."

Wow! Now, *that* is a remarkable promise.

God doesn't just forgive, he forgets. For all the things he does do, this is one thing he refuses to do. He refuses to keep a list of my wrongs.

GOD CAME NEAR

God refuses to keep a list of our wrongs. Have you extended the same generosity to others? Why or why not?

The Big Choice

If you don't want to serve the LORD,
you must choose for yourselves today whom you will serve.

JOSHUA 24:15

G od's invitation is clear and nonnegotiable. He gives all and
we give him all. Simple and absolute. He is clear in what
he asks and clear in what he offers. The choice is up to us.
Isn't it incredible that God leaves the choice to us? Think about it.
There are many things in life we can't choose. We can't, for example,
choose the weather. We can't control the economy.

We can't choose whether we are born with a big nose or blue
eyes or a lot of hair. We can't even choose how people respond to us.

But we can choose where we spend eternity. The big choice
God leaves to us. The critical decision is ours.

That is the only decision that really matters.

AND THE ANGELS WERE SILENT

How do we choose where we will spend eternity? Have
you made this choice?

_____

_____

_____

_____

_____

_____

A Personal Path

You, LORD, give perfect peace to those
who keep their purpose firm and put their trust in you.

ISAIAH 26:3 TEV

When David volunteered to go mano a mano with Goliath, King Saul tried to clothe the shepherd boy with soldier's armor. After all, Goliath stood over nine feet tall. He wore a bronze helmet and a 125-pound coat of mail. He bore bronze leggings and carried a javelin and a spear with a 15-pound head (1 Samuel 17:4–7). And David? David had a slingshot. This is a VW Bug playing blink with an eighteen-wheeler. When Saul saw David, pimpled, and Goliath, rippled, he did what any Iron Age king would do. "Saul gave David his own armor—a bronze helmet and a coat of mail" (1 Samuel 17:38 NLT).

But David rejected the armor, selected the stones, lobotomized the giant, and taught us a powerful lesson: what fits others might not fit you. Indeed what fits *the king* might not fit you. Just because someone gives you advice, a job, or a promotion, you don't have to accept it. Let your uniqueness define your path of life.

CURE FOR THE COMMON LIFE

Why is it more important to heed God's will than human advice?

Needed: One Great Savior

All have sinned and are not good enough
for God's glory, and all need to be made right
with God by his grace, which is a free gift.

ROMANS 3:23–24

The supreme force in salvation is God's grace. Not our works. Not our talents. Not our feelings. Not our strength.

Salvation is God's sudden, calming presence during the stormy seas of our lives. We hear his voice; we take the step.

We, like Paul, are aware of two things: we are great sinners and we need a great savior.

We, like Peter, are aware of two facts: we are going down and God is standing up. So we . . . leave behind the *Titanic* of self-righteousness and stand on the solid path of God's grace.

And, surprisingly, we are able to walk on water. Death is disarmed. Failures are forgivable. Life has real purpose. And God is not only within sight, he is within reach.

IN THE EYE OF THE STORM

When we stand on the solid path of God's grace we find that life has real purpose. How is this statement true in your life?

_____

_____

_____

_____

_____

The Intersection of Love

Though He was crucified in weakness,
yet He lives by the power of God.

2 CORINTHIANS 13:4 NKJV

The cross. Can you turn any direction without seeing one? Perched atop a chapel. Carved into a graveyard headstone. Engraved in a ring or suspended on a chain. The cross is the universal symbol of Christianity. An odd choice, don't you think? Strange that a tool of torture would come to embody a movement of hope.

Why is the cross the symbol of our faith? To find the answer look no further than the cross itself. Its design couldn't be simpler. One beam horizontal—the other vertical. One reaches out—like God's love. The other reaches up—as does God's holiness. One represents the width of his love; the other reflects the height of his holiness. The cross is the intersection. The cross is where God forgave his children without lowering his standards.

HE CHOSE THE NAILS

Explain how the holiness of God and his love intersect on the cross.

_____

_____

_____

_____

Dealing with the Past

Don't get angry. Don't be upset; it only leads to trouble.

PSALM 37:8

Anger. It's easy to define: the noise of the soul. *Anger.* The unseen irritant of the heart. *Anger.* The relentless invader of silence.

The louder it gets the more desperate we become.

Some of you are thinking . . . *you don't have any idea how hard my life has been.* And you're right, I don't. But I have a very clear idea how miserable your future will be unless you deal with your anger.

X-ray the world of the vengeful and behold the tumor of bitterness: black, menacing, malignant. Carcinoma of the spirit. Its fatal fibers creep around the edge of the heart and ravage it. Yesterday you can't alter, but your reaction to yesterday you can. The past you cannot change, but your response to your past you can.

WHEN GOD WHISPERS YOUR NAME

Explain how anger makes life miserable. How does God want us to deal with anger?

_____

_____

_____

_____

_____

_____

The Angels Offer Worship

All the angels stood around the throne . . .
saying: "Amen! Blessing and glory and wisdom . . .
be to our God forever and ever."
REVELATION 7:11–12 NKJV

Only one sight enthralls angels—God's face. They know that he is Lord of all.

And as a result, they worship him. Whether in the temple with Isaiah or the pasture with the Bethlehem shepherds, angels worship.

"All the angels stood around the throne . . . saying: 'Amen! Blessing and glory and wisdom, thanksgiving and honor and power and might, be to our God forever and ever. Amen'" (Revelation 7:11–12 NKJV).

Doesn't their worship proclaim volumes about God's beauty? Angels could gaze at the Grand Tetons and Grand Canyon, Picasso paintings and the Sistine Chapel, but they choose, instead, to fix their eyes on the glory of God. They can't see enough of him, and they can't be silent about what they see.

COME THIRSTY

Write your own description of the glory of God.

Who Is My Brother?

"Lord, how many times shall I
forgive my brother when he sins against me?"
Jesus answered, ". . . seventy-seven times."

MATTHEW 18:21–22 NIV

Seems to me God gives a lot more grace than we'd ever imagine. We could do the same.

I'm not for watering down the truth or compromising the gospel. But if a fellow with a pure heart calls God *Father*, can't I call that same man *Brother*? If God doesn't make doctrinal perfection a requirement for family membership, should I?

And if we never agree, can't we agree to disagree? If God can tolerate my mistakes, can't I tolerate the mistakes of others? If God allows me with my foibles and failures to call him *Father*, shouldn't I extend the same grace to others?

WHEN GOD WHISPERS YOUR NAME

When God has lavished his grace on us, why do we tend to be so miserly with ours?

Stubborn Love

"He was lost, but now he is found!"

LUKE 15:24

Jesus summarized God's stubborn love with a parable. He told about a teenager who decided that life at the farm was too slow for his tastes. So with pockets full of inheritance money, he set out to find the big time. What he found instead were hangovers, fair-weather friends, and long unemployment lines. When he had had just about as much of the pig's life as he could take, he swallowed his pride, dug his hands deep into his empty pockets, and began the long walk home, all the while rehearsing a speech that he planned to give to his father.

He never used it. Just when he got to the top of the hill, his father, who'd been waiting at the gate, saw him. The boy's words of apology were quickly muffled by the father's words of forgiveness.

If you ever wonder how God can use you to make a difference in your world, . . . look at the forgiveness found in those open arms and take courage.

NO WONDER THEY CALL HIM THE SAVIOR

What does God's stubborn love mean to you?

_____

_____

_____

_____

Living in God's Presence

Pray in the Spirit at all times with all kinds of prayers,
asking for everything you need.

EPHESIANS 6:18

How do I live in God's presence? How do I detect his unseen hand on my shoulder and his inaudible voice in my ear? How can you and I grow familiar with the voice of God? Here are a few ideas:

Give God your waking thoughts. Before you face the day, face the Father. Before you step out of bed, step into his presence.

Give God your waiting thoughts. Spend time with him in silence.

Give God your whispering thoughts. Imagine considering every moment as a potential time of communion with God.

Give God your waning thoughts. At the end of the day, let your mind settle on him. Conclude the day as you began it: talking to God.

JUST LIKE JESUS

How can you give your waking thoughts, waiting thoughts,
whispering thoughts, and waning thoughts to God?

_____

_____

_____

_____

_____

_____

God Is Enough

Because your love is better than life, my lips will glorify you. . . .
My soul will be satisfied as with the richest of foods.

PSALM 63:3, 5 NIV

When it comes to love: *Be careful.*

Before you walk down the aisle, take a good long look around. Make sure this is God's intended place for you. And, if you suspect it isn't, get out. Don't force what is wrong to be right. Be careful.

And, until love is stirred, let God's love be enough for you. There are seasons when God allows us to feel the frailty of human love so we'll appreciate the strength of his love. Didn't he do this with David? Saul turned on him. Michal, his wife, betrayed him. Jonathan and Samuel were David's friends, but they couldn't follow him into the wilderness. Betrayal and circumstances left David alone. Alone with God. And, as David discovered, God was enough. David wrote these words in a desert: "Because your love is better than life, my lips will glorify you. My soul will be satisfied as with the richest of foods."

A LOVE WORTH GIVING

What circumstances in life remind you that God's love is enough?

_____

_____

_____

_____

A Heavenly Perspective

*"Ask, and God will give to you. Search, and you will find.
Knock, and the door will open for you."*

MATTHEW 7:7

Go back and report to John what you hear and see: The blind receive sight, the lame walk . . . and the good news is preached to the poor" (Matthew 11:4–5).

This was Jesus' answer to John's agonized query from the dungeon of doubt: "Are you the one who was to come, or should we expect someone else?" (v. 3).

We don't know how John received Jesus' message, but we can imagine. I like to think of a slight smile coming over his lips as he heard what his Master said. For now he understood. It wasn't that Jesus was silent; it was that John had been listening for the wrong answer. John had been listening for an answer to his earthly problems, while Jesus was busy resolving his heavenly ones.

That's worth remembering the next time you hear the silence of God.

THE APPLAUSE OF HEAVEN

*What will you do the next time you hear the silence of God?
Why does God allow the times of agonized questioning?*

_____

_____

_____

_____

_____

The Path of Righteousness

He leads me in the paths of righteousness.

PSALM 23: NKJV

It was, at once, history's most beautiful and most horrible moment. Jesus stood in the tribunal of heaven. Sweeping a hand over all creation, he pleaded, "Punish me for their mistakes. See the murderer? Give me his penalty. The adulteress? I'll take her shame. The bigot, the liar, the thief? Do to me what you would do to them. Treat me as you would a sinner."

And God did. "For Christ died for sins once for all, the righteous for the unrighteous, to bring you to God" (1 Peter 3:18 NIV).

The path of righteousness is a narrow, winding trail up a steep hill. At the top of the hill is a cross. At the base of the cross are bags. Countless bags full of innumerable sins. Calvary is the compost pile for guilt. Would you like to leave yours there as well?

TRAVELING LIGHT

Are you carrying bags of guilt around in your life? What does God want you to do with them?

God Calls Your Name

"This is what the Lord God says:
I, myself, will search for my sheep and take care of them."

Ezekiel 34:11

He's waiting for you. God is standing on the porch of heaven, expectantly hoping, searching the horizon for a glimpse of his child. You're the one God is seeking.

God is the waiting Father, the caring Shepherd in search of his lamb. His legs are scratched, his feet are sore, and his eyes are burning. He scales the cliffs and traverses the fields. He explores the caves. He cups his hands to his mouth and calls into the canyon.

And the name he calls is yours.

The message is simple: God gave up his Son in order to rescue all his sons and daughters. To bring his children home. He's listening for your answer.

And the Angels Were Silent

What is your answer to God's invitation? Is he still waiting for your answer?

_____

_____

_____

_____

_____

_____

The Savior Won

God has made this Jesus, whom you crucified, both Lord and Christ.
ACTS 2:36 NIV

A transformed group stood beside a transformed Peter as he announced: "Therefore let all Israel be assured of this: God has made this Jesus, whom you crucified, both Lord and Christ" (Acts 2:36).

No timidity in his words. No reluctance. About three thousand people believed his message.

The apostles sparked a movement. The people became followers of the Death-conqueror. They couldn't hear enough or say enough about him. People began to call them "Christ-ians." Christ was their model, their message. They preached "Jesus Christ and him crucified" (1 Corinthians 2:2 NIV) not for the lack of another topic, but because they couldn't exhaust this one.

What unlocked the doors of the apostles' hearts?

Simple. They saw Jesus. They encountered the Christ. Their sins collided with their Savior and their Savior won!

SIX HOURS ONE FRIDAY

Christ was the model and the message of the first Christians. How does this apply to your life?

A Little Light, Please

Jesus went to them,
walking on the sea. . . . And they cried out in fear.
MATTHEW 14:25–26 NKJV

Every so often a storm will come, and I'll look up into the blackening sky and say, "God, a little light, please?"

The light came for the disciples. A figure came to them walking on the water. It wasn't what they expected. Perhaps they were looking for angels to descend or heaven to open. We don't know what they were looking for. But one thing is for sure, they weren't looking for Jesus to come walking on the water.

And since Jesus came in a way they didn't expect, they almost missed seeing the answer to their prayers.

And unless we look and listen closely, we risk making the same mistake. God's lights in our dark nights are as numerous as the stars, if only we'll look for them.

IN THE EYE OF THE STORM

Sometimes we become so preoccupied with the stormy darkness
that we miss God's light. How can we avoid this mistake?

_____

_____

_____

_____

_____

_____

Why Worship?

*With my mouth will I make known
Your faithfulness to all generations.*

PSALM 89:1 NKJV

During our summer vacation I took advantage of the occasion to solicit a sailing lesson. Ever puzzled by the difference in leeward, starboard, and stern, I asked the crew a few questions. After a while the captain offered, "Would you like to sail us home?" He assured me I would have no trouble. "Target that cliff," he instructed. "Set your eyes and the boat on it."

I found the instruction hard to follow. Other sights invited my attention: the rich mahogany of the deck, rich foam cresting on the waves. I wanted to look at it all. But look too long and risk losing the course. The boat stayed on target as long as I set my eyes beyond the vessel.

Worship helps us do this in life. It lifts our eyes off the boat with its toys and passengers and sets them "on the realities of heaven, where Christ sits at God's right hand in the place of honor and power" (Colossians 3:1 NLT).

CURE FOR THE COMMON LIFE

Explain how worship can help us keep our focus on Christ.

Peace Treaties of Love

Be sure that no one pays back wrong for wrong, but always try to do what is good for each other and for all people.

1 THESSALONIANS 5:15

Jesus described for his followers what he came to do. He came to build a relationship with people. He came to take away enmity, to take away the strife, to take away the isolation that existed between God and man. Once he bridged that, once he overcame that, he said, "I call you friends" (John 5:15).

In repairing a relationship, it's essential to realize that no friendship is perfect, no marriage is perfect, no person is perfect. With the resolve that you are going to make a relationship work, you can develop peace treaties of love and tolerance and harmony to transform a difficult situation into something beautiful.

WALKING WITH THE SAVIOR

What can you do to turn difficult relationships in your life into beautiful relationships?

_____

_____

_____

_____

_____

_____

What Love Does

"I was without clothes, and you gave me something to wear."

MATTHEW 25:36

What if you were given the privilege of Mary? What if God himself were placed in your arms as a naked baby? Would you not do what she did? "She wrapped the baby with pieces of cloth" (Luke 2:7).

The baby Jesus, still wet from the womb, was cold and chilled. So this mother did what any mother would do; she did what love does: She covered him.

Wouldn't you cherish an opportunity to do the same? You have one. Such opportunities come your way every day. Jesus said, "I was without clothes, and you gave me something to wear. I tell you the truth, anything you did for even the least of my people here, you also did for me" (Matthew 25:36, 40).

A LOVE WORTH GIVING

List ways you can reach out to clothe the "least" of this world.

_____

_____

_____

_____

_____

_____

A High-Stakes Mission

*"Don't be afraid of people, who can kill the body but
cannot kill the soul. The only one you should fear is the one
who can destroy the soul and the body in hell."*

MATTHEW 10:28

Hell's misery is deep, but not as deep as God's love.

So how do we apply this [truth]? If you are saved, it should cause you to rejoice. You've been rescued. A glance into hell leads the believer to rejoice. But it also leads the believer to redouble his efforts to reach the lost. To understand hell is to pray more earnestly and to serve more diligently. Ours is a high-stakes mission.

And the lost? What is the meaning of this message for the unprepared? Heed the warnings and get ready. This plane won't fly forever. "Death is the destiny of every man; the living should take this to heart" (Ecclesiastes 7:2 NIV).

WHEN CHRIST COMES

"To understand hell is to pray more earnestly and to serve more diligently." Explain what that statement means.

_____

_____

_____

_____

_____

_____

God's Surprises

No one has ever imagined what
God has prepared for those who love him.

1 CORINTHIANS 2:9

Have you got God figured out? Have you got God captured on a flowchart and frozen on a flannelboard? If so, then listen. Listen to God's surprises.

Hear the rocks meant for the body of the adulterous woman drop to the ground.

Listen as the Messiah whispers to the Samaritan woman, "I who speak to you am he" (John 4:26 NIV).

Listen to the widow from Nain eating dinner with her son who is supposed to be dead.

God appearing at the strangest of places. Doing the strangest of things. Stretching smiles where there had hung only frowns. Placing twinkles where there were only tears.

SIX HOURS ONE FRIDAY

What are some of the surprising things you have seen God do in your life? In the lives of others? How do these affect you?

What Is Your Price?

"Life is not measured by how much one owns."

LUKE 12:15

Jesus had a definition for *greed*. He called it the practice of measuring life by possessions.

Greed equates a person's worth with a person's purse.

1. You got a lot = you are a lot.

2. You got a little = you are little.

The consequence of such a philosophy is predictable. If you are the sum of what you own, then by all means own it all. No price is too high. No payment is too much.

Greed is not defined by what something costs; it is measured by what it costs you.

If anything costs you your faith or your family, the price is too high.

WHEN GOD WHISPERS YOUR NAME

Do you ever fall into society's trap of measuring a person's worth with a person's purse? Why is this so repugnant to God?

_____

_____

_____

_____

_____

_____

God in the Ordinary

In Christ we can come before God with freedom and without fear.

EPHESIANS 3:12

God calls us in a real world. He doesn't communicate by stacking stars in the heavens or reincarnating grandparents from the grave.

He's not a magician or a good-luck charm or the man upstairs. He is, instead, the Creator of the universe who is right here in the thick of our day-to-day world who speaks to you more through cooing babies and hungry bellies than he ever will through horoscopes, zodiac papers, or weeping Madonnas.

If you get some supernatural vision or hear some strange voice in the night, don't get too carried away. It could be God or it could be indigestion, and you don't want to misinterpret one for the other.

God speaks in our world. We just have to learn to hear him . . . amidst the ordinary.

AND THE ANGELS WERE SILENT

Make a list of some of the ordinary ways you can hear God speak in your world. Are you listening?

Secure in His Grasp

God is strong and can help you not to fall.

JUDE 24

You and I are on a great climb. The wall is high, and the stakes are higher. You took your first step the day you confessed Christ as the Son of God. He gave you his harness—the Holy Spirit. In your hands he placed a rope—his Word.

Your first steps were confident and strong, but with the journey came weariness, and with the height came fear. You lost your footing. You lost your focus. You lost your grip, and you fell. For a moment, which seemed like forever, you tumbled wildly. Out of control. Out of self-control. Disoriented. Dislodged. Falling.

But then the rope tightened, and the tumble ceased. You hung in the harness and found it to be strong. You grasped the rope and found it to be true. And though you can't see your guide, you know him. You know he is strong. You know he is able to keep you from falling.

A GENTLE THUNDER

The Holy Spirit is our guide on the pathway of life.
Describe how he keeps you from falling.

One Explanation

"After I rise from the dead, I will go ahead of you into Galilee."
MATTHEW 26:32

Remember [Christ's] followers' fear at the crucifixion? They ran. Scared as cats in a dog pound.

But fast-forward forty days. Bankrupt traitors have become a force of life-changing fury. Peter is preaching in the very precinct where Christ was arrested. Followers of Christ defy the enemies of Christ. Whip them and they'll worship. Lock them up and they'll launch a jailhouse ministry. As bold after the resurrection as they were cowardly before it.

Explanation:

Greed? They made no money.

Power? They gave all the credit to Christ.

Popularity? Most were killed for their beliefs.

Only one explanation remains—a resurrected Christ and his Holy Spirit. The courage of these men and women was forged in the fire of the empty tomb.

NEXT DOOR SAVIOR

Explain how the Holy Spirit is a great gift from God.

Reflecting God's Glory

*Our faces, then, are not covered. We all show the Lord's glory,
and we are being changed to be like him.*

2 CORINTHIANS 3:18

The purpose of worship is to change the face of the worshiper. That is exactly what happened to Christ on the mountain. Jesus' appearance was changed: "His face became bright like the sun" (Matthew 17:2).

The connection between the face and worship is more than coincidental. Our face is the most public part of our bodies, covered less than any other area. It is also the most recognizable part of our bodies. We don't fill a school annual with photos of people's feet but rather with photos of faces. God desires to take our faces, this exposed and memorable part of our bodies, and use them to reflect his goodness.

JUST LIKE JESUS

Does it matter whether we worship God? Explain why.

_____

_____

_____

_____

_____

_____

_____

_____

When Hopes Don't Happen

In the time of trouble He shall hide me in His pavilion.
PSALM 27:5 NKJV

What do we do with our disappointments? We could do what Miss Havisham did. Remember her in Charles Dickens's *Great Expectations*? Jilted by her fiancé just prior to the wedding, she closed all the blinds in the house, stopped every clock, left the wedding cake on the table to gather cobwebs, and wore her wedding dress until it hung in yellow decay around her shrunken form. Her wounded heart consumed her life.

We can follow the same course.

Or we can follow the example of the apostle Paul. His goal was to be a missionary in Spain, however, God sent him to prison. Sitting in a Roman jail, Paul could have made the same choice as Miss Havisham, but he didn't. Instead he said, "As long as I'm here, I might as well write a few letters." Hence your Bible has the epistles to Philemon, the Philippians, the Colossians, and the Ephesians.

TRAVELING LIGHT

A positive response to disappointment brings joy to our lives and glory to God. Explain why.

Forgiveness Frees the Soul

If you suffer for doing good,
and you are patient, then God is pleased.

1 PETER 2:20

I s there any emotion that imprisons the soul more than the unwillingness to forgive? What do you do when people mistreat you or those you love? Does the fire of anger boil within you, with leaping flames consuming your emotions? Or do you reach somewhere, to some source of cool water and pull out a bucket of mercy—to free yourself?

Don't get on the roller coaster of resentment and anger. You be the one who says, "Yes, he mistreated me, but I am going to be like Christ. I'll be the one who says, 'Forgive them, Father, they don't know what they're doing.'"

WALKING WITH THE SAVIOR

Do you find yourself on the roller coaster of resentment and anger? Explain how forgiving and showing mercy can free you from that roller coaster.

_____

_____

_____

_____

_____

_____

_____

No Strings Attached

*He is the One who loves us, who made us
free from our sins with the blood of his death.*

REVELATION 1:5

When we love with expectations, we say, "I love you. But I'll love you even more if . . . "

Christ's love had none of this. No strings, no expectations, no hidden agendas, no secrets. His love for us was, and is, up front and clear. "I love you," he says. "Even if you let me down. I love you in spite of your failures."

One step behind the expectations of Christ come his forgiveness and tenderness. Tumble off the tightrope of what our Master expects and you land safely in his net of tolerance.

NO WONDER THEY CALL HIM THE SAVIOR

Think of times when you have landed safely in Christ's "net of tolerance." How should this affect the tolerance you show to others?

A Soft Tap at the Door

But be holy in all you do,
just as God, the One who called you, is holy.

1 PETER 1:15

I have something against the lying voices that noise our world. You've heard them. They tell you to swap your integrity for a new sale. To barter your convictions for an easy deal. To exchange your devotion for a quick thrill.

They whisper. They woo. They taunt. They tantalize. They flirt. They flatter. "Go ahead, it's okay." "Don't worry, no one will know."

The world rams at your door; Jesus taps at your door. The voices scream for your allegiance; Jesus softly and tenderly requests it. The world promises flashy pleasure; Jesus promises a quiet dinner . . . with God.

Which voice do you hear?

IN THE EYE OF THE STORM

What happens when we listen to the lying voices in our noisy world? How do we become more sensitive to the quiet voice of God?

Go First to God

"This is my commitment to my people: removal of their sins."
ROMANS 11:27 MSG

God does more than forgive our mistakes; he removes them! We simply have to take them to him.

He not only wants the mistakes we've made. He wants the ones we are making! Are you making some? Are you drinking too much? Are you cheating at work or cheating at marriage? Are you mismanaging money? Are you mismanaging your life?

If so, don't pretend nothing is wrong. Don't pretend you don't fall. Don't try to get back in the game. Go first to God. The first step after a stumble must be in the direction of the cross.

HE CHOSE THE NAILS

Do you know someone who is struggling with mistakes? Are you? Why is it important not to pretend with God but to be honest about our mistakes?

God, the Savior

"Those who believe in the Son have eternal life,
but those who do not obey the Son will never have life."

JOHN 3:36

When does salvation come?

When we look to Christ. When we embrace him as Savior. Astonishingly simple, isn't it? Claim the great promise of John 3:16: "God loved the world so much that he gave his one and only Son so that whoever believes in him may not be lost, but have eternal life."

God, the Lover. God, the Giver. God, the Savior.

And man, the believer. And for those who believe, he has promised a new birth.

But despite the simplicity, there are still those who don't believe. They don't trust the promise.

If only they would try. If only they would test it. But God is as polite as he is passionate. He never forces his way in. The choice is theirs.

A GENTLE THUNDER

Think of individuals you know who still don't believe the simple message of salvation. Pray for them and think of ways to reach out to them.

Abounding Grace

The more we see our sinfulness,
the more we see God's abounding grace.

ROMANS 5:20 TLB

To abound is to have a surplus, an abundance, an extravagant portion. Should the fish in the Pacific worry that it will run out of ocean? No. Why? The ocean abounds with water. Need the lark be anxious about finding room in the sky to fly? No. The sky abounds with space.

Should the Christian worry that the cup of mercy will run empty? He may. For he may not be aware of God's abounding grace. Are you? Are you aware that the cup God gives you overflows with mercy? Or are you afraid your cup will run dry? Your warranty will expire? Are you afraid your mistakes are too great for God's grace?

God is not a miser with his grace. Your cup may be low on cash or clout, but it is overflowing with mercy.

TRAVELING LIGHT

Do you ever worry that you will use up all of God's grace?
Why is this foolish?

_____

_____

_____

_____

July

Jesus spoke to them, saying,
"Be of good cheer! It is I; do not be afraid."

—MATTHEW 14:27 NKJV

Judgment Is God's Job

Wait for the LORD, and he will make things right.

PROVERBS 20:22

Some of you are in the courtroom. The courtroom of complaint. Some of you are rehashing the same hurt every chance you get with anyone who will listen.

For you, I have this question: Who made you God? I don't mean to be cocky, but why are you doing his work for him?

"Vengeance is Mine," God declared. "I will repay" (Hebrews 10:30 NKJV).

Judgment is God's job. To assume otherwise is to assume God can't do it.

Revenge is irreverent. To forgive someone is to display reverence. Forgiveness is not saying the one who hurt you was right. Forgiveness is stating that God is faithful and he will do what is right.

WHEN GOD WHISPERS YOUR NAME

Do you find yourself "doing God's work for him"? In other words, do you find yourself judging others? Why is this a waste of time?

_____

_____

_____

_____

_____

Spiritual Water

"The water I give will become a spring
of water gushing up inside . . . giving eternal life."
JOHN 4:14

Deprive your body of necessary fluid, and your body will tell you.

Deprive your soul of spiritual water, and your soul will tell you. Dehydrated hearts send desperate messages. Snarling tempers. Waves of worry. Growling mastodons of guilt and fear. You think God wants you to live with these? Hopelessness. Sleeplessness. Loneliness. Resentment. Irritability. Insecurity. These are warnings. Symptoms of a dryness deep within.

Treat your soul as you treat your thirst. Take a gulp. Imbibe moisture. Flood your heart with a good swallow of water.

Where do you find water for the soul? "If anyone thirsts, let him come to Me and drink" (John 7:37 NKJV).

COME THIRSTY

Are you living with hopelessness? Sleeplessness? Loneliness?
Resentment? Irritability? Insecurity? What can you do to
treat these symptoms of spiritual dryness?

_____

_____

_____

_____

_____

_____

Your Whispering Thoughts

God, examine me and know my heart;
test me and know my nervous thoughts.

PSALM 139:23

Imagine considering every moment as a potential time of communion with God. By the time your life is over, you will have spent six months at stoplights, eight months opening junk mail, a year and a half looking for lost stuff (double that number in my case), and a whopping five years standing in various lines.

Why don't you give these moments to God? By giving God your whispering thoughts, the common becomes uncommon. Simple phrases such as "Thank you, Father," "Be sovereign in this hour, O Lord," "You are my resting place, Jesus" can turn a commute into a pilgrimage. You needn't leave your office or kneel in your kitchen. Just pray where you are. Let the kitchen become a cathedral or the classroom a chapel. Give God your whispering thoughts.

JUST LIKE JESUS

Five years of standing in various lines—imagine that! How can you give those moments to God?

_____

_____

_____

_____

The Time Line of History

He sent me to preach the Good News . . .
so that cross of Christ would not lose its power.

1 CORINTHIANS 1:17

The cross rests on the time line of history like a compelling diamond. Its tragedy summons all sufferers. Its absurdity attracts all cynics. Its hope lures all searchers.

History has idolized it and despised it, gold-plated it and burned it, worn and trashed it. History has done everything to it but ignore it.

That's the one option that the cross does not offer.

No one can ignore it! You can't ignore a piece of lumber that suspends the greatest claim in history. A crucified carpenter claiming that he is God on earth? Divine? Eternal? The Death-slayer?

To accept or reject Christ without a careful examination of Calvary is like deciding on a car without looking at the engine. Being religious without knowing the cross is like owning a Mercedes with no motor. Pretty package, but where is your power?

NO WONDER THEY CALL HIM THE SAVIOR

"Being religious without knowing the cross is like owning a Mercedes with no motor." What does that mean?

_____

_____

_____

_____

God Changes Our Face

He put a new song in my mouth, a song of praise to our God.

PSALM 40:3

God invites us to see his face so he can change ours. He uses our uncovered faces to display his glory. The transformation isn't easy. The sculptor of Mount Rushmore faced a lesser challenge than does God. But our Lord is up to the task. He loves to change the faces of his children. By his fingers, wrinkles of worry are rubbed away. Shadows of shame and doubt become portraits of grace and trust. He relaxes clenched jaws and smooths furrowed brows. His touch can remove the bags of exhaustion from beneath the eyes and turn tears of despair into tears of peace.

How? Through worship.

We'd expect something more complicated, more demanding. A forty-day fast or the memorization of Leviticus perhaps. No. God's plan is simpler. He changes our faces through worship.

JUST LIKE JESUS

Explain how worshiping God can remove our wrinkles of worry, shadows of shame, clenched jaws, and furrowed brows.

A List of Our Sins

He canceled the record that contained the charges against us.
He . . . destroyed it by nailing it to Christ's cross.

COLOSSIANS 2:14 NLT

ome with me to the hill of Calvary. Watch as the soldiers shove the Carpenter to the ground and stretch his arms against the beams. One presses a knee against a forearm and a spike against a hand. Jesus turns his face toward the nail just as the soldier lifts the hammer to strike it.

The crowd at the cross concluded that the purpose of the pounding was to skewer the hands of Christ to a beam. But they were only half-right. We can't fault them for missing the other half. They couldn't see it.

Between his hand and the wood there was a list. A long list. A list of our mistakes: our lusts and lies and greedy moments and prodigal years. A list of our sins.

The list, however, cannot be read. The words can't be deciphered. The mistakes are covered. The sins are hidden. Those at the top are hidden by his hand; those down the list are covered by his blood.

HE CHOSE THE NAILS

When you think of the blood of Jesus covering your sins
and mistakes, how do you respond?

_____

_____

_____

Finding God's Grace

*You gave me life and showed me kindness, and in
your care you watched over my life.*

JOB 10:12

Discipline is easy for me to swallow. Logical to assimilate. Manageable and appropriate. But God's grace? Anything but. Examples? How much time do you have?

David the psalmist becomes David the voyeur, but by God's grace becomes David the psalmist again.

Peter denied Christ before he preached Christ.

Zacchaeus, the crook. The cleanest part of his life was the money he'd laundered. But Jesus still had time for him.

The thief on the cross: hell-bent and hung-out-to-die one minute, heaven-bound and smiling the next.

Story after story. Prayer after prayer. Surprise after surprise. Seems that God is looking more for ways to get us home than for ways to keep us out. I challenge you to find one soul who came to God seeking grace and did not find it.

WHEN GOD WHISPERS YOUR NAME

*Think of the story of your life. How has God's grace
affected your life?*

_____

_____

_____

_____

_____

Enough for Today

"I will cause food to fall like rain from the sky for all of you. Every day the people must go out and gather what they need for that day."

EXODUS 16:4

God liberated his children from slavery and created a path through the sea. He gave them a cloud to follow in the day and a fire to see at night. And he gave them food. He met their most basic need: He filled their bellies.

Each morning the manna came. Each evening the quail appeared. "Trust me. Trust me and I will give you what you need." The people were told to take just enough for one day. Their needs would be met, one day at a time.

"Just take enough for today," was God's message. "Let me worry about tomorrow."

The Father wanted the people to trust him.

AND THE ANGELS WERE SILENT

God meets our needs one day at a time. How should this affect the way we live?

The Dungeon of Bitterness

"If you forgive others for their sins,
your Father in heaven will also forgive you for your sins."

MATTHEW 6:14

Bitterness is its own prison.

The sides are slippery with resentment. A floor of muddy anger stills the feet. The stench of betrayal fills the air and stings the eyes. A cloud of self-pity blocks the view of the tiny exit above.

Step in and look at the prisoners. Victims are chained to the walls. Victims of betrayal. Victims of abuse.

The dungeon, deep and dark, is beckoning you to enter. You can, you know. You've experienced enough hurt. You can choose, like many, to chain yourself to your hurt. Or you can choose, like some, to put away your hurts before they become hates.

How does God deal with your bitter heart? He reminds you that what you have is more important than what you don't have. You still have your relationship with God. No one can take that.

HE STILL MOVES STONES

Have you ever been in the prison of bitterness? How did God help you deal with your bitterness?

_____

_____

_____

_____

_____

It's Inexplicable

The LORD who saves you is the Holy One of Israel.

ISAIAH 49:7

Even after generations of people had spit in his face, he still loved them. After a nation of chosen ones had stripped him naked and ripped his incarnated flesh, he still died for them. And even today, after billions have chosen to prostitute themselves before the pimps of power, fame, and wealth, he still waits for them.

It is inexplicable. It doesn't have a drop of logic nor a thread of rationality.

And yet, it is that very irrationality that gives the gospel its greatest defense. For only God could love like that.

How absurd to think that such nobility would go to such poverty to share such a treasure with such thankless souls.

But he did.

GOD CAME NEAR

Have you ever been worried or perplexed by the irrationality of God's love? Why should you actually be encouraged by this?

The Perfect Priest

On the day when the Lord Jesus comes . . .
all the people who have believed will be amazed at Jesus.

2 THESSALONIANS 1:10

When we see Christ, what will we see?

We will see the perfect priest. "He was dressed in a long robe and had a gold band around his chest" (Revelation 1:13). The first readers of this message knew the significance of the robe and band. Jesus is wearing the clothing of a priest. A priest presents people to God and God to people.

You have known other priests. There have been others in your life, whether clergy or not, who sought to bring you to God. But they, too, needed a priest. Some needed a priest more than you did. They, like you, were sinful. Not so with Jesus. "Jesus is the kind of high priest we need. He is holy, sinless, pure, not influenced by sinners, and he is raised above the heavens" (Hebrews 7:26).

Jesus is the perfect priest.

WHEN CHRIST COMES

What does it mean to you that Christ, as the perfect priest, represents you to God?

_____

_____

_____

_____

_____

_____

Honest Evaluation

Guide me in your truth and teach me, my God, my Savior.

PSALM 25:5

Raise your hand if any of the following describe you.

You are at peace with everyone. Every relationship as sweet as fudge. Even your old flames speak highly of you. Love all and are loved by all. Is that you?

You have no fears. Call you the Teflon toughie. Wall Street plummets—no problem. Heart condition discovered—yawn. Does this describe you?

You need no forgiveness. Never made a mistake. As square as a game of checkers. As clean as grandma's kitchen. Is that you? No?

Let's evaluate this. A few of your relationships are shaky. You have fears and faults. Hmmm. Do you really want to hang on to your chest of self-reliance? Sounds to me as if you could use a shepherd.

TRAVELING LIGHT

Make a list of some of the reasons why you need a shepherd and beside each write why you are thankful that God is your Shepherd.

_____

_____

_____

_____

_____

_____

Closer Than You Think

Jesus spoke to them, saying,
"Be of good cheer! It is I; do not be afraid."

MATTHEW 14:27 NKJV

When the disciples saw Jesus in the middle of their stormy night, they called him a ghost. A phantom. To them, the glow was anything but God.

When we see gentle lights on the horizon, we often have the same reaction. We dismiss occasional kindness as apparitions, accidents, or anomalies. Anything but God.

And because we look for the bonfire, we miss the candle. Because we listen for the shout, we miss the whisper.

But it is in burnished candles that God comes, and through whispered promises he speaks: "When you doubt, look around; I am closer than you think."

IN THE EYE OF THE STORM

Do you sometimes miss the gentle light of God's loving care because you are looking for the bonfire? Do you miss his gentle whisper? What are the consequences?

_____

_____

_____

_____

_____

_____

Know Your Part

Consider others better than yourselves.

PHILIPPIANS 2:3 NIV

True humility is not thinking lowly of yourself but thinking accurately of yourself. The humble heart does not say, "I can't do anything." But rather, "I can't do everything. I know my part and am happy to do it."

When Paul writes "*consider* others better than yourselves" (Philippians 2:3 NIV, emphasis mine), he uses a verb that means "to calculate," "to reckon." The word implies a conscious judgment resting on carefully weighed facts. To consider others better than yourself, then, is not to say you have no place; it is to say that you know your place. "Don't cherish exaggerated ideas of yourself or your importance, but try to have a sane estimate of your capabilities by the light of the faith that God has given to you" (Romans 12:3 PHILLIPS).

A LOVE WORTH GIVING

"True humility is not thinking lowly of yourself but thinking accurately of yourself." Explain what that statement means.

_____

_____

_____

_____

_____

_____

_____

He Kept the Faith

Continue to have faith and do what you know is right.
Some people have rejected this, and their faith has been shipwrecked.

1 TIMOTHY 1:19

I sit a few feet from a man on death row. Jewish by birth. Tentmaker by trade. Apostle by calling. His days are marked. I'm curious about what bolsters this man as he nears his execution. So I ask some questions.

Do you have family, Paul? *I have none.*

What about your health? *My body is beaten and tired.*

Any awards? *Not on earth.*

Then what do you have, Paul? No belongings. No family. What do you have that matters?

I have my faith. It's all I have. But it's all I need. I have kept the faith.

Paul leans back against the wall of his cell and smiles.

WHEN GOD WHISPERS YOUR NAME

"Faith is all that really matters." What does that statement mean? What does it mean to you personally?

_____

_____

_____

_____

_____

_____

Endure to the End

"Those people who keep their faith until the end will be saved."
MATTHEW 10:22

A re you close to quitting? Please don't do it. Are you discouraged as a parent? Hang in there. Are you weary with doing good? Do just a little more. Are you pessimistic about your job? Roll up your sleeves and go at it again. No communication in your marriage? Give it one more shot.

Remember, a finisher is not one with no wounds or weariness. Quite to the contrary, he, like the boxer, is scarred and bloody. Mother Teresa is credited with saying, "God didn't call us to be successful, just faithful." The fighter, like our Master, is pierced and full of pain. He, like Paul, may even be bound and beaten. But he remains.

The Land of Promise, says Jesus, awaits those who endure. It is not just for those who make the victory laps or drink champagne. No sir. The Land of Promise is for those who simply remain to the end.

NO WONDER THEY CALL HIM THE SAVIOR

Do you know someone who is tired of being faithful? Who feels like quitting? What can you do to encourage that person to hang in there?

_____

_____

_____

_____

A Father's Pride

God is being patient with you. He does not want anyone to be lost,
but he wants all people to change their hearts and lives.

2 PETER 3:9

To those who embrace Christ as Savior, he has promised a new birth.

Does that mean the old nature will never rear its ugly head? Does that mean you will instantly be able to resist any temptation?

To answer that question, compare your new birth in Christ to a newborn baby. Can a newborn walk? Can he feed himself? Can he sing or read or speak? No, not yet. But someday he will.

It takes time to grow. But is the parent in the delivery room ashamed of the baby? Is the mom embarrassed that the infant can't spell . . . that the baby can't walk . . . that the newborn can't give a speech?

Of course not. The parents aren't ashamed; they are proud. They know that growth will come with time. So does God.

A GENTLE THUNDER

God gives us time to grow in our Christian faith. What has he given us to help us mature spiritually?

_____

_____

_____

_____

_____

Christ Came to Serve

They all may call on the name of the LORD,
to serve Him with one accord.

ZEPHANIAH 3:9 NKJV

Jesus came to serve.

He let a woman in Samaria interrupt his rest, a woman in adultery interrupt his sermon, a woman with a disease interrupt his plans, and one with remorse interrupt his meal.

Though none of the apostles washed his feet, he washed theirs. Though none of the soldiers at the cross begged for mercy, he extended it. And though his followers skedaddled like scared rabbits on Thursday, he came searching for them on Easter Sunday. The resurrected King ascended to heaven only after he'd spent forty days with his friends—teaching them, encouraging them . . . serving them.

Why? It's what he came to do. He came to serve.

CURE FOR THE COMMON LIFE

Jesus exemplifies the life of a servant. How can you apply his example to your life?

_____

_____

_____

_____

_____

_____

The Purpose of Life

"Love the Lord your God with all
your heart, all your soul, and all your mind."

MATTHEW 22:37

M ine deep enough in every heart and you'll find it: a longing for meaning, a quest for purpose. As surely as a child breathes, he will someday wonder, "What is the purpose of my life?"

Some search for meaning in a career. "My purpose is to be a dentist." Fine vocation but hardly a justification for existence.

For others, who they are is what they have. They find meaning in a new car or a new house or new clothes. These people are great for the economy and rough on the budget because they are always seeking meaning in something they own. Some try sports, entertainment, cults, sex, you name it.

All mirages in the desert of purpose.

Shouldn't we face the truth? If we don't acknowledge God, we are flotsam in the universe.

IN THE GRIP OF GRACE

Why does acknowledging God give purpose to life?

Sealed with the Spirit

Having believed, you were marked in him
with a seal, the promised Holy Spirit.

EPHESIANS 1:13 NIV

The most famous New Testament "sealing" occurred with the tomb of Jesus. Roman soldiers rolled a rock over the entrance and "set a seal on the stone" (Matthew 27:66 NASB). Archaeologists envision two ribbons stretched in front of the entrance, glued together with hardened wax that bore the imprimatur of the Roman government—SPQR *(Senatus Populusque Romanus)*—as if to say, "Stay away! The contents of this tomb belong to Rome." Their seal, of course, proved futile.

The seal of the Spirit, however, proves forceful. When you accepted Christ, God sealed you with the Spirit. "Having believed, you were marked in him with a seal, the promised Holy Spirit." When hell's interlopers come seeking to snatch you from God, the seal turns them away. He bought you, owns you, and protects you. God paid too high a price to leave you unguarded.

COME THIRSTY

Like the sealed tomb, the seal of the Spirit protects the believer. How does this truth encourage you?

_____

_____

_____

_____

_____

A Big View of God

Holy, holy, holy is the Lord God Almighty.
He was, he is, and he is coming.

REVELATION 4:8

Exactly what is worship? I like King David's definition. "O magnify the LORD with me, and let us exalt His name together" (Psalm 34:3 NASB). Worship is the act of magnifying God. Enlarging our vision of him. Stepping into the cockpit to see where he sits and observe how he works. Of course, his size doesn't change, but our perception of him does. As we draw nearer, he seems larger. Isn't that what we need? A *big* view of God? Don't we have *big* problems, *big* worries, *big* questions? Of course we do. Hence we need a big view of God.

Worship offers that. How can we sing, "Holy, Holy, Holy" and not have our vision expanded?

JUST LIKE JESUS

How would you define worship? How does worship expand your view of God?

_____

_____

_____

_____

_____

_____

The Via Dolorosa

God was in Christ reconciling the world to Himself.

2 CORINTHIANS 5:19 NKJV

The most notorious road in the world is the Via Dolorosa, "the Way of Sorrows." According to tradition, it is the route Jesus took from Pilate's hall to Calvary. The path is marked by stations frequently used by Christians for their devotions. One station marks the passing of Pilate's verdict. Another, the appearance of Simon to carry the cross. There are fourteen stations in all, each one a reminder of the events of Christ's final journey.

Is the route accurate? Probably not. No one knows the exact route Christ followed that Friday.

But we do know where the path actually began.

The path began, not in the court of Pilate, but in the halls of heaven. The Father began his journey when he left his home in search of us. His desire was singular—to bring his children home.

The path to the cross tells us exactly how far God will go to call us back.

HE CHOSE THE NAILS

Describe some ways you can thank Christ for walking the painful path of the cross.

_____

_____

_____

_____

Repentance Is a Decision

*Perhaps you do not understand that God is kind to you
so you will change your hearts and lives.*

ROMANS 2:4

No one is happier than the one who has sincerely repented of wrong. Repentance is the decision to turn from selfish desires and seek God. It is a genuine, sincere regret that creates sorrow and moves us to admit wrong and desire to do better.

It's an inward conviction that expresses itself in outward actions.

You look at the love of God and you can't believe he's loved you like he has, and this realization motivates you to change your life. That is the nature of repentance.

WALKING WITH THE SAVIOR

Explain why "no one is happier than the one who has sincerely repented of wrong."

_____

_____

_____

_____

_____

_____

_____

_____

People Who Make a Difference

"Good people have good things in their hearts."
MATTHEW 12:35

Name the ten wealthiest men in the world.
Name eight people who have won the Nobel or Pulitzer prize.

How did you do? I didn't do well either. With the exception of you trivia hounds, none of us remember the headliners of yesterday too well. Surprising how quickly we forget, isn't it? And what I've mentioned above are no second-rate achievements. These are the best in their fields. But the applause dies. Awards tarnish. Achievements are forgotten.

Here's another quiz. See how you do on this one.

Name ten people who have taught you something worthwhile.
Name five friends who have helped you in a difficult time.

Easier? It was for me too. The lesson? The people who make a difference are not the ones with the credentials, but the ones with the concern.

AND THE ANGELS WERE SILENT

Think of some of the people who have made a difference in your life. Why is it easy for you to remember each of these people?

_____

_____

_____

_____

_____

Knowing God's Will

*"Those who see the Son and believe in him have eternal life. . . .
This is what my Father wants."*

JOHN 6:40

We learn God's will by spending time in his presence. The key to knowing God's heart is having a relationship with him. A *personal* relationship. God will speak to you differently than he will speak to others. Just because God spoke to Moses through a burning bush, that doesn't mean we should all sit next to a bush waiting for God to speak. God used a fish to convict Jonah. Does that mean we should have worship services at Sea World? No. God reveals his heart personally to each person.

For that reason, your walk with God is essential. His heart is not seen in an occasional chat or weekly visit. We learn his will as we take up residence in his house every single day.

Walk with him long enough and you come to know his heart.

THE GREAT HOUSE OF GOD

Have you come to know God's heart? Make a list of the things you have discovered. How can you know his heart better?

_____

_____

_____

_____

_____

The Present-Tense Christ

Jesus Christ is the same yesterday, today, and forever.

HEBREWS 13:8

I am God's Son" (John 10:36).

"I am the resurrection and the life" (John 11:25).

"I am the way, and the truth, and the life" (John 14:6).

"I am the true vine" (John 15:1).

The present-tense Christ. He never says, "I was." We do. We do because "we were." We were younger, faster, prettier. Prone to be people of the past tense, we reminisce. Not God. Unwavering in strength, he need never say, "I was."

From the center of the storm, the unwavering Jesus shouts, "I am." Tall in the Trade Tower wreckage. Bold against the Galilean waves. ICU, battlefield, boardroom, prison cell, or maternity ward—whatever your storm, "I am."

NEXT DOOR SAVIOR

Are there storms in your life right now or in the life of someone who is close to you? How does knowing the present-tense Christ help you to stay calm in the storm?

God's Signature

"Before I made you in your mother's womb, I chose you."

JEREMIAH 1:5

With God in your world, you aren't an accident or an incident; you are a gift to the world, a divine work of art, signed by God.

One of the finest gifts I ever received is a football signed by thirty former professional quarterbacks. There is nothing unique about this ball. For all I know it was bought at a discount sports store. What makes it unique is the signatures.

The same is true with us. In the scheme of nature *Homo sapiens* are not unique. We aren't the only creatures with flesh and hair and blood and hearts. What makes us special is not only our body but the signature of God on our lives. We are his works of art. We are created in his image to do good deeds. We are significant, not because of what we do, but because of whose we are.

IN THE GRIP OF GRACE

What does it mean to you to have the "signature of God" on your life? How does this make you feel about yourself?

_____

_____

_____

_____

_____

_____

God Forgets

Bless the LORD, . . . who forgives all your iniquities.
PSALM 103:2–3 NKJV

God doesn't remember the past. But I do, you do. You still remember. You're like me. You still remember what you did before you changed. In the cellar of your heart lurk the ghosts of yesterday's sins. Sins you've confessed; errors of which you've repented; damage you've done your best to repair.

That horrid lie.

The time you exploded in anger.

Now, honestly. Do you think God was exaggerating when he said he would cast our sins as far as the east is from the west? Do you actually believe he would make a statement like "I will not hold their iniquities against them" and then rub our noses in them whenever we ask for help?

Of course you don't. You and I just need an occasional reminder of God's nature, his forgetful nature.

GOD CAME NEAR

Aren't you glad for God's forgetful nature? How can this be a positive effect on your life?

_____

_____

_____

_____

_____

More Than Meets the Eye

Faith means being sure of the things we hope for
and knowing that something is real even if we do not see it.

HEBREWS 11:1

Faith is trusting what the eye can't see.

Eyes see the prowling lion. Faith sees Daniel's angel.

Eyes see storms. Faith sees Noah's rainbow.

Eyes see giants. Faith sees Canaan.

Your eyes see your faults. Your faith sees your Savior.

Your eyes see your guilt. Your faith sees his blood.

Your eyes look in the mirror and see a sinner, a failure, a promise-breaker. But by faith you look in the mirror and see a robed prodigal bearing the ring of grace on your finger and the kiss of your Father on your face.

WHEN GOD WHISPERS YOUR NAME

Think of a time when you had to trust God for what you couldn't see. How did this affect you?

_____

_____

_____

_____

_____

_____

_____

Guard Against Greed

Whoever loves money never has money enough;
whoever loves wealth is never satisfied with his income.

ECCLESIASTES 5:10 NIV

Greed comes in many forms. Greed for approval. Greed for applause. Greed for status. Greed for the best office, the fastest car, the prettiest date. Greed has many faces, but speaks one language: the language of more. Epicurus noted, "Nothing is enough for the man to whom enough is too little." And what was that observation of John D. Rockefeller's? He was asked, "How much money does it take to satisfy a man?" He answered, "Just a little more." Wise was the one who wrote, "Whoever loves money never has money enough; whoever loves wealth is never satisfied with his income" (Ecclesiastes 5:10 NIV).

Greed has a growling stomach. Feed it, and you risk more than budget-busting debt. You risk losing purpose.

CURE FOR THE COMMON LIFE

Describe some of the faces of greed that you have observed.
What are the results of such greed?

_____

_____

_____

_____

_____

_____

All God's Children

If they could be made God's people by what they did,
God's gift of grace would not really be a gift.

ROMANS 11:6

To whom does God offer his gift? To the brightest? The most beautiful or the most charming? No. His gift is for us all—beggars and bankers, clergy and clerks, judges and janitors. All God's children.

And he wants us so badly, he'll take us in any condition—"as is" reads the tag on our collars. He's not about to wait for us to reach perfection (he knows we'll never get there!). Do you think he's waiting for us to overcome all temptations? Hardly. When we master the Christian walk? Far from it. Remember, Christ died for us when we were still sinners. His sacrifice, then, was not dependent on our performance.

He wants us *now.*

NO WONDER THEY CALL HIM THE SAVIOR

God does not wait until we reach perfection. He accepts us as we are. How does this encourage you for yourself? For your family?

_____

_____

_____

_____

_____

_____

No Limit to His Love

This is how we know what real love is: Jesus gave his life for us.
1 JOHN 3:16

It's nice to be included. You aren't always. Universities exclude you if you aren't smart enough. Businesses exclude you if you aren't qualified enough, and, sadly, some churches exclude you if you aren't good enough.

But though they may exclude you, Christ includes you. When asked to describe the width of his love, he stretched one hand to the right and the other to the left and had them nailed in that position so you would know he died loving you.

But isn't there a limit? Surely there has to be an end to this love. You'd think so, wouldn't you? But David the adulterer never found it. Paul the murderer never found it. Peter the liar never found it. When it came to life, they hit bottom. But when it came to God's love, they never did.

HE CHOSE THE NAILS

We can never find the limit of God's love. How should this affect the way we live?

_____

_____

_____

_____

_____

_____

God Is in Your Corner

He will not leave you or forget you.

DEUTERONOMY 31:8

When I was seven years old, I ran away from home. I'd had enough of my father's rules and decided I could make it on my own, thank you very much. With my clothes in a paper bag, I stormed out the back gate and marched down the alley. [But] I didn't go far. I got to the end of the alley and remembered I was hungry, so I went back home.

Though the rebellion was brief, it was rebellion nonetheless. And had you stopped me on that prodigal path . . . I just might have told you how I felt. I just might have said, "I don't need a father. I'm too big for the rules of my family."

I didn't hear the rooster crow like Peter did. I didn't feel the fish belch like Jonah did. I didn't get a robe and a ring and sandals like the prodigal did. But I learned from my father on earth what those three learned from their Father in heaven. Our God is no fair-weather Father. He's not into this love-'em-and-leave-'em stuff. I can count on him to be in my corner no matter how I perform. You can too.

THE GREAT HOUSE OF GOD

God is always in our corner. What does this say about his character?

_____

_____

_____

_____

God, Your Guardian

He will cover you with his feathers, and
under his wings you can hide.

PSALM 91:4

The image of living beneath *Shaddai's* shadow reminds me of a rained-out picnic. My college friends and I barely escaped a West Texas storm before it pummeled the park where we were spending a Saturday afternoon. As we were leaving, my buddy brought the car to a sudden stop and gestured to a tender sight on the ground. A mother bird sat exposed to the rain, her wing extended over her baby who had fallen out of the nest. The fierce storm prohibited her from returning to the tree, so she covered her child until the wind passed.

From how many winds is God protecting you? His wing, at this moment, shields you. A slanderous critic heading toward your desk is interrupted by a phone call. A burglar en route to your house has a flat tire. A drunk driver runs out of gas before your car passes his. God, your guardian, protects you.

COME THIRSTY

Right this moment and every moment God is protecting you. What does this mean to you?

_____

_____

_____

_____

God Walks Among the Suffering

He took our suffering on him and carried our diseases.

Picture a battleground strewn with wounded bodies, and you see Bethesda. Imagine a nursing home overcrowded and understaffed, and you see the pool. Call to mind the orphans in Bangladesh or the abandoned in New Delhi, and you will see what people saw when they passed Bethesda. As they passed, what did they hear? An endless wave of groans. What did they witness? A field of faceless need. What did they do? Most walked past.

But not Jesus.

He is alone. The people need him—so he's there. Can you picture it? Jesus walking among the suffering.

Little do they know that God is walking slowly, stepping carefully between the beggars and the blind.

HE STILL MOVES STONES

Do you ever feel ill at ease around people in great need? How do you respond to them? How would Christ respond to them?

Contentment

He who follows righteousness and mercy finds life.

PROVERBS 21:21 NKJV

I n our world, contentment is a strange street vendor, roaming, looking for a home, but seldom finding an open door. He moves slowly from house to house, knocking on doors, offering his wares: an hour of peace, a smile of acceptance, a sigh of relief. But his goods are seldom taken. We are too busy to be content.

"Not now, thank you. I've too much to do," we say. "Too many marks to be made, too many achievements to be achieved."

So the vendor moves on. When I asked him why so few welcomed him into their homes, his answer left me convicted. "I charge a high price, you know. My fee is steep. I ask people to trade in their schedules, frustrations, and anxieties. I demand that they put a torch to their fourteen-hour days and sleepless nights. You'd think I'd have more buyers." He scratched his beard, then added pensively, "But people seem strangely proud of their ulcers and headaches."

NO WONDER THEY CALL HIM the SAVIOR

Make a list of things you could do to trade your frustrations and anxieties for peace and rest.

_____

_____

_____

_____

_____

Why Deny?

If we say we have no sin,
we are fooling ourselves, and the truth is not in us.

1 John 1:8

We do ourselves no favors in justifying our deeds or glossing over our sins. Some time ago my daughter Andrea got a splinter in her finger. I took her to the restroom and set out some tweezers, ointment, and a Band-Aid.

She didn't like what she saw. "I just want the Band-Aid, Daddy."

Sometimes we are just like Andrea. We come to Christ with our sin, but all we want is a covering. We want to skip the treatment. We want to hide our sin. And one wonders if God, even in his great mercy, will heal what we conceal.

How can God heal what we deny? How can God touch what we cover up?

A Gentle Thunder

Explain why God cannot heal what we deny or cover up.

_____

_____

_____

_____

_____

_____

_____

You Make the Choice

Be careful what you think, because your thoughts run your life.

PROVERBS 4:23

You are driving to work when the words of your coworker come to mind. He needled you about your performance. He second-guessed your efficiency. Why was he so hard on you? You begin to wonder. *I didn't deserve any of that. Who is he to criticize me? Besides, he has as much taste as a rice cake. Have you seen those shoes he wears?*

At this point you need to make a choice. *Am I going to keep a list of these wrongs?* You can.

Or you can do something else. You can take those thoughts captive. You can defy the culprit. Quote a verse if you have to: "Bless those who persecute you; bless and do not curse" (Romans 12:14 NIV).

You are not a victim of your thoughts. You have a vote. You have a voice.

A LOVE WORTH GIVING

Do you sometimes feel like the victim of your thoughts? Why is it important that we take our thoughts captive?

_____

_____

_____

_____

_____

We Shall See Him

*Now we see a dim reflection, as if we were
looking into a mirror, but then we shall see clearly.*

1 CORINTHIANS 13:12

What will happen when you see Jesus?

You will see unblemished purity and unbending strength. You will feel his unending presence and know his unbridled protection. And—all that he is, you will be, for you will be like Jesus. Wasn't that the promise of John? "We know that when Christ comes again, we will be like him, because we will see him as he really is" (1 John 3:2).

Since you'll be pure as snow, you will never sin again; you will never stumble again; you will never feel lonely again; you will never doubt again.

When Christ comes, you will dwell in the light of God. And you will see him as he really is.

WHEN CHRIST COMES

Make a list of other things that will happen when you see Jesus. Describe what these will mean to you personally.

_____

_____

_____

_____

_____

_____

God Loves Humility

He crowns the humble with salvation.

PSALM 149:4 NIV

With the same intensity that he hates arrogance, God loves humility. The Jesus who said, "I am gentle and humble in heart" (Matthew 11:29 NASB) loves those who are gentle and humble in heart. "Though the LORD is supreme, he takes care of those who are humble" (Psalm 138:6). God says, "I . . . live with people who are . . . humble" (Isaiah 57:15). He also says, "To this one I will look, to him who is humble and contrite" (Isaiah 66:2 NASB). And to the humble, God gives great treasures:

He gives honor: "Humility goes before honor" (Proverbs 15:33 NRSV).

He gives wisdom: "With the humble is wisdom" (Proverbs 11:2 NASB).

He gives direction: "He teaches the humble His way" (Psalm 25:9 NASB).

And most significantly, he gives grace: "God . . . gives grace to the humble" (1 Peter 5:5).

TRAVELING LIGHT

Why does God love and reward humility?

_____

_____

_____

_____

Getting Our Attention

Come back to the LORD your God, because he is kind and shows mercy. He doesn't become angry quickly, and he has great love.

JOEL 2:13

How far do you want God to go in getting your attention? If God has to choose between your eternal safety and your earthly comfort, which do you hope he chooses?

What if he moved you to another land? (As he did Abraham.) What if he called you out of retirement? (Remember Moses?) How about the voice of an angel or the bowel of a fish? (A la Gideon and Jonah.) How about a promotion like Daniel's or a demotion like Samson's?

God does what it takes to get our attention. Isn't that the message of the Bible? The relentless pursuit of God. God on the hunt. God in the search. Peeking under the bed for hiding kids, stirring the bushes for lost sheep.

A GENTLE THUNDER

God is relentless in his pursuit of us. How far has God gone to get your attention or the attention of someone you know? Describe what happened.

Our Loving Father

The Father has loved us so much that we are called children of God.

1 JOHN 3:1

When my oldest daughter, Jenna, was four years old, she came to me with a confession. "Daddy, I took a crayon and drew on the wall." (Kids amaze me with their honesty.)

I sat down and lifted her up into my lap and tried to be wise. "Is that a good thing to do?" I asked her.

"No."

"What does Daddy do when you write on the wall?"

"You spank me."

"What do you think Daddy should do this time?"

"Love."

Don't we all want that? Don't we all long for a father who, even though our mistakes are written all over the wall, will love us anyway?

We do have that type of a father. A father who is at his best when we are at our worst. A father whose grace is strongest when our devotion is weakest.

SIX HOURS ONE FRIDAY

Explain why our heavenly Father is at his best when we are at our worst.

If Only . . .

"Spiritual life comes from the Spirit."

JOHN 3:6

Maybe your past isn't much to brag about. Maybe you've seen raw evil. And now you . . . have to make a choice. Do you rise above the past and make a difference? Or do you remain controlled by the past and make excuses?

Many choose the convalescent homes of the heart. Healthy bodies. Sharp minds. But retired dreams. Back and forth they rock in the chair of regret, repeating the terms of surrender. Lean closely and you will hear them: "If only."

"If only I'd been born somewhere else . . ."

"If only I'd been treated fairly . . ."

Maybe you've used those words. Maybe you have every right to use them. If such is the case, go to John's Gospel and read Jesus' words: "Human life comes from human parents, but spiritual life comes from the Spirit" (John 3:6).

WHEN GOD WHISPERS YOUR NAME

Have you retired your dreams? Are you rocking in the chair of regret? How can the words of John 3:6 help you get up out of that chair?

What Worship Does

You who fear the LORD, praise Him!

PSALM 22:23 NKJV

Worship humbles the smug and lifts the deflated.
Worship adjusts us, lowering the chin of the haughty, straightening the back of the burdened.

Worship properly positions the worshiper. And oh how we need it! We walk through life so bent out of shape. Five-talent folks swaggering: "I bet God's glad to have me." Two-talent folks struggling: "I bet God's sick of putting up with me." So sold on ourselves that we think someone died and made us ruler. Or so down on ourselves that we think everyone died and just left us.

Treat both conditions with worship.

CURE FOR THE COMMON LIFE

Why does worship humble the smug and lift the deflated?

Heed the Signals

Honor God and obey his commands,
because this is all people must do.

ECCLESIASTES 12:13

Here are some God-given, time-tested truths that define the way you should navigate your life. Observe them and enjoy secure passage. Ignore them and crash against the ragged rocks of reality.

- Love God more than you fear hell.

- Make major decisions in a cemetery.

- When no one is watching, live as if someone is.

- Succeed at home first.

- Don't spend tomorrow's money today.

- Pray twice as much as you fret.

- God has forgiven you; you'd be wise to do the same.

IN THE EYE OF THE STORM

Choose one of the "Laws of the Lighthouse" listed above and write how it relates to your life. How has it helped you?

_____

_____

_____

_____

_____

Just Be There

The person who shows mercy can stand without fear at the judgment.

JAMES 2:13

Nothing takes the place of your presence. Letters are nice. Phone calls are special, but being there in the flesh sends a message.

After Albert Einstein's wife died, his sister, Maja, moved in to assist with the household affairs. For fourteen years she cared for him, allowing his valuable research to continue. In 1950 she suffered a stroke and lapsed into a coma. Thereafter, Einstein spent two hours every afternoon reading aloud to her from Plato. She gave no sign of understanding his words, but he read anyway. If she understood anything by his gesture, she understood this—he believed that she was worth his time.

Do you believe in your kids? Then show up. Show up at their games. Show up at their plays. Do you believe in your friends? Then show up. Show up at their graduations and weddings. Spend time with them. You want to bring out the best in someone? Then show up.

A LOVE WORTH GIVING

Make a list of some people who need you to show up for them. Beside each write how you can spend time with that person.

_____

_____

_____

Lifting Heart and Hands

To the King that rules forever, who will never die, who cannot be seen, the only God, be honor and glory forever and ever.

1 TIMOTHY 1:17

The whole purpose of coming before the King is to praise him, to live in recognition of his splendor. Praise—lifting up our heart and hands, exulting with our voices, singing his praises—is the occupation of those who dwell in the kingdom.

Praise is the highest occupation of any being. What happens when we praise the Father? We reestablish the proper chain of command; we recognize that the King is on the throne and that he has saved his people.

WALKING WITH THE SAVIOR

Describe in your own words what happens when you praise the Father. How does this help you in your spiritual walk?

_____

_____

_____

_____

_____

_____

_____

_____

Failures Are Not Fatal

We must pay more careful attention . . .
to what we have heard, so that we do not drift away.

Hebrews 2:1 niv

I f you lose your faith, you will probably do so gradually. You will let a few days slip by without consulting your compass. Your sails will go untrimmed. Your rigging will go unprepared. And worst of all, you will forget to anchor your boat. And, before you know it, you'll be bouncing from wave to wave in stormy seas.

And unless you anchor deep, you could go down.

How do you anchor deep? Look at the verse again: "We must pay more careful attention . . . *to what we have heard.*"

The most reliable anchor points are not recent discoveries, but are time-tested truths that have held their ground against the winds of change. Truths like: My life is not futile. My failures are not fatal. My death is not final.

Attach your soul to these boulders and no wave is big enough to wash you under.

Six Hours One Friday

List some basic time-tested truths from the Word of God.

_____

_____

_____

_____

_____

What Size Is God?

"God can do all things."
MATTHEW 19:26

N ature is God's workshop. The sky is his resume. The universe is his calling card. You want to know who God is? See what he has done. You want to know his power? Take a look at his creation. Curious about his strength? Pay a visit to his home address: 1 Billion Starry Sky Avenue.

He is untainted by the atmosphere of sin, unbridled by the time line of history, unhindered by the weariness of the body.

What controls you doesn't control him. What troubles you doesn't trouble him. What fatigues you doesn't fatigue him. Is an eagle disturbed by traffic? No, he rises above it. Is the whale perturbed by a hurricane? Of course not, he plunges beneath it. Is the lion flustered by the mouse standing directly in his way? No, he steps over it.

How much more is God able to soar above, plunge beneath, and step over the troubles of the earth!

THE GREAT HOUSE OF GOD

How would you describe the power of God?

_____

_____

_____

_____

_____

_____

More Than Family

Each of us finds our meaning and function as a part of his body.
ROMANS 12:5 MSG

I f similar experiences create friendships, shouldn't the church overflow with friendships? With whom do you have more in common than fellow believers? Amazed by the same manger, stirred by the same Bible, saved by the same cross, and destined for the same home. Can you not echo the words of the psalmist? "I am a friend to everyone who fears you, to anyone who obeys your orders" (Psalm 119:63).

The church. More than family, we are friends. More than friends, we are family. God's family of friends.

CURE FOR THE COMMON LIFE

Describe how God's family of friends has been a positive influence in your life.

The Answer to Arguments

Get along with each other, and forgive each other.
If someone does wrong to you,
forgive that person because the Lord forgave you.

COLOSSIANS 3:13

Unity doesn't begin in examining others but in examining self. Unity begins not in demanding that others change, but in admitting that we aren't so perfect ourselves.

The answer to arguments? Acceptance. The first step to unity? Acceptance. Not agreement, acceptance. Not unanimity, acceptance. Not negotiation, arbitration, or elaboration. Those might come later but only after the first step, acceptance.

IN THE GRIP OF GRACE

Explain why acceptance is the first step to unity. Have you experienced this truth yourself? Why or why not?

_____

_____

_____

_____

_____

_____

_____

_____

_____

God Created All Things

By Him all things were created, both in the heavens and on earth,
visible and invisible, whether thrones or dominions or rulers or
authorities—all things have been created through Him and for Him.

COLOSSIANS 1:16 NASB

What a phenomenal list! Heavens and earth. Visible and invisible. Thrones, dominions, rulers, and authorities. No thing, place, or person omitted. The scale on the sea urchin. The hair on the elephant hide. The hurricane that wrecks the coast, the rain that nourishes the desert, the infant's first heartbeat, the elderly person's final breath—all can be traced back to the hand of Christ, the firstborn of creation.

Firstborn in Paul's vernacular has nothing to do with birth order. Firstborn refers to order of rank. As one translation states: "He ranks higher than everything that has been made" (v.15). Everything? Find an exception. Peter's mother-in-law has a fever; Jesus rebukes it. A tax needs to be paid; Jesus pays it by sending first a coin and then a fisherman's hook into the mouth of a fish. Jesus bats an eyelash, and nature jumps.

NEXT DOOR SAVIOR

What is your response to God's creative power?

_____

_____

_____

_____

Christ's Ultimate Aim

"He came to serve others and to
give his life as a ransom for many people."

MARK 10:45

One of the incredible abilities of Jesus was to stay on target. His life never got off track. He kept his life on course.

As Jesus looked across the horizon of his future, he could see many targets. Many flags were flapping in the wind, each of which he could have pursued. He could have been a political revolutionary. He could have been content to be a teacher and educate minds. But in the end he chose to be a Savior and save souls.

Anyone near Christ for any length of time heard it from Jesus himself. "The Son of Man came to find lost people and save them" (Luke 19:10). The heart of Christ was relentlessly focused on one task. The day he left the carpentry shop of Nazareth he had one ultimate aim—the cross of Calvary.

JUST LIKE JESUS

What is your ultimate aim in life? Is your heart focused on this task? Is Christ the center of your goal? If not, consider why he should be.

_____

_____

_____

_____

_____

Bow Before Him

*"God will always give what is right
to his people who cry to him night and day."*

LUKE 18:7

J esus tends to his sheep. And he will tend to you.

If you will let him. How? How do you let him? The steps are so simple.

First, go to him. David would trust his wounds to no other person but God. He said, "*You* anoint my head with oil" (Psalm 23:5 NKJV, emphasis mine). Not, "your prophets," "your teachers," or "your counselors."

Your second step is to assume the right posture. Bow before God.

In order to be anointed, the sheep must stand still, lower their heads, and let the Shepherd do his work. Peter urges us to "be humble under God's powerful hand so he will lift you up when the right time comes" (1 Peter 5:6).

When we come to God, we make requests; we don't make demands. We come with high hopes and a humble heart. We state what we want, but we pray for what is right.

We go to him. We bow before him, and we *trust in him*.

TRAVELING LIGHT

Why are we hesitant to let our Shepherd care for us?

_____

_____

_____

_____

Don't Be Troubled

The person who trusts in the LORD will be blessed.

JEREMIAH 17:7

Just prior to his crucifixion, [Jesus] told his disciples that he would be leaving them. "Where I am going you cannot follow now, but you will follow later" (John 13:36).

Such a statement was bound to stir some questions. Peter spoke for the others and asked, "Lord, why can't I follow you now?" (v. 37).

See if Jesus' reply doesn't reflect the tenderness of a parent to a child: "Don't let your hearts be troubled. Trust in God, and trust in me. There are many rooms in my Father's house; I would not tell you this it if were not true. I am going there to prepare a place for you. I will come back and take you to be with me so that you may be where I am" (John 14:1–3).

Reduce the paragraph to a sentence and it might read: "You do the trusting and I'll do the taking."

WHEN CHRIST COMES

"You do the trusting and I'll do the taking." What does that statement mean to you? How does this make a difference in your daily walk with God?

Consistent Inconsistencies

Strengthen yourselves so that you will
live here on earth doing what God wants.

1 PETER 4:2

I suspect the most consistent thing about life has to be its inconsistency.

It's this eerie inconsistency that keeps all of us, to one degree or another, living our lives on the edge of our chairs.

Yet, it was in this inconsistency that God had his finest hour. Never did the obscene come so close to the holy as it did on Calvary. Never did the good in the world so intertwine with the bad as it did on the cross.

God on a cross. Humanity at its worst. Divinity at its best.

God is not stumped by an evil world. He doesn't gasp in amazement at the depth of our faith or the depth of our failures. He knows the condition of the world . . . and loves it just the same. For just when we find a place where God would never be (like on a cross), we look again and there he is, in the flesh.

NO WONDER THEY CALL HIM THE SAVIOR

"God is not stumped by an evil world." How does that statement encourage you? Why?

_____

_____

_____

_____

No Fears at All

I am the LORD your God, who holds your right hand,
and I tell you, "Don't be afraid. I will help you."

ISAIAH 41:13

Could you use some courage? Are you backing down more than you are standing up? Jesus scattered the butterflies out of the stomachs of his nervous disciples.

We need to remember that the disciples were common men given a compelling task. Before they were the stained-glassed saints in the windows of cathedrals, they were somebody's next-door neighbors trying to make a living and raise a family. They weren't cut from theological cloth or raised on supernatural milk. But they were an ounce more devoted than they were afraid and, as a result, did some extraordinary things.

Earthly fears are no fears at all. Answer the big question of eternity, and the little questions of life fall into perspective.

THE APPLAUSE OF HEAVEN

Could you use some courage to overcome earthly fears? Write some promises from God's Word to encourage you.

_____

_____

_____

_____

_____

_____

God Wants Your List

Love does not keep a record of wrongs.

1 CORINTHIANS 13:5 TEV

Do you remember the story about the man who was bitten by the dog? When he learned the dog had rabies, he began making a list. The doctor told him there was no need to make a will, that rabies could be cured. "Oh, I'm not making a will," he replied. "I'm making a list of all the people I want to bite."

Couldn't we all make such a list? You've already learned, haven't you, that friends aren't always friendly? Neighbors aren't always neighborly? Some workers never work, and some bosses are always bossy?

You've already learned, haven't you, that a promise made is not always a promise kept? Even though they said "yes" on the altar, they may say "no" in the marriage.

You've already learned, haven't you, that we tend to fight back? To keep lists and snarl lips and growl at people we don't like?

God wants your list. He wants you to leave the list at the cross.

HE CHOSE THE NAILS

Why is it important to leave our list of hurts at the cross?

_____

_____

_____

_____

God Gives Rest

*"The teaching that I ask you to accept is easy;
the load I give you to carry is light."*

MATTHEW 11:30

P aul had an interesting observation about the way we treat people. He said it about marriage, but the principle applies in any relationship. "The man who loves his wife loves himself" (Ephesians 5:28). There is a correlation between the way you feel about yourself and the way you feel about others. If you are at peace with yourself—if you like yourself—you will get along with others.

The converse is also true. If you don't like yourself, if you are ashamed, embarrassed, or angry, other people are going to know it.

Which takes us to the question, "How does a person get relief?"

"Come to me, all of you who are tired and have heavy loads, and I will give you rest" (Matthew 11:28). Jesus says he is the solution for weariness of soul.

WHEN GOD WHISPERS YOUR NAME

How do you feel about yourself? Is this reflected in the way you feel about others?

_____

_____

_____

_____

Bending Low

Every knee will bow to the name of Jesus.

PHILIPPIANS 2:9–10

Servants resist stubbornness. Ulrich Zwingli manifested such a spirit. He promoted unity during Europe's great Reformation. At one point he found himself at odds with Martin Luther. Zwingli did not know what to do. He found his answer one morning on the side of a Swiss mountain. He watched two goats traversing a narrow path from opposite directions, one ascending, the other descending. At one point the narrow trail prevented them from passing each other. When they saw each other, they backed up and lowered their heads, as though ready to lunge. But then a wonderful thing happened. The ascending goat lay down on the path. The other stepped over his back. The first animal then arose and continued his climb to the top. Zwingli observed that the goat made it higher because he was willing to bend lower.

Didn't the same happen to Jesus? "God made his name greater than every other name so that every knee will bow to the name of Jesus."

CURE FOR THE COMMON LIFE

"Servants resist stubbornness." Explain what that means.

_____

_____

_____

_____

_____

He's Coming Back

Christ rose first; then when Christ comes back,
all his people will become alive again.

1 CORINTHIANS 15:23 TLB

God has made [a] promise to us. "I will come back . . . ," he assures us. Yes, the rocks will tumble. Yes, the ground will shake. But the child of God needn't fear—for the Father has promised to take us to be with him.

But dare we believe the promise? Dare we trust his loyalty? Isn't there a cautious part of us that wonders how reliable these words may be?

How can we know he will do what he said? How can we believe he will move the rocks and set us free?

Because he's already done it once.

WHEN CHRIST COMES

Explain how we can believe that Christ will come back as he promised. What has he already done to assure us?

_____

_____

_____

_____

_____

_____

_____

God Gives Hope

God will help you overflow with hope in him
through the Holy Spirit's power within you.

ROMANS 15:13 TLB

Heaven's hope does for your world what the sunlight did for my grandmother's cellar. I owe my love of peach preserves to her. She canned her own and stored them in an underground cellar near her West Texas house. It was a deep hole with wooden steps, plywood walls, and a musty smell. As a youngster I used to climb in, close the door, and see how long I could last in the darkness. I would sit silently, listening to my breath and heartbeats, until I couldn't take it anymore and then would race up the stairs and throw open the door. Light would avalanche into the cellar. What a change! Moments before I couldn't see anything—all of a sudden I could see everything.

Just as light poured into the cellar, God's hope pours into your world. Upon the sick, he shines the ray of healing. To the bereaved, he gives the promise of reunion. To the confused, he offers the light of Scripture.

TRAVELING LIGHT

Think of a time when God's light poured into your world.
What effect did this have on you?

_____

_____

_____

_____

August

*But grow in the grace and knowledge of
our Lord and Savior Jesus Christ.*

—2 Peter 3:18 niv

Nothing on Earth Satisfies

*We brought nothing into the world,
so we can take nothing out. But, if we have food
and clothes, we will be satisfied with that.*

1 TIMOTHY 6:7–8

Satisfied? That is one thing we are not. We are not satisfied.

We take a vacation of a lifetime. We satiate ourselves with sun, fun, and good food. But we are not even on the way home before we dread the end of the trip and begin planning another.

We are not satisfied.

As a child we say, "If only I were a teenager." As a teen we say, "If only I were an adult." As an adult, "If only I were married." As a spouse, "If only I had kids."

We are not satisfied. Contentment is a difficult virtue. Why?

Because there is nothing on earth that can satisfy our deepest longing. We long to see God. The leaves of life are rustling with the rumor that we will—and we won't be satisfied until we do.

WHEN GOD WHISPERS YOUR NAME

*What are some ways you are not satisfied? Will you ask
God to fill your voids with his spiritual peace?*

_____

_____

_____

_____

_____

He Did It for You

*All things are worth nothing compared
with the greatness of knowing Christ Jesus my Lord.*

PHILIPPIANS 3:8

Want to know the coolest thing about Christ's coming? Not that the One who hung the galaxies gave it up to hang doorjambs to the displeasure of a cranky client who wanted everything yesterday but couldn't pay for anything until tomorrow.

Not that he refused to defend himself when blamed for every sin of every slut and sailor since Adam.

Not even that after three days in a dark hole he stepped into the Easter sunrise with a smile and a swagger and a question for lowly Lucifer—"Is that your best punch?"

That was cool, incredibly cool.

But want to know the coolest thing about the One who gave up the crown of heaven for a crown of thorns? He did it for you. Just for you.

HE CHOSE THE NAILS

Christ died just for you. What does that say about his great love and grace?

_____

_____

_____

_____

_____

The Master Builder

*He restores my soul; He leads me in
the paths of righteousness for His name's sake.*

PSALM 23:3 NKJV

It's hard to see things grow old. The town in which I grew up is growing old. Some of the buildings are boarded up. Some of the houses are torn down. The old movie house where I took my dates has "For Sale" on the marquee.

I wish I could make it all new again. I wish I could blow the dust off the streets but I can't.

I can't. But God can. "He restores my soul," wrote the shepherd. He doesn't reform; he restores. He doesn't camouflage the old; he restores the new. The Master Builder will pull out the original plan and restore it. He will restore the vigor. He will restore the energy. He will restore the hope. He will restore the soul.

THE APPLAUSE OF HEAVEN

What is the difference between reforming something and restoring it? Explain how this difference is good news for believers.

God's Bottomless Well

*"If anyone believes in me, rivers of living water
will flow out from that person's heart."*

JOHN 7:38

Don't you need regular sips from God's reservoir? I do. In countless situations—stressful meetings, dull days, long drives, demanding trips—and many times a day, I step to the underground spring of God. There I receive anew his work for my sin and death, the energy of his Spirit, his lordship, and his love.

Drink with me from his bottomless **well**. You don't have to live with a dehydrated heart.

Receive Christ's *work* on the cross,
    the *energy* of his Spirit,
      his *lordship* over your life,
        his unending, unfailing *love*.

Drink deeply and often. And out of you will flow rivers of living water.

COME THIRSTY

Have you needed to drink from God's bottomless well lately? Describe how his work, energy, lordship, and love affect your life.

_____

_____

_____

_____

_____

A Raging Fire

Since God has shown us great mercy,
I beg you to offer your lives as a living sacrifice to him.

ROMANS 12:1

Resentment is the cocaine of the emotions. It causes our blood to pump and our energy level to rise. But, also like cocaine, it demands increasingly large and more frequent dosages. There is a dangerous point at which anger ceases to be an emotion and becomes a driving force. A person bent on revenge moves unknowingly further and further away from being able to forgive, for to be without the anger is to be without a source of energy.

Hatred is the rabid dog that turns on its owner.

Revenge is the raging fire that consumes the arsonist.

Bitterness is the trap that snares the hunter.

And mercy is the choice that can set them all free.

THE APPLAUSE OF HEAVEN

Write down some results of hatred, revenge, and bitterness that you have observed. How does mercy bring freedom from these results?

_____

_____

_____

_____

_____

Some Days Never Come

*If we love each other, God lives in us,
and his love is made perfect in us.*

1 John 4:12

Someday. The enemy of risky love is a snake whose tongue has mastered the talk of deception. "Someday," he hisses.

"Someday, I can take her on the cruise."

"Someday, I will have time to call and chat."

"Someday, the children will understand why I was so busy."

But you know the truth, don't you? You know even before I write it. You could say it better than I.

Some days never come. And the price of practicality is sometimes higher than extravagance. But the rewards of risky love are always greater than its cost.

Go to the effort. Invest the time. Write the letter. Make the apology. Take the trip. Purchase the gift. Do it. The seized opportunity renders joy. The neglected brings regret.

And the Angels Were Silent

Make a list of some things you have been putting off until another day. Do you want these to be sources of regret or joy?

_____

_____

_____

_____

_____

You Have Captured God's Heart

As a man rejoices over his new wife,
so your God will rejoice over you.

ISAIAH 62:5

Have you ever noticed the way a groom looks at his bride during the wedding? I have. Perhaps it's my vantage point. As the minister of the wedding, I'm positioned next to the groom.

If the light is just so and the angle just right, I can see a tiny reflection in his eyes. Her reflection. And the sight of her reminds him why he is here. His jaw relaxes and his forced smile softens. He forgets he's wearing a tux. He forgets his sweat-soaked shirt. When he sees her, any thought of escape becomes a joke again. For it's written all over his face, "Who could bear to live without this bride?"

And such are precisely the feelings of Jesus. Look long enough into the eyes of our Savior and, there, too, you will see a bride. Dressed in fine linen. Clothed in pure grace. She is the bride . . . walking toward him.

And who is this bride for whom Jesus longs? You are. You have captured the heart of God.

WHEN CHRIST COMES

God cannot bear to live without you. How do you respond to that thought?

_____

_____

_____

_____

Majestic Message

You will name him Jesus,
because he will save his people from their sins.

MATTHEW 1:21

Many of the names in the Bible that refer to our Lord are nothing less than palatial and august: Son of God, the Lamb of God, the Light of the World, the Resurrection and the Life, the Bright and Morning Star, He That Should Come, Alpha and Omega.

They are phrases that stretch the boundaries of human language in an effort to capture the uncapturable, the grandeur of God. And try as they might to draw as near as they may, they always fall short. Hearing them is somewhat like hearing a Salvation Army Christmas band on the street corner play Handel's *Messiah*. Good try, but it doesn't work. The message is too majestic for the medium.

And such it is with language. The phrase "There are no words to express . . ." is really the only one that can honestly be applied to God. No names do him justice.

GOD CAME NEAR

Write down the seven names of God mentioned above. Beside each, write how the name describes the grandeur of God.

_____

_____

_____

_____

_____

God's Plans

Enjoy serving the LORD, and he will give you what you want.

PSALM 37:4

When we submit to God's plans, we can trust our desires. Our assignment is found at the intersection of God's plan and our pleasures. *What do you love to do? What brings you joy? What gives you a sense of satisfaction?*

Some long to feed the poor. Others enjoy leading the church. Each of us has been made to serve God in a unique way.

The longings of your heart, then, are not incidental; they are critical messages. The desires of your heart are not to be ignored; they are to be consulted. As the wind turns the weather vane, so God uses your passions to turn your life. God is too gracious to ask you to do something you hate.

JUST LIKE JESUS

Consider the longings and desires of your heart. Are you nurturing them under God's guidance or have you ignored them? How can you find the intersection of God's plan and your desires?

_____

_____

_____

_____

_____

_____

The Prison of Want

"Life is not defined by what you have, even when you have a lot."
LUKE 12:15 MSG

Are you in prison? You are if you feel better when you have more and worse when you have less. You are if joy is one delivery away, one transfer away, one award away, or one makeover away. If your happiness comes from something you deposit, drive, drink, or digest, then face it—you are in prison, the prison of want.

That's the bad news. The good news is, you have a visitor. And your visitor has a message that can get you paroled. Make your way to the receiving room. Take your seat in the chair, and look across the table at the psalmist David. He motions for you to lean forward. "I have a secret to tell you," he whispers, "the secret of satisfaction. 'The LORD is my shepherd; I shall not want'" (Psalm 23:1 NKJV).

It's as if he is saying, "What I have in God is greater than what I don't have in life."

You think you and I could learn to say the same?

TRAVELING LIGHT

Explain why what we have in God is greater than anything we don't have in life.

_____

_____

_____

_____

_____

Our Problem Is Sin

Fix your attention on God.
You'll be changed from the inside out.

ROMANS 12:2 MSG

Real change is an inside job. You might alter things a day or two with money and systems, but the heart of the matter is, and always will be the matter of the heart.

Allow me to get specific. Our problem is sin. Not finances. Not budgets. Our problem is sin. We are in rebellion against our Creator. We are separated from our Father. We are cut off from the source of life. A new president or policy won't fix that. It can only be solved by God.

That's why the Bible uses drastic terms like *conversion, repentance,* and *lost* and *found.* Society may renovate, but only God re-creates.

WHEN GOD WHISPERS YOUR NAME

Our problem is sin and rebellion—problems that only God can solve. Explain how this happens. What are the results?

_____

_____

_____

_____

_____

_____

_____

Love Doesn't Boast

[Love] does not boast, it is not proud.

1 CORINTHIANS 13:4 NIV

The humble heart honors others.

Is Jesus not our example? Content to be known as a carpenter. Happy to be mistaken for the gardener. He served his followers by washing their feet. He serves us by doing the same. Each morning he gifts us with beauty. Each Sunday he calls us to his table. Each moment he dwells in our hearts. And does he not speak of the day when he as "the master will dress himself to serve and tell the servants to sit at the table, and he will serve them" (Luke 12:37)?

If Jesus is so willing to honor us, can we not do the same for others? Make people a priority. Accept your part in his plan. Be quick to share the applause. And, most of all, regard others as more important than yourself. Love does. For love "does not boast, it is not proud."

A LOVE WORTH GIVING

Do you make people a priority? Are you quick to share the applause? Why are these things important to God?

_____

_____

_____

_____

_____

Truth in Love

Your kingdom is built on what is right and fair.
Love and truth are in all you do.

PSALM 89:14

The single most difficult pursuit is truth and love.

That sentence is grammatically correct. I know every English teacher would like to pluralize it to read: The most difficult pursuits are those of truth and love. But that's not what I mean to say.

Love is a difficult pursuit.

Truth is a tough one too.

But put them together, pursue truth and love at the same time and hang on, baby, you're in for the ride of your life.

Love in truth. Truth in love. Never one at the expense of the other. Never the embrace of love without the torch of truth. Never the heat of truth without the warmth of love.

To pursue both is our singular task.

THE INSPIRATIONAL STUDY BIBLE

Why is the pursuit of love and truth so difficult?

_____

_____

_____

_____

_____

_____

An Undeserved Gift

*Many people received God's gift of life
by the grace of the one man, Jesus Christ.*

ROMANS 5:15

We take our free gift of salvation and try to earn it or diagnose it or pay for it instead of simply saying "thank you" and accepting it.

Ironic as it may appear, one of the hardest things to do is to be saved by grace. There's something in us that reacts to God's free gift. We have some weird compulsion to create laws, systems, and regulations that will make us "worthy" of our gift.

Why do we do that? The only reason I can figure is pride. To accept grace means to accept its necessity, and most folks don't like to do that. To accept grace also means that one realizes his despair, and most people aren't too keen on doing that either.

NO WONDER THEY CALL HIM THE SAVIOR

"To accept grace means to accept its necessity." Why is that so difficult for most folks to do?

_____

_____

_____

_____

_____

_____

Safe to Believe

When Jesus was raised from the dead
it was a signal of the end of death-as-the-end.

ROMANS 6:8 MSG

Don't you love that sentence? "It was a signal of the end of death-as-the-end." The resurrection is an exploding flare announcing to all sincere seekers that it is safe to believe. Safe to believe in ultimate justice. Safe to believe in eternal bodies. Safe to believe in heaven as our estate and the earth as its porch. Safe to believe in a time when questions won't keep us awake and pain won't keep us down. Safe to believe in open graves and endless days and genuine praise.

Because we can accept the resurrection story, it is safe to accept the rest of the story.

WHEN CHRIST COMES

The resurrection is the announcement to sincere seekers
that it is safe to believe in open graves and endless days.
Explain why. How does this affect your faith?

_____

_____

_____

_____

_____

_____

You Belong to Him

The love of God has been poured out in our hearts by the Holy Spirit.
ROMANS 5:5 NKJV

Deep within you, God's Spirit confirms with your spirit that you belong to him. Beneath the vitals of the heart, God's Spirit whispers, "You are mine. I bought you and sealed you, and no one can take you." The Spirit offers an inward, comforting witness.

He is like a father who walks hand in hand with his little child. The child knows he belongs to his daddy, his small hand happily lost in the large one. He feels no uncertainty about his papa's love. But suddenly the father, moved by some impulse, swings his boy up into the air and into his arms and says, "I love you, Son."

Has the relationship between the two changed? On one level, no. The father is no more the father than he was before the expression of love. But on a deeper level, yes. The dad drenched, showered, and saturated the boy in love. God's Spirit does the same with us. The Holy Spirit pours the love of God in our hearts.

COME THIRSTY

The Holy Spirit pours the love of God into our hearts.
Describe some differences this has made in your life.

_____

_____

_____

_____

The True Son of God

His followers went to him and woke him, saying, "Lord, save us!
We will drown!" Jesus answered, "Why are you afraid?"
MATTHEW 8:25–26

Read this verse: "Then those who were in the boat
worshiped him, saying, 'Truly you are the Son of God'"
(Matthew 14:33 NIV).

After the storm, [the disciples] worshiped him. They had never,
as a group, done that before. Never. Check it out. Open your Bible.
Search for a time when the disciples corporately praised him.

You won't find it.

You won't find them worshiping when he heals the leper.
Forgives the adulteress. Preaches to the masses. They were willing
to follow. Willing to leave family. Willing to cast out demons.
Willing to be in the army.

But only after the incident on the sea did they worship
him. Why?

Simple. This time they were the ones who were saved.

IN THE EYE OF THE STORM

Write a prayer of praise for what Christ has done in your life.

_____

_____

_____

_____

_____

He Took Our Place

Christ . . . changed places with us and put himself under that curse.
GALATIANS 3:13

While on the cross, Jesus felt the indignity and disgrace of a criminal. No, he was not guilty. No, he had not committed a sin. And, no, he did not deserve to be sentenced. But you and I were, we had, and we did. We were left with nothing to offer but a prayer.

"He changed places with us." He wore our sin so we could wear his righteousness.

Though we come to the cross dressed in sin, we leave the cross dressed in the "coat of his strong love" (Isaiah 59:17) and girded with a belt of "goodness and fairness" (Isaiah 11:5) and clothed in "garments of salvation" (Isaiah 61:10 NIV).

Indeed, we leave dressed in Christ himself. "You have all put on Christ as a garment" (Galatians 3:27 NEB).

HE CHOSE THE NAILS

We are dressed in Christ himself. Explain what that means.

_____

_____

_____

_____

_____

_____

_____

A Parent's Precious Prayers

All your children will be taught
by the LORD, and they will have much peace.

ISAIAH 54:13

Never underestimate the ponderings of a Christian parent. Never underestimate the power that comes when a parent pleads with God on behalf of a child. Who knows how many prayers are being answered right now because of the faithful ponderings of a parent ten or twenty years ago? God listens to thoughtful parents.

Praying for our children is a noble task. If what we are doing, in this fast-paced society, is taking us away from prayer time for our children, we're doing too much. There is nothing more special, more precious than time that a parent spends struggling and pondering with God on behalf of a child.

WALKING WITH THE SAVIOR

Do you take time to pray for your children or other family members? Why is it important that we not neglect these prayers?

It Defies Logic

"Here is my servant whom I have chosen. I love him."

MATTHEW 12:18

Those who saw Jesus—really saw him—knew there was something different. At his touch blind beggars saw. At his command crippled legs walked. At his embrace empty lives filled with vision.

He fed thousands with one basket. He stilled a storm with one command. He raised the dead with one proclamation. He changed lives with one request. He rerouted the history of the world with one life, lived in one country, was born in one manger, and died on one hill.

God did what we wouldn't dare dream. He did what we couldn't imagine. He became a man so we could trust him. He became a sacrifice so we could know him. And he defeated death so we could follow him.

It defies logic. It is a divine insanity. A holy incredibility.

Only a Creator beyond the fence of logic could offer such a gift of love.

AND THE ANGELS WERE SILENT

What words would you choose to describe the gift of God's Son?

To See the Unseen

He gives strength to those who are
tired and more power to those who are weak.

ISAIAH 40:29

An example of faith was found on the wall of a concentration camp. On it a prisoner had carved the words:

I believe in the sun, even though it doesn't shine,
I believe in love, even when it isn't shown,
I believe in God, even when he doesn't speak.

I try to imagine the person who etched those words. I try to envision his skeletal hand gripping the broken glass or stone that cut into the wall. I try to imagine his eyes squinting through the darkness as he carved each letter. What hand could have cut such a conviction? What eyes could have seen good in such horror?

There is only one answer: Eyes that chose to see the unseen.

HE STILL MOVES STONES

"Eyes that chose to see the unseen." Explain what that phrase means. In what sense is this the basis of Christian faith?

_____

_____

_____

_____

_____

You Have to Choose

*I" am the way, and the truth, and
the life. The only way to the Father is through me."*

John 14:6

The definitive voice in the universe is Jesus.

He leaves us with two options. Accept him as God, or reject him. There is no third alternative.

Oh, but we try to create one. Suppose I did the same? Suppose you came across me standing on the side of the road. I can go north or south. You ask me which way I'm going. My reply? "I'm going sorth."

Thinking you didn't hear correctly, you ask me to repeat the answer.

"I'm going sorth. I can't choose between north and south, so I'm going both. I'm going sorth."

"You can't do that," you reply. "You have to choose."

"Okay," I concede, "I'll head nouth."

"Nouth is not an option!" you insist. "It's either north or south. You gotta pick."

When it comes to Christ, you've got to do the same.

Next Door Savior

Why is there no alternative to choosing or rejecting Christ?

_____

_____

_____

_____

Infinite Patience

Patience produces character, and character produces hope.
And this hope will never disappoint us.

ROMANS 5:4–5

G od is often more patient with us than we are with ourselves. We assume that if we fall, we aren't born again. If we stumble, then we aren't truly converted. If we have the old desires, then we must not be a new creation.

If you are anxious about this, please remember, "God began doing a good work in you, and I am sure he will continue it until it is finished when Jesus Christ comes again" (Philippians 1:6).

A GENTLE THUNDER

When you stumble in your walk with Christ, do you question your relationship with him? What promises from God's Word can give you assurance of your salvation?

_____

_____

_____

_____

_____

_____

_____

_____

_____

Loving Forgetfulness

*"I will forgive their iniquity,
and their sin I will remember no more."*

JEREMIAH 31:34 NKJV

To love conditionally is against God's nature. Just as it's against your nature to eat trees and against mine to grow wings, it's against God's nature to remember forgiven sins.

You see, God is either the God of perfect grace . . . or he is not God. Grace forgets. Period. He who is perfect love cannot hold grudges. If he does, then he isn't perfect love. And if he isn't perfect love, you might as well put this book down and go fishing, because both of us are chasing fairy tales.

But I believe in his loving forgetfulness. And I believe he has a graciously terrible memory.

GOD CAME NEAR

God has a graciously terrible memory. Explain why that is such good news.

_____

_____

_____

_____

_____

_____

Give God Your Worries

When I kept things to myself, I felt weak deep inside me.
PSALM 32:3

Ask yourself two questions:

Is there any unconfessed sin in my life?

Confession is telling God you did the thing he saw you do. He doesn't need to hear it as much as you need to say it. Whether it's too small to be mentioned or too big to be forgiven isn't yours to decide. Your task is to be honest.

Are there any unsurrendered worries in my heart?

"Give all your worries to him, because he cares about you" (1 Peter 5:7).

The German word for *worry* means "to strangle." The Greek word means "to divide the mind." Both are accurate. Worry is a noose on the neck and a distraction of the mind, neither of which is befitting for joy.

WHEN GOD WHISPERS YOUR NAME

Why it is important to be totally honest with God about your sins and your worries?

_____

_____

_____

_____

_____

_____

Choosing to Be Content

I have learned in whatever state I am, to be content.

Philippians 4:11 NKJV

In his book *Money: A User's Manual*, Bob Russell describes a farmer who once grew discontent with his farm. He griped about the lake on his property always needing to be stocked and managed. And those fat cows lumbered through his pasture. All the fencing and feeding—what a headache!

He called a realtor and made plans to list the farm. A few days later the agent phoned, wanting approval for the advertisement she intended to place in the local paper. She read the ad to the farmer. It described a lovely farm in an ideal location—quiet and peaceful, contoured with rolling hills, carpeted with soft meadows, nourished by a fresh lake, and blessed with well-bred livestock. The farmer said, "Read that ad to me again."

After hearing it a second time, he decided, "I've changed my mind. I'm not going to sell. I've been looking for a place like that all my life."

Cure for the Common Life

How can looking at life or circumstances from a different perspective renew your contentment?

What Are Your Strengths?

We all have different gifts,
each of which came because of the grace God gave us.

ROMANS 12:6

There are some things we want to do but simply aren't equipped to accomplish. I, for example, have the desire to sing. Singing for others would give me wonderful satisfaction. The problem is, it wouldn't give the same satisfaction to my audience.

Paul gives good advice in Romans 12:3: "Have a sane estimate of your capabilities" (PHILLIPS).

In other words, be aware of your strengths. When you teach, do people listen? When you lead, do people follow? When you administer, do things improve? Where are you most productive? Identify your strengths, and then major in them. Failing to focus on our strengths may prevent us from accomplishing the unique tasks God has called us to do.

JUST LIKE JESUS

Are you aware of your strengths? Explain how failing to focus on your strengths can prevent you from accomplishing the unique task God has called you to do.

_____

_____

_____

_____

_____

A Real Friend

A real friend will be more loyal than a brother.

PROVERBS 18:24

To others, Jesus was a miracle worker. To others, Jesus was a master teacher. To others, Jesus was the hope of Israel. But to John, he was all of these and more. To John, Jesus was a friend.

You don't abandon a friend—not even when that friend is dead. John stayed close to Jesus.

He had a habit of doing this. He was close to Jesus in the Upper Room. He was close to Jesus in the Garden of Gethsemane. He was at the foot of the cross at the crucifixion, and he was a quick walk from the tomb at the burial.

Did he understand Jesus? No.

Was he glad Jesus did what he did? No.

But did he leave Jesus? No.

What about you?

HE CHOSE THE NAILS

What does it mean to be a friend of Jesus?

_____

_____

_____

_____

_____

The Temple of God's Spirit

*You should know that your body is a temple for
the Holy Spirit who is in you. You have received the Holy Spirit
from God. So you do not belong to yourselves.*

1 CORINTHIANS 6:19

Y ou will live forever in this body. It will be different, mind
you. What is now crooked will be straightened. What is
now faulty will be fixed. Your body will be different, but
you won't have a different body. You will have this one. Does that
change the view you have of it? I hope so.

God has a high regard for your body. You should as well.
Respect it. I did not say worship it. But I did say respect it. It is, after
all, the temple of God. Be careful how you feed it, use it, and
maintain it. You wouldn't want anyone trashing your home; God
doesn't want anyone trashing his. After all, it is his, isn't it?

WHEN CHRIST COMES

*Do you take care of your body? Make a list of the ways you
treat your body well and another list of ways you could take
better care of your body.*

_____

_____

_____

_____

_____

_____

Headed Home

We are waiting for God to finish making us his
own children, which means our bodies will be made free.

ROMANS 8:23

Aging is God's idea. It's one of the ways he keeps us headed homeward. We can't change the process, but we can change our attitude. Here is a thought. What if we looked at the aging body as we look at the growth of a tulip?

Do you ever see anyone mourning over the passing of the tulip bulb? Do gardeners weep as the bulb begins to weaken? Of course not. We don't purchase tulip girdles or petal wrinkle cream or consult plastic-leaf surgeons. We don't mourn the passing of the bulb; we celebrate it. Tulip lovers rejoice the minute the bulb weakens. "Watch that one," they say. "It's about to blossom."

Could it be heaven does the same? The angels point to our bodies. The more frail we become, the more excited they become. "Watch that lady in the hospital," they say. "She's about to blossom." "Keep an eye on the fellow with the bad heart. He'll be coming home soon."

TRAVELING LIGHT

How does our culture promote a negative view of aging?
How does this contrast with God's view of aging?

_____

_____

_____

_____

God Sees Our Value

*"God does not see the same way people see. People look
at the outside of a person, but the LORD looks at the heart."*

1 SAMUEL 16:7

God sees us with the eyes of a Father. He sees our defects, errors, and blemishes. But he also sees our value.

What did Jesus know that enabled him to do what he did?

Here's part of the answer. He knew the value of people. He knew that each human being is a treasure. And because he did, people were not a source of stress but a source of joy.

IN THE EYE OF THE STORM

What can you do to see others more with God's eyes?

_____

_____

_____

_____

_____

_____

_____

_____

_____

_____

_____

God's View of Your Life

You are my place of safety and protection.
You are my God and I trust you.

PSALM 91:2

Have bad things *really* happened to you? You and God may have different definitions for the word *bad*. Parents and children do. Look up the word *bad* in a middle schooler's dictionary, and you'll read definitions such as "pimple on nose," or "pop quiz in geometry." "Dad, this is really bad!" the youngster says. Dad, having been around the block a time or two, thinks differently. Pimples pass.

What you and I might rate as an absolute disaster, God may rate as a pimple-level problem that will pass. He views your life the way you view a movie after you've read the book. When something bad happens, you feel the air sucked out of the theater. Everyone else gasps at the crisis on the screen. Not you. Why? You've read the book. You know how the good guy gets out of the tight spot. God views your life with the same confidence. He's not only read your story . . . he wrote it.

COME THIRSTY

God has written the story of your life. How does this affect your attitudes about life? The choices you make in life?

_____

_____

_____

_____

Spiritual Bankruptcy

*God will show his mercy forever and
ever to those who worship and serve him.*

Luke 1:50

God does not save us because of what we've done. Only a puny god could be bought with tithes. Only an egotistical god would be impressed with our pain. Only a temperamental god could be satisfied by sacrifices. Only a heartless god would sell salvation to the highest bidders.

And only a great God does for his children what they can't do for themselves.

God's delight is received upon surrender, not awarded upon conquest. The first step to joy is a plea for help, an acknowledgment of moral destitution, an admission of inward paucity. Those who taste God's presence have declared spiritual bankruptcy and are aware of their spiritual crisis. Their pockets are empty. Their options are gone. They have long since stopped demanding justice; they are pleading for mercy.

The Applause of Heaven

Why must we come to God with "empty pockets"? Explain why we have to stop demanding justice and start pleading for mercy.

_____

_____

_____

_____

One Church, One Faith

*"Holy Father, keep through Your name those whom
You have given Me, that they may be one as We are."*

JOHN 17:11 NKJV

"May they all be one," Jesus prayed.

One. Not one in groups of two thousand. But one in One. One church. One faith. One Lord. Not Baptist, not Methodist, not Adventist. Just Christians. No denominations. No hierarchies. No traditions. Just Christ.

Too idealistic? Impossible to achieve? I don't think so. Harder things have been done, you know. For example, once upon a tree, a Creator gave his life for his creation. Maybe all we need are a few hearts that are willing to follow suit.

What about you? Can you build a bridge? Toss a rope? Span a chasm? Pray for oneness?

NO WONDER THEY CALL HIM THE SAVIOR

*Why is the unity of God's church so important to him?
To the message of Christ's love?*

Look for His Likeness

*He will keep his agreement of love for a thousand lifetimes
for people who love him and obey his commands.*

DEUTERONOMY 7:9

We are God's idea. We are his. His face. His eyes. His hands. His touch. We are him. Look deeply into the face of every human being on earth, and you will see his likeness. Though some appear to be distant relatives, they are not. God has no cousins, only children.

We are, incredibly, the body of Christ. And though we may not act like our Father, there is no greater truth than this: We are his. Unalterably. He loves us. Undyingly. Nothing can separate us from the love of Christ (Romans 8:38–39).

A GENTLE THUNDER

"Nothing can separate us from the love of Christ." What does this promise mean to you? What difference has it made in your life?

_____

_____

_____

_____

_____

_____

_____

Store Up the Sweet

Whatever is true, whatever is honorable, . . .
if there is anything worthy of praise, think about these things.

PHILIPPIANS 4:8 RSV

Change the thoughts, and you change the person. If today's thoughts are tomorrow's actions, what happens when we fill our minds with thoughts of God's love? Will standing beneath the downpour of his grace change the way we feel about others?

Paul says absolutely! It's not enough to keep the bad stuff out. We've got to let the good stuff in. It's not enough to keep no list of wrongs. We have to cultivate a list of blessings: "Whatever is true, whatever is honorable, whatever is just, whatever is pure, whatever is lovely, whatever is gracious, if there is any excellence, if there is anything worthy of praise, think about these things" (Philipians 4:8 RSV). *Thinking* conveys the idea of pondering—studying and focusing, allowing what is viewed to have an impact on us.

Rather than store up the sour, store up the sweet.

A LOVE WORTH GIVING

Make a list of blessings God has poured into your life this week. Use that list to fill your mind with good thoughts.

A Place of Permanence

The LORD will always lead you.

ISAIAH 58:11

You've been there. You've escaped the sandy foundations of the valley and ascended his grand outcropping of granite. You've turned your back on the noise and sought his voice. You've stepped away from the masses and followed the Master as he led you up the winding path to the summit.

Gently your Guide invites you to sit on the rock above the tree line and look out with him at the ancient peaks that will never erode. "What is necessary is still what is sure," he confides. "Just remember:

"You'll go nowhere tomorrow that I haven't already been.

"Truth will still triumph.

"The victory is yours."

The sacred summit. A place of permanence in a world of transition.

THE APPLAUSE OF HEAVEN

You can go nowhere tomorrow that Christ has not already been. What does that mean to you? How do you respond to that promise?

I WALK UP THE PATH TO JESUS. HE
DOES NOT FOLLOW ME.
HE WILL LEAD ME FROM THE MASSES,
MEANING AWAY FROM THE TRIVIAL
& BENIGN = THE SUMMIT IS A CLEAR
VIEW AWAY FROM THAT 2017

Known for Humility

Don't cherish exaggerated ideas of yourself or your importance.

ROMANS 12:3 PHILLIPS

The mightiest of the saints were known for their humility. Though Moses had served as prince of Egypt and emancipator of the slaves, the Bible says, "Moses was . . . more humble than anyone else" (Numbers 12:3 NIV).

The apostle Paul was saved through a personal visit from Jesus. He was carried into the heavens and had the ability to raise the dead. But when he introduced himself, he mentioned none of these. He simply said, "I, Paul, am God's slave" (Titus 1:1 MSG).

John the Baptist was a blood relative of Jesus and the first evangelist in history, but he is remembered in Scripture as the one who resolved, "He must increase, but I must decrease" (John 3:30 NKJV).

TRAVELING LIGHT

Can you name other saints of God who could have boasted of themselves but instead chose to boast of God? How can these people serve as examples for us?

_____

_____

_____

_____

_____

Four Habits Worth Having

*But grow in the grace and knowledge of our
Lord and Savior Jesus Christ.*

2 Peter 3:18 NIV

G rowth is the goal of the Christian. Maturity is mandatory. If a child ceased to develop, the parent would be concerned, right?

When a Christian stops growing, help is needed. If you are the same Christian you were a few months ago, be careful. You might be wise to get a checkup. Not on your body, but on your heart. Not a physical, but a spiritual.

May I suggest one?

Why don't you check your habits? Make these four habits regular activities and see what happens.

First, the habit of prayer. Second, the habit of study. Third, the habit of giving. And last of all, the habit of fellowship.

When God Whispers Your Name

Are the four habits (prayer, study, giving, and fellowship) a part of your daily life? List ways you can improve in each.

Nothing to Offer

LORD, I call to you. . . . Listen to me when I call to you.

PSALM 141:1

Nicodemus came to Jesus in the middle of the night. The centurion came in the middle of the day. The leper and the sinful woman appeared in the middle of crowds. Zacchaeus appeared in the middle of a tree. Matthew had a party for him.

The educated. The powerful. The rejected. The sick. The lonely. The wealthy. Who would have ever assembled such a crew? All they had in common were their empty hope chests, long left vacant by charlatans and profiteers. Though they had nothing to offer, they asked for everything: a new birth, a second chance, a fresh start, a clean conscience. And without exception their requests were honored.

SIX HOURS ONE FRIDAY

Think of people you know who have come to Jesus with nothing to offer. What did he give in return?

A Focus to Life

Work as if you were doing it for the Lord, not for people.

COLOSSIANS 3:23

When do we get our first clue that [Jesus] knows he is the Son of God? In the temple of Jerusalem. He is twelve years old. His parents are three days into the return trip to Nazareth before they notice he is missing. They find him in the temple studying with the leaders.

As a young boy, Jesus already senses the call of God. But what does he do next? Recruit apostles and preach sermons and perform miracles? No, he goes home to his folks and learns the family business.

That is exactly what you should do. Want to bring focus to your life? Do what Jesus did. Go home, love your family, and take care of business. *But Max, I want to be a missionary.* Your first mission field is under your roof. What makes you think they'll believe you overseas if they don't believe you across the hall?

JUST LIKE JESUS

"Your first mission field is under your roof." Explain what that statement means. Do you have the right focus in your life?

Honest Worship

Take your everyday, ordinary life . . .
and place it before God as an offering.

ROMANS 12:1 MSG

Honest worship lifts eyes off self and sets them on God. Scripture's best-known worship leader wrote: "Give honor to the LORD, you angels; give honor to the LORD for his glory and strength. Give honor to the LORD for the glory of his name. Worship the LORD in the splendor of his holiness" (Psalm 29:1–2 NLT).

Worship gives God honor, offers him standing ovations.

We can make a big deal about God on Sundays with our songs and on Mondays with our strengths. Every day in every deed. Each time we do our best to thank God for giving his, we worship. "Take your everyday, ordinary life—your sleeping, eating, going-to-work, and walking-around life—and place it before God as an offering" (Romans 12:1 MSG). Worship places God on center stage and us in proper posture.

CURE FOR THE COMMON LIFE

Every day in every deed you can make a big deal about God. Write some examples of how you can do this.

_____

_____

_____

_____

God Is on Our Team

When I was helpless, he saved me.

PSALM 116:6

As youngsters, we neighborhood kids would play street football. The minute we got home from school we'd drop the books and hit the pavement. The kid across the street had a dad with a great arm and a strong addiction to football. As soon as he'd pull in the driveway from work we'd start yelling for him to come and play ball. He couldn't resist. Out of fairness he'd always ask, "Which team is losing?" Then he would join that team, which often seemed to be mine.

His appearance in the huddle changed the whole ball game. He was confident, strong, and most of all, he had a plan. We'd circle around him, and he'd look at us and say, "Okay boys, here is what we are going to do." The other side was groaning before we left the huddle. You see, we not only had a new plan, we had a new leader.

He brought new life to our team. God does precisely the same. We didn't need a new play; we needed a new plan. We didn't need to trade positions; we needed a new player. That player is Jesus Christ, God's firstborn Son.

IN THE GRIP OF GRACE

What does Christ bring to your team?

_____

_____

_____

_____

A Positive Power

Death and life are in the power of the tongue.

PROVERBS 18:21 NKJV

Nathaniel Hawthorne came home heartbroken. He'd just been fired from his job in the custom house. His wife, rather than responding with anxiety, surprised him with joy. "Now you can write your book!"

He wasn't so positive. "And what shall we live on while I'm writing it?"

To his amazement she opened a drawer and revealed a wad of money she'd saved out of her housekeeping budget. "I always knew you were a man of genius," she told him. "I always knew you'd write a masterpiece."

She believed in her husband. And because she did, he wrote. And because he wrote, every library in America has a copy of *The Scarlet Letter* by Nathaniel Hawthorne.

You have the power to change someone's life simply by the words that you speak. "Death and life are in the power of the tongue."

A LOVE WORTH GIVING

Describe a time when someone spoke positive words that changed your life.

Perfected

Their sins and the evil things
they do—I will not remember anymore.

HEBREWS 10:17

W ith one sacrifice he made perfect forever those who are being made holy" (Hebrews 10:14).

Underline the word *perfect*. Note that the word is not *better*. Not *improving*. Not *on the upswing*. God doesn't improve; he perfects. He doesn't enhance; he completes.

Now I realize that there's a sense in which we're imperfect. We still err. We still stumble. We still do exactly what we don't want to do. And that part of us is, according to the verse, "being made holy."

But when it comes to our position before God, we're perfect. When he sees each of us, he sees one who has been made perfect through the One who is perfect—Jesus Christ.

IN THE EYE OF THE STORM

When God sees us, he sees us as perfect through Christ.
Explain what that means. How does this affect your
relationship with God?

_____

_____

_____

_____

_____

_____

Simplify Your Faith

"You have only one Master, the Christ."

MATTHEW 23:10

There are some who position themselves between you and God. There are some who suggest the only way to get to God is through them. There is the great teacher who has the final word on Bible teaching. There is the father who must bless your acts. There is the spiritual master who will tell you what God wants you to do. Jesus' message for complicated religion is to remove these middlemen. "You have only one Master, the Christ."

He's not saying that you don't need teachers, elders, or counselors. He is saying, however, that we are all brothers and sisters and have equal access to the Father. Simplify your faith by seeking God for yourself. No confusing ceremonies necessary. No mysterious rituals required. No elaborate channels of command or levels of access.

You have a Bible? You can study. You have a heart? You can pray. You have a mind? You can think.

AND THE ANGELS WERE SILENT

You can seek God for yourself without any other person or ritual. Describe some of the advantages of this great gift.

Set Apart

*The Spirit produces the fruit of love, joy, peace,
patience, kindness, goodness, faithfulness, gentleness, self-control.*
GALATIANS 5:22–23

In the third century, St. Cyprian wrote to a friend named Donatus:

"This seems a cheerful world, Donatus, when I view it from this fair garden. But if I climbed some great mountain and looked out . . . you know very well what I would see; brigands on the high road, pirates on the seas, in the amphitheaters men murdered to please the applauding crowds.

Yet in the midst of it, I have found a quiet and holy people. They are despised and persecuted, but they care not. They have overcome the world. These people, Donatus, are Christians."

What a compliment! *A quiet and holy people.*

Quiet. Not obnoxious. Not boastful. Not demanding. Just quiet.

Holy. Set apart. Pure. Decent. Honest. Wholesome.

THE INSPIRATIONAL STUDY BIBLE

Quiet. Holy. Pure. Decent. Honest. Wholesome. What adjectives would you add to that list?

_____

_____

_____

_____

God's Poetry

We are His workmanship.

EPHESIANS 2:10 NKJV

Scripture calls the church a poem. "We are His workmanship" (Ephesians 2:10). *Workmanship* descends from the Greek word *poeo* or *poetry*. We are God's poetry! What Longfellow did with pen and paper, our Maker does with us. We express his creative best.

You aren't God's poetry. I'm not God's poetry. *We* are God's poetry. Poetry demands variety. "God works through different men in different ways, but it is the same God who achieves his purposes through them all" (1 Corinthians 12:6 PHILLIPS). God uses all types to type his message. Logical thinkers. Emotional worshipers. Dynamic leaders. Docile followers. The visionaries who lead, the studious who ponder, the generous who pay the bills. Alone, we are meaningless symbols on a page. But collectively, we inspire.

CURE FOR THE COMMON LIFE

"Alone, we are meaningless symbols on a page. But collectively, we inspire." Describe ways you have experienced this in your life.

_____

_____

_____

_____

_____

Rescued by Heaven

*"I tell you the truth, whoever hears what I say
and believes in the One who sent me has eternal life."*

JOHN 5:24

When you recognize God as Creator, you will admire him. When you recognize his wisdom, you will learn from him. When you discover his strength, you will rely on him. But only when he saves you will you worship him.

It's a "before and after" scenario. Before your rescue, you could easily keep God at a distance. Sure he was important, but so was your career. Your status. Your salary.

Then came the storm . . . the rage . . . the fight . . . the ripped moorings. Despair fell like a fog; your bearings were gone. In your heart, you knew there was no exit.

Turn to your career for help? Only if you want to hide from the storm . . . not escape it. Lean on your status for strength? A storm isn't impressed with your title.

Suddenly you are left with one option: God.

IN THE EYE OF THE STORM

Do you remember a time when you finally realized that God was the one option? Describe how you came to that conclusion.

_____

_____

_____

_____

The Christ of Your Mondays

I can do all things through Christ who strengthens me.

PHILIPPIANS 4:13 NKJV

Stand and consider:

- The Hubble Space Telescope sends back infrared images of faint galaxies that are perhaps twelve billion light-years away (twelve billion times six trillion miles).
- Astronomers venture a feeble estimate that the number of stars in the universe equals the number of grains of sand on all the beaches of the world.
- The star Betelgeuse has a diameter of 100 million miles, which is larger than the earth's orbit around the sun.

Why the immensity? Why such vast, unmeasured, unexplored, "unused" space? So that you and I, freshly stunned, could be stirred by this resolve: "I can do all things through Christ who strengthens me." The Christ of the galaxies is the Christ of your Mondays.

NEXT DOOR SAVIOR

How does it encourage you to know that the Christ of the galaxies is the Christ of your Mondays?

Let the Redeemed Say So

You have begun to live the new life, in which you are being made new and are becoming like the One who made you.

COLOSSIANS 3:10

I wonder if Jesus doesn't muster up a slight smile as he sees his lost sheep come straggling into the fold—the beaten, broken, dirty sheep who stands at the door looking up at the Shepherd, asking, "Can I come in? I don't deserve it, but is there room in your kingdom for one more?" The Shepherd looks down at the sheep and says, "Come in, this is your home."

Salvation is the process that's done, that's secure, that no one can take away from you. Sanctification is the lifelong process of being changed from one degree of glory to the next, growing in Christ, putting away the old, taking on the new.

The psalmist David would tell us that those who have been redeemed will say so! If we're not saying so, perhaps it's because we've forgotten what it is like to be redeemed. Let the redeemed of the earth say so!

WALKING WITH THE SAVIOR

Describe how you have put away the old and taken on the new.

_____

_____

_____

_____

_____

_____

He Cares About You

Anyone who is having troubles should pray.

JAMES 5:13

Have you taken your disappointments to God? You've shared them with your neighbor, your relatives, your friends. But have you taken them to God? James says, "Anyone who is having troubles should pray" (James 5:13).

Before you go anywhere else with your disappointments, go to God.

Maybe you don't want to trouble God with your hurts. *After all, he's got famines and pestilence and wars; he won't care about my little struggles,* you think. Why don't you let him decide that? He cared enough about a wedding to provide the wine. He cared enough about Peter's tax payment to give him a coin. He cared enough about the woman at the well to give her answers. "He cares about you" (1 Peter 5:7).

TRAVELING LIGHT

Do you sometimes think that God is too busy running the world to be concerned with your struggles? How does this affect your confidence in him?

God Energizes Our Efforts

*We proclaim him, admonishing and teaching everyone
with all wisdom, so that we may present everyone perfect in Christ.
To this end I labor, struggling with all his energy,
which so powerfully works in me.*

COLOSSIANS 1:28–29 NIV

L ook at Paul's aim, *to present everyone perfect in Christ.* Paul dreamed of the day each person would be safe in Christ. What was his method? *Counseling and teaching.* Paul's tools? Verbs. Nouns. Sentences. Lessons. The same equipment you and I have.

Was it easier then than now? Don't think so. Paul called it work. *To this end I labor,* he wrote. Labor means work. Work means homes visited, people taught, classes prepared.

How did he do it? What was his source of strength? He worked with *all the energy he so powerfully works in me.*

As Paul worked, so did God. And as you work, so does the Father.

WHEN GOD WHISPERS YOUR NAME

*Do you have opportunities to labor for Christ? Explain how God
will accomplish this work by his strength, not yours.*

_____

_____

_____

_____

_____

Run to Him!

His love has taken over our lives; GOD's faithful ways are eternal.
PSALM 117:2 MSG

God's love for you is not dependent on how you look, how you think, how you act, or how perfect you are. His love is absolutely nonnegotiable and nonreturnable. Ours is a faithful God.

No matter what you do, no matter how far you fall, no matter how ugly you become, God has a relentless, undying, unfathomable, unquenchable love from which you cannot be separated. Ever!

Run to Jesus. Jesus wants you to go to him. He wants to become the most important person in your life, the greatest love you'll ever know. He wants you to love him so much that there's no room in your heart and in your life for sin. Invite him to take up residence in your heart.

THE INSPIRATIONAL STUDY BIBLE

God's love is absolutely nonnegotiable and nonreturnable. Explain why that is such good news.

_____

_____

_____

_____

_____

God Knows What's Best

Trust the LORD with all your heart,
and don't depend on your own understanding.

PROVERBS 3:5

The problem with this world is that it doesn't fit. Oh, it will do for now, but it isn't tailor-made. We were made to live with God, but on earth we live by faith. We were made to live forever, but on this earth we live but for a moment.

We must trust God. We must trust not only that he does what is best but that he knows what is ahead. Ponder the words of Isaiah 57:1–2: "The good men perish; the godly die before their time and no one seems to care or wonder why. No one seems to realize that God is taking them away from the evil days ahead. For the godly who die shall rest in peace" (TLB).

My, what a thought. God is taking them away from the evil days ahead. Could death be God's grace? Could the funeral wreath be God's safety ring? As horrible as the grave may be, could it be God's protection from the future?

"Trust in God," Jesus urges, "and trust in me" (John 14:1).

A GENTLE THUNDER

We must trust not only that God does what is best but that he knows what is ahead. Describe what that means to you.

_____

_____

_____

_____

Working to Please God

Work as if you were serving the Lord,
not as if you were serving only men and women.

EPHESIANS 6:7

What if everyone worked with God in mind? Suppose no one worked to satisfy self or please the bottom line but everyone worked to please God.

Many occupations would instantly cease: drug trafficking, thievery, prostitution, nightclub and casino management. Certain careers, by their nature, cannot please God. These would cease.

Certain behaviors would cease as well. If I'm repairing a car for God, I'm not going to overcharge his children. If I'm painting a wall for God, you think I'm going to use paint thinner?

Imagine if everyone worked for the audience of One. Every nurse, thoughtful. Every officer, careful. Every professor, insightful. Every salesperson, delightful. Every teacher, hopeful. Every lawyer, skillful.

Impossible? Not entirely. All we need is someone to start a worldwide revolution. Might as well be us.

CURE FOR THE COMMON LIFE

Do you work for an audience of One? What difference does this make in the way you work?

Changed to His Likeness

By his power to rule all things, he will change our simple bodies and make them like his own glorious body.

What do we know about our resurrected bodies? They will be unlike any we have ever imagined.

Will we look so different that we aren't instantly recognized? PerhaPsalm (We may need nametags.) Will we be walking through walls? Chances are we'll be doing much more.

Will we still bear the scars from the pain of life? The marks of war. The disfigurements of disease. The wounds of violence. Will these remain on our bodies? That is a very good question. Jesus, at least for forty days, kept his. Will we keep ours? On this issue, we have only opinions, but my opinion is that we won't. Peter tells us that "by his wounds you have been healed" (1 Peter 2:24 NIV). In heaven's accounting, only one wound is worthy to be remembered. And that is the wound of Jesus. Our wounds will be no more.

WHEN CHRIST COMES

Only one wound is worthy to be remembered. And that is the wound of Jesus. What does that statement mean?

_____

_____

_____

_____

Filled to Overflowing

My cup overflows with blessings.

PSALM 23:5 NLT

The overflowing cup was a powerful symbol in the days of David. Hosts in the ancient East used it to send a message to the guest. As long as the cup was kept full, the guest knew he was welcome. But when the cup sat empty, the host was hinting that the hour was late. On those occasions, however, when the host really enjoyed the company of the person, he filled the cup to overflowing. He didn't stop when the wine reached the rim; he kept pouring until the liquid ran over the edge of the cup and down on the table.

Have you noticed how wet your table is? God wants you to stay. Your cup overflows with joy. Overflows with grace.

You have a place at God's table. And he is filling your cup to overflowing.

TRAVELING LIGHT

Make a list of some of the overflowing blessings God has poured into your life. How do you respond to him?

The Courtroom of the World

*"You will be my witnesses—in Jerusalem, in all of Judea,
in Samaria, and in every part of the world."*

ACTS 1:8

We are witnesses. And like witnesses in a court, we are called to testify, to tell what we have seen and heard. And we are to speak truthfully. Our task is not to whitewash nor bloat the truth. Our task is to tell the truth. Period.

There is, however, one difference between the witness in court and the witness for Christ. The witness in court eventually steps down from the witness chair, but the witness for Christ never does. Since the claims of Christ are always on trial, court is perpetually in session, and we remain under oath.

JUST LIKE JESUS

Describe a time when you were called to testify for Christ. What did that mean to you? How did it affect your life? The lives of others?

_____

_____

_____

_____

_____

_____

_____

Unfailing Love

"I will forgive them for leaving me and will love them freely."

HOSEA 14:4

Are you convinced that you have never lived a loveless day? Not one. Never unloved. Those times you deserted Christ? He loved you. You hid from him; he came looking for you.

And those occasions you denied Christ? Though you belonged to him, you hung with them, and when his name surfaced, you cursed like a drunken sailor. God let you hear the crowing of conscience and feel the heat of tears. But he never let you go. Your denials cannot diminish his love.

Nor can your doubts. You've had them. You may have them even now. While there is much we cannot know, may never know, can't we be sure of this? Doubts don't separate doubters from God's love.

COME THIRSTY

What difference would it make in the lives of people you know if each one believed they had never lived a loveless day?

_____

_____

_____

_____

_____

The Choice Is Ours

"I will make you my promised bride forever.
I will be good and fair; I will show you my love and mercy."

HOSEA 2:19

For all its peculiarities and unevenness, the Bible has a simple story. God made man. Man rejected God. God won't give up until he wins him back.

God will whisper. He will shout. He will touch and tug. He will take away our burdens; he'll even take away our blessings. If there are a thousand steps between us and him, he will take all but one. But he will leave the final one for us. The choice is ours.

Please understand. His goal is not to make you happy. His goal is to make you his. His goal is not to get you what you want; it is to get you what you need.

A GENTLE THUNDER

God's goal is not to get you what you want; it is to get you what you need. How does that affect the way you respond to circumstances in life?

_____

_____

_____

_____

_____

_____

Claiming Courage

You will teach me how to live a holy life.

PSALM 16:11

Are you a brief journey away from painful encounters? Are you only steps away from the walls of your own heartache? Learn a lesson from your Master. Don't march into battle with the Enemy without first claiming the courage from God's promises. May I give you a few examples?

When you are confused: "'I know what I am planning for you,' says the LORD. 'I have good plans for you, not plans to hurt you'" (Jeremiah 29:11).

If you feel weighted by yesterday's failures: "So now, those who are in Christ Jesus are not judged guilty" (Romans 8:1).

On those nights when you wonder where God is: "I am the Holy One, and I am among you" (Hosea 11:9).

AND THE ANGELS WERE SILENT

God's promises are as true today as when they were first recorded in his Word. Write some promises that have helped you on the journey of life.

_____

_____

_____

_____

_____

September

*Let us hold firmly to the hope that we have confessed,
because we can trust God to do what he promised.*

—Hebrews 10:23

God Makes Us Right Again

Create in me a pure heart,
God, and make my spirit right again.

PSALM 51:10

We are thirsty.

Not thirsty for fame, possessions, passion, or romance. We've drunk from those pools. They are saltwater in the desert. They don't quench—they kill.

"Blessed are those who hunger and thirst for righteousness. . . ." (Matthew 5:6 NIV).

Righteousness. That's it. That's what we are thirsty for. We're thirsty for a clean conscience. We crave a clean slate. We yearn for a fresh start. We pray for a hand that will enter the dark cavern of our world and do for us the one thing we can't do for ourselves—make us right again.

THE APPLAUSE OF HEAVEN

What is the definition of righteousness? Why do we hunger and thirst for it? Where do we find it?

_____

_____

_____

_____

_____

_____

_____

The Power to Love

This is what God commands: . . . that we love each other.

1 JOHN 3:23

Does bumping into certain people leave you brittle, breakable, and fruitless? Do you easily fall apart? If so, your love may be grounded in the wrong soil. It may be rooted in their love (which is fickle) or in your resolve to love (which is frail). John urges us to "rely on the love *God* has for us" (1 John 4:16 NIV, emphasis mine). He alone is the power source.

Many people tell us to love. Only God gives us the power to do so.

We know what God wants us to do. "This is what God commands: that we love each other" (1 John 3:23). But how can we? How can we be kind to the vow breakers? To those who are unkind to us? How can we be patient with people who have the warmth of a vulture and the tenderness of a porcupine? How can we forgive the moneygrubbers and backstabbers we meet, love, and marry? How can we love as God loves? We want to. We long to. But how can we?

By living loved.

A LOVE WORTH GIVING

Explain what "living loved" means.

_____

_____

_____

_____

_____

Governed by Love

In Christ we are set free by the blood of his death,
and so we have forgiveness of sins.

EPHESIANS 1:7

J esus spoke of freedom, but he spoke of a different kind of freedom: the type of freedom that comes not through power but through submission. Not through control but through surrender. Not through possessions but through open hands.

God wants to emancipate his people; he wants to set them free. He wants his people to be not slaves but sons. He wants them governed not by law but by love.

We have been liberated from our own guilt and our own legalism. We have the freedom to pray and the freedom to love the God of our heart. And we have been forgiven by the only One who could condemn us. We are truly free!

WALKING WITH THE SAVIOR

Describe what it means to be free in Christ. Explain how
this freedom comes through love, not by law.

The Thorns of Sin

*Evil people's lives are like paths covered with thorns and tra*Psalm
PROVERBS 22:5

The fruit of sin is thorns—spiny, prickly, cutting thorns.

I emphasize the "point" of the thorns to suggest a point you may have never considered: If the fruit of sin is thorns, isn't the thorny crown on Christ's brow a picture of the fruit of our sin that pierced his heart?

What is the fruit of sin? Step into the briar patch of humanity and feel a few thistles. Shame. Fear. Disgrace. Discouragement. Anxiety. Haven't our hearts been caught in these brambles?

The heart of Jesus, however, had not. He had never been cut by the thorns of sin. What you and I face daily, he never knew. Anxiety? He never worried! Guilt? He was never guilty! Fear? He never left the presence of God! Jesus never knew the fruits of sin . . . until he became sin for us.

HE CHOSE THE NAILS

"Jesus never knew the fruits of sin until he became sin for us." What benefits do we enjoy because he was willing to become sin for us?

_____

_____

_____

_____

_____

A Life Free of Clutter

"Your heart will be where your treasure is."
MATTHEW 6:21

The most powerful life is the most simple life. The most powerful life is the life that knows where it's going, that knows where the source of strength is, and the life that stays free of clutter and happenstance and hurriedness.

Being busy is not a sin. Jesus was busy. Paul was busy. Peter was busy. Nothing of significance is achieved without effort and hard work and weariness. Being busy, in and of itself, is not a sin. But being busy in an endless pursuit of *things* that leave us empty and hollow and broken inside—that cannot be pleasing to God.

One source of man's weariness is the pursuit of things that can never satisfy; but which one of us has not been caught up in that pursuit at some time in our lives? Our passions, possessions, and pride—these are all *dead* things. When we try to get life out of dead things, the result is only weariness and dissatisfaction.

WALKING WITH THE SAVIOR

What can you do to pursue a more simple life, to keep your life free of clutter and hurriedness?

Examine Your Tools

Kindle afresh the gift of God which is in you.
2 TIMOTHY 1:6 NASB

When I was six years old, my father built us a house. *Architectural Digest* didn't notice, but my mom sure did. Dad constructed it, board by board, every day after work. My youth didn't deter him from giving me a job. He tied an empty nail apron around my waist, placed a magnet in my hands, and sent me on daily patrols around the building site, carrying my magnet only inches off the ground.

One look at my tools and you could guess my job. Stray-nail collector.

One look at yours and the same can be said. Brick by brick, life by life, God is creating a kingdom, a "spiritual house" (1 Peter 2:5 CEV). He entrusted you with a key task in the project. Examine your tools and discover it. Your ability unveils your destiny.

CURE FOR THE COMMON LIFE

What "tools" has God placed in your life? Are you using these tools? Why or why not?

_____

_____

_____

_____

_____

God, Our Defender

He is my defender; I will not be defeated.

PSALM 62:6

Here is a big question. What is God doing when you are in a bind? When the lifeboat springs a leak? When the rip cord snaps? When the last penny is gone before the last bill is paid?

I know what we are doing. Nibbling on nails like corn on the cob. Pacing floors. Taking pills.

But what does God do?

He fights for us. He steps into the ring and points us to our corner and takes over. "Remain calm; the LORD will fight for you" (Exodus 14:14).

His job is to fight. Our job is to trust.

Just trust. Not direct. Or question. Our job is to pray and wait.

WHEN GOD WHISPERS YOUR NAME

What is God doing when you are pacing the floor? Why do we nibble our nails rather than trust him and wait?

_____

_____

_____

_____

_____

_____

Dare to Dream

"God can do things that are not possible for people to do."

LUKE 18:27

God always rejoices when we dare to dream. In fact, we are much like God when we dream. The Master exults in newness. He delights in stretching the old. He wrote the book on making the impossible possible.

Examples? Check the Book.

Eighty-year-old shepherds don't usually play chicken with Pharaohs, but don't tell that to Moses.

Teenage shepherds don't normally have showdowns with giants, but don't tell that to David.

Night-shift shepherds don't usually get to hear angels sing and see God in a stable, but don't tell that to the Bethlehem bunch.

And for sure don't tell that to God. He's made an eternity out of making the earthbound airborne. And he gets angry when people's wings are clipped.

AND THE ANGELS WERE SILENT

Do you have a dream in your heart? Write down that dream and add some things you could do to bring that dream to pass.

_____

_____

_____

_____

_____

Don't Panic

Let us hold firmly to the hope that we have confessed,
because we can trust God to do what he promised.

HEBREWS 10:23

Your disappointments too heavy? Read the story of the Emmaus-bound disciples. The Savior they thought was dead now walked beside them. He entered their house and sat at their table. And something happened in their hearts. "It felt like a fire burning in us when Jesus talked to us on the road and explained the Scriptures to us" (Luke 24:32).

Next time you're disappointed, don't panic. Don't give up. Just be patient and let God remind you he's still in control. It ain't over till it's over.

HE STILL MOVES STONES

The choice is panic or peace. Is there a situation in your life that causes you to panic? How does Christ want you to respond to that situation?

_____

_____

_____

_____

_____

_____

_____

He Weeps with Us

Jesus wept.

JOHN 11:35 NKJV

Jesus weeps. He sits between Mary and Martha, puts an arm around each, and sobs.

He weeps with them.

He weeps for them.

He weeps with you.

He weeps for you.

He weeps so we will know: Mourning is not disbelieving. Flooded eyes don't represent a faithless heart. A person can enter a cemetery Jesus-certain of life after death and still have a Twin Tower crater in the heart. Christ did. He wept, and he knew he was ten minutes from seeing a living Lazarus!

And his tears give you permission to shed your own. Grief does not mean you don't trust; it simply means you can't stand the thought of another day without the Lazarus of your life. If Jesus gave the love, he understands the tears. So grieve, but don't grieve like those who don't know the rest of this story.

NEXT DOOR SAVIOR

Explain why remembering the tears that Jesus shed can bring comfort to us.

The Wages of Deceit

No one who is dishonest will live in my house;
no liars will stay around me.

PSALM 101:7

More than once I've heard people refer to the story [of Ananias and Sapphira] with a nervous chuckle and say, "I'm glad God doesn't still strike people dead for lying." I'm not so sure he doesn't. It seems to me that the wages of deceit is still death. Not death of the body, perhaps, but the death of:

a marriage—Falsehoods are termites in the trunk of the family tree.

a conscience—The tragedy of the second lie is that it is always easier to tell than the first.

a career—Just ask the student who got booted out for cheating or the employee who got fired for embezzlement if the lie wasn't fatal.

We could also list the deaths of intimacy, trust, peace, credibility, and self-respect. But perhaps the most tragic death that occurs from deceit is our [Christian] witness. The court won't listen to the testimony of a perjured witness. Neither will the world.

JUST LIKE JESUS

Explain the importance of living without deceit before the world.

_____

_____

_____

Heaven Knows Your Heart

Naked a man comes from his mother's womb,
and as he comes, so he departs.

ECCLESIASTES 5:15 NIV

Think for just a moment about the things you own. Think about the house you have, the car you drive, the money you've saved. Think about the stocks you've traded and the clothes you've purchased. Envision all your stuff, and let me remind you of two biblical truths.

Your stuff isn't yours. Ask any coroner. No one takes anything with him. When one of the wealthiest men in history, John D. Rockefeller, died, his accountant was asked, "How much did John D. leave?" The accountant's reply? "All of it."

All that stuff—it's not yours. And you know what else about all that stuff? *It's not you.* Who you are has nothing to do with the clothes you wear or the car you drive. Jesus said, "Life is not defined by what you have, even when you have a lot" (Luke 12:15 MSG). Heaven does not know you as the fellow with the nice suit or the woman with the big house or the kid with the new bike. Heaven knows your heart.

TRAVELING LIGHT

Do you tend to think that the things you own define you? Explain why this is not accurate.

_____

_____

_____

_____

God Loves the Truth

The LORD hates those who tell lies
but is pleased with those who keep their promises.

PROVERBS 12:22

Our Master has a strict honor code. From Genesis to Revelation, the theme is the same: God loves the truth and hates deceit. In 1 Corinthians 6:9–10 Paul lists the type of people who will not inherit the kingdom of God. The covey he portrays is a ragged assortment of those who sin sexually, worship idols, take part in adultery, sell their bodies, get drunk, rob people, and—there it is—*lie about others.*

Such rigor may surprise you. *You mean my fibbing and flattering stir the same heavenly anger as adultery and aggravated assault?* Apparently so.

Why the hard line? Why the tough stance?

For one reason: dishonesty is absolutely contrary to the character of God.

JUST LIKE JESUS

Why is dishonesty contrary to the character of God?

_____

_____

_____

_____

_____

_____

Love Is Patient

Let your patience show itself perfectly in what you do.

JAMES 1:4

Some time ago our church staff attended a leadership conference. Especially interested in one class, I arrived early and snagged a front-row seat. As the speaker began, however, I was distracted by a couple of voices in the back of the room. Two guys were mumbling to each other. I was giving serious thought to shooting a glare over my shoulder when the speaker offered an explanation. "Forgive me," he said. "I forgot to explain why the two fellows at the back of the class are talking. One of them is an elder at a new church in Romania. He has traveled here to learn about church leadership. But he doesn't speak English, so the message is being translated."

All of a sudden everything changed. Patience replaced impatience. Why? Because patience always hitches a ride with understanding. "A man of understanding holds his tongue" (Proverbs 11:12 NIV). Don't miss the connection between understanding and patience. Before you blow up, listen up. Before you strike out, tune in.

A LOVE WORTH GIVING

Explain the connection between understanding and patience.

_____

_____

_____

_____

Blessed Are the Focused

Each of you has received a gift to use to serve others.
1 PETER 4:10

There is only so much sand in the hourglass. Who gets it? You know what I'm talking about, don't you?

"The PTA needs a new treasurer. With your background and experience and talent and wisdom and love for kids and degree in accounting, *you* are the perfect one for the job!"

It's tug-of-war, and you are the rope.

"Blessed are the meek," Jesus said (Matthew 5:5 NIV). The word *meek* does not mean weak. It means focused. It is a word used to describe a domesticated stallion. Power under control.

Blessed are those who recognize their God-given responsibilities. Blessed are those who acknowledge that there is only one God and have quit applying for his position. Blessed are those who know what on earth they are on earth to do and set themselves about the business of doing it.

IN THE EYE OF THE STORM

Do you find yourself torn between what others want you to do and what God wants you to do? How do you determine what are your God-given responsibilities?

_____

_____

_____

_____

_____

The Reality of Faith

Surely this was a righteous man.

LUKE 23:47 NIV

If it is true that a picture paints a thousand words, then there was a Roman centurion who got a dictionary full. All he did was see Jesus suffer. He never heard him preach or saw him heal or followed him through the crowds. He never witnessed him still the wind; he only witnessed the way he died. But that was all it took to cause this weatherworn soldier to take a giant step in faith. "Surely this was a righteous man."

That says a lot, doesn't it? It says the rubber of faith meets the road of reality under hardship. It says the trueness of one's belief is revealed in pain. Genuineness and character are unveiled in misfortune. Faith is at its best, not in three-piece suits on Sunday mornings or at VBS on summer days, but at hospital bedsides, cancer wards, and cemeteries.

NO WONDER THEY CALL HIM THE SAVIOR

"The trueness of one's belief is revealed in pain." Write how that statement applies to your life or the life of someone you know.

_____

_____

_____

_____

_____

Fear and Faith

About midnight Paul and Silas were praying
and singing songs to God as the other prisoners listened.

ACTS 16:25

Great acts of faith are seldom born out of calm calculation. It wasn't logic that caused Moses to raise his staff on the bank of the Red Sea.

It wasn't medical research that convinced Naaman to dip seven times in the river.

It wasn't common sense that caused Paul to abandon the Law and embrace grace.

And it wasn't a confident committee that prayed in a small room in Jerusalem for Peter's release from prison. It was a fearful, desperate band of backed-into-a-corner believers. It was a church with no options. A congregation of have-nots pleading for help.

And never were they stronger.

At the beginning of every act of faith, there is often a seed of fear.

IN THE EYE OF THE STORM

"Great acts of faith are seldom born out of calm calculation."
Explain what that statement means. What does it mean to
you personally?

_____

_____

_____

_____

_____

The Departure Date

*Your life is like a mist. You can
see it for a short time, but then it goes away.*

JAMES 4:14

Y ou, as all God's children, live one final breath from your
own funeral.

Which, from God's perspective, is nothing to grieve. He
responds to these grave facts with this great news: "The day you die
is better than the day you are born" (Ecclesiastes 7:1 NLT). Now
there is a twist. Heaven enjoys a maternity-ward reaction to
funerals. Angels watch body burials the same way grandparents
monitor delivery-room doors. "He'll be coming through any
minute!" They can't wait to see the new arrival. While we're driving
hearses and wearing black, they're hanging pink and blue streamers
and passing out cigars. We don't grieve when babies enter the
world. The hosts of heaven don't weep when we leave it.

COME THIRSTY

*Have you recently lost a loved one? How does your perspective
of that loss change with the reminder that the hosts of heaven
don't weep when we leave this world?*

_____

_____

_____

_____

_____

Who Can Fathom Eternity?

God has planted eternity in the hearts of men.

ECCLESIASTES 3:11 TLB

I t doesn't take a wise person to know that people long for more than earth. When we see pain, we yearn. When we see hunger, we question why. Senseless deaths. Endless tears, needless loss.

We have our moments. The newborn on our breast, the bride on our arm, the sunshine on our back. But even those moments are simply slivers of light breaking through heaven's window. God flirts with us. He tantalizes us. He romances us. Those moments are appetizers for the dish that is to come.

"No one has ever imagined what God has prepared for those who love him" (1 Corinthians 2:9).

What a breathtaking verse! Do you see what it says? *Heaven is beyond our imagination.* At our most creative moment, at our deepest thought, at our highest level, we still cannot fathom eternity.

WHEN GOD WHISPERS YOUR NAME

How do you imagine heaven? Are you glad to know it is beyond your imagination? Why? How can this encourage you in your faith?

Is It Loving?

[Love] is not rude.

1 CORINTHIANS 13:5 NIV

When defining what love is not, Paul put *rudeness* on the list. "It is not rude." The Greek word for *rude* means shameful or disgraceful behavior.

An example of rudeness was recently taken before the courts in Minnesota. A man fell out of his canoe and lost his temper. Though the river was lined with vacationing families, he polluted the air with obscenities. Some of those families sued him. He said, "I have my rights."

God calls us to a higher, more noble concern. Not "What are my rights?" but "What is loving?"

Do you have the right to dominate a conversation? Yes, but is it loving to do so?

Is it within your rights to bark at the clerk or snap at the kids? Yes. But is it loving to act this way?

A LOVE WORTH GIVING

Make a list of situations that would apply to doing what is loving rather than what is your right.

_____

_____

_____

_____

_____

_____

From the Inside Out

*"I will ask the Father, and he will give you
another Helper to be with you forever—the Spirit of truth."*

JOHN 14:16–17

D o-it-yourself Christianity is not much encouragement to
the done-in and worn-out.

Self-sanctification holds little hope for the addict. At
some point we need more than good advice; we need help.
Somewhere on this journey home we realize that a fifty-fifty
proposition is too little. We need more.

We need help. Help from the inside out. Not near us. Not
above us. Not around us. But in us. In the part of us we don't
even know. In the heart no one else has seen. In the hidden
recesses of our being dwells, not an angel, not a philosophy, not
a genie, but God.

WHEN GOD WHISPERS YOUR NAME

*We need help from the inside out. Where do we find this
help? What are the results?*

_____

_____

_____

_____

_____

_____

An Open Door

Now in Christ Jesus, you who
were far away from God are brought near.

EPHESIANS 2:13

Nothing remains between you and God but an open door. Something happened in the death of Christ that opened the door for you and me. And that something is described by the writer of Hebrews.

"So, brothers and sisters, we are completely free to enter the Most Holy Place without fear because of the blood of Jesus' death. We can enter through a new and living way that Jesus opened for us. It leads through the curtain—Christ's body" (Hebrews 10:19–20).

To the original readers, those last four words were explosive: "the curtain—Christ's body." According to the writer, the curtain equals Jesus. Hence, whatever happened to the flesh of Jesus happened to the curtain. What happened to his flesh? It was torn. Torn by the whips, torn by the thorns. Torn by the weight of the cross and the point of the nails. But in the horror of his torn flesh, we find the splendor of the open door.

HE CHOSE THE NAILS

What does the "splendor of the open door" provide for
God's children? How do you respond to this?

_____

_____

_____

_____

The Ultimate Triumph

"Unless a grain of wheat falls into the earth and dies, it remains a single grain of wheat; but if it dies, it brings a good harvest."

JOHN 12:24 PHILLIPS

We do all we can to live and not die. God, however, says we must die in order to live. When you sow a seed, it must die in the ground before it can grow. What we see as the ultimate tragedy, he sees as the ultimate triumph.

And when a Christian dies, it's not a time to despair, but a time to trust. Just as the seed is buried and the material wrapping decomposes, so our fleshly body will be buried and will decompose. But just as the buried seed sprouts new life, so our body will blossom into a new body.

The seed buried in the earth will blossom in heaven. Your soul and body will reunite, and you will be like Jesus.

WHEN CHRIST COMES

Death is not a time to despair for the Christian but a time to trust. What does that mean? Describe how this has been true in your life.

Too Incredible

"The One who comes from above is greater than all."

JOHN 3:31

The idea that a virgin would be selected by God to bear himself. The notion that God would don a scalp and toes and two eyes. The thought that the King of the universe would sneeze and burp and get bit by mosquitoes. It's too incredible. Too revolutionary. We would never create such a Savior. We aren't that daring.

When we create a redeemer, we keep him safely distant in his faraway castle. We allow him only the briefest of encounters with us. We permit him to swoop in and out with his sleigh before we can draw too near. We wouldn't ask him to take up residence in the midst of a contaminated people. In our wildest imaginings we wouldn't conjure a king who becomes one of us.

But God did.

AND THE ANGELS WERE SILENT

Why is it so surprising to us that God would take up residence in the midst of our contaminated world? Why is it such good news?

_____

_____

_____

_____

_____

Sweeter After a Rest

"In six days the LORD made everything. . . .
On the seventh day he rested."

EXODUS 20:11

Time has skyrocketed in value. The value of any commodity depends on its scarcity. And time that once was abundant now is going to the highest bidder.

When I was ten years old, my mother enrolled me in piano lessons. Spending thirty minutes every afternoon tethered to a piano bench was a torture.

Some of the music, though, I learned to enjoy. I hammered the staccatos. I belabored the crescendos. But there was one instruction in the music I could never obey to my teacher's satisfaction. The *rest*. The zigzagged command to do nothing. What sense does that make? Why sit at the piano and pause when you can pound?

"Because," my teacher patiently explained, "music is always sweeter after a rest."

It didn't make sense to me at age ten. But now, a few decades later, the words ring with wisdom—divine wisdom.

THE APPLAUSE OF HEAVEN

How do you make time for rest? Why is this wise for your spiritual and physical well-being?

_____

_____

_____

_____

The Lamb of God

*At noon the whole country was covered
with darkness, which lasted for three hours.*

MATTHEW 27:45 TEV

O f course the sky is dark; people are killing the Light of
the World.

The universe grieves. God said it would. "On that day . . .
I will make the sun go down at noon, and darken the earth in broad
daylight. . . . I will make it like the mourning for an only son, and
the end of it like a bitter day" (Amos 8:9–10 RSV).

The sky weeps. And a lamb bleats. Remember the time of the
scream? "At about three o'clock Jesus cried out" (Matthew 27:46
TEV). Three o'clock in the afternoon, the hour of the temple
sacrifice. Less than a mile to the east, a finely clothed priest leads a
lamb to the slaughter, unaware that his work is futile. Heaven is not
looking at the lamb of man but at "the Lamb of God, who takes
away the sin of the world" (John 1:29 RSV).

NEXT DOOR SAVIOR

*Describe what the death of Christ means to you personally.
Write a short psalm of praise to thank him.*

The Power of Your Hands

But those who do right will continue to do right,
and those whose hands are not dirty with sin will grow stronger.

JOB 17:9

What if someone were to film a documentary on your hands? What if a producer were to tell your story based on the life of your hands? What would we see? As with all of us, the film would begin with an infant's fist, then a close-up of a tiny hand wrapped around mommy's finger. Then what? Holding on to a chair as you learned to walk?

Were you to show the documentary to your friends, you'd be proud of certain moments: your hands extending with a gift, placing a ring on another's finger, doctoring a wound, preparing a meal. And then there are other scenes. Hands taking more often than giving, demanding instead of offering.

Oh, the power of our hands. Leave them unmanaged and they become weapons: clawing for power, strangling for survival, seducing for pleasure. But manage them and our hands become instruments of grace—not just tools in the hands of God, but God's very hands.

JUST LIKE JESUS

Describe how God uses your hands.

_____

_____

_____

_____

A Second Chance

"I came to give life—life in all its fullness."

JOHN 10:10

Not many second chances exist in the world today. Just ask the kid who didn't make the little league team or the fellow who got the pink slip or the mother of three who got dumped for a "pretty little thing."

Not many second chances. Nowadays it's more like, "It's now or never." "Around here we don't tolerate incompetence." "Gotta get tough to get along." "Not much room at the top." "Three strikes and you're out." "It's a dog-eat-dog world!"

Jesus would say, "Then don't live with the dogs." That makes sense, doesn't it? Why let a bunch of other failures tell you how much of a failure you are?

It's not every day that you find someone who will give you a second chance—much less someone who will give you a second chance every day. But in Jesus, you find both.

NO WONDER THEY CALL HIM THE SAVIOR

Write about specific times when you have been grateful for God's second chance.

_____

_____

_____

_____

To Tell the Truth

Speak the truth to one another.

EPHESIANS 4:25 TJB

Are you in a dilemma, wondering if you should tell the truth or not? The question to ask in such moments is, "Will God bless my deceit? Will he, who hates lies, bless a strategy built on lies? Will the Lord, who loves the truth, bless the business of falsehoods? Will God honor the career of the manipulator?" I don't think so either.

Examine your heart. Ask yourself some tough questions.

Am I being completely honest with my spouse and children? Are my relationships marked by candor? What about my work or school environment? Am I honest in my dealings? Am I a trustworthy student? An honest taxpayer?

Do you tell the truth . . . always?

If not, start today. Don't wait until tomorrow. The ripple of today's lie is tomorrow's wave and next year's flood.

JUST LIKE JESUS

Are you completely honest in your relationships? How can this affect your life?

_____

_____

_____

_____

_____

_____

Obsessed with Stuff

"Be on your guard against every form of greed."
LUKE 12:15 NASB

In 1900 the average person living in the United States wanted seventy-two different things and considered eighteen of them essential. Today the average person wants five hundred things and considers one hundred of them essential.

Our obsession with stuff carries a hefty price tag. Eighty percent of us battle the pressure of overdue bills. We spend 110 percent of our disposable income trying to manage debt. And who can keep up? We no longer measure ourselves against the Joneses next door but against the star on the screen or the stud on the magazine cover. Hollywood's diamonds make yours look like a gumball-machine toy. Who can satisfy Madison Avenue? No one can. For that reason Jesus warns, "Be on your guard against every form of greed" (Luke 12:15 NASB).

CURE FOR THE COMMON LIFE

How does our culture entice you to want more and more stuff? What can you do to guard against this obsession?

_____

_____

_____

_____

_____

_____

What a God!

LORD God All-Powerful, who is like you?
LORD, you are powerful and completely trustworthy.

PSALM 89:8

Ponder the achievement of God.

He doesn't condone our sin, nor does he compromise his standard.

He doesn't ignore our rebellion, nor does he relax his demands.

Rather than dismiss our sin, he assumes our sin and, incredibly, sentences himself.

God's holiness is honored. Our sin is punished . . . and we are redeemed.

God does what we cannot do so we can be what we dare not dream: perfect before God.

IN THE GRIP OF GRACE

Rather than dismiss our sin, Christ assumes our sin.
Explain how that happens. What are the results?

_____

_____

_____

_____

_____

_____

A Symbol of Love

He is not here; he has risen from the dead.

LUKE 24:6

When John arrived at the empty tomb, the burial wraps had not been ripped off and thrown down. They were still in their original state! The linens were undisturbed. The graveclothes were still rolled and folded.

How could this be?

If for some reason friends or foes had unwrapped the body, would they have been so careful as to dispose of the clothing in such an orderly fashion? Of course not! But if neither friend nor foe took the body, who did?

Through the rags of death, John saw the power of life. Odd, don't you think, that God would use something as sad as a burial wrap to change a life?

But God is given to such practices:

In his hand empty wine jugs at a wedding become a symbol of power.

The coin of a widow becomes a symbol of generosity.

And a tool of death is a symbol of his love.

HE CHOSE THE NAILS

Make a list of things that symbolize God's love.

_____

_____

_____

_____

God's Name in Your Heart

The name of the LORD is a strong tower;
the righteous run to it and are safe.

PROVERBS 18:10 NKJV

When you are confused about the future, go to your *Jehovah-raah*, your caring Shepherd. When you are anxious about provision, talk to *Jehovah-jireh*, the Lord who provides. Are your challenges too great? Seek the help of *Jehovah-shalom*, the Lord is peace. Is your body sick? Are your emotions weak? *Jehovah-rophe*, the Lord who heals you, will see you now. Do you feel like a soldier stranded behind enemy lines? Take refuge in *Jehovah-nissi*, the Lord your Banner.

Meditating on the names of God reminds you of the character of God. Take these names and bury them in your heart.

God is
> the Shepherd who guides,
> the Lord who provides,
> the Voice who brings peace in the storm,
> the Physician who heals the sick, and
> the Banner that guides the soldier.

THE GREAT HOUSE OF GOD

Describe what each name of God means to you.

_____

_____

_____

_____

The Pot of Prayer

I will go to the altar of God, to God who is my joy and happiness.

PSALM 43:4

Let's say a stress stirrer comes your way. The doctor decides you need an operation. She detects a lump and thinks it best that you have it removed. So there you are, walking out of her office. You've just been handed this cup of anxiety. What are you going to do with it? You can place it in one of two pots.

You can dump your bad news in the vat of worry and pull out the spoon. Turn on the fire. Stew on it. Stir it. Mope for a while. Brood for a time. Won't be long before you'll have a delightful pot of pessimism.

How about a different idea? The pot of prayer. Before the door of the doctor's office closes, give the problem to God. "I receive your lordship. Nothing comes to me that hasn't passed through you." In addition, stir in a healthy helping of gratitude.

Your part is prayer and gratitude. God's part? Peace and protection.

COME THIRSTY

Do you tend to react to stress by stirring the pot of pessimism or the pot of prayer? What are the results?

A Load Too Heavy

Do not be bitter or angry or mad.
Never shout angrily or say things to hurt others.

EPHESIANS 4:31

Oh, the gradual grasp of hatred. Its damage begins like the crack in my windshield. Thanks to a speeding truck on a gravel road, my window was chipped. With time the nick became a crack, and the crack became a winding tributary. I couldn't drive my car without thinking of the jerk who drove too fast. Though I've never seen him, I could describe him. He is some deadbeat bum who cheats on his wife, drives with a six-pack on the seat, and keeps the television so loud the neighbors can't sleep.

Ever heard the expression "blind rage"?

Let me be very clear. Hatred will sour your outlook and break your back. The load of bitterness is simply too heavy. Your knees will buckle under the strain, and your heart will break beneath the weight. The mountain before you is steep enough without the heaviness of hatred on your back. The wisest choice—the *only* choice—is for you to drop the anger. You will never be called upon to give anyone more grace than God has already given you.

IN THE GRIP OF GRACE

Explain why God's grace helps us give grace.

_____

_____

_____

_____

Jesus Planned It All

Look, the Lamb of God,
who takes away the sin of the world!

JOHN 1:29

Jesus planned his own sacrifice. It means Jesus intentionally planted the tree from which his cross would be carved.

It means he willingly placed the iron ore in the heart of the earth from which the nails would be cast.

It means he voluntarily placed his Judas in the womb of a woman.

It means Christ was the one who set in motion the political machinery that would send Pilate to Jerusalem.

And it also means he didn't have to do it—but he did.

GOD CAME NEAR

"Jesus planned his own sacrifice." Make a list of some of the ways he did this. Then describe why he did all this.

_____

_____

_____

_____

_____

_____

_____

_____

Imagine Seeing God

May the LORD bless you from
Mount Zion, he who made heaven and earth.

PSALM 134:3

The Hebrew writer gives us a *National Geographic* piece on heaven. Listen to how he describes the mountaintop of Zion. He says when we reach the mountain we will have come to "the city of the living God. To thousands of angels gathered together with joy. To the meeting of God's firstborn children whose names are written in heaven" (Hebrews 12:22–23).

What a mountain! Won't it be great to see the angels? To finally know what they look like and who they are?

Imagine the meeting of the firstborn. A gathering of all God's children. No jealousy. No competition. No division. We will be perfect . . . sinless.

And imagine seeing God. Finally, to gaze in the face of your Father. To feel the Father's gaze upon you. Neither will ever cease.

WHEN GOD WHISPERS YOUR NAME

Make a list of some things you are anticipating about heaven.

_____

_____

_____

_____

_____

_____

Submerged in Mercy

[God] has not punished us as our sins should be punished.

PSALM 103:10

D o you really think you haven't done things that hurt Christ? Have you ever been dishonest with his money? That's cheating.

Ever gone to church to be seen rather than to see him? Hypocrite.

Ever broken a promise you've made to God?

Don't you deserve to be punished? And yet, here you are. Reading this book. Breathing. Still witnessing sunsets and hearing babies gurgle. Still watching the seasons change. There are no lashes on your back or hooks in your nose or shackles on your feet. Apparently God hasn't kept a list of your wrongs.

Listen. You have not been sprinkled with forgiveness. You have not been spattered with grace. You have not been dusted with kindness. You have been immersed in it. You are submerged in mercy. You are a minnow in the ocean of his mercy. Let it change you!

A LOVE WORTH GIVING

You have been immersed in God's forgiveness and grace. How does that affect your life?

_____

_____

_____

_____

_____

Focus on God's Majesty

You have not seen Christ, but still you
love him. You cannot see him now, but you believe in him.

1 PETER 1:8

S ome years ago a sociologist accompanied a group of mountain climbers on an expedition. Among other things, he observed a distinct correlation between cloud cover and contentment. When there was no cloud cover and the peak was in view, the climbers were energetic and cooperative. When the gray clouds eclipsed the view of the mountaintop, though, the climbers were sullen and selfish.

The same thing happens to us. As long as our eyes are on God's majesty there is a bounce in our step. But let our eyes focus on the dirt beneath us and we will grumble about every rock and crevice we have to cross. For this reason Paul urged, "Don't shuffle along, eyes to the ground, absorbed with the things right in front of you. Look up, and be alert to what is going on around Christ—that's where the action is. See things from his perspective" (Colossians 3:2 MSG).

THE GREAT HOUSE OF GOD

Why is it better to focus on God's majesty than the muck of life?

_____

_____

_____

_____

_____

A Pasture for the Soul

He lets me rest in green pastures.

PSALM 23:2

For a field to bear fruit, it must occasionally lie fallow. And for you to be healthy, you must rest. Slow down, and God will heal you. He will bring rest to your mind, to your body, and most of all to your soul. He will lead you to green pastures.

Green pastures were not the natural terrain of Judea. The hills around Bethlehem where David kept his flock were not lush and green. Even today they are white and parched. Any green pasture in Judea is the work of some shepherd. He has cleared the rough, rocky land. Stumps have been torn out, and brush has been burned.

With his own pierced hands, Jesus created a pasture for the soul. He tore out the thorny underbrush of condemnation. He pried loose the huge boulders of sin. In their place he planted seeds of grace and dug ponds of mercy.

And he invites us to rest there.

TRAVELING LIGHT

Write some reminders of ways you can slow down and find spiritual rest.

_____

_____

_____

_____

_____

Guard the Gateway

*The devil, your enemy, goes around like a roaring
lion looking for someone to eat. Refuse to give in to him,
by standing strong in your faith.*

1 PETER 5:8–9

You've got to admit, some of our hearts are trashed out. Let any riffraff knock on the door, and we throw it open. Anger shows up, and we let him in. Revenge needs a place to stay, so we have him pull up a chair. Pity wants to have a party, so we show him the kitchen. Lust rings the bell, and we change the sheets on the bed. Don't we know how to say no?

Many don't. For most of us, thought management is, well, unthought of. We think much about time management, weight management, personnel management, even scalp management. But what about thought management? Shouldn't we be as concerned about managing our thoughts as we are managing anything else? Jesus was. Like a trained soldier at the gate of a city, he stood watch over his mind. He stubbornly guarded the gateway of his heart.

If he did, shouldn't we?

JUST LIKE JESUS

Why is "thought management" a good idea?

_____

_____

_____

_____

_____

At Home with His Love

"Abide in My love."
JOHN 15:9 NASB

When you abide somewhere, you live there. You grow familiar with the surroundings. You don't pull in the driveway and ask, "Where is the garage?" You don't consult the blueprint to find the kitchen. To abide is to be at home.

To abide in Christ's love is to make his love your home. Not a roadside park or hotel room you occasionally visit, but your preferred dwelling. You rest in him. Eat in him. When thunder claps, you step beneath his roof. His walls secure you from the winds. His fireplace warms you from the winters of life. As John urged, "We take up permanent residence in a life of love" (1 John 4:16 MSG).

You abandon the old house of false love and move into his home of real love.

COME THIRSTY

Think of the home of God's love. Make a list of some of the blessings you would find in that house.

Looking Up

Lord, show us the Father. That is all we need.

JOHN 14:8

Biographies of bold disciples begin with chapters of honest terror. Fear of death. Fear of failure. Fear of loneliness. Fear of a wasted life. Fear of failing to know God.

Faith begins when you see God on the mountain and you are in the valley and you know that you're too weak to make the climb. You see what you need . . . you see what you have . . . and what you have isn't enough to accomplish anything.

Moses had a sea in front and an enemy behind. The Israelites could swim or they could fight. But neither option was enough.

Paul had mastered the Law. He had mastered the system. But one glimpse of God convinced him that sacrifice and symbols were not enough.

Faith that begins with fear will end up nearer the Father.

IN THE EYE OF THE STORM

Describe a time when you were in the valley and you "saw God on the mountain." What happened? How did this affect you?

_____

_____

_____

_____

_____

_____

"God Knows Me"

You number my wanderings; put my tears into Your bottle.

PSALM 56:8 NKJV

God knows you. He engraved your name on his hands and keeps your tears in a bottle (Isaiah 49:16; Psalm 56:8).

God knows you. And he is near you! How far is the Shepherd from the sheep (John 10:14)? The branch from the vine (John 15:5)? That's how far God is from you. He is near. See how these four words look taped to your bathroom mirror: "God is for me" (Psalm 56:9 NKJV).

And his kingdom needs you. The poor need you; the lonely need you; the church needs you . . . the cause of God needs you. You are part of "the overall purpose he is working out in everything and everyone" (Ephesians 1:12 MSG). The kingdom needs you to discover and deploy your unique skill. Use it to make much out of God. Get the word out. God is with us; we are not alone.

CURE FOR THE COMMON LIFE

"God is for you." How does that statement make you feel? What difference can this make in your life?

Trust God with the Future

"Don't let your hearts be troubled.
Trust in God, and trust in me."

JOHN 14:1

Our [little] minds are ill-equipped to handle the thoughts of eternity. When it comes to a world with no boundaries of space and time, we don't have the hooks for those hats. Consequently, our Lord takes the posture of a parent. *Trust me.*

Don't be troubled by the return of Christ. Don't be anxious about things you cannot comprehend. For the Christian, the return of Christ is not a riddle to be solved or a code to be broken, but rather a day to be anticipated.

WHEN CHRIST COMES

Do you respond to Christ's return with anxiety or anticipation? How does he want you to respond? Why?

_____

_____

_____

_____

_____

_____

_____

_____

Refuse Trashy Thoughts

As he thinks in his heart, so is he.

PROVERBS 23:7 NKJV

To listen to our vocabulary you'd think we are the victims of our thoughts. "Don't talk to me," we say. "I'm in a bad mood." As if a mood were a place to which we were assigned ("I can't call you. I'm in Bosnia.") rather than an emotion we permit.

Or we say, "Don't mess with her. She has a bad disposition." Is a disposition something we "have"? Like a cold or the flu? Are we the victims of the emotional bacteria of the season? Or do we have a choice?

Paul says we do: "We capture every thought and make it give up and obey Christ" (2 Corinthians 10:5).

Do you hear some battlefield jargon in that passage—"capture every thought," "make it give up," and "obey Christ"? You get the impression that we are the soldiers and the thoughts are the enemies. Our assignment is to protect the boat and refuse entrance to trashy thoughts. The minute they appear we go into action. "This heart belongs to God," we declare, "and you aren't getting on board."

A Love Worth Giving

Explain why you do not have to be the victim of your thoughts and emotions.

In the Arms of God

"Everyone who lives and believes in me will never die."

JOHN 11:26

We don't like to say good-bye to those whom we love. Whether it be at a school or a cemetery, separation is tough. It is right for us to weep, but there is no need for us to despair. They had pain here. They have no pain there. They struggled here. They have no struggles there. You and I might wonder why God took them home. But they don't. They understand. They are, at this very moment, at peace in the presence of God.

When it is cold on earth, we can take comfort in knowing that our loved ones are in the warm arms of God. And when Christ comes, we will hold them too.

WHEN CHRIST COMES

It is always a struggle to say good-bye to our loved ones. How does knowing they are in the arms of God make it easier?

_____

_____

_____

_____

_____

_____

_____

Get Over Yourself

In humility consider others better than yourselves.
PHILIPPIANS 2:3 NIV

Columnist Rick Reilly gave this advice to rookie professional athletes: "Stop thumping your chest. The line blocked, the quarterback threw you a perfect spiral while getting his head knocked off, and the good receiver blew the double coverage. Get over yourself."

The truth is, every touchdown in life is a team effort. Applaud your teammates. An elementary-age boy came home from the tryouts for the school play. "Mommy, Mommy," he announced, "I got a part. I've been chosen to sit in the audience and clap and cheer." When you have a chance to clap and cheer, do you take it? If you do, your head is starting to fit your hat size.

TRAVELING LIGHT

Is it easy for you to sit on the sidelines and clap and cheer for others on your team or is this difficult for you? Which is wiser?

_____

_____

_____

_____

_____

_____

The Best Is Yet to Be

*"I will also give to each one who wins
the victory a white stone with a new name written on it."*

REVELATION 2:17

Makes sense. Fathers are fond of giving their children special names. Princess. Tiger. Sweetheart. Bubba. Angel.

Isn't it incredible to think that God has saved a name just for you? One you don't even know? We've always assumed that the name we got is the name we will keep. Not so. The road ahead is so bright a fresh name is needed. Your eternity is so special no common name will do.

So God has one reserved just for you. There is more to your life than you ever thought. There is more to your story than what you have read.

And so I plead. Be there when God whispers your name.

WHEN GOD WHISPERS YOUR NAME

God will give you a new name for all eternity. How does this demonstrate his love for you?

Go the Distance

"Those people who keep their faith until the end will be saved."
MATTHEW 24:13

Jesus doesn't say if you succeed you will be saved. Or if you come out on top you will be saved. He says if you endure. An accurate rendering would be, "If you hang in there until the end . . . if you go the distance."

The Brazilians have a great phrase for this. In Portuguese, a person who has the ability to hang in and not give up has *garra*. *Garra* means "claws." What imagery! A person with *garra* has claws that burrow into the side of the cliff and keep him from falling.

So do the saved. They may get close to the edge; they may even stumble and slide. But they will dig their nails into the rock of God and hang on.

Jesus gives you this assurance. Hang on. He'll make sure you get home.

AND THE ANGELS WERE SILENT

List some practical things you can do to "dig your nails into the rock of God."

_____

_____

_____

_____

_____

Radical Reconstruction

*"Rejoice and be glad, because you have
a great reward waiting for you in heaven."*

MATTHEW 5:12

In the Sermon on the mount, what Jesus promises is not a gimmick to give you goose bumps nor a mental attitude that has to be pumped up at pep rallies. No, Matthew 5 describes God's radical reconstruction of the heart.

Observe the sequence. First, we recognize we are in need (we're poor in spirit). Next, we repent of our self-sufficiency (we mourn). We quit calling the shots and surrender control to God (we're meek). So grateful are we for his presence that we yearn for more of him (we hunger and thirst). As we grow closer to him, we become more like him. We forgive others (we're merciful). We change our outlook (we're pure in heart). We love others (we're peacemakers). We endure injustice (we're persecuted).

It's no casual shift of attitude. It is a demolition of the old structure and a creation of the new. The more radical the change, the greater the joy. And it's worth every effort, for this is the joy of God.

THE APPLAUSE OF HEAVEN

Describe how God's radical reconstruction has affected you.

_____

_____

_____

_____

_____

A Place to Heal

Christ gave those gifts to prepare God's holy people
for the work of serving, to make the body of Christ stronger.

EPHESIANS 4:12

He grants gifts so we can "*prepare* God's holy people." Paul reached into a medical dictionary for this term. Doctors used it to describe the setting of a broken bone. Broken people come to churches. Not with broken bones, but broken hearts, homes, dreams, and lives. They limp in on fractured faith, and if the church operates as the church, they find healing. Pastor-teachers touch and teach. Gospel bearers share good news. Prophets speak words of truth. Visionaries dream of greater impact. Some administer. Some pray. Some lead. Some follow. But all help to heal brokenness: "to make the body of Christ stronger."

Don't miss it. No one is strong all the time. Don't miss the place to find your place and heal your hurts.

CURE FOR THE COMMON LIFE

Do you know someone who is living with a broken heart or home or dream? What can you do to reach out to heal that brokenness?

God Knows What He's Doing

Surely I spoke of things I did not understand;
I talked of things too wonderful for me to know.

JOB 42:3

It's easy to thank God when he does what we want. But God doesn't always do what we want. Ask Job.

His empire collapsed, his children were killed, and what was a healthy body became a rage of boils. From whence came this torrent? From whence will come any help?

Job goes straight to God and pleads his case. His head hurts. His body hurts. His heart hurts.

And God answers. Not with answers but with questions. An ocean of questions.

After several dozen questions . . . Job has gotten the point. What is it?

The point is this: God owes no one anything. No reasons. No explanations. Nothing. If he gave them, we couldn't understand them.

God is God. He knows what he is doing. When you can't trace his hand, trust his heart.

THE INSPIRATIONAL STUDY BIBLE

What do you know about the character of God that enables you to trust his heart?

_____

_____

_____

_____

God Goes with Us

"I am with you and will watch over you wherever you go."
GENESIS 28:15 NIV

When God calls us into the deep valley of death, he will be with us. Dare we think that he would abandon us in the moment of death? Would the shepherd require his sheep to journey to the highlands alone? Of course not. Would God require his child to journey to eternity alone? Absolutely not! He is with you!

What God said to Moses, he says to you: "My Presence will go with you, and I will give you rest" (Exodus 33:14 NIV).

What God said to Jacob, he says to you: "I am with you and will watch over you wherever you go" (Genesis 28:15 NIV).

What God said to Joshua, he says to you: "As I was with Moses, so I will be with you; I will never leave you nor forsake you" (Joshua 1:5 NIV).

TRAVELING LIGHT

Read each of the three verses in the text again and write out the phrase in each that assures us of God's presence. How do you respond to these promises?

The CEO of Heaven

Be careful what you think, because your thoughts run your life.

God wants you to "think and act like Christ Jesus" (Philippians 2:5). But how? The answer is surprisingly simple. We can be transformed if we make one decision: *I will submit my thoughts to the authority of Jesus.*

Jesus claims to be the CEO of heaven and earth. He has the ultimate say on everything, especially our thoughts. He has more authority, for example, than your parents. Your parents may say you are no good, but Jesus says you are valuable, and he has authority over parents.

Jesus also has authority over your ideas. Suppose you have an idea that you want to rob a grocery store. Jesus, however, has made it clear that stealing is wrong. If you have given him authority over your ideas, then the idea of stealing cannot remain in your thoughts.

To have a pure heart, we must submit all thoughts to the authority of Christ. If we are willing to do that, he will change us to be like him.

JUST LIKE JESUS

Have you submitted all your thoughts to the authority of Christ? Explain why this is necessary if we are to become like him.

_____

_____

_____

_____

Receive God's Hope

Come near to God, and God will come near to you.

Your toughest challenge is nothing more than bobby pins and rubber bands to God. *Bobby pins and rubber bands?*

My older sister used to give them to me when I was a child. I would ride my tricycle up and down the sidewalk, pretending that the bobby pins were keys and my trike was a truck. But one day I lost the "keys." Crisis! What was I going to do? My search yielded nothing but tears and fear. But when I confessed my mistake to my sister, she just smiled. Being a decade older, she had a better perspective.

God has a better perspective as well. With all due respect, our severest struggles are, in his view, nothing worse than lost bobby pins and rubber bands. He is not confounded, confused, or discouraged.

Receive his hope, won't you? Receive it because you need it. Receive it so you can share it.

A LOVE WORTH GIVING

God is not confounded, confused, or discouraged by the things that happen to you. How does this give you hope?

_____

_____

_____

_____

Victory over Death

Death, where is your victory?
Death, where is your pain?

1 CORINTHIANS 15:55

The fire that lit the boiler of the New Testament church was an unquenchable belief that if Jesus had been only a man, he would have stayed in the tomb. The earliest Christians couldn't stay silent about the fact that the One they saw hung on a cross walked again on the earth and appeared to five hundred people.

Let us ask our Father humbly, yet confidently in the name of Jesus, to remind us of the empty tomb. Let us see the victorious Jesus: the Conqueror of the tomb, the One who defied death. And let us be reminded that we, too, will be granted that same victory!

WALKING WITH THE SAVIOR

Jesus defied death. He conquered the tomb. Why should this encourage you? What does it mean to you personally?

_____

_____

_____

_____

_____

_____

Six Hours One Friday

He really was the Son of God!

MATTHEW 27:54

To the casual observer the six hours are mundane.

God is on a cross. The Creator of the universe is being executed.

Spit and blood are caked to his cheeks, and his lips are cracked and swollen. Thorns rip his scalp. His lungs scream with pain. His legs knot with cramps. Taut nerves threaten to snap as pain twangs her morbid melody. Yet, death is not ready. And there is no one to save him, for he is sacrificing himself.

It is no normal six hours . . . it is no normal Friday.

Let me ask you a question: What do you do with that day in history? What do you do with its claims?

If it really happened, if God did commandeer his own crucifixion, if he did turn his back on his own Son, those six hours were no normal six hours. They were the most critical hours in history.

SIX HOURS ONE FRIDAY

The death of God's Son on a cross marks the most critical hours in history. Explain why.

_____

_____

_____

_____

God, Our Father

Remember, O LORD, Your tender mercies
and Your lovingkindnesses, for they are from of old.

PSALM 25:6 NKJV

Recently, my daughter Jenna and I spent several days in the old city of Jerusalem. One afternoon, as we were exiting the Jaffa gate, we found ourselves behind an orthodox Jewish family—a father and his three small girls. One of the daughters, perhaps four or five years of age, fell a few steps behind and couldn't see her father. "Abba!" she called to him. He spotted her and immediately extended his hand.

When the signal changed, he led her and her sisters through the intersection. In the middle of the street, he reached down and swung her up into his arms and continued their journey.

Isn't that what we all need? An abba who will hear when we call? Who will take our hand when we are weak? Who will guide us through the hectic intersections of life? Don't we all need an abba who will swing us up into his arms and carry us home? We all need a father.

THE GREAT HOUSE OF GOD

Why does God want us to call on him for our needs? What has he provided for you as your Abba?

_____

_____

_____

_____

Uniquely You

"He gave . . . to each according to his own ability."
MATTHEW 25:15 NKJV

Da Vinci painted one *Mona Lisa*. Beethoven composed one Fifth Symphony. And God made one version of you. He custom designed you for a one-of-a-kind assignment. Mine like a gold digger the unique-to-you nuggets from your life.

When God gives an assignment, he also gives the skill. Study your skills, then, to reveal your assignment.

Look at you. Your uncanny ease with numbers. Your quenchless curiosity about chemistry. Others stare at blueprints and yawn; you read them and drool. "I was made to do this," you say.

Our Maker gives assignments to people, "to each according to each one's unique ability." As he calls, he equiPsalm Look back over your life. What have you consistently done well? What have you loved to do? Stand at the intersection of your affections and successes and find your uniqueness.

CURE FOR THE COMMON LIFE

Make another list of the things you love to do. Write a statement of the ways God is using or could use your affections and successes in this world.

_____

_____

_____

_____

October

We know the love that God
has for us, and we trust that love.

—1 John 4:16

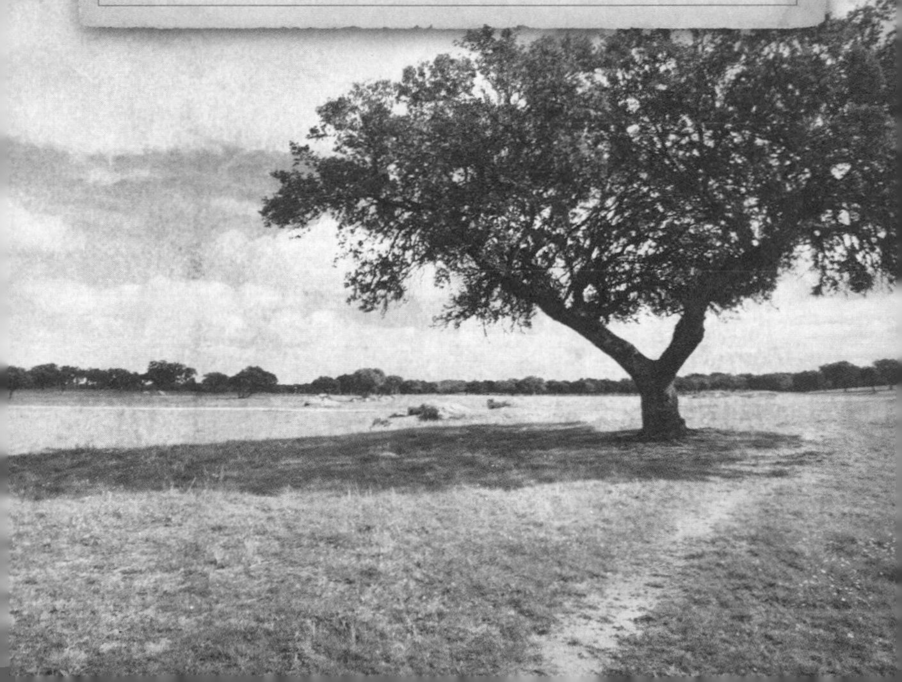

A Daily Blessing

*I ask the Father in his great glory to give you
the power to be strong inwardly through his Spirit.*

EPHESIANS 3:16

Here is a scene repeated in Brazil thousands of times daily. It's early morning. Time for young Marcos to leave for school. As he gathers his books and heads for the door, he pauses by his father's chair. He searches his father's face. *Benção, Pai?* Marcos asks. *(Blessing, Father?)*

The father raises his hand. *Deus te abençoe, meu filho,* he assures. *(God bless you, my son.)*

Father and child part for the day, a blessing requested, a blessing willingly given.

We should do the same. Like the child longing for the father's favor, each of us needs a daily reminder of our heavenly Father's love.

31 DAYS OF BLESSING

Make a list of some of the ways God has blessed your life. Write a note of praise to him for his goodness.

_____

_____

_____

_____

_____

_____

Is That All There Is?

Christ died for our sins in accordance with the Scriptures.

1 CORINTHIANS 15:3 ESV

Maybe you've gone through the acts of religion and faith and yet found yourself more often than not at a dry well. Prayers seem empty. Goals seem unthinkable. Christianity becomes a warped record full of highs and lows and off-key notes.

Is this all there is? Sunday attendance. Pretty songs. Faithful tithings. Golden crosses. Three-piece suits. Big choirs. Leather Bibles. It is nice and all, but . . . where is the heart of it?

Think about these words from Paul in 1 Corinthians, chapter 15. "For I delivered to you as of first importance what I also received, that Christ died for our sins in accordance with the Scriptures" (v. 3 ESV).

There it is. Almost too simple. Jesus was killed, buried, and resurrected. Surprised? The part that matters is the cross. No more and no less.

NO WONDER THEY CALL HIM THE SAVIOR

"The part that matters is the cross." Explain what that sentence means.

A Life of Service

We are many, but in Christ we are all
one body. Each one is a part of that body.

ROMANS 12:5

God has enlisted us in his navy and placed us on his ship. The boat has one purpose—to carry us safely to the other shore.

This is no cruise ship; it's a battleship. We aren't called to a life of leisure; we are called to a life of service. Each of us has a different task. Some, concerned with those who are drowning, are snatching people from the water. Others are occupied with the enemy, so they man the cannons of prayer and worship. Still others devote themselves to the crew, feeding and training the crew members.

Though different, we are the same. Each can tell of a personal encounter with the captain, for each has received a personal call.

We each followed him across the gangplank of his grace onto the same boat. There is one captain and one destination. Though the battle is fierce, the boat is safe, for our captain is God. The ship will not sink. For that, there is no concern.

IN THE GRIP OF GRACE

Describe your place of service on God's ship.

_____

_____

_____

_____

_____

A Personal Invitation

"Come to me . . . and I will give you rest."

MATTHEW 11:28

When Jesus says, "Come to me," he doesn't say come to religion, come to a system, or come to a certain doctrine. This is a very personal invitation to a God, an invitation to a Savior.

Our God is not aloof—he's not so far above us that he can't see and understand our problems. Jesus isn't a God who stayed on the mountaintop—he's a Savior who came down and lived and worked with the people. Everywhere he went, the crowds followed, drawn together by the magnet that was—and is—the Savior.

The life of Jesus Christ is a message of hope, a message of mercy, a message of life in a dark world.

THE INSPIRATIONAL STUDY BIBLE

Make a list of aspects of the message of Jesus Christ that personally bring you hope.

_____

_____

_____

_____

_____

_____

_____

God's Highest Dream

It is not our love for God; it is God's love for us
in sending his Son to be the way to take away our sins.

1 JOHN 4:10

We have attempted to reach the moon but scarcely made it off the ground. We tried to swim the Atlantic, but couldn't get beyond the reef. We have attempted to scale the Everest of salvation, but we have yet to leave the base camp, much less ascend the slope. The quest is simply too great. We don't need more supplies or muscle or technique; we need a helicopter.

Can't you hear it hovering?

"God has a way to *make people right with him*" (Romans 3:21, emphasis mine). How vital that we embrace this truth. God's highest dream is not to make us rich, not to make us successful or popular or famous. God's dream is to make us right with him.

IN THE GRIP OF GRACE

God's highest dream is not to make us rich, but to make us right with him. Does this make sense to most people? Why or why not? Does it make sense to you? Explain.

_____

_____

_____

_____

_____

The Journey to the Cross

This was God's plan which he had made long ago;
he knew all this would happen.

ACTS 2:23

Jesus died . . . on purpose. No surprise. No hesitation. No faltering.

You can tell a lot about a person by the way he dies. And the way Jesus marched to his death leaves no doubt: he had come to earth for this moment. Read the words of Peter. "Jesus was given to you, and with the help of those who don't know the law, you put him to death by nailing him to a cross. But this was God's plan which he had made long ago; he knew all this would happen" (Acts 2:23).

No, the journey to the cross didn't begin in Jericho. It didn't begin in Galilee. It didn't begin in Nazareth. It didn't even begin in Bethlehem.

The journey to the cross began long before. As the echo of the crunching of the fruit was still sounding in the garden, Jesus was leaving for Calvary.

AND THE ANGELS WERE SILENT

Describe how Christ's journey to the cross shows God's great love.

_____

_____

_____

_____

_____

The Doorway to Your Heart

*If people's thinking is controlled by
the sinful self, there is death. But if their thinking is
controlled by the Spirit, there is life and peace.*

ROMANS 8:6

Your heart is a fertile greenhouse ready to produce good fruit. Your mind is the doorway to your heart—the strategic place where you determine which seeds are sown and which seeds are discarded. The Holy Spirit is ready to help you manage and filter the thoughts that try to enter. He can help you guard your heart.

He stands with you on the threshold. A thought approaches, a questionable thought. Do you throw open the door and let it enter? Of course not. You "fight to capture every thought until it acknowledges the authority of Christ" (2 Corinthians 10:5 PHILLIPS). You don't leave the door unguarded. You stand equipped with handcuffs and leg irons, ready to capture any thought not fit to enter.

JUST LIKE JESUS

Explain how your mind is the doorway to your heart. How can you let the Holy Spirit help you guard your thoughts?

_____

_____

_____

_____

_____

An Uncommon Call

The Spirit has given each of us a special way of serving others.
1 CORINTHIANS 12:7 CEV

You have one. A divine spark. An uncommon call to an uncommon life. "The Spirit has given each of us a *special way* of serving others." So much for the excuse "I don't have anything to offer." Did the apostle Paul say, "The Spirit has given *some* of us . . ."? Or, "The Spirit has given *a few* of us . . ."? No. "The Spirit has given *each of us* a special way of serving others." Enough of this self-deprecating "I can't do anything."

And enough of its arrogant opposite: "I have to do everything." No, you don't! You're not God's solution to society, but a solution in society. Imitate Paul, who said, "Our goal is to stay within the boundaries of God's plan for us" (2 Corinthians 10:13 NLT). Clarify your contribution.

Don't worry about skills you don't have. Don't covet strengths others do have. Just extract your uniqueness.

CURE FOR THE COMMON LIFE

Do you ever worry about the skills you don't have? What is a better attitude to have toward your uniqueness?

We Need a Great Savior

[Peter] shouted, "Lord, save me!" Immediately Jesus
reached out his hand and caught Peter.

MATTHEW 14:30–31

We come to Christ in an hour of deep need. We abandon the boat of good works. We realize, like Peter, that spanning the gap between us and Jesus is a feat too great for our feet. So we beg for help. Hear his voice. And step out in fear, hoping that our little faith will be enough.

Faith is a desperate dive out of the sinking boat of human effort and a prayer that God will be there to pull us out of the water. Paul wrote about this kind of faith:

"For it is by grace you have been saved, through faith—and this not from yourselves, it is the gift of God—not by works, so that no one can boast" (Ephesians 2:8–9 NIV).

IN THE EYE OF THE STORM

Why do we tend to prefer good works to faith? Explain
why this is not God's plan.

_____

_____

_____

_____

_____

_____

_____

He Was Reachable

The Word became flesh and dwelt among us.

JOHN 1:14 NKJV

The Word became flesh," John said. In other words, he was touchable, approachable, reachable. And, what's more, he was ordinary. If he were here today you probably wouldn't notice him as he walked through a shopping mall. He wouldn't turn heads by the clothes he wore or the jewelry he flashed.

"Just call me Jesus," you can almost hear him say.

He was the kind of fellow you'd invite to watch the Rams-Giants game at your house. He'd wrestle on the floor with your kids, doze on your couch, and cook steaks on your grill. He'd laugh at your jokes and tell a few of his own. And when you spoke, he'd listen to you as if he had all the time in eternity.

And one thing's for sure, you'd invite him back.

GOD CAME NEAR

How does it encourage you to realize that Jesus was touchable and reachable?

Entering His Presence

For to me, to live is Christ and to die is gain.

PHILIPPIANS 1:21 NIV

J ust as a parent needs to know that his or her child is safe at school, we long to know that our loved ones are safe in death. We long for the reassurance that the soul goes immediately to be with God. But dare we believe it? Can we believe it? According to the Bible we can.

Scripture is surprisingly quiet about this phase of our lives. When speaking about the period between the death of the body and the resurrection of the body, the Bible doesn't shout; it just whispers. But at the confluence of these whispers, a firm voice is heard. This authoritative voice assures us that, at death, the Christian immediately enters into the presence of God and enjoys conscious fellowship with the Father and with those who have gone before.

WHEN CHRIST COMES

"At death, the Christian immediately enters into the presence of God." What does that promise mean to you? Does it encourage you?

_____

_____

_____

_____

_____

A Finished Work

God began doing a good work in you,
and I am sure he will continue it until it is finished.

PHILIPPIANS 1:6

The message of Jesus to the religious person is simple: It's not what you do. It's what I do. I have moved in.

Religious rule-keeping can sap your strength. It's endless. There is always another class to attend, Sabbath to obey, Ramadan to observe. No prison is as endless as the prison of perfection. Her inmates find work but never find peace. How could they? They never know when they are finished.

Christ, however, gifts you with a finished work. He fulfilled the law for you. Bid farewell to the burden of religion. Gone is the fear that having done everything, you might not have done enough. You climb the stairs, not by your strength, but his. God pledges to help those who stop trying to help themselves.

NEXT DOOR SAVIOR

Have you ever felt burdened by religious rule-keeping?
Why is it so exhausting? Why is it pointless?

Time Slips By

*In the past you wasted too much time doing
what nonbelievers enjoy.*

1 PETER 4:3

As we get older, our vision should improve. Not our vision of earth, but our vision of heaven. Those who have spent their life looking for heaven gain a skip in their step as the city comes into view. After Michelangelo died, someone found in his studio a piece of paper on which he had written a note to his apprentice. In the handwriting of his old age the great artist wrote: "Draw, Antonio, draw, and do not waste time."

Well-founded urgency, Michelangelo. Time slips. Days pass. Years fade. And life ends. And what we came to do must be done while there is time.

HE STILL MOVES STONES

Do you sense an urgency to spend your life for God? How does this affect your daily decisions?

_____

_____

_____

_____

_____

_____

_____

Everything You Need

*My God will use his wonderful riches
in Christ Jesus to give you everything you need.*

PHILIPPIANS 4:19

May I meddle for a moment? What is the one thing separating you from joy? How do you fill in this blank: "I will be happy when _____"? When I am healed. When I am promoted. When I am married. When I am single. When I am rich. How would you finish that statement?

Now, with your answer firmly in mind, answer this. If your ship never comes in, if your dream never comes true, if the situation never changes, could you be happy? If not, then you need to know what you have in your Shepherd.

You have a God who hears you, the power of love behind you, the Holy Spirit within you, and all of heaven ahead of you. If you have the Shepherd, you have grace for every sin, direction for every turn, a candle for every corner, and an anchor for every storm. You have everything you need.

TRAVELING LIGHT

*If you have the Shepherd, you have everything you need.
Explain what that statement means.*

Praise to God

Let us always offer to God our sacrifice of praise.

HEBREWS 13:15

You are a great God.
Your character is holy.
Your truth is absolute.
Your strength is unending.
Your discipline is fair.
Your provisions are abundant for our needs.
Your light is adequate for our path.
Your grace is sufficient for our sins.
You are never early, never late.
You sent your Son in the fullness of time and will return at
    the consummation of time.
Your plan is perfect.
Bewildering. Puzzling. Troubling.
But perfect.

"HE REMINDED US OF YOU"
(A PRAYER FOR A FRIEND)

*God's plan may be puzzling and troubling at times, but it is
always perfect. How does this affect the way you respond to
life's circumstances?*

Our Courteous Christ

"The Son of Man did not come to be served, but to serve."
MARK 10:45 NKJV

I had never thought much about the courtesy of Christ before, but as I began looking, I realized that Jesus makes Emily Post look like Archie Bunker.

He always knocks before entering. He doesn't have to. He owns your heart. If anyone has the right to barge in, Christ does. But he doesn't. That gentle tap you hear? It's Christ. "Behold, I stand at the door and knock" (Revelation 3:20 NASB). And when you answer, he awaits your invitation to cross the threshold.

And when he enters, he always brings a gift. Some bring Chianti and daisies. Christ brings "the gift of the Holy Spirit" (Acts 2:38). And, as he stays, he serves. "For even the Son of Man did not come to be served, but to serve" (Mark 10:45 NIV). If you're missing your apron, you'll find it on him. He's serving the guests as they sit (John 13:4–5). He won't eat until he's offered thanks, and he won't leave until the leftovers are put away (Matthew 14:19–20).

A LOVE WORTH GIVING

Christ served and gave and waited on others. How does this affect the way you treat others?

_____

_____

_____

_____

A Home for Your Heart

*Those who go to God Most High
for safety will be protected by the Almighty.*

PSALM 91:1

Chances are you've given little thought to housing your soul. We create elaborate houses for our bodies, but our souls are relegated to a hillside shanty where the night winds chill us and the rain soaks us. Is it any wonder the world is so full of cold hearts?

Doesn't have to be this way. We don't have to live outside. It's not God's plan for your heart to roam as a Bedouin. God wants you to move in out of the cold and live . . . with him. Under his roof there is space available. At his table a plate is set. In his living room a wingback chair is reserved just for you. And he'd like you to take up residence in his house. Why would he want you to share his home?

Simple, he's your Father.

THE GREAT HOUSE OF GOD

Have you "moved in out of the cold" and taken up residence with God? How has this changed your life?

_____

_____

_____

_____

_____

_____

Jesus Dispels Doubt

They were fearful and terrified. . . . But Jesus said,
"Why are you troubled? . . . It is I myself!"

Luke 24:37–39

They had betrayed their Master. When Jesus needed them they had scampered. And now they were having to deal with the shame.

Seeking forgiveness, but not knowing where to look for it, the disciples came back. They gravitated to that same Upper Room that contained the sweet memories of broken bread and symbolic wine.

They came back. Each with a scrapbook full of memories and a thin thread of hope. Each knowing that it is all over, but in his heart hoping that the impossible will happen once more. "If I had just one more chance."

And just when the gloom gets good and thick, just when their wishful thinking is falling victim to logic, just when someone says, "How I'd give my immortal soul to see him one more time," a familiar face walks through the wall.

My, what an ending. Or, better said, what a beginning!

NO WONDER THEY CALL HIM THE SAVIOR

Christ always *extends mercy. What does this mean to you?*

Waiting Forwardly

The day of the Lord will come like a thief. The skies will disappear with a loud noise. . . . So what kind of people should you be?

2 PETER 3:10–11

Great question. What kind of people should we be? Peter tells us: "You should live holy lives and serve God, as you wait for and look forward to the coming of the day of God" (2 Peter 3:11–12).

Hope of the future is not a license for irresponsibility in the present. Let us wait forwardly, but let us wait.

But for most of us, waiting is not our problem. Or, maybe I should state, waiting is our problem. We are so good at waiting that we don't wait forwardly. We forget to look. We are too content. We seldom search the skies. We seldom, if ever, allow the Holy Spirit to interrupt our plans and lead us to worship so that we might see Jesus.

WHEN CHRIST COMES

What determines whether we are living a holy life? Do we live this life by our own effort? Explain.

_____

_____

_____

_____

_____

_____

Help from the Holy Spirit

The Spirit comes to the aid of our weakness.

ROMANS 8:26 NEB

The Spirit comes to the aid of our weakness. What a sentence worthy of a highlighter. Who does not need this reminder? Weak bodies. Weak wills. Weakened resolves. We've known them all. The word *weakness* can refer to physical infirmities, as with the invalid who had been unable to walk for thirty-eight years (John 5:5), or spiritual impotence, as with the spiritually "helpless" of Romans 5:6.

Whether we are feeble of soul or body or both, how good to know it's not up to us. The Spirit himself is pleading for us.

COME THIRSTY

The Spirit himself is pleading before the throne of God on behalf of our weaknesses. Explain how this is such a comfort to us.

_____

_____

_____

_____

_____

_____

_____

_____

_____

Finding Good in the Bad

Wish good for those who harm you;
wish them well and do not curse them.

ROMANS 12:14

It would be hard to find someone worse than Judas. Some say he was a good man with a backfired strategy. I don't buy that. The Bible says, "Judas . . . was a thief" (John 12:6). The man was a crook. Somehow he was able to live in the presence of God and experience the miracles of Christ and remain unchanged. In the end he decided he'd rather have money than a friend, so he sold Jesus for thirty pieces of silver. Judas was a scoundrel, a cheat, and a bum. How could anyone see him any other way?

I don't know, but Jesus did. Only inches from the face of his betrayer, Jesus looked at him and said, "Friend, do what you came to do" (Matthew 26:50). What Jesus saw in Judas as worthy of being called a friend, I can't imagine. But I do know that Jesus doesn't lie, and in that moment he saw something good in a very bad man. He can help us do the same with those who hurt us.

JUST LIKE JESUS

Are there people who have hurt you? Why does God want you to call them "friend"?

You Can Trust Him

We can come before God's throne where there is grace.
There we receive mercy . . . to help us when we need it.

HEBREWS 4:16

Why did Jesus live on the earth as long as he did? Couldn't his life have been much shorter? Why not step into our world just long enough to die for our sins and then leave? Why not a sinless year or week? Why did he have to live a life? To take on our sins is one thing, but to take on our sunburns, our sore throats? To experience death, yes—but to put up with life? To put up with long roads, long days, and short tempers? Why did he do it?

Because he wants you to trust him.

He has been where you are and can relate to how you feel. And if his life on earth doesn't convince you, his death on the cross should. He understands what you are going through. Our Lord does not patronize us or scoff at our needs. He responds "generously to all without finding fault" (James 1:5 NIV).

HE CHOSE THE NAILS

Does knowing that Christ experienced life as we know it here on earth help you to trust him? Explain why.

A Faithful Father

*He is a faithful God who
does no wrong, who is right and fair.*

DEUTERONOMY 32:4

To recognize God as Lord is to acknowledge that he is sovereign and supreme in the universe. To accept him as Savior is to accept his gift of salvation offered on the cross. To regard him as Father is to go a step further. Ideally, a father is the one in your life who provides and protects. This is exactly what God has done.

He has provided for your needs (Matthew 6:25–34).

He has protected you from harm (Psalm 139:5).

He has adopted you (Ephesians 1:5). And he has given you his name (1 John 3:1).

God has proven himself as a faithful father. Now it falls to us to be trusting children.

HE STILL MOVES STONES

Write out each of the verses mentioned above. Describe what each one says God has done for you. How do you want to respond to his provision?

Religion by Computer

"Those who believe in the Son have eternal life."

JOHN 3:36

Computerized Christianity. Push the right buttons, enter the right code, insert the correct data, and bingo, print out your own salvation.

You do your part and the Divine Computer does his. No need to pray (after all, you control the keyboard). No emotional attachment necessary (who wants to hug circuits?). And worship? Well, worship is a lab exercise—insert the rituals and see the results.

Religion by computer. That's what happens when . . .

you replace the living God with a cold system;

you replace inestimable love with a pro forma budget;

you replace the ultimate sacrifice of Christ with the puny achievements of man.

AND THE ANGELS WERE SILENT

Has worship become a ritual for you? Write some of the ways God has shown his love to you and your family and let this rekindle your joy of worship.

The Voice of Adventure

The LORD is my light and my salvation—whom shall I fear?
PSALM 27:1 NIV

Jesus says the options are clear. On one side there is the voice of safety. You can build a fire in the hearth, stay inside, and stay warm and dry for what you don't try, right? You can't fall if you don't take a stand, right? You can't lose your balance if you never climb, right? So don't try it. Take the safe route.

Or you can hear the voice of adventure—God's adventure. Instead of building a fire in your hearth, build a fire in your heart. Follow God's impulses. Adopt the child. Move overseas. Teach the class. Change careers. Run for office. Make a difference. Sure it isn't safe, but what is?

HE STILL MOVES STONES

Why do we always tend to choose the side of safety? Is there a fire in your heart? What can you do to step out into God's adventure for your life?

Jesus Resisted Temptation

*He was tempted in every way that
we are, but he did not sin.*

HEBREWS 4:15

When his accusers called him a servant of Satan, Jesus demanded to see their evidence. "Which one of you convicts Me of sin?" he dared (John 8:46 NASB). Ask my circle of friends to point out my sin, and watch the hands shoot up. When those who knew Jesus were asked this same question, no one spoke. Christ was followed by disciples, analyzed by crowds, criticized by family, and scrutinized by enemies, yet not one person would remember him committing even one sin. He was never found in the wrong place. Never said the wrong word. Never acted the wrong way. He never sinned. Not that he wasn't tempted, mind you. He was "tempted in every way that we are, but he did not sin."

Lust wooed him. Greed lured him. Power called him. Jesus—the human—was tempted. But Jesus—the holy God—resisted.

NEXT DOOR SAVIOR

Jesus was tempted but never yielded to temptation. Explain how this can help us ask for his power to resist temptation.

Call It Grace

Being made right with God by his grace,
we could have the hope of receiving the life that never ends.

TITUS 3:7

You may be decent. You may pay taxes and kiss your kids and sleep with a clean conscience. But apart from Christ you aren't holy. So how can you go to heaven?

Only believe. Accept the work already done, the work of Jesus on the cross.

Accept the goodness of Jesus Christ. Abandon your own works and accept his. Abandon your own decency and accept his. Stand before God in his name, not yours.

It's that easy? There was nothing easy about it at all. The cross was heavy, the blood was real, and the price was extravagant. It would have bankrupted you or me, so he paid it for us. Call it simple. Call it a gift. But don't call it easy.

Call it what it is. Call it grace.

A GENTLE THUNDER

Our decency, our goodness, our works can never meet God's standard. Only Christ is qualified. Explain why we can never earn salvation.

_____

_____

_____

_____

_____

An Act of Grace

"I lay down my life for the sheep."
JOHN 10:15 NIV

Our Master lived a three-dimensional life. He had as clear a view of the future as he did of the present and the past.

This is why the ropes used to tie his hands and the soldiers used to lead him to the cross were unnecessary. They were incidental. Had they not been there, had there been no trial, no Pilate and no crowd, the very same crucifixion would have occurred. Had Jesus been forced to nail himself to the cross, he would have done it. For it was not the soldiers who killed him, nor the screams of the mob: It was his devotion to us.

So call it what you wish: an act of grace; a plan of redemption; a martyr's sacrifice. But whatever you call it, don't call it an accident. It was anything but that.

GOD CAME NEAR

The death of Christ was not an accident but an act of devotion. Write a few sentences explaining the meaning of that statement.

_____

_____

_____

_____

_____

God Is Your Home

"God is spirit, and those who worship him
must worship in spirit and truth."

JOHN 4:24

Don't think you are separated from God, he at the top end of a great ladder, you at the other. Dismiss any thought that God is on Venus while you are on earth. Since God is spirit (John 4:24), he is next to you: God himself is our roof. God himself is our wall. And God himself is our foundation.

Moses knew this. "Lord," he prayed, "you have been our home since the beginning" (Psalm 90:l). What a powerful thought: God as your home. Your home is the place where you can kick off your shoes and eat pickles and crackers and not worry about what people think when they see you in your bathrobe.

Your home is familiar to you. No one has to tell you how to locate your bedroom. God can be equally familiar to you. With time you can learn where to go for nourishment, where to hide for protection, where to turn for guidance. Just as your earthly house is a place of refuge, so God's house is a place of peace. God's house has never been plundered; his walls have never been breached.

THE GREAT HOUSE OF GOD

What steps can you take to know God better?

_____

_____

_____

_____

Take Risks for God

"Well done, good and faithful servant; you were faithful over a few things, I will make you ruler over many things."

MATTHEW 25:21 NKJV

Use your uniqueness to take great risks for God!

If you're great with kids, volunteer at the orphanage.

If you have a head for business, start a soup kitchen.

If God bent you toward medicine, dedicate a day or a decade to AIDS patients.

The only mistake is not to risk making one.

He lavished you with strengths in this life and a promise of the next. Go out on a limb; he won't let you fall. Take a big risk; he won't let you fail. He invites you to dream of the day you feel his hand on your shoulder and his eyes on your face. "Well done," he will say, "good and faithful servant."

CURE FOR THE COMMON LIFE

Are you afraid of taking great risks for God? Why or why not? How can you use your uniqueness for him?

A Treasure Map

In the beginning there was the Word.
The Word was with God, and the Word was God.

JOHN 1:1

The Bible has been banned, burned, scoffed, and ridiculed. Scholars have mocked it as foolish. Kings have branded it as illegal. A thousand times over the grave has been dug and the dirge has begun, but somehow the Bible never stays in the grave. Not only has it survived, it has thrived. It is the single most popular book in all of history. It has been the bestselling book in the world for years!

There is no way on earth to explain it. Which perhaps is the only explanation. The answer? The Bible's durability is not found on earth; it is found in heaven. For the millions who have tested its claims and claimed its promises there is but one answer—the Bible is God's book and God's voice .

The purpose of the Bible is to proclaim God's plan and passion to save his children. That is the reason this book has endured through the centuries. It is the treasure map that leads us to God's highest treasure, eternal life.

THE INSPIRATIONAL STUDY BIBLE

Describe some of the treasures you have found in God's Word.

_____

_____

_____

_____

Absurdities and Ironies

"Father, 'into your Hands I commit My spirit.'"

LUKE 23:46 NKJV

As Christ gave his final breath, the earth gave a sudden stir. A rock rolled, and a soldier stumbled. Then, as suddenly as the silence was broken, the silence returned. And now all is quiet. The mocking has ceased. There is no one to mock.

The soldiers are busy with the business of cleaning up the dead. Two men have come. Dressed well and meaning well, they are given the body of Jesus.

And we are left with the relics of his death.

Three nails in a bin.

Three cross-shaped shadows.

A braided crown with scarlet tips.

Bizarre, isn't it? The thought that this blood is not man's blood but God's?

Crazy, isn't it? To think that these nails held your sins to a cross?

Absurdities and ironies. The hill of Calvary is nothing if not both.

HE CHOSE THE NAILS

What do the images of Christ's death mean to you?

_____

_____

_____

_____

Salvation Celebration

"Rejoice that your names are written in heaven."

LUKE 10:20 NIV

According to Jesus our decisions have a thermostatic impact on the unseen world. Our actions on the keyboard of earth trigger hammers on the piano strings of heaven. Our obedience pulls the ropes which ring the bells in heaven's belfries. Let a child call and the ear of the Father inclines. And, most important, let a sinner repent, and every other activity ceases, and every heavenly being celebrates.

We don't always share such enthusiasm, do we? When you hear of a soul saved, do you drop everything and celebrate? Is your good day made better or your bad day salvaged? We may be pleased—but exuberant? When a soul is saved, the heart of Jesus becomes the night sky on the Fourth of July, radiant with explosions of cheer.

Can the same be said about us?

JUST LIKE JESUS

Do you remember the day you repented before the throne of the Father? How can you celebrate when others repent?

_____

_____

_____

_____

_____

_____

God's Mighty Angels

The angels are spirits who serve God and
are sent to help those who will receive salvation.

HEBREWS 1:14

Chiffon wings and meringue sweetness? Perhaps for angels in the gift books and specialty shops, but God's angels are marked by indescribable strength. Paul says Christ "will come with his mighty angels" (2 Thessalonians 1:7 NLT). From the word translated *mighty*, we have the English word *dynamic*. Angels pack dynamic force. It took only one angel to slay the firstborn of Egypt and only one angel to close the mouths of the lions to protect Daniel. David called angels "mighty creatures who carry out his plans, listening for each of his commands" (Psalm 103:20 NLT).

No need for you to talk to angels; they won't listen. Their ears incline only to God's voice. They are "spirits who serve God," responding to his command and following only his directions. Jesus said they "always see the face of my Father in heaven" (Matthew 18:10 NIV). Only one sound matters to angels—God's voice.

COME THIRSTY

What new insight have you gained from these comments?

_____

_____

_____

_____

The Gift of God's Smile

*We do not make requests of you because
we are righteous, but because of your great mercy.*

DANIEL 9:18 NIV

I f only, when God smiles and says we are saved, we'd salute him, thank him, and live like those who have just received a gift from the commander in chief.

We seldom do that, though. We prefer to get salvation the old-fashioned way: We earn it. To accept grace is to admit failure, a step we are hesitant to take. We opt to impress God with how good we are rather than confessing how great he is. We dizzy ourselves with doctrine. Burden ourselves with rules. Think that God will smile on our efforts.

He doesn't.

God's smile is not for the healthy hiker who boasts that he made the journey alone. It is, instead, for the crippled leper who begs God for a back on which to ride.

IN THE EYE OF THE STORM

Why do we opt to impress God with how good we are rather than confess how great he is?

_____

_____

_____

_____

_____

_____

Room for Miracles

*I [Thomas] will not believe it until I see the nail marks
in his hands and . . . put my hand into his side."*

JOHN 20:25

In our world of budgets, long-range planning, and computers, don't we find it hard to trust in the unbelievable? Don't most of us tend to scrutinize life behind furrowed brows and walk with cautious steps? It's hard for us to imagine that God can surprise us. To make a little room for miracles today, well, it's not sound thinking.

We make the same mistake that Thomas made: we forget that "impossible" is one of God's favorite words.

How about you? How is your imagination these days? When was the last time you let some of your dreams elbow out your logic? When was the last time you imagined the unimaginable? Has it been a while since you claimed God's promise to do "more than anything we can ask or imagine" (Ephesians 3:20)?

NO WONDER THEY CALL HIM THE SAVIOR

*Record some instances when God has shown you that
"impossible" is one of his favorite words.*

_____

_____

_____

_____

_____

Confident in the Father

The LORD comforts his people
and will have pity on those who suffer.

ISAIAH 49:13

I f you'll celebrate a marriage anniversary alone this year, [God] speaks to you.

If your child made it to heaven before making it to kindergarten, he speaks to you.

If your dreams were buried as they lowered the casket, God speaks to you.

He speaks to all of us who have stood or will stand in the soft dirt near an open grave. And to us he gives this confident word: "I want you to know what happens to a Christian when he dies so that when it happens, you will not be full of sorrow, as those are who have no hope. For since we believe that Jesus died and then came back to life again, we can also believe that when Jesus returns, God will bring back with him all the Christians who have died" (1 Thessalonians 4:13–14 TLB).

WHEN CHRIST COMES

Have you stood near an open grave? How did you feel?
What is God's promise of comfort to you?

_____

_____

_____

_____

_____

Love Rejoices in Truth

Love does not delight in evil but rejoices with the truth.

1 CORINTHIANS 13:6 NIV

In this verse lies a test for love.

Here's an example. A classic one. A young couple are on a date. His affection goes beyond her comfort zone. She resists. But he tries to persuade her with the oldest line in the book: "But I love you. I just want to be near you. If you loved me . . ."

That siren you hear? It's the phony-love detector. This guy doesn't love her. He may love her body. He may love boasting to his buddies about his conquest. But he doesn't love her. True love will never ask the "beloved" to do what he or she thinks is wrong.

Do you want to know if your love for someone is true? If your friendship is genuine? Ask yourself: Do I influence this person to do what is right?

A LOVE WORTH GIVING

Do you influence your friends to do what is right? Why or why not? How do your friends influence you?

It's Called "Choice"

To choose life is to love the LORD your God,
obey him, and stay close to him.

He placed one scoop of clay upon another until a form lay lifeless on the ground.

All were silent as the Creator reached in himself and removed something yet unseen. "It's called 'choice.' The seed of choice."

Within the man, God had placed a divine seed. A seed of his *self*. The God of might had created earth's mightiest. The Creator had created, not a creature, but another creator. And the One who had chosen to love had created one who could love in return.

Now it's our choice.

IN THE EYE OF THE STORM

God did not want robots to respond to his love. He wanted humans to choose his love. Explain how this indicates the depth of his love for you. Does he love even those who choose not to love him?

_____

_____

_____

_____

_____

_____

Fretting Is Futile

"You cannot add any time to your life by worrying about it."
MATTHEW 6:27

No one has to remind you of the high cost of anxiety. (But I will anyway.) Worry divides the mind. The biblical word for *worry* (*merimnao*) is a compound of two Greek words, *merizo* ("to divide") and *nous* ("the mind"). Anxiety splits our energy between today's priorities and tomorrow's problems. Part of our mind is on the now; the rest is on the not yet. The result is half-minded living.

That's not the only result. Worrying is not a disease, but it causes diseases. It has been connected to high blood pressure, heart trouble, blindness, migraine headaches, thyroid malfunctions, and a host of stomach disorders.

Anxiety is an expensive habit. Of course, it might be worth the cost if it worked. But it doesn't. Our frets are futile. Worry has never brightened a day, solved a problem, or cured a disease.

TRAVELING LIGHT

Describe some of the high costs of anxiety. Now write how your life might change if you decided to worry less.

Do Something

Faith that does nothing is dead!

JAMES 2:26

Faith is not the belief that God will do what you want. Faith is the belief that God will do what is right. God is always near and always available. Just waiting for your touch. So let him know. Demonstrate your devotion:

> Write a letter.
>
> Ask forgiveness.
>
> Be baptized.
>
> Feed a hungry person.
>
> Pray.
>
> Teach.
>
> Go.

Do something that demonstrates faith. For faith with no effort is no faith at all. *God will respond.* He has never rejected a genuine gesture of faith. Never.

HE STILL MOVES STONES

Make a list of things you can do to demonstrate your faith. How do you want God to respond?

_____

_____

_____

_____

_____

_____

Brag About That!

Don't praise yourself. Let someone else do it.

PROVERBS 27:2

Demanding respect is like chasing a butterfly. Chase it, and you'll never catch it. Sit still, and it may light on your shoulder. The French philosopher Blaise Pascal asked, "Do you wish people to speak well of you? Don't speak well of yourself." Maybe that's why the Bible says, "Don't praise yourself. Let someone else do it."

Do you feel a need for affirmation? Does your self-esteem need attention? You don't need to drop names or show off. You need only pause at the base of the cross and be reminded of this: The Maker of the stars would rather die for you than live without you. And that is a fact. So if you need to brag, brag about that.

TRAVELING LIGHT

Does it lift your sense of self-worth to know that the Maker of the stars was willing to die for you? Explain why.

A Crisp View of God

*LORD, even when I have trouble
all around me, you will keep me alive.*

PSALM 138:7

There is a window in your heart through which you can see God. Once upon a time that window was clear. Your view of God was crisp. You could see God as vividly as you could see a gentle valley or hillside.

Then, suddenly, the window cracked. A pebble broke the window. A pebble of pain.

And suddenly God was not so easy to see. The view that had been so crisp had changed.

You were puzzled. God wouldn't allow something like this to happen, would he?

When you can't see him, trust him. . . . Jesus is closer than you've ever dreamed.

IN THE EYE OF THE STORM

Has the window of your heart ever been cracked by a pebble of pain? What is the most helpful way to respond at those times? What is the most harmful?

_____

_____

_____

_____

_____

_____

"Come to Me"

*"Come to me, all of you who are tired
and have heavy loads, and I will give you rest."*

MATTHEW 11:28

"Come to me." The invitation is to come to him. Why him? He offers the invitation as a penniless rabbi in an oppressed nation. He has no political office, no connections with the authorities in Rome. He hasn't written a best seller or earned a diploma.

Yet, he dares to look into the leathery faces of farmers and tired faces of housewives and offer rest. He looks into the disillusioned eyes of a preacher or two from Jerusalem. He gazes into the cynical stare of a banker and the hungry eyes of a bartender and makes this paradoxical promise: "Take my yoke upon you and learn from me, for I am gentle and humble in heart, and you will find rest for your souls" (Matthew 11:29 NIV).

The people came. They came out of the cul-de-sacs and office complexes of their day. They brought him the burdens of their existence, and he gave them not religion, not doctrine, not systems, but rest.

SIX HOURS ONE FRIDAY

Write a note of thanksgiving to Christ for his rest.

In a Word

"He who overcomes, and keeps My works until the end,
to him I will give power over the nations."

REVELATION 2:26 NKJV

Think for a moment about this question: What if God weren't here on earth? You think people can be cruel now; imagine us without the presence of God. You think we are brutal to each other now; imagine the world without the Holy Spirit. You think there is loneliness and despair and guilt now; imagine life without the touch of Jesus. No forgiveness. No hope. No acts of kindness. No words of love. No more food given in his name. No more songs sung to his praise. No more deeds done in his honor. If God took away his angels, his grace, his promise of eternity, and his servants, what would the world be like?

In a word, hell.

JUST LIKE JESUS

Make your own list of things that would be missing from life
without the touch of Jesus. How does this encourage you?

_____

_____

_____

_____

_____

_____

_____

Jesus Knows

"I am the one God chose and sent into the world."

JOHN 10:36

God with us.

He knows hurt. His siblings called him crazy.

He knows hunger. He made a meal out of wheat-field grains.

He knows exhaustion. So sleepy, he dozed in a storm-tossed boat.

Most of all, he knows sin. Not his own, mind you. But he knows yours.

Every lie you've told.

Person you've hurt.

Promise you've broken.

Every deed you've committed against God—for all sin is against God—Jesus knows. He knows them better than you do. He knows their price. Because he paid it.

CURE FOR THE COMMON LIFE

How do you respond when you realize that God knows all your sins better than you do? Explain why.

What Heaven Holds

"There is joy in the presence of the angels
of God when one sinner changes his heart and life."

LUKE 15:10

Why do Jesus and his angels rejoice over one repenting sinner? Can they see something we can't? Do they know something we don't? Absolutely. They know what heaven holds.

Heaven is populated by those who let God change them. Arguments will cease, for jealousy won't exist. Suspicions won't surface, for there will be no secrets. Every sin is gone. Every insecurity is forgotten. Every fear is past. Pure wheat. No weeds. Pure gold. No alloy. Pure love. No lust. Pure hope. No fear. No wonder the angels rejoice when one sinner repents; they know another work of art will soon grace the gallery of God. They know what heaven holds.

JUST LIKE JESUS

Do you know someone who has repented of sin and come to God? Describe how the hand of God has changed that life.

_____

_____

_____

_____

_____

The Embers of Love

God has given us the Holy Spirit, who fills our hearts with his love.
ROMANS 5:5 CEV

What if you're married to someone you don't love—or who doesn't love you? Many choose to leave. That may be the step you take. But if it is, take at least a thousand others first. And bathe every one of those steps in prayer. Love is a fruit of the Spirit. Ask God to help you love as he loves. "God has given us the Holy Spirit, who fills our hearts with his love." Ask everyone you know to pray for you. Your friends. Your family. Your church leaders. Get your name on every prayer list available. And, most of all, pray for and, if possible, with your spouse. Ask the same God who raised the dead to resurrect the embers of your love.

Isn't it good to know that even when we don't love with a perfect love, he does? God always nourishes what is right. He always applauds what is right. He has never done wrong, led one person to do wrong, or rejoiced when anyone did wrong. For he is love.

A LOVE WORTH GIVING

God loves with a perfect love even when we do not. How does this encourage you about people and circumstances in your life?

No Secrets from God

If anyone belongs to Christ, there is a new creation.
The old things have gone; everything is made new!

2 CORINTHIANS 5:17

Have you been there? Have you felt the ground of conviction give way beneath your feet? The ledge crumbles, your eyes widen, and down you go. *Poof!*

Now what do you do? When we fall, we can dismiss it. We can deny it. We can distort it. Or we can deal with it.

We keep no secrets from God. Confession is not telling God what we did. He already knows. Confession is simply agreeing with God that our acts were wrong.

How can God heal what we deny? How can God grant us pardon when we won't admit our guilt? Ahh, there's that word: guilt. Isn't that what we avoid? Guilt. Isn't that what we detest? But is guilt so bad? What does guilt imply if not that we know right from wrong, that we aspire to be better than we are? That's what guilt is: a healthy regret for telling God one thing and doing another.

A GENTLE THUNDER

What is the dictionary definition of guilt? How would you describe it? Explain why guilt can be a good thing.

"No More"

*The Lord himself will come down from heaven
with a loud command.*

1 Thessalonians 4:16

Have you ever wondered what that command will be? It will be the inaugural word of heaven. It will be the first audible message most have heard from God. It will be the word that closes one age and opens a new one.

I think I know what the command will be. I could very well be wrong, but I think the command that puts an end to the pains of the earth and initiates the joys of heaven will be two words: "No more."

The King of kings will raise his pierced hand and proclaim, "No more."

The angels will stand and the Father will speak, "No more."

Every person who lives and who ever lived will turn toward the sky and hear God announce, "No more."

No more loneliness.

No more tears.

No more death. No more sadness. No more crying. No more pain.

And the Angels Were Silent

What things would you add to the list of "no more"?

_____

_____

_____

_____

A Gentle Lamb

Where God's love is, there is no fear,
because God's perfect love drives out fear.

1 JOHN 4:18

A lot of us live with a hidden fear that God is angry at us. Somewhere, sometime, some Sunday school class or some television show convinced us that God has a whip behind his back, a paddle in his back pocket, and he's going to nail us when we've gone too far.

No concept could be more wrong! Our Savior's Father is very fond of us and only wants to share his love with us.

We have a Father who is filled with compassion, a feeling Father who hurts when his children hurt. We serve a God who says that even when we're under pressure and feel like nothing is going to go right, he is waiting for us, ready to embrace us whether we succeed or fail.

He doesn't come quarreling and wrangling and forcing his way into anyone's heart. He comes into our hearts like a gentle lamb, not a roaring lion.

WALKING WITH THE SAVIOR

Why is it important to know that God embraces us whether we succeed or fail?

_____

_____

_____

_____

Give Up Your Life

He gave up his place with God and made himself nothing.

PHILIPPIANS 2:7

God grants us an uncommon life to the degree we surrender our common one. "If you try to keep your life for yourself, you will lose it. But if you give up your life for me, you will find true life" (Matthew 16:25 NLT).

Jesus did. He "made Himself of no reputation, taking the form of a bondservant, and coming in the likeness of men. . . . He humbled Himself and became obedient to the point of death" (Philippians 2:7–8 NKJV).

No one in Nazareth saluted him as the Son of God. He did not stand out in his elementary-classroom photograph, demanded no glossy page in his high school annual. Friends knew him as a woodworker, not star hanger. His looks turned no heads; his position earned him no credit. "He gave up his place with God and made himself nothing."

God hunts for those who will do likewise—people through whom he can deliver Christ into the world.

CURE FOR THE COMMON LIFE

Explain why God is looking for people who are willing to become nothing.

God's Faithfulness

My God will use his wonderful riches in
Christ Jesus to give you everything you need.

PHILIPPIANS 4:19

God's faithfulness has never depended on the faithfulness of his children. He is faithful even when we aren't. When we lack courage, he doesn't. He has made a history out of using people in spite of people.

Need an example? The feeding of the five thousand. It's the only miracle, aside from those of the final week, recorded in all four Gospels. Why did all four writers think it worth repeating? Perhaps they wanted to show how God doesn't give up even when his people do.

When the disciples didn't pray, Jesus prayed. When the disciples didn't see God, Jesus sought God. When the disciples were weak, Jesus was strong. When the disciples had no faith, Jesus had faith.

I simply think God is greater than our weakness. In fact, I think it is our weakness that reveals how great God is.

God is faithful even when his children are not.

A GENTLE THUNDER

In what areas of life do you need a great God? A faithful God?

_____

_____

_____

_____

_____

Words of Hope

Everything that was written in the past was
written to teach us, so that . . . we might have hope.

ROMANS 15:4 NIV

Encourage those who are struggling. Don't know what to say?
Then open your Bible.

To the grief stricken: "God has said, 'Never will I leave
you; never will I forsake you'" (Hebrews 13:5 NIV).

To the guilt ridden: "There is now no condemnation for those
who are in Christ Jesus" (Romans 8:1 NIV).

To the jobless: "In all things God works for the good of those
who love him" (Romans 8:28 NIV).

To those who feel beyond God's grace: "Whoever believes in
him shall not perish but have eternal life" (John 3:16 NIV).

Your Bible is a basket of blessings. Won't you share one?

A LOVE WORTH GIVING

Your Bible is a basket of blessings. Make a list of some of
the blessings you can share with a friend in need.

A Heart like His

From this time on we do not think of anyone as the world does.

2 CORINTHIANS 5:16

Ask God to help you have his eternal view of the world. His view of humanity is starkly simple. From his perspective every person is either:

Entering through the small gate or the wide gate (Matthew 7:13–14).

Heaven called or hell bound (Mark 16:16).

Our ledger, however, is cluttered with unnecessary columns. Is he rich? Is she pretty? What work does he do? What color is her skin? Does she have a college degree? These matters are irrelevant to God.

To have a heart like his is to look into the faces of the saved and rejoice! They are just one grave away from being just like Jesus. To have a heart like his is to look into the faces of the lost and pray. For unless they turn, they are one grave away from torment.

JUST LIKE JESUS

When you have a heart like Jesus, how will you respond to the saved? How will you respond to the lost?

_____

_____

_____

_____

_____

Choose Love

Those who live in love live in God.

1 JOHN 4:16

From the file entitled "It Ain't Gonna Happen," I pull and pose this suggestion. Let's make Christ's command a federal law. Everyone has to make God's love his or her home. Let it herewith be stated and hereby declared:

> *No person may walk out into the world to begin the day until he or she has stood beneath the cross to receive God's love.*

Cabbies. Presidents. Preachers. Tooth pullers and truck drivers. All required to linger at the fountain of his favor until all thirst is gone.

Don't you ache for the change we'd see? Less honking and locking horns, more hugging and helping kids. We'd pass fewer judgments and more compliments. Forgiveness would skyrocket.

Wild idea? I agree. God's love can't be legislated, but it can be chosen. Choose it, won't you? For Christ's sake, and yours, choose it.

COME THIRSTY

Have you chosen to stand at the foot of the cross to receive God's love? How has this affected your life?

_____

_____

_____

_____

_____

A Plate of Experiences

"I have good plans for you, not plans to hurt you."

JEREMIAH 29:11

Last night during family devotions, I called my daughters to the table and set a plate in front of each. In the center of the table I placed a collection of food: some fruit, some raw vegetables, and some Oreo cookies. "Every day," I explained, "God prepares for us a plate of experiences. What kind of plate do you most enjoy?"

The answer was easy. Sara put three cookies on her plate. Some days are like that, aren't they? Some days are "three-cookie days." Many are not. Sometimes our plate has nothing but vegetables—twenty-four hours of celery, carrots, and squash. Apparently God knows we need some strength, and though the portion may be hard to swallow, isn't it for our own good? Most days, however, have a bit of it all.

The next time your plate has more broccoli than apple pie, remember who prepared the meal. And the next time your plate has a portion you find hard to swallow, talk to God about it. Jesus did.

THE GREAT HOUSE OF GOD

What is the wise way to handle dull, difficult, and even dreary days?

_____

_____

_____

_____

_____

OCTOBER 29 🌙 EVENING

Work Can Be Worship

Everything you do or say should be done to obey Jesus your Lord.
COLOSSIANS 3:17

Have you seen the painting *The Angelus* by Jean-Francois Millet? It portrays two peasants praying in their field. A church steeple sits on the horizon, and a light falls from heaven. The rays do not fall on the church, however. They don't fall on the bowed heads of the man and woman. The rays of the sun fall on the wheelbarrow and the pitchfork at the couple's feet.

God's eyes fall on the work of our hands. Our Wednesdays matter to him as much as our Sundays. He blurs the secular and sacred. One stay-at-home mom keeps this sign over her kitchen sink: "Divine tasks performed here, daily." An executive hung this plaque in her office: "My desk is my altar." Both are correct. With God, our work matters as much as our worship. Indeed, work can be worship.

CURE FOR THE COMMON LIFE

Do you view your work as worship? Why or why not?

633

Love Is All You'll Find

We know the love that God has for us, and we trust that love.

Water must be wet. A fire must be hot. You can't take the wet out of water and still have water. You can't take the heat out of fire and still have fire.

In the same way, you can't take the love out of [God] and still have him exist. For he was and is Love.

Probe deep within him. Explore every corner. Search every angle. Love is all you find. Go to the beginning of every decision he has made and you'll find it. Go to the end of every story he has told and you'll see it.

Love.

No bitterness. No evil. No cruelty. Just love. Flawless love. Passionate love. Vast and pure love. He is love.

IN THE EYE OF THE STORM

"You can't take the love out of God and still have him exist." Explain what that statement means. How does it affect the way you respond to people and events in life?

_____

_____

_____

_____

_____

_____

Life Is Long Enough

*All the days planned for me were
written in your book before I was one day old.*

PSALM 139:16

No person lives one day more or less than God intends. "All the days planned for me were written in your book before I was one day old."

But her days here were so few . . .

His life was so brief . . .

To us it seems that way. We speak of a short life, but compared to eternity, who has a long one? A person's days on earth may appear as a drop in the ocean. Yours and mine may seem like a thimbleful. But compared to the Pacific of eternity, even the years of Methuselah filled no more than a glass.

In God's plan every life is long enough and every death is timely. And though you and I might wish for a longer life, God knows better.

TRAVELING LIGHT

*"In God's plan every life is long enough." How does that
statement relate to your life? To the lives of people you hold dear?*

Everyone Will See Him

*"After I go and prepare a place
for you, I will come back and take you to be
with me so that you may be where I am."*

JOHN 14:3

Someday, according to Christ, he will set us free. He will come back.

In the blink of an eye, as fast as the lightning flashes from the east to the west, he will come back. And everyone will see him—you will, I will. Bodies will push back the dirt and break the surface of the sea. The earth will tremble, the sky will roar, and those who do not know him will shudder. But in that hour you will not fear, because you know him.

WHEN CHRIST COMES

In the blink of an eye Christ will return. How does that affect the way you live? Explain why.

_____

_____

_____

_____

_____

_____

_____

The Muck and Mire

*God will show his mercy forever and
ever to those who worship and serve him.*

Luke 1:50

For thirty-three years he would feel everything you and I have ever felt. He felt weak. He grew weary. He was afraid of failure. He was susceptible to wooing women. He got colds, burped, and had body odor. His feelings got hurt.

To think of Jesus in such a light is—well, it seems almost irreverent, doesn't it? It's not something we like to do; it's uncomfortable. It is much easier to keep the humanity out of the incarnation. Clean the manure from around the manger. Wipe the sweat out of his eyes. Pretend he never snored or blew his nose or hit his thumb with a hammer.

He's easier to stomach that way. There is something about keeping him divine that keeps him distant, packaged, predictable.

But don't do it. For heaven's sake, don't. Let him be as human as he intended to be. Let him into the mire and muck of our world. For only if we let him in can he pull us out.

God Came Near

Why does Christ want you to let him into the muck and mire of your world?

637

November

*"Then you will know the truth,
and the truth will make you free."*

—John 8:32

Take Jesus at His Word

*In all these things we have full victory
through God who showed his love for us.*

ROMANS 8:37

When it comes to healing our spiritual condition, we don't have a chance. We might as well be told to pole-vault the moon. We don't have what it takes to be healed. Our only hope is that God will do for us what he did for the man at Bethesda—that he will step out of the temple and step into our ward of hurt and helplessness.

Which is exactly what he has done.

I wish we would take Jesus at his word.

When he says we're forgiven, let's unload the guilt.

When he says we're valuable, let's believe him.

When he says we're provided for, let's stop worrying.

God's efforts are strongest when our efforts are useless.

HE STILL MOVES STONES

*When Jesus says you're forgiven, do you unload your guilt?
How does this affect your peace of mind?*

_____

_____

_____

_____

_____

A Love That Never Fails

You show unfailing love to your anointed . . .
PSALM 18:50 NLT

Some of you are so thirsty for this type of love. A love that never fails. Those who should have loved you didn't. Those who could have loved you didn't. You were left at the hospital. Left at the altar. Left with an empty bed. Left with a broken heart. Left with your question "Does anybody love me?"

Please listen to heaven's answer. God loves you. Personally. Powerfully. Passionately. Others have promised and failed. But God has promised and succeeded. He loves you with an unfailing love. And his love—if you will let it—can fill you and leave you with a love worth giving.

So come. Come thirsty and drink deeply.

A LOVE WORTH GIVING

Has human love ever failed you? How does God's promise of unfailing love encourage you?

Sinner, Set Free

"Then you will know the truth, and the truth will make you free."

JOHN 8:32

Think of it this way. Sin put you in prison. Sin locked you behind the bars of guilt and shame and deception and fear. Sin did nothing but shackle you to the wall of misery. Then Jesus came and paid your bail. He served your time; he satisfied the penalty and set you free. Christ died, and when you cast your lot with him, your old self died too.

The only way to be set free from the prison of sin is to serve its penalty. In this case the penalty is death. Someone has to die, either you or a heaven-sent substitute. You cannot leave prison unless there is a death. But that death has occurred at Calvary. And when Jesus died, you died to sin's claim on your life. You are free.

IN THE GRIP OF GRACE

Christ paid the penalty for your sin. You are free from sin's claim on your life. Why is this such good news? What are the benefits to you?

_____

_____

_____

_____

_____

_____

God Entered Time

They will sing about what the LORD has done,
because the LORD's glory is great.

PSALM 138:5

When God entered time and became a man, he who was boundless became bound. For more than three decades, his once limitless reach would be limited to the stretch of an arm, his speed checked to the pace of human feet.

I wonder, was he ever tempted to reclaim his boundlessness? When the rain chilled his bones, was he tempted to change the weather? When the heat parched his lips, did he give thought to popping over to the Caribbean for some refreshment?

If ever he entertained such thoughts, he never gave in to them. Not once did Christ use his supernatural powers for personal comfort. With one word he could've transformed the hard earth into a soft bed, but he didn't. With a wave of his hand, he could've boomeranged the spit of his accusers back into their faces, but he didn't. With an arch of his brow, he could've paralyzed the hand of the soldier as he braided the crown of thorns. But he didn't.

HE CHOSE THE NAILS

Although Christ could have used his power for personal comfort, he never did. Why is that to our benefit?

_____

_____

_____

_____

Are You Listening?

"Everyone who asks will receive. Everyone who searches will find."

MATTHEW 7:8

Once there was a man who dared God to speak: *Burn the bush like you did for Moses, God. And I will follow. Collapse the walls like you did for Joshua, God. And I will fight. Still the waves like you did on Galilee, God. And I will listen.*

And so the man sat by a bush, near a wall, close to the sea and waited for God to speak.

And God heard the man, so God answered. He sent fire, not for a bush, but for a church. He brought down a wall, not of brick, but of sin. He stilled a storm, not of the sea, but of a soul.

And God waited for the man to respond. And he waited . . . and waited.

But because the man was looking at bushes and not hearts, bricks and not lives, seas and not souls, he decided that God had done nothing.

Finally he looked to God and asked, *Have you lost your power?*

And God looked at him and said, *Have you lost your hearing?*

A GENTLE THUNDER

Sometimes God is answering our prayer but it seems he has done nothing. How should we respond?

_____

_____

_____

_____

God Uses the Common

"Those who try to keep their lives will lose them.
But those who give up their lives will save them."

LUKE 17:33

Heaven may have a shrine to honor God's uncommon use of the common.

It's a place you won't want to miss. Stroll through and see Rahab's rope, Paul's bucket, David's sling, and Samson's jawbone. Wrap your hand around the staff that split the sea and smote the rock. Sniff the ointment that soothed Jesus' skin and lifted his heart.

I don't know if these items will be there. But I am sure of one thing—the people who used them will.

The risk takers: Rahab who sheltered the spy. The brethren who smuggled Paul.

The conquerors: David, slinging a stone. Samson, swinging a bone. Moses, lifting a rod.

The caregivers: Mary at Jesus' feet. What she gave cost much, but somehow she knew what he would give would cost more.

AND THE ANGELS WERE SILENT

What names of common people would you add to the list
of risk takers, conquerors, and caregivers?

_____

_____

_____

_____

Run the Race

Let us run the race that is before us and never give up.

HEBREWS 12:1

The word *race* is from the Greek *agon,* from which we get the word *agony.* The Christian's race is not a jog but rather a demanding and grueling, sometimes agonizing race. It takes a massive effort to finish strong.

Likely you've noticed that many don't? Surely you've observed there are many on the side of the trail? They used to be running. There was a time when they kept the pace. But then weariness set in. They didn't think the run would be this tough.

By contrast, Jesus' best work was his final work, and his strongest step was his last step. Our Master is the classic example of one who endured. He could have quit the race. But he didn't.

JUST LIKE JESUS

It takes a massive effort to finish strong in the spiritual race. Is it important to you to endure to the end? What steps can you take to build your spiritual stamina?

Glimpses of God's Image

Everything comes from God alone. Everything lives by his power, and everything is for his glory.

ROMANS 11:36 TLB

The breath you just took? God gave that. The blood that just pulsed through your heart? Credit God. The light by which you read and the brain with which you process? He gave both. Everything comes from him . . . and exists for him. We exist to exhibit God, to display his glory. We serve as canvases for his brushstroke, papers for his pen, soil for his seeds, glimpses of his image.

CURE FOR THE COMMON LIFE

Think of your life as a canvas for God's brushstroke. How would you describe the image he is creating of your life?

Got It All Figured Out

I look at your heavens, which you made with
your fingers. . . . But why are people important to you?

PSALM 8:3–4

We understand how storms are created. We map solar systems and transplant hearts. We measure the depths of the oceans and send signals to distant planets. We have studied the system and are learning how it works.

And, for some, the loss of mystery has led to the loss of majesty. The more we know, the less we believe. Strange, don't you think? Knowledge of the workings shouldn't negate wonder. Knowledge should stir wonder. Who has more reason to worship than the astronomer who has seen the stars?

Ironically, the more we know, the less we worship. We are more impressed with our discovery of the light switch than with the One who invented electricity. Rather than worship the Creator, we worship the creation (Romans 1:25).

No wonder there is no wonder. We've figured it all out.

IN THE GRIP OF GRACE

Rather than worship the Creator, we worship the creation.
Explain what that statement means. What are the results?

_____

_____

_____

_____

Our Ultimate Dilemma

"I am the resurrection and the life.
He who believes in me will live, even though he dies."

JOHN 11:25 NIV

Her words were full of despair. "If you had been here . . ."
(John 11:21). She stares into the Master's face with
confused eyes. She'd been strong long enough; now it
hurt too badly. Lazarus was dead. Her brother was gone. And the
one man who could have made a difference didn't. He hadn't even
made it for the burial. Something about death makes us accuse God
of betrayal. "If God were here there would be no death!" we claim.

You see, if God is God anywhere, he has to be God in the face
of death. Pop psychology can deal with depression. Pep talks can
deal with pessimism. Prosperity can handle hunger. But only God
can deal with our ultimate dilemma—death. And only the God of
the Bible has dared to stand on the canyon's edge and offer an
answer. He has to be God in the face of death. If not, he is not God
anywhere.

GOD CAME NEAR

Only God can deal with our ultimate dilemma—death.
How have you experienced that truth in your own life or
the life of a friend?

_____

_____

_____

The High Cost of Getting Even

*Do not try to punish others when they wrong you, but wait
for God to punish them with his anger.*

ROMANS 12:19

H ave you ever noticed in the western movies how the bounty hunter travels alone? It's not hard to see why. Who wants to hang out with a guy who settles scores for a living? Who wants to risk getting on his bad side? More than once I've heard a person spew his anger. He thought I was listening, when really I was thinking, *I hope I never get on his list.* Cantankerous sorts, these bounty hunters. Best leave them alone. Hang out with the angry and you might catch a stray bullet. Debt-settling is a lonely occupation. It's also an unhealthy occupation. . . .

If you're out to settle the score, you'll never rest. How can you? For one thing, your enemy may never pay up. As much as you think you deserve an apology, your debtor may not agree. The racist may never repent. The chauvinist may never change. As justified as you are in your quest for vengeance, you may never get a penny's worth of justice. And if you do, will it be enough?

THE GREAT HOUSE OF GOD

*Debt-settling is a lonely and unhealthy occupation. Why is
that? Do you know anyone who fits that description?*

_____

_____

_____

_____

The Shepherd Leads

He makes me to lie down in green pastures;
He leads me beside the still waters.

PSALM 23:2 NKJV

I n the second verse of the Twenty-third Psalm, David the poet becomes David the artist. His quill becomes a brush, his parchment a canvas, and his words paint a picture. A flock of sheep on folded legs, encircling a shepherd. Bellies nestled deep in the long shoots of grass. A still pond on one side, the watching shepherd on the other. "He makes me to lie down in green pastures; He leads me beside the still waters."

Note the two pronouns preceding the two verbs. *He* makes me . . . *He* leads me.

Who is the active one? Who is in charge? The Shepherd. The Shepherd selects the trail and prepares the pasture. The sheep's job—our job—is to watch the Shepherd.

TRAVELING LIGHT

How can you keep your eyes on the Shepherd? How can you let him be in charge of your life?

God Loves You Dearly

We love because God first loved us.

1 JOHN 4:19

Untethered by time, he sees us all. From the backwoods of Virginia to the business district of London, from the Vikings to the astronauts, from the cave dwellers to the kings. From the hut-builders to the finger-pointers to the rock-stackers, he sees us. Vagabonds and ragamuffins all, he saw us before we were born.

And he loves what he sees. Flooded by emotion. Overcome by pride, the Star Maker turns to us, one by one, and says, "You are my child. I love you dearly. I'm aware that someday you'll turn from me and walk away. But I want you to know, I've already provided you a way back."

IN THE GRIP OF GRACE

God loves you dearly. How do you respond to such love? What difference does it make in your life?

_____

_____

_____

_____

_____

_____

_____

_____

Courteous Conduct

Be wise in the way you act with people who are not believers.
COLOSSIANS 4:5

Those who don't believe in Jesus note what we do. They make decisions about Christ by watching us. When we are kind, they assume Christ is kind. When we are gracious, they assume Christ is gracious. But if we are brash, what will people think about our King? When we are dishonest, what assumption will an observer make about our Master? No wonder Paul says, "Be wise in the way you act with people who are not believers, making the most of every opportunity. When you talk, you should always be kind and pleasant so you will be able to answer everyone in the way you should" (Colossians 4:5–6). Courteous conduct honors Christ.

It also honors his children. When you surrender a parking place to someone, you honor him. When you return a borrowed book, you honor the lender. When you make an effort to greet everyone in the room, especially the ones others may have overlooked, you honor God's children.

A LOVE WORTH GIVING

Make a list of the ways your life has honored Christ in the past few days.

Finishing Strong

Think about Jesus' example. He held on while wicked people
were doing evil things to him. So do not get tired and stop trying.

HEBREWS 12:3

Heaven was not foreign to Jesus. He is the only person to live on earth *after* he had lived in heaven. As believers, you and I will live in heaven after time on earth, but Jesus did just the opposite. He knew heaven before he came to earth. He knew what awaited him upon his return. And knowing what awaited him in heaven enabled him to bear the shame on earth.

He "accepted the shame as if it were nothing because of the joy that God put before him" (Hebrews 12:2). In his final moments, Jesus focused on the joy God put before him. He focused on the prize of heaven. By focusing on the prize, he was able not only to finish the race but to finish it strong.

JUST LIKE JESUS

Jesus was able to bear shame on earth knowing what
awaited him in heaven. Do you know what awaits you in
heaven? How does that encourage you?

_____

_____

_____

_____

_____

_____

In the Beginning . . .

In him there was life, and that life was the light of all people.

JOHN 1:4

I've always perceived the apostle John as a fellow who viewed life simply. "Right is right and wrong is wrong, and things aren't nearly as complicated as we make them out to be."

For example, defining Jesus would be a challenge to the best of writers, but John handles the task with casual analogy. The Messiah, in a word, was "the Word." A walking message. A love letter. Be he a fiery verb or a tender adjective, he was, quite simply, a word.

And life? Well, life is divided into two sections, light and darkness. If you are in one, you are not in the other and vice versa.

Next question?

NO WONDER THEY CALL HIM THE SAVIOR

John described Jesus as "the Word." Make a list of words you would use to describe Jesus and what he means to you.

A Compassionate God

He comforts us every time we have trouble,
so when others have trouble, we can comfort them.

2 CORINTHIANS 1:4

My child's feelings are hurt. I tell her she's special.

My child is injured. I do whatever it takes to make her feel better.

My child is afraid. I won't go to sleep until she is secure.

I'm not a hero. . . . I'm a parent. When a child hurts, a parent does what comes naturally. He helps.

Why don't I let my Father do for me what I am more than willing to do for my own children?

I'm learning. Being a father is teaching me that when I am criticized, injured, or afraid, there is a Father who is ready to comfort me. There is a Father who will hold me until I'm better, help me until I can live with the hurt, and who won't go to sleep when I'm afraid of waking up and seeing the dark.

Ever.

THE APPLAUSE OF HEAVEN

Describe how it helps you to know that your heavenly Father is ready to comfort you and help you.

_____

_____

_____

_____

_____

It's Not Up to You

The Spirit speaks to God for his people in the way God wants.
ROMANS 8:27

None of us pray as much as we should, but all of us pray more than we think, because the Holy Spirit turns our sighs into petitions and tears into entreaties. He speaks for you and protects you. He makes sure you get heard.

Now, suppose a person never learns about the sealing and intercession of the Spirit. This individual thinks that salvation security resides in self, not God, that prayer power depends on the person, not the Spirit. What kind of life will this person lead? A parched and prayerless one.

But what if you believe in the work of the Spirit? Will you be different as a result? You bet your sweet Sunday you will. Your shoulders will lift as you lower the buckling weight of self-salvation. Your knees will bend as you discover the buoyant power of the praying Spirit. Higher walk. Deeper prayers. And, most of all, a quiet confidence that comes from knowing it's not up to you.

COME THIRSTY

The Holy Spirit speaks for you and protects you. What does that statement mean to you?

The Verdict

*Jesus said [to her], "I also don't judge you guilty.
You may go now, but don't sin anymore."*

JOHN 8:11

If you have ever wondered how God reacts when you fail, frame the words [of that verse] and hang them on the wall. Read them. Ponder them.

Or better still, take him with you to your canyon of shame. Invite Christ to journey with you . . . to stand beside you as you retell the events of the darkest nights of your soul.

And then listen. Listen carefully. He's speaking. "I don't judge you guilty."

And watch. Watch carefully. He's writing. He's leaving a message. Not in the sand, but on a cross.

Not with his hand, but with his blood.

His message has two words: Not guilty.

HE STILL MOVES STONES

Think of Christ's hand writing those two words for you: Not guilty. How does that make you feel? How do you respond to such merciful love?

_____

_____

_____

_____

_____

_____

He Understands

*"God even knows how many hairs
are on your head. So don't be afraid."*

MATTHEW 10:30–31

Why did Jesus grow weary in Samaria (John 4:6), disturbed in Nazareth (Mark 6:6), and angry in the temple (John 2:15)? Why was he sleepy in the boat on the Sea of Galilee (Mark 4:38), sad at the tomb of Lazarus (John 11:35), and hungry in the wilderness (Matthew 4:2)?

Why? Why did he endure all these feelings? Because he knew you would feel them too.

He knew you would be weary, disturbed, and angry. He knew you'd be sleepy, grief-stricken, and hungry. He knew you'd face pain. If not the pain of the body, the pain of the soul . . . pain too sharp for any drug. He knew you'd face thirst. If not a thirst for water, at least a thirst for truth, and the truth we glean from the image of a thirsty Christ is—he understands.

And because he understands, we can come to him.

HE CHOSE THE NAILS

Make a list of some of the things Christ endured here on earth that qualify him to understand your feelings.

_____

_____

_____

_____

He Wore Our Coat

*They have washed their robes and
made them white in the blood of the Lamb.*

REVELATION 7:14

God has only one requirement for entrance into heaven: that we be clothed in Christ.

Listen to how Jesus describes the inhabitants of heaven: "They will walk with me and wear white clothes, because they are worthy" (Revelation 3:4).

Listen to the description of the elders: "Around the throne there were . . . twenty-four elders. They were dressed in white and had golden crowns on their heads" (v. 4:4).

All are dressed in white. The saints. The elders. How would you suppose Jesus is dressed? In white? "He is dressed in a robe dipped in blood, and his name is the Word of God" (v. 19:13).

Why is Christ's robe not white? Why is his cloak not spotless? Why is his garment dipped in blood? Paul says simply, "He changed places with us" (Galatians 3:13).

He wore our coat of sin to the cross.

WHEN CHRIST COMES

Christ wore your coat of sin to the cross. How would you describe such love?

_____

_____

_____

_____

Who Does the Saving?

A person is made right with God
through faith, not through obeying the law.

ROMANS 3:28

I
f we are saved by good works, we don't need God—weekly reminders of the dos and don'ts will get us to heaven. If we are saved by suffering, we certainly don't need God. All we need is a whip and a chain and the gospel of guilt. If we are saved by doctrine, then, for heaven's sake, let's study! We don't need God; we need a lexicon.

But be careful, student. For if you are saved by having exact doctrine, then one mistake would be fatal. That goes for those who believe we are made right with God through deeds. I hope the temptation is never greater than the strength. If it is, a bad fall could be a bad omen. And those who think we are saved by suffering, take caution as well, for you never know how much suffering is required.

It took Paul decades to discover what he wrote in only one sentence: "A person is made right with God through faith." Not through good works, suffering, or study.

AND THE ANGELS WERE SILENT

Explain why we can never pay for the gift of salvation.

_____

_____

_____

_____

Honest with God

If you hide your sins, you will not succeed.

PROVERBS 28:13

Our [high school] baseball coach had a firm rule against chewing tobacco. We had a couple of players who were known to sneak a chew, and he wanted to call it to our attention.

He got our attention, all right. Before long we'd all tried it. A sure test of manhood was to take a chew when the pouch was passed down the bench. I had barely made the team; I sure wasn't going to fail the test of manhood.

One day I'd just popped a plug in my mouth when one of the players warned, "Here comes the coach!" Not wanting to get caught, I did what came naturally; I swallowed. *Gulp.*

I added new meaning to the Scripture, "I felt weak deep inside me. I moaned all day long" (Psalm 32:3). I paid the price for hiding my disobedience.

My body was not made to ingest tobacco. Your soul was not made to ingest sin.

May I ask a frank question? Are you keeping any secrets from God? Take a pointer from a nauseated third baseman. You'll feel better if you get it out.

IN THE GRIP OF GRACE

Why is it always better to be totally honest with God?

_____

_____

_____

Let Him Change Your Mind

Set your mind on the things above,
not on the things that are on earth.

COLOSSIANS 3:2 NASB

G od changes the man by changing the mind. And how does it happen? By considering the glory of Christ.

To behold him is to become like him. As Christ dominates your thoughts, he changes you from one degree of glory to another until—hang on!—you are ready to live with him.

Heaven is the land of sinless minds. Absolute trust. No fear or anger. Shame and second-guessing are practices of a prior life. Heaven will be wonderful, not because the streets are gold, but because our thoughts will be pure.

So what are you waiting on? Give him your best thoughts, and see if he doesn't change your mind.

NEXT DOOR SAVIOR

In heaven our thoughts will be pure. Write down some
reasons you are looking forward to that.

Saying "Thank You"

Thank the LORD because he is good. His love continues forever.

PSALM 106:1

Worship is when you're aware that what you've been given is far greater than what you can give. Worship is the awareness that were it not for his touch, you'd still be hobbling and hurting, bitter and broken. Worship is the half-glazed expression on the parched face of a desert pilgrim as he discovers that the oasis is not a mirage.

Worship is the "thank you" that refuses to be silenced.

We have tried to make a science out of worship. We can't do that. We can't do that any more than we can "sell love" or "negotiate peace."

Worship is a voluntary act of gratitude offered by the saved to the Savior, by the healed to the Healer, and by the delivered to the Deliverer.

IN THE EYE OF THE STORM

How would you describe worship? List some examples of worship in the Bible that are meaningful to you.

_____

_____

_____

_____

_____

_____

_____

Claim God's Forgiveness

For as many of you as were baptized into Christ have put on Christ.
GALATIANS 3:27 RSV

Y ou read it right. We have "put on" Christ. When God looks at us he doesn't see us; he sees Christ. We "wear" him. We are hidden in him; we are covered by him. As the song says, "Dressed in his righteousness alone, faultless to stand before the throne."

Presumptuous, you say? Sacrilegious? It would be if it were my idea. But it isn't; it's his. We are presumptuous not when we marvel at his grace, but when we reject it. And we're sacrilegious not when we claim his forgiveness, but when we allow the haunting sins of yesterday to convince us that God forgives but he doesn't forget.

Do yourself a favor. Remember . . . he forgot.

GOD CAME NEAR

Do you sometimes forget that God always forgets the sins of yesterday? Write a note of thanksgiving to him for his great forgetfulness.

A Place for the Weary

Do not lose the courage you
had in the past, which has a great reward.

HEBREWS 10:35

I s there anything more frail than a bruised reed? Look at the bruised reed at the water's edge. A once slender and tall stalk of sturdy river grass, it is now bowed and bent.

Are you a bruised reed? Was it so long ago that you stood so tall, so proud?

Then something happened. You were bruised . . .

by harsh words

by a friend's anger

by a spouse's betrayal. . . .

The bruised reed. Society knows what to do with you. The world will break you off; the world will snuff you out.

But the artists of Scripture proclaim that God won't. Painted on canvas after canvas is the tender touch of a Creator who has a special place for the bruised and weary of the world. A God who is the friend of the wounded heart.

HE STILL MOVES STONES

Are you a bruised reed? What would you like God to do to help you?

_____

_____

_____

_____

God with Us

"They shall call His name Immanuel,"
which is translated, "God with us."

MATTHEW 1:23 NKJV

G od's treatment for insignificance won't lead you to a bar or
dating service, a spouse or social club. God's ultimate cure
for the common life takes you to a manger. The babe of
Bethlehem. Immanuel. Remember the promise of the angel?
"'Behold, the virgin shall be with child, and bear a Son, and they
shall call His name Immanuel,' which is translated, 'God with us'"
(Matthew 1:23 NKJV).

Immanuel. The name appears in the same Hebrew form as it
did two thousand years ago. *Immanu* means "with us." *El* refers to
Elohim, or God. Not an "above us God" or a "somewhere in the
neighborhood God." He came as the "with us God." God with us.

Not "God with the rich" or "God with the religious." But God
with *us*. All of us. Russians, Germans, Buddhists, Mormons, truck
drivers and taxi drivers, librarians. God with *us*.

CURE FOR THE COMMON LIFE

God is with all of us, not just some of us. Explain why that
is such good news.

667

Fix Your Eyes on Jesus

*May he enlighten the eyes of your mind
so that you can see what hope his call holds for you.*

EPHESIANS 1:18 TJB

What [does] it mean to be just like Jesus? The world has never known a heart so pure, a character so flawless. His spiritual hearing was so keen he never missed a heavenly whisper. His mercy so abundant he never missed a chance to forgive. No lie left his lips, no distraction marred his vision. He touched when others recoiled. He endured when others quit. Jesus is the ultimate model for every person. God urges you to fix your eyes upon Jesus. Heaven invites you to set the lens of your heart on the heart of the Savior and make him the object of your life.

JUST LIKE JESUS

"Set the lens of your heart on the heart of the Savior."
Explain what this means. What steps can you take to do this?

_____

_____

_____

_____

_____

_____

_____

The Drama of Redemption

With one sacrifice he made perfect forever
those who are being made holy.

HEBREWS 10:14

We would have scripted the moment differently. Ask us how a God should redeem his world, and we will show you! White horses, flashing swords. Evil flat on his back. God on his throne.

But God on a cross?

A split-lipped, puffy-eyed, blood-masked God on a cross?

Sponge thrust in his face?

Spear plunged in his side?

Dice tossed at his feet?

No, we wouldn't have written the drama of redemption this way. But, then again, we weren't asked to. These players and props were heaven picked and God ordained. We were not asked to design the hour.

But we have been asked to respond to it.

HE CHOSE THE NAILS

How do you respond to God's plan of salvation?

God Knows the Answers

*If any of you needs wisdom,
you should ask God for it.*

JAMES 1:5

Thomas came with doubts. Did Christ turn him away?
Moses had his reservations. Did God tell him to go home?
Job had his struggles. Did God avoid him?
Paul had his hard times. Did God abandon him?

No. God never turns away the sincere heart. Tough questions don't stump God. He invites our probing.

Mark it down. God never turns away the honest seeker. Go to God with your questions. You may not find all the answers, but in finding God, you know the One who does.

WALKING WITH THE SAVIOR

Do you have questions you are afraid to ask God? How can you overcome this fear?

_____

_____

_____

_____

_____

_____

_____

_____

Take Heart!

May the Lord lead your hearts into God's love and Christ's patience.

2 THESSALONIANS 3:5

The majority is not always right. If the majority had ruled, the children of Israel never would have left Egypt. They would have voted to stay in bondage. If the majority had ruled, David never would have fought Goliath. His brothers would have voted for him to stay with the sheep. What's the point? You must listen to your own heart.

God says you're on your way to becoming a disciple when you can keep a clear head and a pure heart.

Do you ever wonder if everything will turn out right as long as you do everything right? Do you ever try to do something right and yet nothing seems to turn out like you planned? Take heart—when people do what is right, God remembers.

THE INSPIRATIONAL STUDY BIBLE

Have you ever found it hard to listen to your own heart because the majority disagreed? Write how you can learn to listen to your own heart.

Spiritual Life from the Spirit

Now we do not live following our sinful selves,
but we live following the Spirit.

ROMANS 8:4

Perhaps your childhood memories bring more hurt than inspiration. The voices of your past cursed you, belittled you, ignored you. At the time, you thought such treatment was typical. Now you see it isn't.

And now you find yourself trying to explain your past. Do you rise above the past and make a difference? Or do you remain controlled by the past and make excuses?

Think about this. Spiritual life comes from the Spirit! Your parents may have given you genes, but God gives you grace. Your parents may be responsible for your body, but God has taken charge of your soul. You may get your looks from your mother, but you get eternity from your Father, your heavenly Father. And God is willing to give you what your family didn't.

WHEN GOD WHISPERS YOUR NAME

What can you do to let God give you what your family didn't?

_____

_____

_____

_____

_____

_____

Go with Your Heart

After Mary saw Jesus, she went and told his followers,
who were very sad and were crying.

MARK 16:10

Tears represent the heart, the spirit, and the soul of a person. To put a lock and key on your emotions is to bury part of your Christlikeness!

Especially when you come to Calvary.

You can't go to the cross with just your head and not your heart. It doesn't work that way. Calvary is not a mental trip. It's not an intellectual exercise. It's not a divine calculation or a cold theological principle.

It's a heart-splitting hour of emotion.

Don't walk away from it dry-eyed and unstirred. Don't just straighten your tie and clear your throat. Don't allow yourself to descend Calvary cool and collected.

Please . . . pause. Look again.

Those are nails in those hands. That's God on that cross. It's us who put him there.

NO WONDER THEY CALL HIM THE SAVIOR

Why do we need to come to the cross with both head and heart?

_____

_____

_____

_____

_____

It's Your Choice

"If people want to follow me, they must give up the things they want. They must be willing even to give up their lives to follow me."

MARK 8:34

On one side stands the crowd.
Jeering. Baiting. Demanding.
On the other stands a peasant.
Swollen lips. Lumpy eye. Lofty promise.
One promises acceptance, the other a cross.
One offers flesh and flash, the other offers faith.
The crowd challenges, "Follow us and fit in."
Jesus promises, "Follow me and stand out."
They promise to please. God promises to save.
God looks at you and asks, "Which will be your choice?"

A GENTLE THUNDER

The crowd invites you to fit in. Jesus promises you will stand out. Which choice is easier? Which do you choose? Why?

_____

_____

_____

_____

_____

_____

When Love Is Real

Rejoice with those who rejoice, and weep with those who weep.

ROMANS 12:15 NASB

The summer before my eighth-grade year I made friends with a guy named Larry. He was new to town, so I encouraged him to go out for our school football team.

The result was a good news–bad news scenario. The good news? He made the cut. The bad news? He won my position. I tried to be happy for him, but it was tough.

A few weeks into the season Larry fell off a motorcycle and broke a finger. I remember the day he stood at my front door holding up his bandaged hand. "Looks like you're going to have to play."

I tried to feel sorry for him, but it was hard. The passage was a lot easier for Paul to write than it was for me to practice. "Rejoice with those who rejoice, and weep with those who weep."

You want to plumb the depths of your love for someone? How do you feel when that person succeeds?

A LOVE WORTH GIVING

Do you find it easy to rejoice with those who rejoice and weep with those who weep? Why or why not?

_____

_____

_____

_____

What Makes God, God?

If we are not faithful, he will still be faithful,
because he cannot be false to himself.

2 TIMOTHY 2:13

G od's blessings are dispensed according to the riches of his grace, not according to the depth of our faith.

Why is that important to know? So you won't get cynical. Look around you. Aren't there more mouths than bread? Aren't there more wounds than physicians? Aren't there more who need the truth than those who tell it?

So what do we do? Throw up our hands and walk away? Tell the world we can't help them?

No, we don't give up. We look up. We trust. We believe. And our optimism is not hollow. Christ has proven worthy. He has shown that he never fails. That's what makes God, God.

A GENTLE THUNDER

Have you ever felt like throwing up your hands and walking away? What is the only reliable solution?

_____

_____

_____

_____

_____

_____

Timely Help

We will find grace to help us when we need it.

HEBREWS 4:16 NLT

God's help is timely. He helps us the same way a father gives plane tickets to his family. When I travel with my kids, I carry all our tickets in my satchel. When the moment comes to board the plane, I stand between the attendant and the child. As each daughter passes, I place a ticket in her hand. She, in turn, gives the ticket to the attendant. Each one receives the ticket in the nick of time.

What I do for my daughters God does for you. He places himself between you and the need. And at the right time, he gives you the ticket. Wasn't this the promise he gave his disciples? "When you are arrested and judged, don't worry ahead of time about what you should say. Say whatever is *given you to say at that time*, because it will not really be you speaking; it will be the Holy Spirit" (Mark 13:11, emphasis mine).

God leads us. He will do the right thing at the right time.

TRAVELING LIGHT

How will we live if we believe that God will do the right thing at the right time?

_____

_____

_____

_____

Run to Jesus

If we live, we are living for the Lord,
and if we die, we are dying for the Lord.

ROMANS 14:8

D
o you wonder where you can go for encouragement and motivation? Go back to that moment when you first saw the love of Jesus Christ. Remember the day when you were separated from Christ? You knew only guilt and confusion and then—a light. Someone opened a door and light came into your darkness, and you said in your heart, "I am redeemed!"

Run to Jesus. Jesus wants you to go to him. He wants to become the most important person in your life, the greatest love you'll ever know. He wants you to love him so much that there's no room in your heart and in your life for sin. Invite him to take up residence in your heart.

WALKING WITH THE SAVIOR

"God wants you to love him so much that there's no room in your heart for sin." Explain what that means.

Do You Doubt?

Anyone who doubts is like a wave in the sea,
blown up and down by the wind.

JAMES 1:6

Doubt. He's a nosy neighbor. He's an unwanted visitor. He's an obnoxious guest.

He'll pester you. He'll irritate you. He'll criticize your judgment. His aim is not to convince you but to confuse you. He doesn't offer solutions; he only raises questions.

Had any visits from this fellow lately? If you find yourself going to church in order to be saved and not because you are saved, then you've been listening to him. If you find yourself doubting God could forgive you again for that, you've been sold some snake oil. If you are more cynical about Christians than sincere about Christ, then guess who came to dinner?

I suggest you put a lock on your gate. I suggest you post a "Do Not Enter" sign on your door.

SIX HOURS ONE FRIDAY

Think of a time when you let doubts enter your mind. What were the results?

A Diligent Search

Anyone who comes to God must believe that he is real and that he rewards those who truly want to find him.

HEBREWS 11:6

One translation renders Hebrews 11:6: "God . . . rewards those who earnestly seek him" (NIV). I like the King James translation: "He is a rewarder of them that *diligently* seek him" (emphasis mine).

Diligently—what a great word. Be diligent in your search. Be hungry in your quest, relentless in your pilgrimage. Let this book be but one of dozens you read about Jesus. Step away from the puny pursuits of possessions and positions, and seek your King.

Don't be satisfied with angels. Don't be content with stars in the sky. Seek him out as the shepherds did. Long for him as Simeon did. Worship him as the wise men did. Do as John and Andrew did: ask for his address. Do as Matthew: invite Jesus into your house. Imitate Zacchaeus. Risk whatever it takes to see Christ.

JUST LIKE JESUS

Are you diligently seeking to live for Christ? How can you be more diligent?

_____

_____

_____

_____

_____

_____

God Became One of Us

"I came that they may have life and have it abundantly."

JOHN 10:10 ESV

For thousands of years, God gave us his voice. Prior to Bethlehem, he gave his messengers, his teachers, his words. But in the manger, God gave us himself.

Many people have trouble with such a teaching. Islam sees God as one who sends others. He sends angels, prophets, books, but God is too holy to come to us himself. For God to touch the earth would be called a "shirk." People who claim that God has touched the earth shirk God's holiness; they make him gross. They blaspheme him.

Christianity, by contrast, celebrates God's great descent. His nature does not trap him in heaven, but leads him to earth. In God's great gospel, he not only sends, he becomes; he not only looks down, he lives among; he not only talks to us, he lives with us as one of us.

CURE FOR THE COMMON LIFE

Christianity celebrates God's descent from heaven to earth. Explain why this is such a contrast to many other religions.

When God Says No

*"Whoever comes to me will never be hungry,
and whoever believes in me will never be thirsty."*

JOHN 6:35

There are times when the one thing you want is the one thing
you never get.

You pray and wait.

No answer.

You pray and wait.

May I ask a very important question? What if God says no?

What if the request is delayed or even denied? When God says
no to you, how will you respond? If God says, "I've given you my
grace, and that is enough," will you be content?

Content. That's the word. A state of heart in which you would be
at peace if God gave you nothing more than he already has.

IN THE GRIP OF GRACE

*When you pray for something, do you decide at the time
what the answer will be? What if God gives a different
answer? Will you be content if he says no?*

_____

_____

_____

_____

_____

_____

The Final Gathering

*"Always be ready, because you don't know the day your
ord will come."*

MATTHEW 24:42

Every person who has ever lived will be present at that final gathering. Every heart that has ever beat. Every mouth that has ever spoken. On that day you will be surrounded by a sea of people. Rich, poor. Famous, unknown. Kings, bums. Brilliant, demented. All will be present. And all will be looking in one direction. All will be looking at him. Every human being.

"The Son of Man will come again in his great glory" (Matthew 25:31).

You won't look at anyone else. No side glances to see what others are wearing. No whispers about new jewelry or comments about who is present. At this, the greatest gathering in history, you will have eyes for only One—the Son of Man. Wrapped in splendor. Shot through with radiance. Imploded with light and magnetic in power.

AND THE ANGELS WERE SILENT

Describe the beauty of Christ's radiance that all will behold.

A Passion for Excellence

In Christ Jesus, God made us to do good works,
which God planned in advance for us to live our lives doing.

EPHESIANS 2:10

The push for power has come to shove. And most of us are either pushing or being pushed.

I might point out the difference between a passion for excellence and a passion for power. The desire for excellence is a gift of God, much needed in society. It is characterized by respect for quality and a yearning to use God's gifts in a way that pleases him.

But there is a canyon of difference between doing your best to glorify God and doing whatever it takes to glorify yourself. The quest for excellence is a mark of maturity. The quest for power is childish.

THE APPLAUSE OF HEAVEN

Describe the difference between glorifying God and glorifying self.

_____

_____

_____

_____

_____

_____

_____

The Best Way to Face Life

Teach us how short our lives really are so that we may be wise.

PSALM 90:12

In a life marked by doctor appointments, dentist appointments, and school appointments, there is one appointment that none of us will miss, the appointment with death. "Everyone must die once, and after that be judged by God" (Hebrews 9:27 TEV). Oh, how we'd like to change that verse. Just a word or two would suffice. "*Nearly everyone* must die . . ." or "*Everyone but me* must die . . ." or "*Everyone who forgets to eat right and take vitamins must die . . .*" But those are not God's words. In his plan everyone must die, even those who eat right and take their vitamins.

Exercise may buy us a few more heartbeats. Medicine may grant us a few more breaths. But in the end, there is an end. And the best way to face life is to be honest about death.

TRAVELING LIGHT

"The best way to face life is to be honest about death."
What does that sentence mean to you?

A True Family

"My true brother and sister and
mother are those who do what God wants."

MARK 3:35

Does Jesus have anything to say about dealing with difficult relatives? Is there an example of Jesus bringing peace to a painful family? Yes there is.

His own.

It may surprise you to know that Jesus had a family at all! You may not be aware that Jesus had brothers and sisters. He did. Quoting Jesus' hometown critics, Mark wrote, "[Jesus] is just the carpenter, the son of Mary and the brother of James, Joseph, Judas, and Simon. And his sisters are here with us" (Mark 6:3).

And it may surprise you to know that his family was less than perfect. They were. If your family doesn't appreciate you, take heart; neither did Jesus'.

[Yet] he didn't try to control his family's behavior, nor did he let their behavior control his. He didn't demand that they agree with him. He didn't sulk when they insulted him. He didn't make it his mission to try to please them.

HE STILL MOVES STONES

How would Christ respond to your family?

_____

_____

_____

_____

Why Did He Do It?

Being with you will fill me with joy; at your right hand I will find pleasure forever.

PSALM 16:11

Holiday travel. It isn't easy. Then why do we do it? Why cram the trunks and endure the airports? You know the answer. We love to be with the ones we love.

The four-year-old running up the sidewalk into the arms of Grandpa.

The cup of coffee with Mom before the rest of the house awakes.

That moment when, for a moment, everyone is quiet as we hold hands around the table and thank God for family and friends and pumpkin pie.

We love to be with the ones we love.

May I remind you? So does God. He loves to be with the ones he loves. How else do you explain what he did? Between him and us there was a distance—a great span. And he couldn't bear it. He couldn't stand it. So he did something about it.

"He gave up his place with God and made himself nothing."

NEXT DOOR SAVIOR

What did God do to be with the ones he loves?

_____

_____

_____

_____

Heavenly Rewards

"When the master comes and finds the
servant doing his work, the servant will be blessed."

MATTHEW 24:46

The stadium is packed today. Since Friday, [Mark] McGwire has hit not one or two home runs, but three. For thirty-seven years, no one could hit more than sixty-one homers in one season; now the St. Louis slugger has hit sixty-eight. And he isn't finished. The fans are on their feet before he comes to bat; they stay on their feet long after he crosses the plate.

Not everyone can be a Mark McGwire. For every million who aspire, only one achieves. The vast majority of us don't hit the big ball, don't feel the ticker tape, don't wear the gold medal, don't give the valedictory address.

And that's okay. We understand that in the economy of earth, there are a limited number of crowns.

The economy of heaven, however, is refreshingly different. Heavenly rewards are not limited to a chosen few, but "to all those who have waited with love for him to come again" (2 Timothy 4:8).

WHEN CHRIST COMES

In heaven we will all win a prize. How does that make you feel?

_____

_____

_____

_____

A Useful Vessel

"If you give up your life for me, you will find true life."

MATTHEW 16:25 NLT

When you're full of yourself, God can't fill you. But when you empty yourself, God has a useful vessel. Your Bible overflows with examples of those who did.

In his Gospel, Matthew mentions his own name only twice. Both times he calls himself a tax collector. In his list of apostles, he assigns himself the eighth spot.

John doesn't even mention his name in his Gospel. The twenty appearances of "John" all refer to the Baptist. John the apostle simply calls himself "the other disciple" or the "disciple whom Jesus loved."

Luke wrote two of the most important books in the Bible but never once penned his own name.

CURE FOR THE COMMON LIFE

Why is it such a struggle for most of us to be empty of ourselves? Why is this necessary before God can use us?

The Bridge of Confession

I said, "I will confess my sins to the LORD," and you forgave my guilt.

PSALM 32:5

Once there were a couple of farmers who couldn't get along with each other. A wide ravine separated their two farms, but as a sign of their mutual distaste for each other, each constructed a fence on his side of the chasm to keep the other out.

In time, however, the daughter of one met the son of the other, and the couple fell in love. Determined not to be kept apart by the folly of their fathers, they tore down the fence and used the wood to build a bridge across the ravine.

Confession does that. Confessed sin becomes the bridge over which we can walk back into the presence of God.

IN THE GRIP OF GRACE

Why is the "bridge" of confession so important to a vital Christian life? How does unconfessed sin affect our relationship with God?

_____

_____

_____

_____

_____

_____

A Plea for Mercy

The Lord is not . . . willing that any
should perish but that all should come to repentance.

2 PETER 3:9 NKJV

What of those who die with no faith? My husband never prayed. My grandpa never worshiped. My mother never opened a Bible, much less her heart. What about the one who never believed?

How do we know he didn't?

Who among us is privy to a person's final thoughts? Who among us knows what transpires in those final moments? Are you sure no prayer was offered? Eternity can bend the proudest knees. Could a person stare into the yawning canyon of death without whispering a plea for mercy? And could our God, who is partial to the humble, resist it?

He couldn't on Calvary. The confession of the thief on the cross was both a first and final one. But Christ heard it. Christ received it. Maybe you never heard your loved one confess Christ, but who's to say Christ didn't?

TRAVELING LIGHT

How does it comfort you to know that God hears even the smallest plea for mercy?

We Need a Shepherd

The LORD is my shepherd; I have everything I need.

PSALM 23:1

S heep aren't smart. They tend to wander into running creeks for water, then their wool grows heavy and they drown. They need a shepherd to lead them to "calm water" (Psalm 23:2). They have no natural defense—no claws, no horns, no fangs. They are helpless. Sheep need a shepherd with a "rod and . . . shepherd's staff" (v. 23:4) to protect them. They have no sense of direction. They need someone to lead them "on paths that are right" (v. 23:3).

So do we. We, too, tend to be swept away by waters we should have avoided. We have no defense against the evil lion who prowls about seeking whom he might devour. We, too, get lost.

We need a shepherd. We need a shepherd to care for us and to guide us. And we have one. One who knows us by name.

A GENTLE THUNDER

We have a Shepherd who cares for us and guides us. Does that mean we are not responsible for our actions? What is our responsibility?

_____

_____

_____

_____

_____

He Didn't Quit

He came to that which was his own,
but his own did not receive him.

JOHN 1:11 NIV

Lee Ielpi is a retired firefighter, a New York City firefighter. He gave twenty-six years to the city. But on September 11, 2001, he gave much more. He gave his son. Jonathan Ielpi was a fireman as well. When the Twin Towers fell, he was there.

Firefighters are a loyal clan. When one perishes in the line of duty, the body is left where it is until a firefighter who knows the person can come and quite literally pick it up. Lee made the discovery of his son's body his personal mission. He dug daily with dozens of others at the sixteen-acre graveyard. On Tuesday, December 11, three months after the disaster, his son was found. And Lee was there to carry him out.

The father didn't quit. Why? Because his love for his son was greater than the pain of the search. Can't the same be said about Christ? Why didn't he quit? Because the love for his children was greater than the pain of the journey.

A LOVE WORTH GIVING

Write a psalm of praise to Christ for his great love.

_____

_____

_____

_____

Nothing Less than Jesus

*"I have obeyed my Father's commands,
and I remain in his love. In the same way, if you obey
my commands, you will remain in my love."*

JOHN 15:10

God rewards those who seek him. Not those who seek doctrine or religion or systems or creeds. Many settle for these lesser passions, but the reward goes to those who settle for nothing less than Jesus himself. And what is the reward? What awaits those who seek Jesus? Nothing short of the heart of Jesus. "And as the Spirit of the Lord works within us, we become more and more like him" (2 Corinthians 3:18 TLB).

Can you think of a greater gift than to be like Jesus? Christ felt no guilt; God wants to banish yours. Jesus had no bad habits; God wants to remove yours. Jesus had no fear of death; God wants you to be fearless. Jesus had kindness for the diseased and mercy for the rebellious and courage for the challenges. God wants you to have the same.

He wants you to be just like Jesus.

JUST LIKE JESUS

God wants you to be just like Jesus. How is he accomplishing this in your life?

Descend into God's Love

I want nothing on earth besides you.

PSALM 73:25

My friend Keith took his wife, Sarah, to Cozumel, Mexico, to celebrate their anniversary. Sarah loves to snorkel. Give her fins, a mask, and a breathing tube, and watch her go deep. Down she swims, searching for the mysteries below.

Keith's idea of snorkeling includes fins, a mask, and a breathing tube, but it also includes a bellyboard. The surface satisfies him.

Sarah, however, convinced him to take the plunge. Forty feet offshore, she shouted for him to paddle out. He did. The two plunged into the water where she showed him a twenty-foot-tall submerged cross. "If I'd had another breath," he confessed, "the sight would have taken it away."

Jesus waves for you to descend and see the same. Forget surface glances. No more sunburned back. Go deep. Take a breath and descend so deeply into his love that you see nothing else.

COME THIRSTY

List some terms to describe the depth of God's love.

_____

_____

_____

_____

Lay Down Your Cares

Praise the Lord, God our Savior, who helps us every day.

PSALM 68:19

Perhaps the heaviest burden we try to carry is the burden of mistakes and failures. What do you do with your failures?

Even if you've fallen, even if you've failed, even if everyone else has rejected you, Christ will not turn away from you. He came first and foremost to those who have no hope. He goes to those no one else would go to and says, "I'll give you eternity."

Only you can surrender your concerns to the Father. No one else can take those away and give them to God. Only you can cast all your anxieties on the One who cares for you. What better way to start the day than by laying your cares at his feet?

WALKING WITH THE SAVIOR

Have you laid your cares at Christ's feet? Or are you trying to carry the burden of mistakes and failures? Why is it better to cast our anxieties on him? Explain.

_____

_____

_____

_____

_____

_____

_____

Saying Yes to God's Purpose

*"I must preach the kingdom of God . . .
because for this purpose I have been sent."*

Luke 4:43 nkjv

After Christ's forty-day pause in the wilderness, the people of Capernaum "tried to keep Him from leaving them; but He said to them, 'I must preach the kingdom of God to the other cities also, because for this purpose I have been sent.'"

He resisted the undertow of the people by anchoring to the rock of his purpose: employing his uniqueness to make a big deal out of God everywhere he could.

And aren't you glad he did? Suppose he had heeded the crowd and set up camp in Capernaum, reasoning, "I thought the whole world was my target and the cross my destiny. But the entire town tells me to stay in Capernaum. Could all these people be wrong?"

Yes, they could! In defiance of the crowd, Jesus said no to good things so he could say yes to the right thing: his unique call.

Cure for the Common Life

Have you had to say no to some good things in order to fulfill God's purpose for your life? How has this helped you stay true to your purpose?

Ponder the Love of God

*I pray that you . . . will have the power to understand
the greatness of Christ's love—how wide
and how long and how high and how deep that love is.*

EPHESIANS 3:18

There is no way our little minds can comprehend the love of
God. But that didn't keep him from coming.

From the cradle in Bethlehem to the cross in Jerusalem
we've pondered the love of our Father. What can you say to that
kind of emotion? Upon learning that God would rather die than
live without you, how do you react? How can you begin to explain
such passion?

IN THE GRIP OF GRACE

*How do you respond to God's love? What do you say to his
passionate grace? Write a note of thanksgiving for his
goodness to you.*

_____

_____

_____

_____

_____

_____

_____

A Fountain of Love

This is real love—not that we loved God, but that he loved us and sent his Son as a sacrifice to take away our sins.

1 JOHN 4:10 NLT

You've had enough of human love. Haven't you? Enough guys wooing you with Elvis-impersonator sincerity. Enough tabloids telling you that true love is just a diet away. Enough helium-filled expectations of bosses and parents and pastors. Enough mornings smelling like the mistakes you made while searching for love the night before.

Don't you need a fountain of love that won't run dry? You'll find one on a stone-cropped hill outside Jerusalem's walls where Jesus hangs, cross-nailed and thorn-crowned. When you feel unloved, ascend this mount. Meditate long and hard on heaven's love for you. Both eyes beaten shut, shoulders as raw as ground beef, lips bloody and split. Fists of hair yanked from his beard. Gasps of air escaping his lungs. As you peer into the crimsoned face of heaven's only Son, remember this: "God showed his great love for us by sending Christ to die for us while we were still sinners" (Romans 5:8 NLT).

COME THIRSTY

Describe some of the differences between God's love and human love.

_____

_____

_____

_____

December

The ways of God are without fault.

—Psalm 18:30

The Winner's Circle

The Lord will reward everyone for whatever
good he does, whether he is slave or free.

EPHESIANS 6:8 NIV

For all we don't know about the next life, this much is certain. The day Christ comes will be a day of reward. Those who went unknown on earth will be known in heaven. Those who never heard the cheers of men will hear the cheers of angels. Those who missed the blessing of a father will hear the blessing of their heavenly Father. The small will be great. The forgotten will be remembered. The unnoticed will be crowned and the faithful will be honored.

The winner's circle isn't reserved for a handful of the elite, but for a heaven full of God's children who "will receive the crown of life that God has promised to those who love him" (James 1:12 NIV).

WHEN CHRIST COMES

What has God promised to those who love him? How does that make you feel?

_____

_____

_____

_____

_____

Christmas Every Day

Sing praises to the LORD. . . .
Tell the nations what he has done.

PSALM 9:11

You have Christmas every day. Your gift bears, not toys and books, but God himself!

His work: on the cross and in the resurrection. As a result, your sin brings no guilt, and the grave brings no fear.

His energy: it's not up to you. You can do all things through Christ, who gives you strength.

His lordship: he is in charge of you and looks out for you.

His love: what can separate you from it?

Who could imagine such gifts? Who could imagine not opening them?

COME THIRSTY

Make a list of the ways you have been helped through the gifts of God's work, his energy, his lordship, and his love.

God Is for You

He will rejoice over you.

ZEPHANIAH 3:17

G od is *for* you. Turn to the sidelines; that's God cheering your run. Look past the finish line; that's God applauding your steps. Listen for him in the bleachers, shouting your name. Too tired to continue? He'll carry you. Too discouraged to fight? He's picking you up. God is for you.

God is for *you.* Had he a calendar, your birthday would be circled. If he drove a car, your name would be on his bumper. If there's a tree in heaven, he's carved your name in the bark.

"Can a mother forget the baby at her breast and have no compassion on the child she has borne?" God asks in Isaiah 49:15 (NIV). What a bizarre question. Can you mothers imagine feeding your infant and then later asking, "What was that baby's name?" No. I've seen you care for your young. You stroke the hair, you touch the face, you sing the name over and over. Can a mother forget? No way. But "even if she could forget, I will not forget you," God pledges (v. 49:15).

IN THE GRIP OF GRACE

Write out Isaiah 49:15. Explain what it means to you.

_____

_____

_____

_____

A Bouquet of Blessings

Happy is the person who trusts the LORD.

PSALM 40:4

S uppose you dwell in a high-rise apartment. On the window sill of your room is a solitary daisy. This morning you picked the daisy and pinned it on your lapel.

But as soon as you're out the door, people start picking petals off your daisy. Someone snags your subway seat. Petal picked. You're blamed for the bad report of a coworker. More petals. By the end of the day, you're down to one. You're only one petal-snatching away from a blowup.

What if the scenario was altered slightly? Let's add one character. The kind man in the apartment next door runs a flower shop. Every night on the way home he stops at your place with a fresh bouquet. Because of him, your apartment has a sweet fragrance, and your step has a happy bounce. Let someone mess with your flower, and you've got a basketful to replace it!

God hand-delivers a bouquet to your door every day. Open it! Take them! Then, when rejections come, you won't be left short-petaled.

A LOVE WORTH GIVING

List some blessings God has included in the bouquet of your life.

_____

_____

_____

_____

The Cure for Disappointment

The ways of God are without fault.

PSALM 18:30

When God doesn't do what we want, it's not easy. Never has been. Never will be. But faith is the conviction that God knows more than we do about this life and He will get us through it.

Remember, disappointment is cured by revamped expectations.

I like the story about the fellow who went to the pet store in search of a singing parakeet. Seems he was a bachelor and his house was too quiet. The store owner had just the bird for him, so the man bought it.

The next day the bachelor came home from work to a house full of music. He went to the cage to feed the bird and noticed for the first time that the parakeet had only one leg.

He felt cheated that he'd been sold a one-legged bird, so he called and complained.

"What do you want," the store owner responded, "a bird who can sing or a bird who can dance?"

Good question for times of disappointment.

HE STILL MOVES STONES

What is the wise way to handle disappointment?

_____

_____

_____

_____

Water for the Soul

"If anyone thirsts, let him come to Me and drink."

JOHN 7:37 NKJV

Are you *anyone*? If so, then step up to the well. You qualify for his water.

All ages are welcome. Both genders invited. No race excluded. Scoundrels. ScamPsalm Rascals and rubes. All welcome. You don't have to be rich to drink, religious to drink, successful to drink; you simply need to follow the instructions on what—or better, *who*—to drink. Him. In order for Jesus to do what water does, you must let him penetrate your heart. Deep, deep inside.

Internalize him. Ingest him. Welcome him into the inner workings of your life. Let Christ be the water of your soul.

COME THIRSTY

What can you do to make Christ the water of your soul?

_____

_____

_____

_____

_____

_____

_____

The Soul Killer

When people sin, they earn what sin pays—death.

ROMANS 6:23

Sin does to a life what shears do to a flower. A cut at the stem separates a flower from the source of life. Initially the flower is attractive, still colorful and strong. But watch that flower over a period of time, and the leaves will wilt and the petals will drop. No matter what you do, the flower will never live again. Surround it with water. Stick the stem in soil. Baptize it with fertilizer. Glue the flower back on the stem. Do what you wish. The flower is dead.

A dead soul has no life.

Cut off from God, the soul withers and dies. The consequence of sin is not a bad day or a bad mood but a dead soul. The sign of a dead soul is clear: poisoned lips and cursing mouths, feet that lead to violence and eyes that don't see God.

The finished work of sin is to kill the soul.

IN THE GRIP OF GRACE

"Cut off from God, the soul withers and dies." Explain why.

_____

_____

_____

_____

_____

_____

God Is Eternal

God is . . . greater than we can understand!
No one knows how old he is.

JOB 36:26

Scripture says that the number of God's years is unsearchable. We may search out the moment the first wave slapped on a shore or the first star burst in the sky, but we'll never find the first moment when God was God, for there is no moment when God was not God. He has never *not been*, for he is eternal. God is not bound by time.

But when Jesus came to the earth, all this changed. He heard for the first time a phrase never used in heaven: "Your time is up." As a child, he had to leave the temple because his time was up. As a man, he had to leave Nazareth because his time was up. And as a Savior, he had to die because his time was up. For thirty-three years, the stallion of heaven lived in the corral of time.

HE CHOSE THE NAILS

Think of the sacrifice Jesus made to live within the constraints of time. How do you respond to his great sacrifices of love for you?

God's Thoughts

LORD, you have done such great things! How deep are your thoughts!

PSALM 92:5

God's thoughts are not our thoughts, nor are they even like ours. We aren't even in the same neighborhood. We're thinking, *Preserve the body*; he's thinking, *Save the soul.* We dream of a pay raise. He dreams of raising the dead. We avoid pain and seek peace. God uses pain to bring peace. "I'm going to live before I die," we resolve. "Die, so you can live," he instructs. We love what rusts. He loves what endures. We rejoice at our successes. He rejoices at our confessions. We show our children the Nike star with the million-dollar smile and say, "Be like Mike." God points to the crucified Carpenter with bloody lips and a torn side and says, "Be like Christ."

THE GREAT HOUSE OF GOD

How do your thoughts typically compare with God's thoughts? Make comparisons between the two. Then make a list of God-thoughts that you want to replace your own thoughts.

_____

_____

_____

_____

_____

_____

Magnify Your Maker

If anyone ministers, let him do it as with the ability
which God supplies, that in all things God may be glorified.

1 PETER 4:11 NKJV

God endows us with gifts so we can make him known. Period. God endues the Olympian with speed, the salesman with savvy, the surgeon with skill. Why? For gold medals, closed sales, or healed bodies? Only partially.

The big answer is to make a big to-do out of God. Brandish him. Herald him. "God has given gifts to each of you from his great variety of spiritual gifts. Manage them well. Then God will be given glory" (1 Peter 4:10–11 NLT).

Live so that "he'll get all the credit as the One mighty in everything—encores to the end of time. Oh, yes!" (1 Peter 4:11 MSG). Exhibit God with your uniqueness. When you magnify your Maker with your strengths, when your contribution enriches God's reputation, your days grow suddenly sweet.

CURE FOR THE COMMON LIFE

Are you exhibiting God with your uniqueness? Why or why not? How would you like to use your gifts for him?

_____

_____

_____

_____

_____

A Heavenly Affirmation

I will be your father.

2 CORINTHIANS 6:18

Each of us has a fantasy that our family will be like the Waltons, an expectation that our dearest friends will be our next of kin. Jesus didn't have that expectation. Look how he defined his family: "My true brother and sister and mother are those who do what God wants" (Mark 3:35).

When Jesus' brother didn't share his convictions, he didn't try to force them. He recognized that his spiritual family could provide what his physical family didn't.

We can't control the way our family responds to us. When it comes to the behavior of others toward us, our hands are tied. We have to move beyond the naive expectation that if we do good, people will treat us right. The fact is they may and they may not—we cannot control how people respond to us.

Let God give you what your family doesn't. If your earthly father doesn't affirm you, then let your heavenly Father take his place.

[And] don't lose heart. God still changes families.

HE STILL MOVES STONES

What can God give you that your family doesn't?

_____

_____

_____

_____

The Master Plan

It was the LORD's will to crush him.

ISAIAH 53:10 NIV

The cross was no accident.

Jesus' death was not the result of a panicking, cosmological engineer. The cross wasn't a tragic surprise. Calvary was not a knee-jerk response to a world plummeting toward destruction. It wasn't a patch-job or a stop-gap measure. The death of the Son of God was anything but an unexpected peril.

No, it was part of a plan. It was a calculated choice. "It was the LORD's will to crush him." The cross was drawn into the original blueprint. It was written into the script. The moment the forbidden fruit touched the lips of Eve, the shadow of a cross appeared on the horizon. And between that moment and the moment the man with the mallet placed the spike against the wrist of God, a master plan was fulfilled.

GOD CAME NEAR

Do you know people who think Calvary was a tragic surprise for God? How can you explain to them that it was all part of God's plan?

No Worries in Heaven

[God] will wipe away every tear from their eyes,
and there will be no more death, sadness, crying, or pain.

REVELATION 21:4

What have you done today to avoid death? Likely a lot. You've popped pills, pumped pecs, passed on the pie, and pursued the polyunsaturates. Why? Why the effort? Because you are worried about staying alive. That won't be a worry in heaven.

In fact, you won't be worrying at all. Some of you moms worry about your kids getting hurt. You won't worry in heaven. In heaven we'll feel no pain. Some of you fellows worry about getting old. You won't in heaven. We'll all be ceaselessly strong.

We are not made of steel; we are made of dust. And this life is not crowned with life; it is crowned with death.

The next life, however; is different. Jesus urged the Christians in Smyrna to "be faithful; even if you have to die, and I will give you the crown of life" (Revelation 2:10).

WHEN CHRIST COMES

Make of list of other things you won't be bothered with in heaven.

_____

_____

_____

_____

_____

_____

Deliver Christ to the World

*I work . . . using Christ's great strength
that works so powerfully in me.*

COLOSSIANS 1:29

The virgin birth is more, much more, than a Christmas story; it is a picture of how close Christ will come to you. The first stop on his itinerary was a womb. Where will God go to touch the world? Look deep within Mary for an answer.

Better still, look deep within yourself. What he did with Mary, he offers to us! He issues a Mary-level invitation to all his children. "If you'll let me, I'll move in!"

What is the mystery of the gospel? "Christ in you, the hope of glory" (Colossians 1:27 NIV).

Christ grew in Mary until he had to come out. Christ will grow in you until the same occurs. He will come out in your speech, in your actions, in your decisions. Every place you live will be a Bethlehem, and every day you live will be a Christmas. You, like Mary, will deliver Christ into the world.

NEXT DOOR SAVIOR

Can you think of ways Christ wants to use you to touch the world?

_____

_____

_____

_____

Prayer Reminds Us

When a believing person prays, great things happen.

JAMES 5:16

P rayer is the recognition that if God had not engaged himself in our problems, we would still be lost in the blackness. It is by his mercy that we have been lifted up. Prayer is that whole process that reminds us of who God is and who we are.

I believe there's great power in prayer. I believe God heals the wounded, and that he can raise the dead. But I don't believe we tell God what to do and when to do it.

God knows that we, with our limited vision, don't even know that for which we should pray. When we entrust our requests to him, we trust him to honor our prayers with holy judgment.

WALKING WITH THE SAVIOR

Prayer reminds us of who God is and who we are. Explain what that means. Why can we trust his judgment in answering our prayers?

_____

_____

_____

_____

_____

_____

Slow Down and Rest

"Six days you shall labor and do all your work,
but the seventh day is the Sabbath of the LORD your God. In it you
shall do no work: you, nor your son, nor your daughter."

EXODUS 20:9–10 NKJV

God knows us so well. He can see the store owner reading this verse and thinking, *Somebody needs to work that day. If I can't, my son will.* So God says, Nor your son. *Then my daughter will.* Nor your daughter. *I guess I'll have to send my cow to run the store, or maybe I'll find some stranger to help me.* No, God says. One day of the week you will say no to work and yes to worship. You will slow and sit down and lie down and rest.

Still we object. "What about my grades?" "I've got my sales quota." We offer up one reason after another, but God silences them all with a poignant reminder: "In six days the LORD made the heavens and the earth, the sea, and all that is in them, and rested the seventh day" (Exodus 20:11 NIV). God's message is plain: "If creation didn't crash when I rested, it won't crash when you do."

Repeat these words after me: It is not my job to run the world.

TRAVELING LIGHT

Why do we tend to think it's our job to run the world?
How does this affect the way we treat the Sabbath?

_____

_____

_____

_____

Grace upon Grace

*I have learned to be satisfied with the things
I have and with everything that happens.*

PHILIPPIANS 4:11

Test this question: What if God's only gift to you were his grace to save you? Would you be content? You beg him to save the life of your child. You plead with him to keep your business afloat. You implore him to remove the cancer from your body. What if his answer is, "My grace is enough." Would you be content?

You see, from heaven's perspective, grace is enough. If God did nothing more than save us from hell, could anyone complain? Having been given eternal life, dare we grumble at an aching body? Having been given heavenly riches, dare we bemoan earthly poverty?

If you have eyes to read these words, hands to hold this book, the means to own this volume, he has already given you grace upon grace.

IN THE GRIP OF GRACE

Make a list of some of the ways God has already given you "grace upon grace."

_____

_____

_____

_____

A Proper Perspective

Do nothing from selfishness or empty conceit, but with humility of mind regard one another as more important than yourselves.

PHILIPPIANS 2:3 NASB

At first glance the standard in that verse seems impossible to meet. Nothing? We shouldn't do *anything* for ourselves? No new dress or suit. What about going to school or saving money—couldn't all of these things be considered selfish?

They could, unless we are careful to understand what Paul is saying. The word the apostle uses for *selfishness* shares a root form with the words *strife* and *contentious*. It suggests a self-preoccupation that hurts others. A divisive arrogance. In fact, first-century writers used the word to describe a politician who procured office by illegal manipulation or a harlot who seduced the client, demeaning both herself and him.

Looking after your personal interests is proper life management. Doing so to the exclusion of the rest of the world is selfishness.

A LOVE WORTH GIVING

Name some of the differences between a careful self-interest and a self-preoccupation that hurts others.

_____

_____

_____

_____

Prepared like a Bride

The bride belongs only to the bridegroom.

JOHN 3:29

John's descriptions of the future [in the book of Revelation] steal your breath. His depiction of the final battle is graphic. Good clashes with evil. The sacred encounters the sinful. The pages howl with the shrieks of dragons and smolder with the coals of fiery pits. But in the midst of the battlefield there is a rose. John describes it in chapter 21:

> *I saw the holy city, the new Jerusalem, coming down out of heaven from God. It was prepared as a bride dressed for her husband.* (v. 2)

In this final mountaintop encounter, God pulls back the curtain and allows the warrior to peek into the homeland. When given the task of writing down what he sees, John chooses the most beautiful comparison earth has to offer. The Holy City, John says, is like "a bride beautifully dressed for her husband" (NLT).

THE APPLAUSE OF HEAVEN

List some comparisons between a beautiful bride and the Holy City. How does this encourage you?

_____

_____

_____

_____

_____

What Friends Do

A friend loves you all the time.

PROVERBS 17:17

One gets the impression that to John, Jesus was above all a loyal companion. Messiah? Yes. Son of God? Indeed. Miracle worker? That too. But more than anything Jesus was a pal. Someone you could go camping with or bowling with or count the stars with.

Now what do you do with a friend? (Well, that's rather simple too.) You stick by him.

Maybe that is why John is the only one of the twelve who was at the cross. He came to say good-bye. By his own admission he hadn't quite put the pieces together yet. But that didn't really matter. As far as he was concerned, his closest friend was in trouble and he came to help.

"Can you take care of my mother?"

Of course. That's what friends are for.

NO WONDER THEY CALL HIM THE SAVIOR

John was the friend Jesus trusted to care for his mother. What can you do to be a friend others can count on in times of need?

_____

_____

_____

_____

Just Pray

Anyone who is having troubles should pray.
Anyone who is happy should sing praises.

JAMES 5:13

D o you want to know how to deepen your prayer life? Pray. Don't prepare to pray. Just pray. Don't read about prayer. Just pray. Don't attend a lecture on prayer or engage in discussion about prayer. Just pray.

Posture, tone, and place are personal matters. Select the form that works for you. But don't think about it too much. Don't be so concerned about wrapping the gift that you never give it. Better to pray awkwardly than not at all.

And if you feel you should only pray when inspired, that's okay. Just see to it that you are inspired every day.

WHEN GOD WHISPERS YOUR NAME

Do you ever find yourself so concerned about the form of your prayer that you don't offer it all? Why is it better to pray awkwardly than not at all?

_____

_____

_____

_____

_____

_____

God's Ways Are Right

"When you pass through the waters, I will be with you;
and through the rivers, they will not overflow you."

ISAIAH 43:2–3 NASB

God knows what is best. No struggle will come your way apart from his purpose, presence, and permission. What encouragement this brings! You are never the victim of nature or the prey of fate. Chance is eliminated. You are more than a weather vane whipped about by the winds of fortune. Would God truly abandon you to the whims of drug-crazed thieves, greedy corporate raiders, or evil leaders? Perish the thought!

We live beneath the protective palm of a sovereign King who superintends every circumstance of our lives and delights in doing us good.

Nothing comes your way that has not first passed through the filter of his love.

COME THIRSTY

Nothing comes into your life that has not passed through the filter of God's love. How does that make you feel? How does it help you to face the difficulties of life?

_____

_____

_____

_____

_____

God Isn't Hard to Find

*Surely your goodness and love will follow me all the days of my life,
and I will dwell in the house of the LORD forever.*

PSALM 23:6 NIV

What a surprising way to describe God. A God who pursues us.

Dare we envision a mobile, active God who chases us, tracks us, following us with goodness and mercy all the days of our lives? He's not hard to find. He's there in Scripture, looking for Adam and Eve. They're hiding in the bushes, partly to cover their bodies, partly to cover their sin. Does God wait for them to come to him? No, the words ring in the garden. "Where are you?" God asks (Genesis 3:9), beginning his quest to redeem the heart of man. A quest to follow his children until his children follow him.

THE GIFT FOR ALL PEOPLE

God pursues us. How does this demonstrate his great love for us? Have you felt him pursuing you? Explain.

_____

_____

_____

_____

_____

_____

_____

Prophecy Fulfilled

Those who look to the LORD will praise him.

PSALM 22:26

The fulfillment of Scripture is a recurring theme in the passion. Why, in his final moments, was Jesus determined to fulfill prophecy? He knew we would doubt. He knew we would question. And since he did not want our heads to keep his love from our hearts, he used his final moments to offer proof that he was the Messiah. He systematically fulfilled centuries-old prophecies.

Did you know that in his life Christ fulfilled 332 distinct prophecies in the Old Testament? What are the mathematical possibilities of all these prophecies being fulfilled in the life of one man?

$$\frac{1}{\begin{array}{c}840,000,000,000,000,000,000,000,\\000,000,000,000,000,000,000,000,000,\\000,000,000,000,000,000,000,000,000,\\000,000,000,000,000,000\end{array}}$$

(That's ninety-seven zeroes!) Amazing!

He Chose the Nails

Why should we be encouraged to know that Christ's life fulfilled so many prophecies?

_____

_____

_____

The Unspeakable Price

*To all who did accept him and believe in him he gave
the right to become children of God.*

JOHN 1:12

While we lived in Rio de Janeiro, we met several American families who came to Brazil to adopt children. They would spend days, sometimes weeks, immersed in a different language and a strange culture. They fought the red tape and paid the large fees, all with the hope of taking a child [home] to the United States.

Hasn't God done the same for us? He entered our culture, battled the resistance, and paid the unspeakable price which adoption required. Legally we are his. He owns us. We have every legal privilege accorded to [his] child. We are just waiting for him to return. We are, as Paul said, "waiting for God to finish making us his own children" (Romans 8:23).

WHEN CHRIST COMES

What does it mean to be adopted by God? List some of the privileges you have as his child.

_____

_____

_____

_____

_____

_____

A Well of Optimism

"You must change and become like little children.
Otherwise, you will never enter the kingdom of heaven."

MATTHEW 18:3

Bedtime is a bad time for kids. No child understands the logic of going to bed while there is energy left in the body or hours left in the day.

My children are no exception. A few years ago, after many objections and countless groans, the girls were finally in their gowns, in their beds, and on their pillows. I slipped into the room to give them a final kiss. Andrea, the five-year-old, was still awake, just barely, but awake. After I kissed her, she lifted her eyelids one final time and said, "I can't wait until I wake up."

Oh, for the attitude of a five-year-old! That simple uncluttered passion for living that can't wait for tomorrow. A philosophy of life that reads, "Play hard, laugh hard, and leave the worries to your father." A bottomless well of optimism flooded by a perpetual spring of faith. Is it any wonder Jesus said we must have the heart of a child before we can enter the kingdom of heaven?

AND THE ANGELS WERE SILENT

How is being optimistic similar to having the heart of a child?

Every Child Has a Name

*"I am the good shepherd. I know my sheep,
as the Father knows me. And my sheep know me."*

JOHN 10:14–15

The shepherd knows his sheep. He calls them by name.

When we see a crowd, we see exactly that, a crowd. We see people, not persons, but people. A herd of humans. A flock of faces. That's what we see.

But not so with the Shepherd. To him every face is different. Every face is a story. Every face is a child. Every child has a name.

The shepherd knows his sheep. He knows each one by name. The Shepherd knows you. He knows your name. And he will never forget it.

WHEN GOD WHISPERS YOUR NAME

God knows your name. You are special to him. How does that make you feel? How do you respond?

_____

_____

_____

_____

_____

_____

_____

_____

Facing the Facts

How precious also are Your thoughts to me,
O God! How great is the sum of them!

PSALM 139:17 NKJV

Aging is a universal condition. But the way we try to hide it, you would think it was a plague!

There are girdles which compact the middle-age spread for both sexes. There are hair transplants, wigs, toupees, and hair pieces. Dentures bring youth to the mouth, wrinkle cream brings youth to the face, and color in a bottle brings youth to the hair.

All to hide what everyone already knows—we're getting older.

Just when the truth about life sinks in, God's truth starts to surface. He takes us by the hand and dares us not to sweep the facts under the rug but to confront them with him at our side.

Aging? A necessary process to pass on to a better world.

Death? Merely a brief passage, a tunnel.

Self? Designed for a purpose, purchased by God himself.

There, was that so bad?

GOD CAME NEAR

How does the attitude of our culture toward aging contrast with God's?

_____

_____

_____

A Broken Heart?

The LORD hates what evil people do,
but he loves those who do what is right.

PROVERBS 15:9

Perhaps the wound is old. A parent abused you. A teacher slighted you. A mate betrayed you. And you are angry.

Or perhaps the wound is fresh. The friend who owes you money just drove by in a new car. The boss who hired you with promises of promotions has forgotten how to pronounce your name. And you are hurt.

Part of you is broken, and the other part is bitter. Part of you wants to cry, and part of you wants to fight. There is a fire burning in your heart. It's the fire of anger.

And you are left with a decision. "Do I put the fire out or heat it up? Do I get over it or get even? Do I release it or resent it? Do I let my hurts heal, or do I let hurt turn into hate?"

Unfaithfulness is wrong. Revenge is bad. But the worst part of all is that, without forgiveness, bitterness is all that is left.

THE APPLAUSE OF HEAVEN

Do you have a fire burning in your heart? What will you choose to do with it?

_____

_____

_____

_____

God Sent Himself

The Word became flesh and dwelt among us.

JOHN 1:14 NKJV

Don't we love the word *with*? "Will you go *with* me?" we ask. "To the store, to the hospital, through my life?" God says he will. "I am *with* you always," Jesus said before he ascended to heaven, "to the very end of the age" (Matthew 28:20 NIV). Search for restrictions on the promise; you'll find none. You won't find "I'll be with you if you behave . . . when you believe. I'll be with you on Sundays in worship . . . at mass." No, none of that. There's no withholding tax on God's *with* promise. He is *with* us.

God is with us.

Prophets weren't enough. Apostles wouldn't do. Angels won't suffice. God sent more than miracles and messages. He sent himself; he sent his Son. "The Word became flesh and dwelt among us."

CURE FOR THE COMMON LIFE

How does God's faithfulness compare with people whose loyalty can be fickle?

Words of Promise

God has given a son to us. . . . His name will be
Wonderful Counselor, Powerful God . . . Prince of Peace.

ISAIAH 9:6

Every Christmas I read this reminder that came in the mail several years ago:

If our greatest need had been information, God would have sent an educator. If our greatest need had been technology, God would have sent us a scientist. If our greatest need had been money, God would have sent us an economist. But since our greatest need was forgiveness, God sent us a Savior.

—ROY LESSIN, *God Sent Us a Savior*

Christmas cards. Punctuated promises. Phrases filled with the reason we do it all anyway.

He became like us, so we could become like him.

Angels still sing and the star still beckons.

He loves each one of us like there was only one of us to love.

WHEN GOD WHISPERS YOUR NAME

"He became like us, so we could become like him." Explain what that statement means. Describe how it is true in your life.

_____

_____

_____

_____

What to Do with Worries

God did not keep back his own Son, but he gave him for us.
If God did this, won't he freely give us everything else?

ROMANS 8:32 CEV

What do we do with . . . worries? Take your anxieties to the cross—literally. Next time you're worried about your health or house or finances or flights, take a mental trip up the hill. Spend a few moments looking again at the pieces of passion.

Run your thumb over the tip of the spear. Balance a spike in the palm of your hand. Read the wooden sign written in your own language. And as you do, touch the velvet dirt, moist with the blood of God.

Blood he bled for you.

The spear he took for you.

The nails he felt for you.

The sign he left for you.

He did all of this for you. Knowing this, knowing all he did for you there, don't you think he'll look out for you here?

HE CHOSE THE NAILS

How does Christ's work on the cross help you trust in his loving care?

_____

_____

_____

_____

Because of Our Need

"For God did not send His Son into the world to condemn the world, but that the world through Him might be saved. "

JOHN 3:17 NKJV

C an you imagine prospective parents saying, "We'd like to adopt Johnny, but first we want to know a few things. Does he have a house to live in? Does he have money for tuition? Does he have a ride to school every morning and clothes to wear every day? Can he prepare his own meals and mend his own clothes?"

No agency would stand for such talk. Its representative would lift her hand and say, "Wait a minute. You don't understand. You don't adopt Johnny because of what he has; you adopt him because of what he needs. He needs a home."

The same is true with God. He doesn't adopt us because of what we have. He doesn't give us his name because of our wit or wallet or good attitude. Adoption is something we receive, not something we earn.

THE GREAT HOUSE OF GOD

God does not adopt us because of what we have but because of what we need. Why is this good news for us?

_____

_____

_____

_____

_____

God's Love

God is love.

1 JOHN 4:16

The supreme surprise of God's love? It has nothing to do with you. Others love you because of you, because your dimples dip when you smile or your rhetoric charms when you flirt. Some people love you because of you. Not God. He loves you because he is he. He loves you because he decides to. Self-generated, uncaused, and spontaneous, his constant-level love depends on his choice to give it. "The LORD did not set his affection on you and choose you because you were more numerous than other peoples, for you were the fewest of all peoples. But it was because the LORD loved you" (Deuteronomy 7:7–8 NIV).

You don't influence God's love. You can't impact the treeness of a tree, the skyness of the sky, or the rockness of a rock. Nor can you affect the love of God.

COME THIRSTY

You cannot influence God's love. While that may sound discouraging, why is it actually an uplifting thought?

_____

_____

_____

_____

_____

Room for God?

"Here I am! I stand at the door and knock."

REVELATION 3:20

Some of the saddest words on earth are: "We don't have room for you."

Jesus knew the sound of those words. He was still in Mary's womb when the innkeeper said, "We don't have room for you."

And when he was hung on the cross, wasn't the message one of utter rejection? "We don't have room for you in this world."

Even today Jesus is given the same treatment. He goes from heart to heart, asking if he might enter.

Every so often, he is welcomed. Someone throws open the door of his or her heart and invites him to stay. And to that person Jesus gives this great promise: "There are many rooms in my Father's house" (John 14:2).

What a delightful promise he makes us! We make room for him in our hearts, and he makes room for us in his house.

WHEN CHRIST COMES

Have you made room in your heart for Christ? Describe how this has changed your life. How would your life be different without him?

_____

_____

_____

_____

_____

God Uses People

Happy are those who are helped by the God of Jacob.

PSALM 146:5

Until he was eighty years old he looked like he wouldn't amount to much more than a once-upon-a-time prince turned outlaw. Would you choose a wanted murderer to lead a nation out of bondage? Would you call upon a fugitive to carry the Ten Commandments? God did. And he called him, of all places, right out of the sheep pasture. Called his name through a burning bush. Scared old Moses right out of his shoes! There, with knees knocking and "Who me?" written all over his face, Moses agreed to go back into the ring.

The reassuring lesson is clear. God used (and uses!) people to change the world. People! Not saints or superhumans or geniuses, but people. Crooks, creeps, lovers, and liars—he uses them all. And what they may lack in perfection, God makes up for in love.

NO WONDER THEY CALL HIM THE SAVIOR

God uses people to change the world. Does he use only perfect people or superhumans or geniuses? Why is this good news for all of us?

Down on Your Knees

God is against the proud, but he gives grace to the humble.

JAMES 4:6

A small cathedral outside Bethlehem marks the supposed birthplace of Jesus. Behind a high altar in the church is a cave, a little cavern lit by silver lamps.

You can enter the main edifice and admire the ancient church. You can also enter the quiet cave where a star embedded in the floor recognizes the birth of the King. There is one stipulation, however. You have to stoop. The door is so low you can't go in standing up.

The same is true of the Christ. You can see the world standing tall, but to witness the Savior, you have to get [down] on your knees.

THE APPLAUSE OF HEAVEN

To witness the Savior, you have to get down on your knees. Explain what that statement means. How do we apply this to our attitudes and actions?

_____

_____

_____

_____

_____

_____

_____

_____

When the Time Comes

*"God will help you deal with whatever
hard things come up when the time comes."*

MATTHEW 6:34 MSG

That last phrase is worthy of your highlighter: "when the
time comes."

"I don't know what I'll do if my husband dies." You will,
when the time comes.

"When my children leave the house, I don't think I can take it."
It won't be easy, but strength will arrive *when the time comes.*

"I could never lead a church. There is too much I don't know."
You may be right. Or you may be wanting to know everything too
soon. Could it be that God will reveal answers to you *when the
time comes?*

The key is this: Meet today's problems with today's strength.
Don't start tackling tomorrow's problems until tomorrow. You do
not have tomorrow's strength yet. You simply have enough for today.

TRAVELING LIGHT

*We often try to tackle tomorrow's struggles in the strength
of today. Why doesn't that work?*

_____

_____

_____

_____

The Gift Is God-Given

*Every good action and every perfect gift is from God.
These good gifts come down from the Creator of the sun, moon,
and stars, who does not change like their shifting shadows.*

JAMES 1:17

The conclusion is unavoidable: self-salvation simply does not work. Man has no way to save himself.

But Paul announces that God has a way. Where man fails God excels. Salvation comes from heaven downward, not earth upward. "Every good action and every perfect gift is from God" (James 1:17).

Please note: Salvation is God-given, God-driven, God-empowered, and God-originated. The gift is not from man to God. It is from God to man.

IN THE GRIP OF GRACE

Did God give us the gift of salvation because we deserved it? Would this ever have been possible? Explain.

_____

_____

_____

_____

_____

_____

_____

Made by the Master

You knit me together in my mother's womb.

PSALM 139:13 NIV

Knitted together" is how the psalmist described the process of God making man. Not manufactured or mass-produced, but knitted. Each thread of personality tenderly intertwined. Each string of temperament deliberately selected.

God as Creator. Pensive. Excited. Inventive.

An artist, brush on palette, seeking the perfect shade.

A composer, fingers on keyboard, listening for the exact chord.

A poet, pen poised on paper, awaiting the precise word.

The Creator, the Master Weaver, threading together the soul.

Each one different. No two alike. None identical.

SIX HOURS ONE FRIDAY

Picture God deliberately and carefully creating each person. What is the significance of this to your life? How does it affect your attitude toward your unique life?

_____

_____

_____

_____

_____

An Extra-Ordinary Night

Today your Savior was born in the town of David.
He is Christ, the Lord.

LUKE 2:11

An ordinary night with ordinary sheep and ordinary shepherds. And were it not for a God who loves to hook an "extra" on the front of the ordinary, the night would have gone unnoticed. The sheep would have been forgotten, and the shepherds would have slept the night away.

But God dances amidst the common. And that night he did a waltz.

The black sky exploded with brightness. Trees that had been shadows jumped into clarity. Sheep that had been silent became a chorus of curiosity. One minute the shepherd was dead asleep, the next he was rubbing his eyes and staring into the face of an alien.

The night was ordinary no more.

The angel came in the night because that is when lights are best seen and that is when they are most needed. God comes into the common for the same reason. His most powerful tools are the simplest.

THE APPLAUSE OF HEAVEN

Why would God "dance amidst the common"?

_____

_____

_____

_____

_____

Gifted to Give

*A spiritual gift is given to each of us
as a means of helping the entire church.*

1 CORINTHIANS 12:7 NLT

When you place your trust in Christ, he places his Spirit in you. And when the Spirit comes, he brings gifts, housewarming gifts of sorts. "A spiritual gift is given to each of us as a means of helping the entire church" (1 Corinthians 12:7 NLT). Remember, God prepacked you with strengths. When you become a child of God, the Holy Spirit requisitions your abilities for the expansion of God's kingdom, and they become spiritual gifts. The Holy Spirit may add other gifts according to his plan. But no one is gift deprived.

Lonely? God is with you.

Depleted? He funds the overdrawn.

Weary of an ordinary existence? Your spiritual adventure awaits.

The cure for the common life begins and ends with God.

CURE FOR THE COMMON LIFE

Are there things you are longing to do for God? What steps can you take to step out into that spiritual adventure?

_____

_____

_____

_____

_____

The Gift of Grace

Those who find me find life,
and the LORD will be pleased with them.

PROVERBS 8:35

Grace is created by God and given to man. On the basis of this point alone, Christianity is set apart from any other religion in the world. Every other approach to God is a bartering system; if I do this, God will do that. I'm either saved by works (what I do), emotions (what I experience), or knowledge (what I know).

By contrast, Christianity has no whiff of negotiation at all. Man is not the negotiator; indeed, man has no grounds from which to negotiate.

IN THE GRIP OF GRACE

Describe some of the blessings we enjoy because our approach to God is not a bartering system. Explain the benefit of having no grounds for negotiation.

_____

_____

_____

_____

_____

_____

_____

A Leaf of Hope

When the dove returned to [Noah] in the evening,
there in its beak was a freshly plucked olive leaf!

GENESIS 8:11 NIV

An olive leaf. Noah would have been happy to have the bird but to have the leaf! This leaf was more than foliage; this was promise. The bird brought more than a piece of a tree; it brought hope. For isn't that what hope is? Hope is an olive leaf— evidence of dry land after a flood.

Don't we love the olive leaves of life? "It appears the cancer may be in remission." "I can help you with those finances." "We'll get through this together."

What's more, don't we love the doves that bring them? When the father walks his son through his first broken heart, he gives him an olive leaf. When the wife of many years consoles the wife of a few months, when she tells her that conflicts come and all husbands are moody and these storms pass, you know what she is doing? She is giving an olive leaf.

We love olive leaves. And we love those who give them.

A LOVE WORTH GIVING

Have you received an "olive leaf" of hope? Describe how that experience encouraged you.

_____

_____

_____

_____

God's Great Gifts

Thanks be to God for his gift that is too wonderful for words.

2 CORINTHIANS 9:15

W hy did he do it? A shack would have sufficed, but he gave us a mansion. Did he have to give the birds a song and the mountains a peak? Was he required to put stripes on the zebra and the hump on the camel? Why wrap creation in such splendor? Why go to such trouble to give such gifts?

Why do you? You do the same. I've seen you searching for a gift. I've seen you stalking the malls and walking the aisles. I'm not talking about the obligatory gifts. I'm talking about that extra-special person and that extra-special gift. Why do you do it? You do it so the heart will stop. You do it so the jaw will drop. You do it to hear those words of disbelief, "You did this for *me*?"

That's why you do it. And that is why God did it. Next time a sunrise steals your breath or a meadow of flowers leaves you speechless, remain that way. Say nothing and listen as heaven whispers, "Do you like it? I did it just for you."

THE GREAT HOUSE OF GOD

Describe how God has come near to you. How has this made a difference in your life?

_____

_____

_____

_____

_____

Love That Lasts Forever

Love never fails.

1 CORINTHIANS 13:8 NIV

"L ove," Paul says, "never fails."

The verb Paul uses for the word *fail* is used elsewhere to describe the demise of a flower as it falls to the ground, withers, and decays. It carries the meaning of death and abolishment. God's love, says the apostle, will never fall to the ground, wither, and decay. By its nature, it is permanent. It is never abolished.

Love "will last forever" (NLT).

It "never dies" (MSG).

It "never ends" (RSV).

Love "is eternal" (TEV).

God's love "will never come to an end" (NEB).

Governments will fail, but God's love will last. Crowns are temporary, but love is eternal. Your money will run out, but his love never will.

A LOVE WORTH GIVING

Write a note of thanks to God for the gift of his eternal love

The Promise Remains

Joseph was the husband of Mary,
and Mary was the mother of Jesus. Jesus is called the Christ.

MATTHEW 1:16

Seems like the only common bond between [Jesus' ancestors] was a promise. A promise from heaven that God would use them to send his Son.

Why did God use these people? Didn't have to. Could have just laid the Savior on a doorstep. Would have been simpler that way. And why does God tell us their stories?

Simple. He wants us to know that when the world goes wild, he stays calm.

Want proof? Read the last name on the list [of Jesus' lineage]. In spite of all the crooked halos and tasteless gambols of his people, the last name on the list is the first one promised—Jesus.

No more names are listed. No more are needed. As if God is announcing to a doubting world, "See, I did it. Just like I said I would."

WHEN GOD WHISPERS YOUR NAME

God is holy. We are sinful. Does this mean it is impossible for us to come to him? Or does it emphasize our need to come to him? Explain.

_____

_____

_____

_____

His Name Is Jesus

Joseph . . . took to him his wife, and
did not know her till she had brought forth
her firstborn Son. And he called His name JESUS.

MATTHEW 1:24–25 NKJV

Joseph tanked his reputation. He swapped his *tsadiq* diploma for a pregnant fiancée and an illegitimate son and made the big decision of discipleship. He placed God's plan ahead of his own.

Rather than make a name for himself, he made a home for Christ. And because he did, a great reward came his way. "He called His name JESUS."

Queue up the millions who have spoken the name of Jesus, and look at the person selected to stand at the front of the line. Joseph. Of all the saints, sinners, prodigals, and preachers who have spoken the name, Joseph, a blue-collar, small-town construction worker, said it first. He cradled the wrinkle-faced Prince of Heaven and, with an audience of angels and pigs, whispered, "Jesus . . . You'll be called Jesus."

CURE FOR THE COMMON LIFE

Joseph set aside his own plans for life and willingly accepted the task God called him to do. How does he serve as an example for us today?

_____

_____

_____

God Became a Man

He gave up his divine privileges; he took the humble position as a slave and was born as a human being.

PHILIPPIANS 2:7 NLT

It all happened in a most remarkable moment . . . a moment like no other.

God became a man. Divinity arrived. Heaven opened herself and placed her most precious one in a human womb.

The omnipotent, in one instant, became flesh and blood. The One who was larger than the universe became a microscopic embryo. And he who sustains the world with a word chose to be dependent upon the nourishment of a young girl.

God had come near.

GOD CAME NEAR

Describe how the birth of Jesus speaks of God's love.

_____

_____

_____

_____

_____

_____

_____

_____

_____

God Came Near

His kingdom will never end.

LUKE 1:33

She looks into the face of the baby. Her son. Her Lord. His Majesty. At this point in history, the human being who best understands who God is and what he is doing is a teenage girl in a smelly stable. She can't take her eyes off him. Somehow Mary knows she is holding God. So this is he. She remembers the words of the angel. "His kingdom will never end."

He looks like anything but a king. His face is prunish and red. His cry, though strong and healthy, is still the helpless and piercing cry of a baby. And he is absolutely dependent upon Mary for his well-being.

Majesty in the midst of the mundane. Holiness in the filth of sheep manure and sweat. Divinity entering the world on the floor of a stable, through the womb of a teenager and in the presence of a carpenter.

She touches the face of the infant-God.

GOD CAME NEAR

We, too, can touch God as we reach out in compassion to others. Describe how you can touch lives with God's loving care.

_____

_____

_____

_____

The Strength of God's Love

God shows his great love for us in this way:
Christ died for us while we were still sinners.

ROMANS 5:8

C an anything make me stop loving you?" God asks. "Watch me speak your language, sleep on your earth, and feel your hurts. Behold the Maker of sight and sound as he sneezes, coughs, and blows his nose. You wonder if I understand how you feel? Look into the dancing eyes of the kid in Nazareth; that's God walking to school. Ponder the toddler at Mary's table; that's God spilling his milk.

"You wonder how long my love will last? Find your answer on a splintered cross, on a craggy hill. That's me you see up there, your Maker, your God, nail-stabbed and bleeding. Covered in spit and sin-soaked.

"That's your sin I'm feeling. That's your death I'm dying. That's your resurrection I'm living. That's how much I love you."

IN THE GRIP OF GRACE

Write a note of thanks to God for his amazing love.

_____

_____

_____

_____

_____

_____

Facing Fear

*"Father, if you are willing,
take away this cup of suffering."*

Luke 22:42

Jesus was more than anxious; he was afraid.

How remarkable that Jesus felt such fear. But how kind that he told us about it. We tend to do the opposite. Gloss over our fears. Cover them up. Keep our sweaty palms in our pockets, our nausea and dry mouths a secret. Not so with Jesus. We see no mask of strength. But we do hear a request for strength.

"Father, if you are willing, take away this cup of suffering." The first one to hear his fear is his Father. He could have gone to his mother. He could have confided in his disciples. He could have assembled a prayer meeting. All would have been appropriate, but none were his priority. He went first to his Father.

Traveling Light

Where did Jesus go with his fear? Did he try to hide his fear? How do his actions show us how to handle our fears?

_____

_____

_____

_____

_____

Admission into Joy

You . . . clothed me in happiness.

PSALM 30:11

The first step to joy is a plea for help, an acknowledgment of moral destitution, an admission of inward paucity. Those who taste God's presence have declared spiritual bankruptcy and are aware of their spiritual crisis. Their cupboards are bare. Their pockets are empty. Their options are gone. They have long since stopped demanding justice; they are pleading for mercy.

They ask God to do for them what they can't do without him. They have seen how holy God is and how sinful they are.

Oh, the irony of God's delight—born in the parched soil of destitution rather than the fertile ground of achievement.

It's a different path, a path we're not accustomed to taking. We don't often declare our impotence. Admission of failure is not usually admission into joy. Complete confession is not commonly followed by total pardon. But then again, God has never been governed by what is common.

THE APPLAUSE OF HEAVEN

What have you asked God to do for you that you can't do without him?

_____

_____

_____

_____

_____

A Free Choice

God did not choose us to suffer his anger
but to have salvation through our Lord Jesus Christ.

1 THESSALONIANS 5:9

We don't like to talk about hell, do we? In intellectual circles the topic of hell is regarded as primitive and foolish. It's not logical. "A loving God wouldn't send people to hell." So we dismiss it.

But to dismiss it is to dismiss a core teaching of Jesus. The doctrine of hell is not one developed by Paul, Peter, or John. It is taught by Jesus himself.

And to dismiss it is to dismiss much more. It is to dismiss the presence of a loving God and the privilege of a free choice. Let me explain. We are free either to love God or not. He invites us to love him. He urges us to love him. He came that we might love him. But, in the end, the choice is yours and mine. For him to take that choice from each of us, to force us to love him, would be less than love.

God explains the benefits, outlines the promises, and articulates very clearly the consequences. And then, in the end, he leaves the choice to us.

AND THE ANGELS WERE SILENT

What are the benefits of choosing to love God? The consequences of rejecting him?

_____

_____

_____

_____

Immersed in Grace

He called you to share in his glory in Christ,
a glory that will continue forever.

1 PETER 5:10

To believe we are totally and eternally debt free is seldom easy. Even if we've stood before the throne and heard it from the King himself, we still doubt. As a result, many are forgiven only a little, not because the grace of the King is limited, but because the faith of the sinner is small. God is willing to forgive all. He's willing to wipe the slate completely clean. He guides us to a pool of mercy and invites us to bathe. Some plunge in, but others just touch the surface. They leave feeling unforgiven.

Where the grace of God is missed, bitterness is born. But where the grace of God is embraced, forgiveness flourishes.

The more we immerse ourselves in grace, the more likely we are to give grace.

IN THE GRIP OF GRACE

Why are we more likely to give grace if we immerse ourselves in God's grace?

A Tiny Seed, a Tiny Deed

Do not despise . . . small beginnings,
for the LORD rejoices to see the work begin.

ZECHARIAH 4:10 NLT

Against a towering giant, a brook pebble seems futile. But God used it to topple Goliath. Compared to the tithes of the wealthy, a widow's coins seem puny. But Jesus used them to inspire us.

Moses had a staff.

David had a sling.

Samson had a jawbone.

Rahab had a string.

Mary had some ointment.

Dorcas had a needle.

All were used by God.

What do you have?

God inhabits the tiny seed, empowers the tiny deed. Don't discount the smallness of your deeds.

CURE FOR THE COMMON LIFE

Make a list of some small things in your life that God could use to inspire others.

_____

_____

_____

_____

_____

God Changes Families

*They all continued praying together with some
women, including Mary the mother of Jesus, and Jesus' brothers.*

ACTS 1:14

G od has proven himself as a faithful father. Now it falls
to us to be trusting children. Let God give you what
your family doesn't. Let him fill the void others have
left. Rely upon him for your affirmation and encouragement.
Look at Paul's words: "you are God's child, and *God will give you
the blessing he promised*, because you are his child" (Galatians 4:7,
emphasis mine).

Having your family's approval is desirable but not necessary for
happiness and not always possible. Jesus did not let the difficult
dynamic of his family overshadow his call from God. And because
he didn't, [his family] chapter has a happy ending.

He gave them space, time, and grace. And because he did, they
changed. One brother became an apostle (Galatians 1:19) and
others became missionaries (1 Corinthians 9:5).

HE STILL MOVES STONES

*Do you rely upon God for your affirmation and encouragement
or do you rely on others? Explain why it is far better to rely
upon God's approval.*

_____

_____

_____

_____

Homesick for Heaven

Our homeland is in heaven.

PHILIPPIANS 3:20

This home we're in won't last forever. Birthdays remind us of that.

Not long ago I turned fifty. I'm closer to ninety than I am to infancy. All those things they say about aging are coming true. I'm patting myself less on the back and more under the chin. I have everything I had twenty years ago, except now it's all lower. The other day I tried to straighten out the wrinkles in my socks and found out I wasn't wearing any.

Aging. It's no fun. The way we try to avoid it, you'd think we could. We paint the body, preserve the body, protect the body. And well we should. These bodies are God's gifts. We should be responsible. But we should also be realistic. This body must die so the new body can live. "Flesh and blood cannot have a part in the kingdom of God. Something that will ruin cannot have a part in something that never ruins" (1 Corinthians 15:50).

TRAVELING LIGHT

God wants us to take care of our bodies, but at the same time he wants us to be realistic about growing old. Explain why those who love God do not need to be afraid of growing old.

Our Goal

"All I have is yours, and all you have is mine.
And my glory is shown through them."

JOHN 17:10

God is in the business of changing the face of the world. Let me be very clear. This change is his job, not ours. Our goal is not to make our faces radiant. Not even Jesus did that. Matthew says, "Jesus' appearance was changed" (Matthew 17:2) not "Jesus changed his appearance." Moses didn't even know his face was shining (Exodus 34:29). Our goal is not to conjure up some fake, frozen expression. Our goal is simply to stand before God with a prepared and willing heart and then let God do his work.

And he does. He wipes away the tears. He mops away the perspiration. He softens our furrowed brows. He touches our cheeks. He changes our faces as we worship.

JUST LIKE JESUS

When we stand before God with a willing heart, he does his work. He wipes our tears, he softens our furrowed brows. Make a list of some of the ways God has touched your life.

_____

_____

_____

_____

_____

_____

The God Who Follows

The upright shall dwell in Your presence.

PSALM 140:13 NKJV

Lazarus was three days dead in a sealed tomb when he heard a voice, lifted his head, and looked over his shoulder and saw Jesus standing. God had followed him into death.

Peter had denied his Lord and gone back to fishing when he heard his name and looked over his shoulder and saw Jesus cooking breakfast. God had followed him in spite of his failure.

God is the God who follows. I wonder . . . have you sensed him following you? We often miss him. But he comes.

Through the kindness of a stranger. The majesty of a sunset. The mystery of romance. Through the question of a child or the commitment of a spouse. Through a word well spoken or a touch well timed, have you sensed his presence?

TRAVELING LIGHT

Think of a time when you sensed God's presence following you, touching your life. What impact did that experience have on you?

_____

_____

_____

_____

_____

_____

Wistful Words

"I leave you peace; my peace I give you. I do not give it to you as the world does. So don't let your hearts be troubled or afraid."

If only you knew that I came to help and not condemn. If only you knew that tomorrow will be better than today. If only you knew the gift I have brought: eternal life. If only you knew I want you safely home."

If only you knew.

What wistful words to come from the lips of God. How kind that he would let us hear them. How crucial that we pause to hear them. If only we knew to trust. Trust that God is in our corner. Trust that God wants what is best.

If only we could learn to trust him.

A GENTLE THUNDER

Why is it important that we learn to trust God? How can this make a difference in our daily lives? Why does God want us to trust him more and more?

Our Sure God

*Surely goodness and mercy shall follow me all the days of my life;
and I will dwell in the house of the LORD forever.*

Look at the first word: *surely*. David didn't say, "*Maybe* goodness and mercy shall follow me." Or "*Possibly* goodness and mercy shall follow me." Or "*I have a hunch* that goodness and mercy shall follow me." David could have used one of those phrases. But he didn't. He believed in a sure God, who makes sure promises and provides a sure foundation. David would have loved the words of one of his great-great-grandsons, the apostle James. He described God as the One "with whom there is never the slightest variation or shadow of inconsistency" (James 1:17 PHILLIPS).

Our moods may shift, but God's doesn't. Our minds may change, but God's doesn't. Our devotion may falter, but God's never does. Even if we are faithless, he is faithful, for he cannot betray himself (2 Timothy 2:13). He is a sure God.

TRAVELING LIGHT

We serve a sure God. Why is this consistency such wonderful news for us?

Visit the all new

graceforthemoment.com

and sign up to receive a free "Grace Thought"

from Max Lucado in your

e-mail box every week!

ACKNOWLEDGMENTS

Grateful acknowledgment is made to the following publishers for permission to reprint this copyrighted material. All copyrights are held by the author, Max Lucado.

The Applause of Heaven (Nashville: Word, 1990).

In the Eye of the Storm (Nashville: Word, 1991).

He Still Moves Stones (Nashville: Word, 1993).

Walking with the Savior (Wheaton: Tyndale House, 1993).

How to Study the Bible (Nashville: Word, 1994).

When God Whispers Your Name (Nashville: Word, 1994).

31 Days of Blessing (MaxLucado.com, 1995).

The Inspirational Study Bible (Nashville: W Publishing Group, 1995).

A Gentle Thunder (Nashville: Word, 1995).

In the Grip of Grace (Nashville: Word, 1996).

The Great House of God (Nashville: Word, 1997).

Just Like Jesus (Nashville: Word, 1998).

When Christ Comes (Nashville: Word, 1999).

The Gift for All People (Sisters, Ore.: Multnomah Publishers, Inc., 1999).

Traveling Light (Nashville: W Publishing Group, 2000).

He Chose the Nails (Nashville: W Publishing Group, 2000).

A Love Worth Giving (Nashville: W Publishing Group, 2002).

Safe in the Shepherd's Arms (Nashville: Thomas Nelson, 2002).

And the Angels Were Silent (Nashville: W Publishing Group, 2003).

God Came Near (Nashville: W Publishing Group, 2003).

Next Door Savior (Nashville: W Publishing Group, 2003).

No Wonder They Call Him the Savior (Nashville: W Publishing Group, 2003).

Six Hours One Friday (Nashville: W Publishing Group, 2003).

Come Thirsty (Nashville: W Publishing Group, 2004).

Cure for the Common Life (Nashville: W Publishing Group, 2005).

31 Days of Blessing (Nashville: W Publishing Group, 1995).

The Inspirational Study Bible (Nashville: Thomas Nelson, 1995).

"He Reminded Us of You: A Prayer for a Friend" (Max's Eulogy for Charles "Kip" Jordan, delivered in Dallas, TX, November 1997).

Brand-New 365-Day Devotional
from MAX LUCADO

Here's a reminder for anxious days, lonely days, struggling days:
You are not alone. *God Is with You Every Day* offers 365 devotions
and scriptures to serve as daily, tangible reminders that God is
indeed with you every day, every step of the way.

———————